'Aotearoa New Zealand is a curiously neglected case in migration studies, despite the significance of immigration in the country's social, economic and political development. This book will make a significant contribution towards filling this gap.'

— Antje Ellermann, Founder and Co-Director, Centre for Migration Studies, University of British Columbia

'This is an impressive review of international migration policy in Aotearoa New Zealand with particular reference to the forty years between 1981 and 2020. It makes a distinctive contribution by situating much of the discussion in the context of the perspectives and policy interventions of successive Ministers of Immigration since the mid-1970s. As someone with more than fifty years of research experience in the field, I found the narrative that the authors have developed is novel, very comprehensive, well argued and interesting to read.'

— Richard Bedford, QSO, Emeritus Professor, University of Waikato and AUT

'*Edges of Empire* is the first book-length study to chronicle the evolution of migration policy governance in Aotearoa New Zealand in the neo-liberal period, against the backdrop of treatymaking involving Māori and complex external relationships with peoples of the Pacific Islands. It boldly responds to the challenge to migration scholars to attend to the colonial in multiple sites and at different scales. The book is also unique in its use of interviews with successive ministers of migration to centre the analysis. In all these ways, Collins, Gamlen and Vallelly have produced a highly original and timely scholarly intervention.'

— Leah F. Vosko, FRSC, Distinguished Research Professor of Political Economy, York University

'Drawing on the personalised accounts of successive Ministers of Immigration, *Edges of Empire* offers a unique analysis of New Zealand's migration policies. At its core, the book outlines how the politics of markets, multiculturalism, and an enduring imperial agenda has shaped migration over the past forty years. It is also one of those rare accounts that threads the Crown's relationship with tangata whenua in unfolding immigration histories. Collins, Gamlen and Vallelly adeptly blend academic thoroughness and storytelling to deliver an immersive and thought-provoking critique of New Zealand's contemporary migration.'

— Rachel Simon-Kumar, Professor and Co-Director, Centre for Asian and Ethnic Minority Health Research and Evaluation, University of Auckland

EDGES OF EMPIRE

EDGES OF EMPIRE

THE POLITICS OF IMMIGRATION IN AOTEAROA NEW ZEALAND, 1980-2020

FRANCIS L. COLLINS
ALAN GAMLEN
NEIL VALLELLY

AUCKLAND
UNIVERSITY
PRESS

First published 2025
Auckland University Press
Waipapa Taumata Rau
University of Auckland
Private Bag 92019
Auckland 1142
New Zealand
www.aucklanduniversitypress.co.nz

ISBN 978 1 77671 112 3

A catalogue record for this book is available from the National Library of New Zealand

Design by Seven
Cover illustration by Seven

This book is printed on FSC® certified paper

Printed in Malaysia by Papercraft Sdn Bhd

Contents

List of Figures and Tables

Introduction

nternational migration is often a highly politicised issue. Indeed, because international migration involves the movement of people between territories and across borders, it is fundamentally involved in determinations of who is included within nations and communities and under what conditions. Migration is also never far from headline news; some politicians have built their careers on trumpeting pro- or anti-immigration slogans, and migration has important impacts on national society and economy as well as the geopolitical positions of countries. Given this public visibility and governmental importance, it is quite remarkable in a country like Aotearoa New Zealand,[1] which experiences so much migration by international standards, that a relatively open stance towards migration has become such a consistent feature of government policy. This is one of the central concerns in this book, which is based on interviews with former New Zealand Ministers of Immigration between 1981 and 2020 – a period of substantial change in migration policy, patterns, and outcomes within this part of the world.

In Aotearoa New Zealand, immigration policy has become bipartisan – both major political parties largely agree on general principles – and institutionalised, in that there is a significant bureaucratic apparatus maintaining a consistent focus on particular approaches to immigration. There is no doubt that immigration policy has changed enormously in this country over the last two centuries, and especially over the last four decades, and has had a range of profound impacts on New Zealand's society, economy, and place in the world. But the ideological basis for policy and policy change in recent decades has been relatively undisturbed, irrespective of which political party is in government. Oppositional voices to immigration policy have emerged from those outside of this established

1   In this book we use the term 'New Zealand', and sometimes 'Aotearoa New Zealand'. New Zealand is the official, internationally recognised name for the country and is a referent for the state in the form of the New Zealand Government. Use of the term Aotearoa is becoming increasingly common at the time of writing. In the context of this book, however, we only use 'Aotearoa New Zealand' intermittently since our emphasis is on the contemporary government of immigration in this country that is directed under the authority of the New Zealand Government. Indeed, as the subsequent chapters will show, immigration policy is an area where the redress of colonialism remains underdeveloped.

political order, but they have generally been dismissed unless they hold what are deemed to be common-sense positions.

Meanwhile, the politics of making immigration policy have taken place elsewhere – in the relationships between officials and elected politicians, in the international conference circuits where migration policies are traded and exchanged by professional experts, in the pressure on New Zealand to conform to the protocols of its super-powerful security allies, where there is a constant risk of migration being portrayed as out of control, and in growing questions about how to reconcile New Zealand's past and ongoing dependence on large-scale immigration with the nation-state's founding document, Te Tiriti o Waitangi (hereafter Te Tiriti), and the English-language version, The Treaty of Waitangi (hereafter The Treaty).

Edges of Empire tells the story of immigration policymaking in Aotearoa New Zealand through the narrative accounts of fifteen former Ministers of Immigration and the political, economic, and social contexts within which they worked. Our focus is on the four decades between 1980 and 2020, a period of economic upheaval and social change during neoliberalism, globalisation, and resurgent forms of nationalism and racism. During this time, migration policies in Aotearoa New Zealand have become increasingly economistic, securitised, and managerial, with significant implications for nation- and state-building. From a primarily bicultural, Māori, and White settler nation until the 1980s, Aotearoa New Zealand has dramatically diversified ethnically, demographically, and socio-economically – through immigration policies that prioritise economic contributions and permit immigration of all nationalities. In the same period, Aotearoa New Zealand's relationships with states and populations in the Pacific have been reconfigured through restrictive labour migration policies, and immigration from Asia and other parts of the world has been met with racism and anti-immigration sentiment, while emigration of New Zealand citizens to Australia has been a recurrent source of anxiety for the public and politicians.

Placing Ministers of Immigration at the core of this book brings unique insight into the story of immigration policymaking and its implications. Much has been written about the details of immigration policy, the effects it has in migrants' lives, the public discourses about the role of migration, and the shifting demographic, social, economic, and cultural makeup of Aotearoa New Zealand. The ideas, imaginations, and experiences of those who have overseen immigration policymaking, however, have not been the subject of much detailed academic analysis. Centring the accounts of Ministers of Immigration demonstrates how policymaking is made across governments of all stripes, with cross-party collaboration and consensus being a significant feature, and changes in policy often driven by bureaucratic thinking, emulation, experimentation, and creative responses to unanticipated problems. The consensus on immigration policy often emanates from elsewhere, in the international environment, which penetrates the status quo through the professional discourse that goes on in university economics and social science departments, think-tanks, and consultancies, and calcifies into the standard practice of government agencies.

Rather than distinct political agendas, the story of immigration policymaking in this book highlights how ideas from neoliberal economic thought and the experience of (and pressure from) other nations have been key drivers for the development of many migration settings. Articulations of multiculturalism, neoliberalism, globalisation, securitisation, and managerialism – terms that we introduce in subsequent sections – have incrementally been assembled as part of a twenty-first-century migration regime that has multiple genealogies and is deeply embedded into a range of societal and governmental spheres. Simultaneously, our account highlights how immigration policy has operated as part of the legacy of the country's settler colonial formation, which is arguably expressed in the fact that Māori have never been formally consulted for their views on whether and how immigration policy aligns with Te Tiriti, and in New Zealand's unequal relations with Pacific peoples and nations. We give emphasis to Māori interventions that are relevant to immigration policy at key points throughout this book, although we also note (following Kukutai and Rata 2017) that there has been an obscuration of Māori interests and claims in relation to immigration since the signing of Te Tiriti in 1840 (see also New Zealand Productivity Commission 2022). However, our account is based on interviews with former ministers, whom we did not ask much about matters relating to Māori. Only one of our interviewees clearly identified as Māori, and so our account of Māori perspectives and actions regarding immigration and immigration policy is not extensive. We do not seek to suggest that our own lack of coverage of these issues indicates the absence of Māori voices and contributions in the politics of immigration. We also have our own perspectives on coloniality and the role of Māori in relation to immigration policy, as we explain in the relevant sections of the book.

Edges of Empire is composed of six chapters that explore the transformation of New Zealand migration governance with an emphasis on the last four decades. Each chapter is situated in a particular historical period and in relation to specific former Ministers of Immigration. After providing a *longue durée* account of the 'imperial migration regime' that was crafted in the nineteenth century, we explore the neoliberal revolution in the 1980s, the assertion of globalisation in the 1990s, new forms of managerialism and securitisation in the early twenty-first century, and the shift from settler immigration towards temporary migration in the years leading up to the Covid-19 border closure in 2020. Across these periods we give precedence to the perspectives and insights of former ministers interviewed in this project, and situate their commentaries in relation to research on migration, policy and public discourse, and selected historical records (although we do not attempt a detailed historiographical approach). Our aim in presenting the book in this way is to document the accounts of these ministers as important figures in the evolution of migration governance in Aotearoa New Zealand, to record key moments in the country's shifting approach to migration, and to examine the diversity of influences on the formulation of policies of regulating migration here. Our hope is that *Edges of Empire* offers value not only from an academic standpoint of better understanding immigration policy development in this part of the world, but also offers an opportunity to represent the first-hand accounts of key government ministers in a way that contributes to public insight and debate around international migration in other parts of the world, many of which continue to look to countries like New Zealand as examples of 'best practice' in migration policymaking. Before we delve into these stories and histories of immigration policymaking, we first introduce Aotearoa New Zealand and its position at the edges of empire, speak to the politics of governing migration, and outline the structure and content of this book.

Edges of Empire

Our account of the stories and histories of migration governance in Aotearoa New Zealand between 1980 and 2020 speaks to this country's position *at the edges of empire*. The first of these was the British Empire, which began to dominate New Zealand in the early nineteenth century. However, by 1973, less than a decade prior to our starting point of 1980, Britain had largely withdrawn from its own empire and entered the European Economic Community (EEC), marking the cumulative closure of New Zealand's political-economic dependence on the imperial metropole. Imperial disintegration had been apparent since the end of World War I and accelerated rapidly after World War II, but in many respects, New Zealand had hung on to the receding edges of the British Empire for as long as it could, cherishing the Empire's political, social, and cultural legitimation of the settler colonial state and society. Immigration policy was a major part of this story. The New Zealand Government removed permit-free access to British and Irish nationals only shortly after the UK acceded to the EEC. The following decade, the 1987 Immigration Act would finally remove all reference to 'traditional source country' criteria that privileged British and Irish immigrants, which had been a cornerstone of immigration policy and population growth since the early days of colonial government.

Despite its geopolitical disintegration, the British Empire persists through its language, culture, and institutions. We remain at the edges of empire and its unequal inheritances (Jacobs 2002). 'The new age of empire', as Andrews (2021) describes it, reminds us that even when empires formally end, the legacies of colonialism – including racism – do not. Instead, they continue to shape societies, in part through their deep embeddedness in post-colonial institutions, including in geopolitical and geoeconomic relationships (see also Koram 2022). Even as the British Empire is increasingly framed as historical, much of its legacy has been taken over and repurposed by a US-led geopolitical alliance that links the old imperial metropole with its Anglosphere settler colonies, New Zealand, Australia, and Canada, forming what is known as the 'Five Eyes' alliance (US, UK, Australia, Canada, and New Zealand) because of its shared signals intelligence capabilities, born in the post-war period. New Zealand typically operates at the edges of this super-powerful alliance, which has an increasingly important migration-specific component, known as the 'Migration Five'. New Zealand engages tentatively with the twenty-first-century imperial undertakings of China and India too – but the shared institutions, social norms, and cultures of the old Anglo Empire are still the most powerful drivers in the circulation of immigration policy and border-security 'best practices' among this newly reconfigured group comprising Britain and its former 'White Dominions'. We recognise that, even today, these practices continue to privilege access for English-speaking, Western, and by implication 'White' people (though 'Whiteness' itself is a category of racialisation that articulates with other global claims to racial and geopolitical superiority).

This country's position at the edges of empire is not only a matter of the temporal margin of imperial expansion, disintegration, and reconfiguration. Rather it also reflects a deeper history of seemingly always being at the periphery, part of empire while always sitting outside its main body. When Te Tiriti was signed on 6 February 1840, there were barely 2000 non-Māori in Aotearoa New Zealand, most of whom were British and had found their way to 'the South Seas' to make a fragile and often outlaw living beyond the thresholds of expanding European authority. Some lived among and many traded with Māori, who numbered approximately 90,000 people (Pool 1991). Māori hapū (sub-tribe) and whānau (extended family networks) comprised culturally, economically, and politically diverse social groups that cumulatively territorialised the entirety of the archipelago that later became known as New Zealand (Anderson et al. 2015). It would not be until 1858 that British settlers reached population parity, in part because of significant Māori population decline through war, disease, and resource loss (Pool 1991). Even with the signing of Te Tiriti, the establishment of colonial government, and the development of commercial settlement, British sovereignty remained contested, and empire was more myth than reality, at least until the conclusion of the New Zealand Wars in the early 1870s (Belich 2002b; O'Malley 2019).

Like other settler states established in the mid-to-late-nineteenth-century 'low point of imperial expansion' (Perry 2001: 13), Aotearoa New Zealand was geographically and symbolically at the edges of empire (Ashton 2015; Ballantyne 2015; Paul et al. 2017; Salesa 2011).[2] The islands now known as New Zealand are some 14,000 nautical miles from the imperial metropole in London and in the nineteenth century would take up to six months to reach by arduous sea voyage. From the perspective of imperial authority, the colonial periphery of New Zealand was a far-flung outpost, on the edge of the world economy. The 'geographical remoteness of New Zealand from the United Kingdom favoured an experiment in nation-building' (Farmer 1985: 59) wherein immigration was the central pillar in the constitution of a European society at what was seen as the ends of the earth. Colonial governments set about reworking the peripheral position of New Zealand through immigration policy, facilitating and subsidising the arrival of tens of thousands of White settlers, appropriating Indigenous land by any means necessary to make way for settlement, and rolling out British colonial law, language, and institutions across the country. Immigration policy would assure that the new settlers would be White and preferably British. Racist policies restricted all other arrivals across the nineteenth and early-to-mid-twentieth centuries, especially the Chinese. For its colonial imagineers (Barber 2020) and dominion executors (Belich 2002b), New Zealand was to become a 'Better Britain', and 'The Great Britain of the South Seas' – overcoming geohistorical periphery

2   There is a veritable sub-genre of texts that address 'the edge(s) of empire', or that engage in related notions of margins, peripheries, outposts, and frontiers. Many such texts examine imperial histories and geographies that overlap with our account of New Zealand (Ashton 2015; Ballantyne 2015; Mayell 2004; Paul et al. 2017; Salesa 2011; Storey 2016), at least the initial period we cover in the nineteenth-to-mid-twentieth centuries, in places like British Columbia (Perry 2001), Australia (Jacobs 2002), and Fiji (Banivanua 2009) that became part of the British Empire, as well as places articulated into other imperial formations (e.g., Nugent 1997; Parker 2002; among others). Like other scholars, we also see the edge(s) of empire as a heuristic device, one that pays attention to its potential to reveal the formations of regimes (Reed 2020), to see the fragility of empire and the ongoingness and legacies of imperialism, in its peripheries as well as its core (Jacobs 2002).

through the assertion of White Britishness as core to emergent colonial, dominion, and national society.

At least since World War II, New Zealand settler governments have been faced with the disintegration of the British Empire with which they had long desired closer relations. Having been at the periphery during the apogee of imperialism, New Zealand felt new pressures to reconfigure internal and external relations during the post-war era. Māori in the post-World War II period grew increasingly assertive about their sovereignty (Walker 1990) and New Zealand developed an enhanced role in the Pacific (Ratuva 2022). Geopolitical and geoeconomic relationships with the Asian region have become more important since Britain joined the EEC in 1973 (Larner 1998). Immigration policy has articulated with these shifts at the historical edges of empire – through the opening of labour migration pathways for Pacific peoples since the 1950s, a declining reliance on British settlers since the 1970s, and a significant transformation of migration policy in the 1980s that led to new, more ethnically diversified patterns of immigration, especially from Asia. By the early twenty-first century, the New Zealand Government was operating immigration policy that was built on neoliberal logics of selecting migrants not on race or nationality, at least on the surface of policy decisions, but on economic value. Migration was now managed to determine migrants' differential inclusion in the economy and society according to this new understanding of their value (Simon-Kumar 2020). By 2018, immigration policy had contributed to a transformation of the country in ethno-demographic terms: far from the mid-twentieth-century years of White settler dominance, Europeans constituted 70.2 per cent of the population, with much larger proportions of Māori (16.5 per cent), Asian (15.1 per cent), and Pacific peoples (8.1 per cent).

White settler anxiety about racialised others – particularly Indigenous peoples and non-White immigrants – has always been striking on these tenuous geohistorical edges of empire (Storey 2016). In the earliest days of British colonisation, public and political anxieties were raised particularly strongly about Chinese immigrants in New Zealand, even though there were very few of them (Ip 2003c). Other groups held under suspicion included Irish Catholics, Dalmatians, Indians, and many others (McCarthy 2022). Following their invitation to migrate to New Zealand to fill labour shortages in the 1950s and 1960s, Pacific people were scapegoats for the economic recession in the 1970s and subject to the racist 'Dawn Raids' deportation campaigns (Anae 2020). Two decades later, the rapid growth in Asian immigration would be framed as an 'invAsian' that seemingly challenged White New Zealand hegemony, facilitating the electoral successes of the still-popular anti-immigration New Zealand

First party (Ng 2017). In the 2010s, migrants of all kinds, but especially those who were not White, were seen as the cause of skyrocketing house prices and the overburdening of schools, hospitals, and infrastructure (Hickey 2016). And in the five decades since the 1970s, a recurrent public and political panic has emerged about the consistent loss of New Zealand citizens through emigration, especially to Australia. These émigrés are demographically replaced by new immigrants, which is often framed as a risk to the long-standing notion that New Zealand should be a nation of White British settlers (Gamlen 2013a).

The political, economic, and social structures that supported the establishment and expansion of the British Empire have legacies that persist through the four decades that are the focus of this book. New Zealand's uptake of a more 'multicultural' and economically focused immigration policy in the 1980s followed the arc of sibling settler colonies Canada and Australia. In the decades prior to and since then, policy exchange between these countries has been a key source of immigration policy development and innovation (Bedford & Spoonley 2014). In the military-security spaces vacated by the disintegrating British Empire, the Five Eyes group, as an Anglosphere imperialistic and transnational administration (Andrews 2021), has taken on greater significance, and New Zealand has become closer to China than many other Western nation-states (Noakes & Burton 2019). Similarly, New Zealand's growing engagement with India and concomitant recognition of diaspora groups in New Zealand highlights how migration and geopolitics are inseparable (Chandramohan 2012). Across these arrangements, though, New Zealand seemingly remains at the edge of imperial formations – at once embracing them but never quite in the centre of any one in particular.

New Zealand's position at the edges of empire makes it a particularly compelling case for examining the development of immigration policy. Being part of empire while always sitting outside the main body of empire offers a kind of liminality (hooks 1992) that provides space to reveal more sharply the regimes that govern population and life (Reed 2020). While the legacies of British imperialism and settler colonialism are palpable in immigration policy across the period we focus on in this research, they also intersect with manifold other political forces. Most notable is the reassertion and reconfiguration of Māori sovereignty over Aotearoa New Zealand, which while often overlooked in migration discussions, raises fundamental questions about who the word 'we' in 'we the people' refers to, and about how identity relates to authority over 'national' borders – both in terms of physical barriers to the territory and in terms of who gets to settle and acquire citizenship (Kukutai and Rata 2017; Matike Mai Aotearoa

2016). Immigration policy in Aotearoa New Zealand has also been subject to the influence of neoliberal political thought and practice, which have wrought their own radical transformations of this country's society and economy since the 1980s (Kelsey 1995). Matters of immigration policy and consequent ethno-demographic diversity have likewise articulated with discourses of globalisation and multiculturalism that have been central justifications for neoliberal shifts in immigration policy in many countries (Mitchell 2004). And more recent transformations in immigration policy that we discuss in this book have seen New Zealand embrace forms of security, managerialism, and growing temporary migration rather than settlement immigration, placing this country at the forefront of reworked settler society formation (Dauvergne 2016). As we demonstrate in this book, these Indigenous, imperial, settler colonial, global, neoliberal, multicultural, security, and managerial imperatives have in different ways come to intersect in the development of a twenty-first-century mode of governing migration that is both indicative of emergent international trends and unique to the context of Aotearoa New Zealand.

Governing Migration

Our attention in this book is squarely on the practices and processes of governing migration and the role of New Zealand Ministers of Immigration in making immigration policy. As such, we are interested in 'who can govern; what governing is; what or who is governed' (Gordon 1991: 3). Focusing on governing migration entails attention to the political rationalities (ways or systems of thinking) that underpin policies, the technologies (such as regulation, monitoring, and enforcement) used to facilitate, limit, and manage migration, and the regimes of governmental practice that emerge through such rationalities and technologies (Walters 2015). Taking this approach, the stories drawn from interviews with Ministers of Immigration, alongside a range of historical and research material, provide important insights into how immigration policymaking happens, its indebtedness to particular ways of thinking about and rationalising migration, and the adoption and creation of systems and techniques for controlling what kind of migration occurs.

In Aotearoa New Zealand, the government of migration is politically vested in the Crown, the 'executive government conducted by Ministers and their public service agencies'. The Immigration Act 2009 stipulates this in stating: 'The purpose of this Act is to manage immigration in a way that balances the national interest, as determined by the Crown, and the rights of individuals.' As part of the executive branch of government, the Minister of Immigration is responsible for implementing the laws made by Parliament. The Minister has overall responsibility for putting immigration laws into action. Ministers achieve this by directing the work of their departments in the civil service, which formulate and enforce specific regulations in line with the relevant Acts. In New Zealand (as in many other countries), immigration law does not spell out exactly how immigration must be regulated, but instead grants the Minister of Immigration and their delegates rather broad powers to execute legislation as they see fit. For most of the period that we study in this book, those public service agencies were the Department of Labour (until 2012) and the Ministry of Business, Innovation and Employment (since 2012), but others, such as the Treasury, the Ministry of Foreign Affairs and Trade, and the Ministry of Social Development, have also exercised influence on migration governance.

In this book, we use the term 'migration policy' rather broadly. For us the word 'migration' encompasses both immigration and emigration – and where necessary we specify which of these two we are talking about. Our use of the word 'policy' requires a bit more background. Many writers use this term to encompass an extremely broad range of governmental institutions and practices, including not just 'policies' in the sense of the formal positions articulated by political parties and governments or their agencies, but also Acts of Parliament or laws. Most migration policies are neither policies nor laws but rather 'regulations': they are rules and directives put in place by authorities that are responsible for implementing laws, such as government departments and courts. Rather than stretching the word 'policy' too far, we tend to use the term 'governance' as an umbrella term for this broad range of institutions and practices. 'Governance' differs from 'government' in that it describes a situation where there is no single authoritative rule maker, but rather multiple overlapping centres of power – such as different institutions, laws, departments, and regulatory codes. It is important to recognise that the existence of government at one level does not rule out governance at other levels. For example, the interactions of individuals within nation-states are ruled over by a government, while the interactions of nation-states in international relations are not regulated by a single authority but instead by a multi-layered regulatory patchwork, and can therefore be referred to as part of 'global governance'.

The broader migration regime that we examine in this book includes not only these elected and official components of government but also other diverse actors and institutions that encourage, enable, channel, and challenge different kinds of migration in different contexts

(Glick Schiller & Salazar 2013). The migration regime that is made visible through the stories of Ministers of Immigration and the historical contexts they speak from is thus not unitary, cohesive, or necessarily coordinated. The nineteenth-to-twentieth-century imperial migration regime that we outline in some detail in Chapter 1, for example, was not a singular and coherent policy vision but rather generated over many decades through ongoing attempts by colonial and dominion governments and other actors to create a White New Zealand by usurping Māori sovereignty, confiscating land for settlement, and excluding non-White peoples. This regime came about over time in increments, drawing on emerging knowledge claims, such as nineteenth-century assertions of White racial superiority, technologies for managing border control such as passports and other travel documentation, and various techniques for determining who could and could not enter the territory of New Zealand. The imperial migration regime also relied on other settler colonial political rationalities and technologies, most notably the Crown acquisition of Māori land for settlers, undertaken through mapping, legislative changes, and, where those failed, through invasion of sovereign territory and subsequent confiscation of land. The succeeding neoliberal migration regime that we trace in Chapters 2–6 has similarly not been a singular achievement but rather has emerged over many decades and involves new forms of knowledge, including experiments in techniques for prioritising economic value and productivity, and the constant adoption and creation of new measures for regulating migration flows and migrant lives.

While this book is aimed at a general readership, we frequently refer to conceptual terminology that helps to name and explain the political, economic, and social forces that constitute government and its effects. In this text, the terms settler colonialism, multiculturalism, neoliberalism, globalisation, securitisation, and migration management are especially salient in drawing attention to the different political rationalities and projects that have shaped and characterised New Zealand migration governance between 1981 and 2020. To facilitate a clear understanding of these terms and their relevance to our discussion in this book, we offer here a brief and accessible overview of each term.

Settler colonialism is a term that describes the form of colonialism that is enacted in Aotearoa New Zealand, in similar British colonial territories including Australia, Canada, and the US (and South Africa, although in different ways), and in other imperial-colonial formations (Veracini 2010). While settler colonisation has many iterations that have emerged across the world at different points historically, the focus in this book is on the specific settler colonial undertakings that emerged within

Aotearoa New Zealand and similar British colonial territories. In these contexts, settler colonialism typically involved the establishment of White settler demographic and then political dominance wherein immigration was a central component in making settler colonial nations, politics, economies, and identities (Wolfe 1999). Settler colonialism has operated through varying mechanisms to displace, usurp, erase, and – in the colonial mindset – 'civilise' such Indigenous peoples and liberate them from what settlers saw as unenlightened savagery. The legacies of settler colonialism are manifest in the institutions, politics, cultures, identity formations, languages, and social mores that characterise countries like Aotearoa New Zealand, even as Indigenous and racialised minorities struggle against the settler state and society (Bell 2014).

In this book, *multiculturalism* refers to particular political claims and projects, especially prominent in contemporary Anglophone settler colonies, that hold that societies and nation-building can be reorganised around the incorporation of ethnically, culturally, and linguistically diverse populations (Hage 2010; Mitchell 2004). As a political project, multiculturalism emerged first in Canada in the 1960s, serving to bring together Anglophone and Francophone White settler populations within a national identity that would then be increasingly opened to diverse immigrant arrivals as race and nationality restrictions were removed from migration policy. Multiculturalism is officially part of Canadian policy, and has been in varying ways in Australia too (Ang & Stratton 1998). Multicultural ideas are found everywhere in New Zealand, but as a policy programme multiculturalism has not been implemented as formally or extensively in New Zealand as in Australia or Canada – in part because of a strong institutional focus on 'biculturalism' stemming from The Treaty (Jones & Johnson 2016; Simon-Kumar 2020). Multiculturalism has been celebrated by its advocates for facilitating inclusion and integration of ethnically diverse populations (Parekh 2000) and criticised by conservative and nationalist political voices for leading to segregation and undermining Western values (Abu-Laban & Stasiulis 1992). For Indigenous peoples, multiculturalism can serve as another layer of settler colonialism, displacing Indigenous struggle through a diversification of populations within countries that are still dominated by White settlers, and their systems and values (Walker 1994). From the critical perspective on migration governance that we develop in this book, multiculturalism has been deployed to facilitate and legitimise neoliberal, economistic migration policies that claim to be less discriminatory but rely on forms of selection and migrant restrictions that work through categories based on nationality and ethnicity (Simon-Kumar 2015).

Neoliberalism is a political project associated with the intellectual and political engagement with building state and legal infrastructure to prioritise the market as the key to effective governance and the enhancement of societies. Neoliberal ideas were crafted initially by a group of Austrian economists and intellectuals in the aftermath of World War I, in the context of the disintegrating Hapsburg Empire and emerging forms of socialism across Europe (Slobodian 2018). The term 'neoliberalism' was coined at the 1938 Walter Lippman Colloquium in Paris, where some of the key figures of what has been termed the 'neoliberal thought collective' first met (Dardot & Laval 2014; Denord 2009). In the post-World War II period, the neoliberal thought collective expanded across Europe – especially after the establishment of the Mont Pèlerin Society in 1947 (Plehwe & Mirowski 2009) – and into North America, most notably at the Chicago School of Economics (Stedman Jones 2012). Far from advocating for a simple reinvigoration of *laissez-faire* liberalism, these thinkers sought to insulate markets from political transformations and democratic demands for wealth redistribution and social justice (Plehwe et al. 2020). And in response to the myriad of economic, political, and social crises of the 1970s, neoliberalism eventually came to serve as the ideological driver for radical political-economic transformations from the 1970s in Latin America, the US, the UK, and Europe, and then across many other parts of the world (Harvey 2005). Aotearoa New Zealand's initial encounter with neoliberalism is often associated with the Fourth Labour Government, which was in office from 1984 to 1990, and the subsequent National Government from 1990 to 1999 (Kelsey 1995), but neoliberal ideas were already circulating in policy circles prior to that time (Alchin 1990; Scollay et al. 2010). While neoliberalism represents diverse and mutating policy approaches (Ong 2006), it is most associated with the roll-back of state regulation of industry and markets, steep reductions in welfare provision, regressive changes to taxation systems, and a roll-out of state and quasi-state functions to actively construct markets that can enhance profitability (Peck & Tickell 2002). The neoliberalisation of migration policy is thus not associated with unfettered movement but rather with the increasing use of human and financial capital measures as the only viable means of selecting eligible long-term immigrants; the construction of migration, employment, and education markets for managing flows of temporary migrants while precluding their inclusion in society; and the extension of border exclusion technologies to reduce irregular migrant arrivals – those who enter a country without official authorisation – that are deemed to be a drain on the state and society.

Closely associated with neoliberal political projects have been a discourse and agenda of *globalisation*, a term that refers to the processes by which the world has become increasingly interconnected in economic, political, social, and cultural terms (Appadurai 1996). In scholarly discussions, globalisation became something of a buzz-word in the 1990s as intellectuals sought to account for and grapple with the end of the 'Cold War' between the US and its Western allies and the Soviet Union and its satellite states and allies. The end of the Cold War was claimed by some to have brought an end to the great geopolitical ideological conflicts of the twentieth century, exemplified by Francis Fukuyama's (1989) purported 'end of history', and manifested the unchallenged ascendency of capitalism and liberal democracy. Critical perspectives on globalisation, however, emphasise that the agenda towards globalisation has been deeply connected to neoliberalism and has been shaped around profoundly uneven and unequal connections between and across places (Massey 1991). Globalisation may be symbolically associated with the hyper-mobile subjects of international business but some of its key manifestations are in forms of globally extended economic activities in developing countries that involve populations whose movements are heavily controlled (Triandafyllidou 2018).

Neoliberalism involves a connection between globalisation and security: on the one hand, it prescribes openness to cross-border flows, and on the other hand, it prescribes active state intervention to secure and protect those flows and the large and powerful organisations that drive them. In exploring this relation in the context of Aotearoa New Zealand we refer to *securitisation*, a term that denotes the introduction, extension, and refinement of border-security technologies to minimise the claimed risks and threats associated with migration, whether political, economic, or safety (Jones 2016). Since the 1990s, there has been an increasing emphasis on border security as a key element for managing purported risks of uncontrolled migration, in terms of both irregular arrivals and those associated with international criminal and terrorist networks. Securitisation has been massively amplified as a response to major terrorist attacks in the US, India, France, and the UK since the early 2000s. Migration and border crossing more generally became increasingly subject to enhanced security protocols at airports, including advanced passenger checks and compulsory screening, even on domestic flights. Other technological developments associated with securitisation include the use of biometrics (Amoore 2006) and more recently algorithmic and other forms of digital automation (Amoore 2024; Collins 2023).

Alongside the restrictionist impulses expressed in securitisation, migration policy since the late 1990s has also been increasingly framed as a 'management' problem. Managerialism has been a common feature of neoliberalism that involves the introduction of private-sector management techniques into wider societal domains (Klikauer 2015), combining 'management's generic tools and knowledge with ideology to establish itself systemically in organizations, public institutions, and society' (Magretta 2012: 4). The introduction of private-sector management practices into public-sector organisations entails an amplified focus on efficiency, productivity, and outcomes; a separation between management and professional experts in the running of organisations; and an ethos of enterprise that involves more market orientation and greater competition for resources (Shepherd 2018). The introduction of managerialism into the circuits of migration policy has occurred through a political discourse of *migration management* that describes efforts to create regimes for regulating borders and mobility that can achieve orderliness and enhanced economic productivity from purposive management of emigration pressures and immigration demands (Geiger & Pécoud 2010). For its advocates, migration management entails a form of 'regulated openness' that has the potential to 'balance the needs and interests of the sending, receiving and transit countries and the migrants themselves' (Ghosh 2007: 107). In practical terms, migration management entails many things that are not always coordinated or complementary – attempts to establish global frameworks for managing migration (Pécoud 2021); the outsourcing of migration regulation and enforcement by nation-states to international organisations (Ashutosh & Mountz 2011) and private firms (Martin 2021); forms of highly regulated circular migration (Basok & Belanger 2016) such as New Zealand's seasonal work programmes with Pacific countries; and a more general policy orientation towards planning, monitoring, evaluating, and closely regulating the flows and conditions of migration to mitigate risk and enhance outcomes (Scheel & Ustek-Spilda 2019). Migration management is in many ways an expression of neoliberalism in that it involves the creation of migration markets that centre a form of private-sector-informed managerialism in the planning and regulation of migration and border crossing. Migration management is also a response to perceived 'emigration pressures' emergent within the context of globalisation, and it is sometimes claimed to be a counterweight to ever-increasing securitisation (Ghosh 2007), although arguably intensified border security goes hand in hand with highly managed programmes for migration (Cobarrubias 2019).

One of the key trends we observe is the increasingly managerial approach to migration policy undertaken by New Zealand governments since the early 1990s. Managing migration in many respects reflected a response to the deregulation of immigration policy in the 1980s, which had opened opportunities for more diverse, multicultural flows of migrants but had not necessarily introduced the requisite technologies for maximising and optimising the economic benefits from migration. Over the 1990s and beyond, governments have frequently drawn on management approaches as part of roll-out neoliberalism that has seen increased regulation of migration entry, conditions, and exit, especially evident in the growth in temporary migration programmes since the mid-2000s. And, in the context of security concerns associated with the global 'war on terror' since the early 2000s, managing migration has operated alongside border securitisation to identify, permit, and manage legitimate migrants and travellers while excluding those who are deemed risky. An important part of this has been to attract and retain the 'top talent' that is supposedly possessed by migrants who are deemed 'highly skilled', often by virtue of racial or cultural characteristics that 'fit' the dominant culture of the destination country. This involves welcoming such individuals and their families through fast tracks into permanent residence and citizenship, while circulating migrants from low-skilled backgrounds – which are often synonymous with non-White, developing countries – through short-term visas that prevent long-term settlement. This approach to determining who legitimately belongs to the nation arguably reflects a modified version of settler colonialism, one where outward racial discrimination has been replaced by neoliberal modes of economic citizenship that often have racialised outcomes (Simon-Kumar 2015; 2020).

There are other important dimensions of migration and migration policymaking that are given less attention in this book, primarily because of limitations in scope and the themes that emerged within interviews. For example, we pay relatively little attention to gender. International migration is gendered (Meares et al. 2010; Piper 2013), and some accounts of Aotearoa New Zealand have given precedence to the gendered patterns of recent immigration (Badkar et al. 2007), the position of women in the multi-locality of households through migration (Ip & Liu 2008), and the gendered character of occupational positions in temporary migration regimes (Howe et al. 2019). It is also notable that during the time of the research for this book only two women were in the position of Minister of Immigration (Annette King for nine months and Lianne Dalziel for four years and two months); this is less combined time than women have been Prime Minister, Minister of Health, Minister of Education, Minister of Police, or Minister of Justice, among other senior ministerial portfolios. While we do not have scope to examine these patterns and their implications in this book, future research, including drawing on this interview archive, could well consider the ways in which immigration policymaking is gendered among politicians as well as in relation to bureaucrats, stakeholders, and various publics.

Narratives of Migration Policymaking

In *Edges of Empire* we are writing about migration governance rather than only about migration itself. Other authors have already paid attention to the detail of immigration policy and its implication for Aotearoa New Zealand. Notably, there are the combined works of Richard Bedford and Paul Spoonley that focus on migration policy and its demographic effects in New Zealand, including their (2012) text *Welcome to Our World? Immigration and the Reshaping of New Zealand*, which we cite often in this book. Julie Fry and Hayden Glass's *Going Places: Migration, Economics and the Future of New Zealand* (2016) and Fry and Peter Wilson's *Better Lives: Migration, Wellbeing and New Zealand* (2018) are two other recent contributions that emphasise the economic contribution of migration to Aotearoa New Zealand. There are also a growing number of book-length accounts of migrant and diasporic community experiences, notably the extensive scholarship of Manying Ip, especially her collection *Unfolding History, Evolving Identity: The Chinese in New Zealand* (2003), which traces the long story of racialisation, community building, and identity development of the earliest non-White immigrants to New Zealand (see also Wang 2018, Liu 2018, and Leckie 2021). Rachel Simon-Kumar, Francis L. Collins, and Wardlow Friesen's collection *Intersections of Inequality, Migration and Diversity: The Politics of Mobility in Aotearoa/New Zealand* (2020) pays special attention to the political constitution of migration and matters of inequality, while Angela McCarthy's recent edited collection provides insight into *Narratives of Migrant and Refugee Discrimination in New Zealand* (2022). Lastly, of note is the short collection *Fair Borders? Migration Policy in the Twenty-First Century* (2017), edited by David Hall, which addresses the notion of fairness in relation to the function of borders in Aotearoa New Zealand, including for Māori, other New Zealand citizens, and migrants themselves.

We draw on insights from and build on these texts throughout this book as we tease out in greater detail than has been done before the stories and histories of migration policymaking in Aotearoa New Zealand from 1981 to 2020. The book also sits alongside international contributions to migration studies that have examined the crafting of migration policy. Antje Ellerman's *The Comparative Politics of Immigration: Policy Choices in Germany, Canada, Switzerland, and the United States* (2021) is one such example, an ambitious multinational comparison that provides insight into the multiple actors, ideas, and institutions involved in developing and influencing migration policy. Natasha T. Duncan's *Immigration*

Policymaking in the Global Era: In Pursuit of Global Talent (2012) zooms in on the UK and Germany and draws on interviews with immigration experts, policy analysts, government officials, and trade union officials, among others, although she draws on the public record to gain insight into the views of politicians (see also Balch 2013 and Spencer 2011 for similar examples). Erica Consterdine's *Labour's Immigration Policy: The Making of the Migration State* (2017) goes further than these texts and includes politicians among her fifty interviews with elite members of the migration policy community. Consterdine's text, focused on the New Labour era in the UK (1997–2010), highlights the value of incorporating an executive perspective in accounts of migration policymaking, in terms of examining how and why particular discourses and technologies are developed, refined, and reworked as part of wider socio-political transformations.

Edges of Empire adds to these important New Zealand and international contributions to migration studies by centring the accounts of Ministers of Immigration and telling the story of migration policymaking by New Zealand governments with an emphasis on the intersecting imperial, settler colonial, global, neoliberal, security, and managerial imperatives that have contributed to the making of a twenty-first-century migration regime. At the centre of the narrative in this book are interviews with fifteen former Ministers of Immigration who were in office between 1981 and 2020. We selected this period for two key reasons. First, we wanted to speak to all former immigration ministers alive at the time of the research – the oldest, Bill Birch (born 1934), having held office from 1990 to 1993. Stan Rodger (born 1940) passed away in 2022 while the writing of this book was underway. Second, and more importantly, we wanted to speak to everyone who had sat across the top of New Zealand's large and long-established migration system during the period of rapid and radical transformation that has taken place since the mid-1980s, when New Zealand abruptly changed from an inward-looking colony of 'better Britons' at the bottom of the world, known as one of the world's most socialist economies, into a neoliberal society, seeking ever-greater openness to the outside world and particularly to its Asian-Pacific neighbourhood.

With these aims in mind, we undertook interviews with: Anthony 'Aussie' Malcolm (1981–1984); Kerry Burke (1984–1987); Stan Rodger (1987–1989); Roger Douglas (1989–1990); Annette King (1990); Bill Birch (1990–1993); Roger Maxwell (1993–1996); Max Bradford (1996–1998); Tuariki Delamere (1998–1999); Lianne Dalziel (1999–2004); David Cunliffe (2005–2007); Clayton Cosgrove (2007–2008); Jonathan Coleman (2008–2011); Michael Woodhouse (2013–2017); and Iain Lees-Galloway (2017–2020). Maurice McTigue, who was Minister of Immigration for only eight months in 1993, did not respond to requests for an interview; Paul Swain (2004–2005) and Nathan Guy (2011–2013) corresponded with us about the possibility of being interviewed but in the end decided not to participate in this project. The interviews we undertook included politicians who have been or are household names in New Zealand as well as politicians whose contribution to migration policymaking and other portfolios and political processes is less well known. In many ways our book therefore documents a crucial period in New Zealand's history – the period of neoliberal globalisation which is arguably bracketed between the formation of the Fourth Labour Government in 1984, when the major liberalisation of immigration policy was initiated, and the Covid-19 pandemic in 2020, when almost all immigration was suspended for a period of two years.

The interviews with former Ministers of Immigration were undertaken by Francis and Alan between December 2019 and February 2021. Our initial plan was to travel around Aotearoa New Zealand to carry out the interviews in person to enhance the rapport and take the time to hear the stories of each former Minister of Immigration. Our journeys in December 2019 initially took us to Christchurch to interview Kerry Burke, to Dunedin to interview Stan Rodger, to Manukau and Pukekohe in Auckland, where we interviewed Roger Douglas and Bill Birch respectively, and to Urenui in Taranaki to interview Roger Maxwell. We were also able to complete an in-person interview with Lianne Dalziel in Christchurch in January 2020. Much like the wider world of immigration, our plans to carry out the remainder of the interviews in person were suspended in March 2020 by the impacts of the Covid-19 global pandemic and government health and border controls. As the pandemic stretched out, we pivoted to undertake interviews on the Zoom video conference platform, except for an in-person interview that Francis undertook with Clayton Cosgrove in Auckland in November 2020. For many of the other participants in this research, online interviews turned out to be more convenient. Many of these more recent former Ministers of Immigration have active and busy careers, so online interviews provided greater flexibility and in many cases did not reduce the detail or candid commentaries offered. We had not planned to interview Aussie Malcolm, but his name kept emerging in the commentaries of other former Ministers of Immigration, and he agreed to participate in an interview that we carried out in December 2020. Fitting the chronology of the ministership, we concluded the interviews with Michael Woodhouse and Iain Lees-Galloway in February 2021.

Interviewing political leaders in the way that we have done for this book has formed only a small component of critical migration research on policymaking internationally (Consterdine 2017; Duncan 2012; Ellerman

2021). In the broader literature in policy studies, there is a substantial body of scholarship that includes as a core method interviewing important public officials (Mosley 2013). The focus of such research has very often been on extending the examination of policy formation and translation beyond questions of what policy is made and why – which can very often be discerned from publicly available materials – towards questions about the *how* of policymaking and administration (Yanow 1996). Yanow (2007: 113), for example, has described the significance of interviews with key actors in political process as an invaluable component of critical and interpretive approaches to policy analysis, especially 'in order to understand how individuals frame policy issues and where these frames come from'. The interviews undertaken for this book have synergies with such approaches. Interviews offered unique insights into the early lives of former Ministers of Immigration, the process of entering politics and becoming Minister of Immigration, the development and implementation of migration policy, relationships with the bureaucracy and other politicians, and the broader political management challenges associated with migration.

Each author of this book has been shaped by very different socio-cultural and professional backgrounds, and our different positionality has influenced our approaches to the material. Francis was born in Wellington in the late 1970s to Pākehā parents and grew up in Los Angeles and Auckland as well as spending significant parts of his adult life in Singapore and South Korea. He is the second of four children and was raised with a strong emphasis on Catholic religion and within Catholic schooling. Francis's ancestors were mainly from Ireland and arrived in New Zealand in the mid-to-late nineteenth century as the full force of settler colonisation was underway. Some of these ancestors came in families and some as individuals, but they were all encouraged to come as part of the project of establishing a White settler colony at the edges of the British Empire, even though as Irish they often had to prove their worthiness as White British subjects. At least one of Francis's ancestors came as a military conscript from colonised Ireland only to fight as a British imperial trooper against Māori in the New Zealand Wars, and then benefited from the gift of stolen land that followed. Indicative of dominant cultural norms in the 1980s, Francis grew up simply thinking he was a New Zealander, with little recognition of the settler colonial racial politics that continue to shape Aotearoa today. Francis came to migration research through training in sociology, media studies, and human geography, with significant exposure to critical and postcolonial social theory and its potential to reveal obscured power relations. This orientation shapes Francis's approach to research, and has been extended and enhanced through collaboration with feminist and postcolonial migration scholars in Asia, and more recently with Indigenous scholars in projects addressing population, diversity, and racism in Aotearoa. His contribution to this book reflects this orientation in the ways in which the text asks difficult and obscured questions about how migration policy is made, how power is exercised through migration and border control, who is excluded from making migration policy, and who benefits from the making of contemporary New Zealand society through migration.

Alan was born in Canada to New Zealand parents of English, Scottish, and Māori ancestry. He is a member of the Tainui confederation of tribes, with whenua in the Coromandel Peninsula. During Alan's early years, the family moved back and forth between Canada (where his father was a mathematics professor) and New Zealand, before permanently returning home when he was seven. Parallel to mainstream schooling in New Zealand from that time, Alan was trained in mau rākau, Te Ataarangi, whaikōrero, kapa haka and other aspects of Māori culture. At Victoria University of Wellington he completed a Bachelor of Arts in History and English Literature, and a Bachelor of Music, majoring in the History and Literature of Music, having first entered university intending to major in performance violin. He then became a books editor at Huia Publishers in Wellington, where he worked on *The Silent Migration*, *Wiremu Tamihana*, and a range of novels, poetry collections, and other works by and about Māori. After Huia, Alan won a Japanese Government research scholarship to study how minority and migrant groups used music to mobilise and advocate for human rights in a highly assimilationist society. While studying, he worked part-time as the editor of a book series on migration for the Japan Centre for Area Studies, and as the travel editor and classical music columnist for a *Time Out* magazine. He then won a Top Achiever Doctoral Scholarship to complete a doctorate in Geography at Oxford University (based at St Antony's College), where he undertook training in both ethnological and statistical methods, as well as the theory and philosophy of social science, based first at the Centre on Migration, Policy and Society and then at the International Migration Institute. He has since lived and worked in the UK, New Zealand, Germany, the US, and Australia. This background of international and interdisciplinary research training has shaped Alan's critical realist epistemology, which underpins his approach to evidence and historical argument in parts of this book.

Neil was born in Northern Ireland and grew up in the final decade of the Troubles – a violent and often deadly conflict between unionists/loyalists who wanted Northern Ireland to remain in the UK and nationalists/republicans who desired a united and sovereign Ireland. At Queen's University Belfast, he studied for a Bachelor of Arts in English Literature and History, focusing primarily on Irish and early modern history. He then completed a Master of Arts in English Literature at Queen's. In 2012, Neil was awarded a Commonwealth Scholarship to undertake his PhD in English Literature at the University of Otago, which he completed in 2015. Since then, Neil's research has moved into the fields of political and critical theory, particularly related to neoliberalism and border regimes, but his training in historical methods and literary analysis remain fundamental to his current scholarly practice, as is evidenced in his contribution to this book.

The participants in this research regularly offered us full and frank accounts of the politics of the day, often interspersed with anecdotes of their encounters with constituents and politicians in New Zealand and abroad, and the challenging scenarios that emerge in cases of ministerial appeals. It was significant that, as researchers initiating and undertaking the interviews, Francis and Alan were positioned as established migration scholars with international reputations, having led major population and migration research institutes and engaged extensively in the past with government agencies and international organisations on migration matters. Our positionality in the research enabled access, but as interpretive policy scholars highlight (Mason-Bish 2019; Mikecz 2012), it also set the scene for robust conversations about policy matters wherein participants were given the opportunity to flesh out their world views, experiences, and motivations, and to respond to critical lines of inquiry about the making of policy and the regulation of migration. While some former ministers were guarded about disclosing sensitive or contentious information, or made it clear that such information was off the record, all were very forthcoming in sharing their stories and perspectives, often extending these to comment on more recent migration policy and political matters. Several of the former ministers, even those who had only recently left the role, commented at the end of the interview that they appreciated the opportunity to 'take a walk down memory lane', as one interviewee put it. Set alongside historical records and published studies that Neil played a pivotal role in researching, summarising, and drafting into an initial historical narrative, the stories and memories of the interviewees provide an important insight into the significant transformation of New Zealand migration governance between 1981 and 2020.

While we maintain the validity of our approach, we acknowledge some methodological limitations. Our primary sources were the ministers, and we did not interview the people who watched and guided those ministers most closely, such as their aides, their civil servants, their shadow counterparts, fellow legislators, political superiors, journalists, or legal experts. Our interviews were, however, supplemented by extensive research on primary sources from the period under examination, including Hansard records of parliamentary debates, government press releases, reports on migration and migration policy developments from the time, and news media reports. We also consulted secondary sources such as published histories. However, despite presenting our narrative chronologically, we did not consult the full range of available primary historical sources. Our analysis and interpretation of the interviews is subjective, and it should be noted that the authors come from different social and disciplinary backgrounds and did not always agree how to interpret the data and which themes to prioritise.

Structure of the Book

Following this introductory chapter, the book shifts firstly to consider the collapse of the imperial migration regime that dominated New Zealand migration governance following the signing of Te Tiriti and the emergence of a new regime amid the neoliberal reworking of society and the economy. Chapters 1, 2, and 3 outline this major transformation in New Zealand's migration regime that took place from the 1970s to the mid-1990s. In Chapter 1, we provide a historical overview of the emergence and consolidation of what we call the imperial migration regime, which was in ascendency in New Zealand from the mid-nineteenth century until the 1970s. Chapter 2 discusses the emergence and contestation of a new political rationality for governing migration couched in an emphasis on multiculturalism and socially liberal principles of non-discrimination that also provided the scope for identifying the economic potential of immigration. Chapter 3 traces the way in which migration policy became explicitly articulated and institutionalised as part of the neoliberalisation of New Zealand society from the late 1980s until the mid-1990s and the emergence of anti-immigrationism as a key part of public discourses around migration.

Chapters 4 to 6 of the book discuss the consolidation of this multicultural-neoliberal migration regime. In Chapter 4, we identify the emergence of a strengthened emphasis on managerialism that manifested in an evolution through adaptation to new realities emerging from the large-scale expansion and diversification of migration that took place from the mid-1990s into the first decade of the twenty-first century. Chapters 5 and 6 explore the growing dysfunction of the migration regime despite ongoing efforts to resolve problems through increasingly micro-level management solutions. These chapters trace the increasing securitisation of migration after the international terrorist attacks of the early 2000s; a renewed emphasis on the emigration of New Zealand citizens; and the rise of temporary migration and concomitant issues of exploitation, national identity, and (non-)citizenship. This part of the book discusses how underlying tensions brought about by record high migration levels placed significant challenges on the ability of Ministers of Immigration, or the bureaucracies they oversaw, to effectively manage the scale and outcomes of migration. We include a brief Coda to explore the Covid-19 pandemic and the response to it, including border closure, immigration suspension, and an opportunity for a reconsideration of migration governance.

Building on the analysis undertaken in these chapters, we conclude the book by drawing attention to the fragments of empire and colonialism in contemporary migration governance, the role of emigration and trans-Tasman connections in immigration settings, and the significance of policy mobility and diffusion. Drawing this analysis together, we return to the observation that, despite being a subject of intense policy and political interest over the course of the four decades between 1981 and 2020, immigration policy in New Zealand is characterised by surprising levels of political consensus. Ministers of Immigration are undoubtedly influential in migration governance and have brought a variety of perspectives and approaches to the role, but fundamental features of immigration policy appear to be institutionalised in such a way that challenges to the status quo are able to be sidelined. This is the outcome of the last four decades of migration policymaking in New Zealand – a seemingly unassailable certainty that migration governance ought to be liberal in a multicultural sense but shaped by taken-for-granted neoliberal political rationalities that prioritise economic and market value.

CHAPTER 1

The Imperial Migration Regime, 1840–1980

The signing of Te Tiriti o Waitangi / The Treaty of Waitangi in 1840 marked a significant historical juncture in the establishment of colonial government and the initiation of large-scale immigration and settlement in New Zealand. At the time of the signing in 1840, the number of non-Māori in New Zealand was around 2000 but would grow to over 700,000 by the late nineteenth century. For the 130 years following the signing of Te Tiriti / The Treaty, New Zealand was shaped by population movement within the British Empire and became dominated by English, Scottish and, to a lesser degree, Irish settlers, and their descendants. The 'imperial migration regime' that emerged then stabilised and declined over this period would fundamentally shape the population, economy, politics, culture, and identity of what became known as New Zealand. From the middle of the nineteenth century, the country was constituted as a White settler colony, tethered to the imperial heartland of Britain.

In the latter half of the twentieth century, the pursuit of population and development took new turns, especially as the British Empire disintegrated in the aftermath of World War II, as New Zealand governments were forced reluctantly into greater independence from an increasingly Europe-oriented UK. From the 1950s onwards, New Zealand continued to be dominated by British as well as wider European immigrant settlement, but there was tentative incorporation of labour migration from neighbouring Pacific countries (including former New Zealand colonies). And since the 1980s, a more globally expansive, economically oriented approach to immigration has led to significant ethno-demographic diversification.

This chapter presents an overview of the historical development of New Zealand's imperial migration regime, covering the 200 years from the late eighteenth to late twentieth centuries.[3] Our account draws on major histories of this period in order to provide sufficient background to the substantive discussion of New Zealand migration policymaking in Chapters 2–6. In this

---

3   This chapter draws extensively on Gamlen and Sherrell's (2022) account of Australia and New Zealand's development as migration states, and our periodisation builds on theirs – as does the wider periodisation we follow throughout this book.

respect, the discussion in this chapter does not engage in historiographical debates about the eighteenth to twentieth centuries in New Zealand. Instead, we draw on major secondary histories by other scholars to provide an overview of key moments in the migration histories of New Zealand, which are arranged temporally into several key periods from early settlement, the signing of Te Tiriti, and processes of immigration throughout the nineteenth century through to twentieth-century consolidation of the imperial migration regime and its disintegration in the 1970s. This account of the imperial migration regime, from its establishment in the nineteenth century to its conclusion in the 1970s and 1980s, provides a background to our more granular account of the dynamic political, economic, and social forces that have constituted New Zealand's immigration policymaking in the late twentieth and early twenty-first centuries.

Early Settlement and Encounters before 1840

Māori settled the archipelago that later became Aotearoa from islands in the eastern Pacific some 800 years ago and became tangata whenua, the Indigenous people (Anderson et al. 2015). The origins of these migrations date back approximately 5000 years in South China and took shape through the navigation and successive settlement of islands in Te Moana-Nui-a-Kiwa (the Pacific Ocean) by the Pacific ancestors of Māori. Māori settlement expanded to encompass the entirety of the major islands in what was to become Aotearoa, and involved adapting tropical lives and practices to a more temperate climate (Anderson 2016; Houkamau 2019).

The first known contact between Māori and Europeans occurred in 1642 with the arrival of Dutch explorer Abel Tasman, who anchored in Te Tai-o-Aorere (now known in English as Tasman Bay) on the northern coast of Te Waipounamu (the South Island). His voyage occurred in the maelstrom of early European imperialism across the world, which was underpinned by claims of racial supremacy and the entitlement to discover and possess Indigenous territories (Attwood 2020; Rata 2020). While other imperial aspirants, including the British, became aware of the 'discovery' of New Zealand, it was more than a century before the British HMS *Endeavour*, captained by James Cook, circumnavigated the country in 1769 as part of a journey that mapped and eventually opened the Pacific to European imperialism and settler colonisation.[4] The French were also engaging in

---

4   It is possible that explorers other than Tasman also reached New Zealand prior to Cook. For example, in 1896 the Italian historian Dom Felice Vaggioli (1896 [2023]: 13) recorded a tradition handed down to Māori in the lower North Island that a European ship arrived well before Cook, bringing dinner plates and iron tools that these tribes still held in their possession in the late nineteenth century.

exploration alongside Cook in 1769, with the *St Jean Baptiste* landing in Doubtless Bay in December of that year (Salmond 1997), followed by the *Mascarin* and the *Marquis de Castro*, commanded by Captain Marion du Fresne in 1772 (Vaggioli, 1896 [2023]). Cook himself visited again in 1772 and 1776, and an increasing number of ships passed through native waters in the following years, with frequent trade emerging across the Tasman to Australia not long after the establishment of the first British penal colony there in 1788. At the time of these early engagements with Europeans, the Māori population has been estimated at 90,000 (Pool 2015).

Starting from at least the late eighteenth century, growing numbers of British subjects were reaching the South Pacific, often via Australia's expanding penal colonies (Salmond 1997). They included mariners, missionaries, whalers, sealers, traders, trappers, fugitives, and *flâneurs* (Gamlen & Sherrell 2022). Māori and these European sojourners and settlers established extensive trading relationships, and, in some instances, early settlers lived among Māori communities. There were also small numbers of Indians in the country in the early nineteenth century, who had absconded from British ships and lived among Māori or European settlements (Ballantyne 2012; Leckie 2022). By the early nineteenth century, Māori had also established trade and interactions beyond their archipelago, including through joining voyages to Europe and regular trading activities in Sydney (O'Malley 2015). While these early interactions represented new global connections, they also led to the spread of European diseases, and increased the availability of muskets, which made the constant intertribal warfare among pre-European Māori far more lethal. These factors led to a substantial decline in the Māori population to approximately 80,000 by 1840 (Ballara 2003; Pool 2015). The population of European settlers continued to grow at a relatively slow rate during the early decades of the nineteenth century, reaching approximately 2000 by 1839. Almost all of these early arrivals were men, two thirds were in the North Island, and around 90 per cent were from the UK (two thirds of those were English – Pool 2015). While trading relationships were seen as beneficial by some Māori (O'Malley 2015), there were also significant concerns among northern rangatira (tribal chiefs) about the destabilising behaviour and impact of early European traders and settlers (Mutu 2022).

By the 1830s, Māori rangatira had become sufficiently concerned about the disruptive impact of early European trade and settlement that they wished to contain the problem (Mutu 2022). At the time, the British were not expressly extending their worldwide colonial project in the islands they called New Zealand. They did, however, appoint James Busby as the 'British Resident' in 1833 to provide some oversight of the tiny but impactful European population (Belich 2002b). While Busby failed to exercise control over contact between peoples and the impact of British on Māori communities, he did have influence. Most notably, Busby's interaction with northern Māori rangatira contributed to He Whakaputanga o te Rangatiratanga o Nu Tīreni, The Declaration of Independence of New Zealand, which was signed by thirty-four Northern rangatira under the auspices of Te Whakaminenga o ngā Hapū o Nu Tīreni (The Gathering of the Hapū of New Zealand). He Whakaputanga has articles that cover independence as a nation, the vesting of collective sovereignty in rangatira, and the establishment of an annual congress, and a fourth article sending the declaration to King William IV and seeking his support (Mutu 2022; O'Malley 2017). According to official state history, this was 'one of the earliest assertions of Māori identity beyond separate iwi and hapū' (Archives New Zealand 2022).

British involvement in New Zealand began to increase in the late 1830s (Belich 2002b), through formal colonial incorporation, growing missionary activity, and the establishment of the private New Zealand Association in 1837 (reconstituted as the New Zealand Company in 1838), which would organise significant immigration in the following decades (Barber 2020). Anglo-French rivalry contributed to British urgency for greater intervention, and many missionaries were advocating for a Protestant colony or protectorate 'that would keep out the papist French, control the agents of vice and facilitate mission work' (Belich 2002b: 182). The British Government acted in June 1839, incorporating New Zealand into an expanded colony of New South Wales. Captain William Hobson was directed by the British Government in August 1839 to negotiate for the sovereignty of New Zealand and to establish a British colony.

1840: Te Tiriti o Waitangi, New Zealand's First Immigration Policy

The signing of The Treaty of Waitangi (English-language version) and Te Tiriti o Waitangi (Māori-language translation) on 6 February 1840 marked a formative moment in the colonisation of Aotearoa New Zealand (Orange 2015). The English version of The Treaty set out the basis of Māori consent and support for British sovereignty and aimed to establish some principles under which the process of colonisation would occur (Belich 2002b). The Māori text of Te Tiriti o Waitangi differed, which contributed to sharp disagreements over the scope of The Treaty and the extent to which it has been honoured that continue to the present day.[5] Nonetheless, by the end of 1840 around 500 Māori rangatira and other leaders had signed Te Tiriti, only thirty-nine of whom signed the English-language version (Waitangi Tribunal 2014). Several powerful rangatira refused to sign, however, including those in Waikato, Taranaki, and the central North Island (Orange 2015).

In addition to its role in legitimising British colonisation, Te Tiriti / The Treaty is also arguably New Zealand's first immigration policy document and is associated with the large-scale immigration that led to European demographic dominance (Kukutai & Rata 2017; New Zealand Productivity Commission 2022; Walker 1994). Indeed, the preamble to The Treaty begins by outlining the urgency of British authority because of the already growing arrival of migrants from Europe and Australia and the need to protect Māori 'just Rights and Property' and 'secure to them the enjoyment of Peace and Good Order' in the context of 'the great number of Her Majesty's Subjects who have already settled in New Zealand and the rapid extension of Emigration both from Europe and Australia which is still in progress'. The centrality of immigration in Te Tiriti / The Treaty is thus evident in several substantive ways.

The significance of Te Tiriti / The Treaty to immigration policy matters has largely been officially ignored until very recently (New Zealand Productivity Commission 2022). There has, however, been growing recognition in recent decades from Māori political leaders (Turia 2007) and academics (Kukutai & Rata 2017; Walker 1994), as well as other researchers (Population Monitoring Group 1991), that Te Tiriti / The Treaty has implications for immigration policy. These assertions have taken place in a context of renewed attention to the significance of The Treaty / Te Tiriti since the establishment of the Waitangi Tribunal in 1975, which has been part of a focus on processes of colonial redress (Orange 2015). Legal advice offered to the New Zealand Productivity Commission's review of immigration policy in 2021 has also highlighted other matters: that there is at least a duty to consult Māori on immigration; that immigration policy decisions around visas, entry permissions, deportations, and other matters relate to the provisions of Article 2 (chiefly authority); and that 'to act consistently with Te Tiriti, it [the Government] ought to consider incorporating Te Tiriti and tikanga [Māori custom] in the development of immigration policy, and empowering Māori to exercise manaakitanga [hospitality] to migrant

---

5   The Treaty / Te Tiriti has been subject to wide-ranging debate (O'Malley et al. 2011), especially in recent decades and in relation to the differing language and meanings of the English version and Māori translation (Kawharu et al. 2005; Ross 1972); the details of these debates are beyond the scope of this short overview.

communities' (Whāia Legal 2021: 2–3). These matters arguably remain unresolved in approaches to immigration policymaking in New Zealand – a point we touch on at various points in our narrative. For the moment, however, we turn to the immigration patterns and policy that emerged in the 130 years that followed the signing of Te Tiriti o Waitangi.

1841–1860: Commercial Settler Colonisation

On 21 May 1840, with the majority of rangatira yet to sign Te Tiriti / The Treaty, Hobson made a proclamation of sovereignty on behalf of Queen Victoria over the whole country of New Zealand (Orange 2015).[6] The signing of Te Tiriti o Waitangi and the claims to sovereignty that were made by the British subsequently marks a formative moment in the settler colonisation of New Zealand and the instigation of large-scale immigration. The Treaty's preamble already noted 'rapid' British emigration to New Zealand, but the scale of immigration of White settlers following 1840 was staggering. From a population of only 2000 at the time of signing, non-Māori (overwhelmingly English) grew in number to 59,000 by 1858 and to 299,000 by 1871. Over the same period, the Māori population declined from 80,000 in 1840 to 47,000 in 1871 due to the combined impacts of disease, war, and loss of resources (Pool 2015). Figure 1.1 visually demonstrates the gravity of this population change.

Commercial plans for large-scale settlement were already well underway as The Treaty was being formed. In 1837, the New Zealand Company received a Royal Charter to advocate settler colonisation of New Zealand. Conceived by Edward Wakefield, the New Zealand Company was one of several schemes designed to promote the settlement of Britain's colonies with enough British migrant labourers and tradespeople to make good the investment of colonial British capital, displace Indigenous peoples, and exploit the 'new' territories (Ballantyne 2014). The New Zealand Company sent its first vessel, the *Tory*, which arrived in what is now Wellington Harbour on 17 August 1839, and its officers set out to purchase large tracts of Māori land, claiming incorrectly to have purchased 20 million acres by October that year (Barber 2020). By the end of 1839, the Company had sent another eight ships, and the first settler colonists – about 1000 of them – arrived in what became known as Wellington in January 1840. Another settlement was established in Whanganui that September, receiving its first settlers in February 1841. The New Zealand Company sent

---

6   The timeline of migration policymaking draws on a series of public and academic sources. For a succinct timeline of these policy changes, see Bellamy 2018.

Figure 1.1. *Māori and Pākehā Population Numbers, 1840–1901*
(**Sources:** *Te Ara – the Encyclopedia of New Zealand*; Papps 1985; Pool 1991)

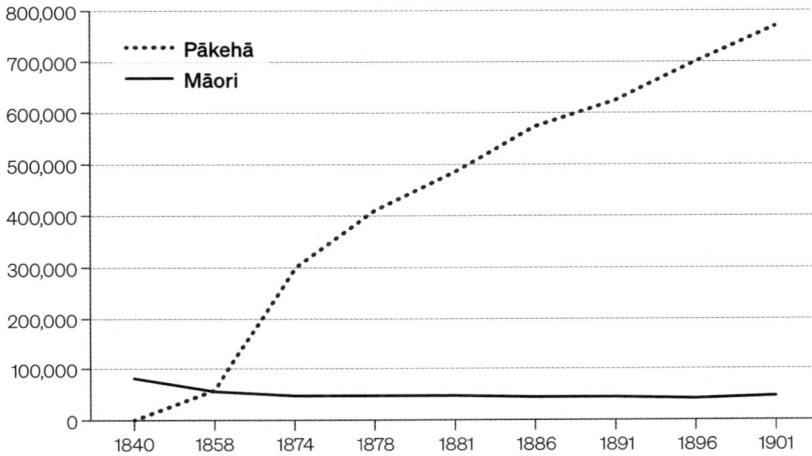

Figure 1.2. *New Zealand Net Migration and Net Migration as a Percentage of Total Population, 1861–2023*
(**Sources:** Gamlen & Sherrell 2022; Statistics New Zealand)

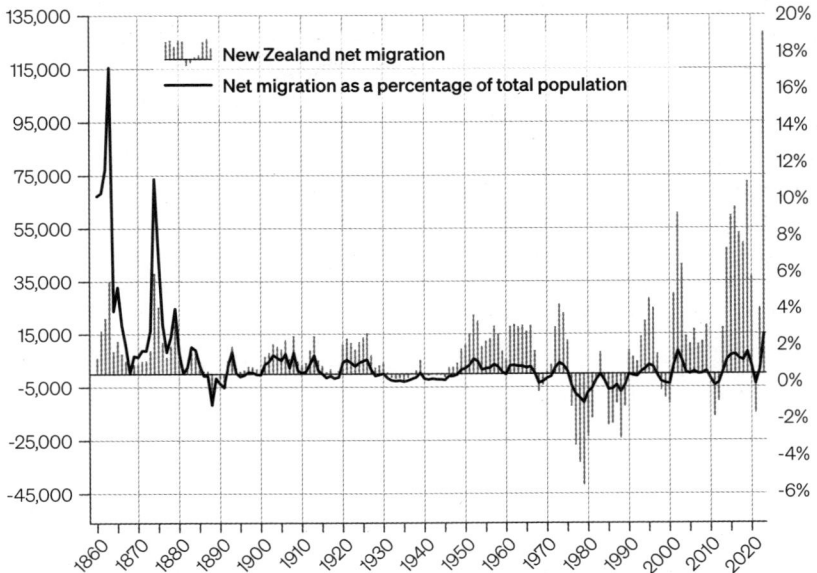

dozens of ships over the subsequent years and brought almost 80 per cent of the 18,000 settlers who arrived in New Zealand in the first twelve years after Te Tiriti o Waitangi (Spoonley & Bedford 2012: 30).

The New Zealand Company – like the new colonial government – was essentially British, but the early settlers themselves were somewhat more diverse. France retained an interest in settling New Zealand, and during August 1840, sixty-three French settlers arrived in Akaroa on the *Comte de Paris*, a ship belonging to the Nanto-Bordelaise Company, a French company seeking to colonise the South Island (Watts 2021). The New Zealand Company also organised recruitment from beyond the UK, including contingents of German settlers in 1843, 1844, and 1850 (Bade 1993), and later arrivals in the 1860s included Bohemian settlers (Procházková 2010). In 1848, the first two settler ships from Scotland arrived in the settlement of Dunedin, which had been established by the Free Church of Scotland and took in some 12,000 settlers over the ensuing ten years (Phillips & Hearn 2008).

After The Treaty, New Zealand became a British colony, initially part of the existing Crown colony of New South Wales and then its own separate colony in 1841 (Orange 2015). In 1854, the country's six new provinces were made responsible for immigration to the fledgling colony and began to develop their own immigration schemes based on the model of the New Zealand Company, with agents in Britain and Ireland offering free or assisted passage and grants of land as part of wider efforts to 'boost' colonial settlement. In the period 1858–70, two thirds of all immigrants went to the Canterbury region (Phillips n.d.). The settlement of the Canterbury region and its main city Christchurch (named after the Oxford University college) took off from 1850, with the arrival of 790 settlers on the famous 'Four Ships': *Randolph*, *Cressy*, *George Seymour*, and *Charlotte James* (Pickles 2016). The Canterbury Association was the largest of a series of provincial schemes that led the first phase of colonial settlement from 1854. Other such provincial immigration schemes were established in Auckland, Hawke's Bay, Southland, Nelson, Taranaki, and Wellington (Phillips & Hearn 2008).

The 1860s: War, Land, and Immigration

The New Zealand Wars, which ran from 1845 to 1872, represented another major turning point in the making of the nation through immigration and the contest over sovereignty between Māori and the Crown (Belich 1986). For historian Vincent O'Malley (2019: 20), 'land and sovereignty were inextricably linked' as causes of war. Immigration and the explosion of White settler populations were also crucial and catalysing ingredients, however, generating demand for land and new claims to political authority. The Crown claimed to have purchased massive tracts of Māori land in the 1840s and 1850s, but many of these claims turned out to be invalid or outright fraudulent. Māori continued to occupy and use many of the territories that settlers claimed to have been sold, and many rangatira became increasingly concerned about both land loss and the seemingly endless arrival of new settlers. Various initiatives arose to actively oppose the British – including the emergence of the Land League to prohibit the sale of Māori land, a Māori King movement to contest Britain's claims to sovereignty, and the Pai Mārire religious movement to reject and expel the foreigners and their culture in its entirety (Belich 2002b).

Military skirmishes over land broke out in various regions during the 1840s, then full-scale war erupted in northern Taranaki in March 1860 after settlers sought to push through a contested land sale at Waitara. The war quickly spread to other regions, as the British authorities moved to simply take the country by force and make way for unimpeded mass British settlement. Māori mounted prolonged, vociferous resistance, won many of the key battles, and taught British officers many durable lessons in military tactics. They were eventually forced into submission by weight of numbers.

During the first half of the 1860s, the Crown relied primarily on British imperial troops and shifting alliances with Māori hapū and iwi. The imperial troops numbered some 12,000 at their height, and 18,000 British soldiers served in New Zealand in total between 1840 and 1870 (O'Malley 2019). Some 40 per cent of imperial troops had been recruited in colonial Ireland, and many of them and other soldiers came from existing postings in other parts of the Empire, notably Australia and India. After concluding military service, many troops were granted confiscated Māori land and remained in New Zealand or sold up and travelled to Australia.

The New Zealand Wars were used to justify Britain's mass confiscation of land for settler colonisation (Williams 1999). For example, in 1863 the New Zealand Settlements Act enabled the confiscation of almost all land belonging to Ngāti Haua and Waikato iwi for the purposes of settlement by European colonists. In the North Island, some 4 million acres were confiscated by 1869. In 1864–65, 3000 settlers arrived under the Waikato immigration scheme (Horn 2014). Auckland's provincial government also recruited settlers as part of the national government's plan to consolidate British superiority. The intention was to bring 20,000 immigrants to Waikato from Cape Colony (in present-day South Africa), Britain, and Ireland, especially labourers (farm and railway workers), mechanics, small farmers, and capitalists (Campbell 1986; Phillips &

Hearn 2008). A larger amount of land would be offered to British and Irish immigrants (10 acres, plus 5 for each child); small farmers would receive 50 acres of land per adult (plus 25 acres for each person between the ages of twelve and seventeen) if they stayed for three years. However, October 1864 saw the failure of the loan system in London through which the Waikato scheme was funded, resulting in its collapse. By this point, however, the scheme had already absorbed some 2000 immigrants from Britain and Ireland, and a further 1000 from Cape Colony.

Meanwhile, spontaneous immigration also took off from the 1860s, leading to a series of settler booms and busts. Some veterans of the gold-rushes in California (1848–55) and Australia (1851–68) continued to New Zealand's South Island gold-rushes from 1861 (Belich 2002b). During the 1860s, net migration increased New Zealand's population by almost 6.5 per cent per year. The churn was high: some 100,000 people re-emigrated, to Australia and other colonies, or returned 'home' to Britain. Streets and buildings in California, Australia, and New Zealand began to look similar, as people circulated among these nodes of British colonisation (Hamer 1990).

Figure 1.3. *New Zealand Net Migration, 1860–1901*
(**Source:** Gamlen & Sherrell 2022)

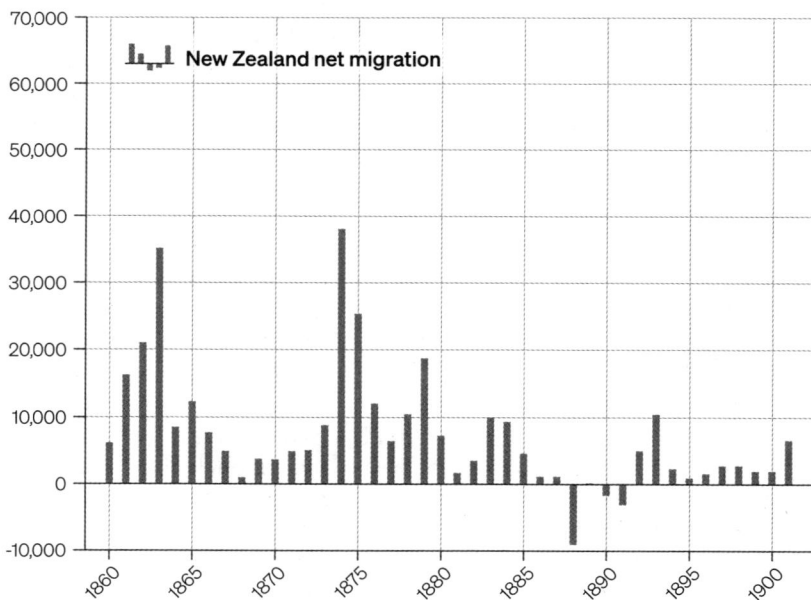

New Zealand's gold-rush was more muted and sporadic than its Australian and California predecessors, but it eventually transformed the colony. Gold was discovered on the banks of the Tuapeka River in Otago in 1861 and by year end some 14,000 prospectors had arrived. From 1861–67, the South Island (where the New Zealand Wars were not occurring) received a burst of 50,000 immigrants, most of them unmarried males, many of whom were attracted by the Otago gold-rush and its various downstream boom industries. The population of Otago itself grew by 400 per cent from 1861–64. A third of the miners hailed from England, but there were large contingents of Irish and Scottish too, as well as Scandinavians, Germans, and Chinese (Eldred-Grigg 2014; Phillips n.d.). The last of these groups, and the most politically oppressed in this early colonial period, were the Chinese, who began arriving towards the end of the Otago rush in 1863, with an estimated 2000 working on New Zealand's goldfields by 1869 (Ip 2003c). The rush itself was largely spent by 1863, but smaller finds emerged for several years, including on the South Island's West Coast in 1864–67 – which drew some 29,000 people, around 12 per cent of New Zealand's entire non-Māori population at that time.

The 1870s: The Great Settler Migration and the First Immigration Ministers

Protracted wars and the slowdown of the Australian and New Zealand gold-rushes led to an economic slump and a decline of immigration to New Zealand from the late 1860s to the early 1870s. From a peak of 35,120 in 1863, net migration fell to below 3800 per year on average from 1867–72, with a nadir in 1868, when there was a net inflow of just 860 people. New Zealand's economy by this time was tiny, and regions like Waikato, which had been thriving parts of the Māori economy prior to the wars, were now in economic depression (O'Malley 2016). While the sugar hit of gold-rushes had brought hopes to the Crown and White settlers of a spectacularly prosperous new Britain in the antipodes, the colony was desperate for more people to expand the economy.

As in other British settler colonies, the government was committed to plans to 'populate or perish', driving a surge in publicly assisted migration in the 1870s (Foks 2022). Colonial Treasurer Julius Vogel asserted that New Zealand was a future 'Britain of the South Seas', with the potential for a large, economically thriving population. Vogel's great public works policy proposed borrowing on the London financial markets to fund new infrastructure (particularly roads, railways, and ports), creating demand for large-scale labour immigration, and satisfying the colony's desire for population growth (Dalziel 2013). The Immigration and Public Works Act passed in 1870, enabling the colonial government to offer free passage to European migrants from 1873. The following year, net migration spiked to over 38,000, equivalent to 11 per cent of the population – a raw intake unequalled for the next thirteen decades. Vogel's scheme transformed New Zealand from a loose constellation of provincial outposts dominated by pork-barrel politics to a fledgling settler colonial state with a centrally administered public infrastructure (Dalziel 2013).

It was in this post-land-war context that, in 1872, the colonial government first established the office of immigration minister, which forms the focus of this book. With the land wars now won, the government was strengthened in its purpose of acquiring Māori land to enable even larger-scale settler colonisation, and the ministerial portfolio of immigration was intimately tied to this project. Many early Ministers of Immigration, such as Maurice O'Rorke (1871–73), Julius Vogel (1873–74), and Harry Atkinson (1874–76), were also simultaneously Minister of Crown Lands or held other senior Cabinet roles, such as Premier (in the case of Vogel) and Treasurer then Premier (in the case of Atkinson). The seniority of the portfolio of immigration and its linkages to land or public works matters continued while George Grey was Premier from 1877 to 1879. Grey's first Minister of Immigration, James McAndrew (1877–78), was simultaneously Minister of Public Works, while Robert Stout (1878–79) was Minister of Lands and Immigration, as well as holding the office of Attorney-General. William Rolleston was Minister of Lands, Immigration and Education (1879–84) and Richmond Hursthouse was briefly Minister of Immigration (as well as Lands and Mines) in 1884. When Stout became Premier (1884–87), John Ballance served as Minister of Immigration (1884–87) while also being Minister of Lands and Native Affairs; he too would later become Premier (1891–93). George Richardson took over as Minister of Immigration and Lands from 1887 to 1891 and also had responsibility for Mines (1887–89) and Agriculture (1889–91).

Despite the creation of this new government immigration portfolio, the great settler migration of the 1870s was itself short-lived. Weak commodity prices soon hit New Zealand's export-dependent economy, driving average net migration back to 6376 in 1877. Net migration rallied briefly in 1878–80, then fell still further, to well under 2000 in 1881. For the next twenty years net migration bubbled around an average of about 2700 per year, only once surpassing 10,000 per year (reaching 10,412 in 1893), and in 1888–91 the colony experienced a net migration loss of around 14,000, with only 764 assisted migrants arriving during this period. No assisted migrants arrived at all in 1892, and assisted migration did not resume until 1904. By the 1890s, New Zealand's first great settler migration was effectively over. Immigration was only part of settler colonisation by this stage, however. With a population of 412,000 non-Māori in 1878, natural increase was now also contributing a growing share to population change (Pool 2015). By 1891, the non-Māori population was 488,000, and by the end of the century it had reached 770,000 (1901). The settlers and their descendants were still overwhelmingly British and Irish. Chinese, the largest non-Māori and non-European group, numbered only 4836 in 1874 (just five of whom were female), and by 1901 that population had decreased to 2902 (36 female), not least because of increasing racist restrictions that characterised the period from 1880 to 1910.

Table 1.1. *Ministers of Immigration, 1872–1981*
(**Sources:** *New Zealand Parliamentary Debates*, Vols. 12–436; *Dictionary of New Zealand Biography*: https://teara.govt.nz/en/biographies)

In Office	Name	Concurrent Major Portfolios	Premier / Prime Minister
1872	John Davies Ormond	Public Works	William Fox
1872	William Fitzherbert	Crown Lands	Edward William Stafford
1872–73	George Maurice O'Rorke	Crown Lands	George Marsden Waterhouse; Julius Vogel
1873–74	Julius Vogel	Premier, Colonial Treasurer	Julius Vogel
1874–76	Harry Albert Atkinson	Colonial Treasurer, Crown Lands	Daniel Pollen; Julius Vogel
1876	John Davies Ormond	Crown Lands	Harry Albert Atkinson
1876–77	Harry Albert Atkinson	Premier, Colonial Treasurer, Crown Lands	Harry Albert Atkinson
1877	Donald Reid	Crown Lands	Harry Albert Atkinson
1877–78	James McAndrew	Crown Lands	George Grey
1878–79	Robert Stout	Attorney-General, Lands	George Grey

1879	William Gisborne	Mines	George Grey
1879–84	William Rolleston	Justice, Lands, Education, Native Affairs	John Hall; Frederick Whitaker; Harry Albert Atkinson
1884	Richmond Hursthouse	Lands	Harry Albert Atkinson
1884–87	John Ballance	Native Affairs, Defence, Lands	Robert Stout
1887–91	George Frederick Richardson	Lands, Mines, Immigration	Harry Albert Atkinson
1891–96	John McKenzie	Lands, Agriculture	John Ballance; Richard John Seddon
1896–1902	William Campbell Walker	Education	Richard John Seddon
1903–6	Richard John Seddon	Prime Minister, Colonial Treasurer, Labour, Defence, Education	Richard John Seddon
1906	Charles Houghton Mills	Trade and Customs	William Hall-Jones
1907–9	James McGowan	Justice, Mines	Joseph George Ward
1909–11	George Fowlds	Education	Joseph George Ward
1911–12	James Carroll (Acting)	Native Affairs	Joseph George Ward
1912	George Warren Russell	Internal Affairs, Public Health	Thomas Mackenzie
1912–15	Francis Henry Dillon Bell	Internal Affairs	William Ferguson Massey
1915	Josiah Alfred Hanan	Education	William Ferguson Massey
1915–20	Francis Henry Dillon Bell	Internal Affairs, Attorney-General, Public Health	William Ferguson Massey

1920–28	William Nosworthy	Agriculture, Finance, Postmaster-General, External Affairs	William Ferguson Massey; Joseph Gordon Coates
1928–30	John George Cobbe	Marine, Industries and Commerce	Joseph Ward
1930–31	Sidney George Smith	Labour	George William Forbes
1931–35	James Alexander Young	Health, Internal Affairs	George William Forbes
1935–40	Hubert Thomas Armstrong	Labour, Employment	Michael Joseph Savage
1940–44	David Wilson	Civil Defence	Peter Fraser
1944–46	Patrick Charles Webb	Labour, Mines, Postmaster-General	Peter Fraser
1947–49	Angus McLagan	Labour, Mines, Employment	Peter Fraser
1949–54	William Sullivan	Labour, Mines, Employment, Housing	Sydney George Holland
1954–57	Josiah Ralph Hanan	Health	Sydney George Holland; Keith Holyoake
1957–60	Frederick Hackett	Labour, Mines	Walter Nash
1960–69	Thomas Philip Shand	Labour, Mines, Electricity	Keith Holyoake
1969–72	John Ross Marshall	Deputy Prime Minister, Overseas Trade, Attorney-General, Labour	Keith Holyoake
1972	David Spence Thomson	Labour	John Ross Marshall
1972–75	Fraser MacDonald Colman	Mines, Postmaster-General	Norman E. Kirk; William E. Rowling
1975–78	Thomas Francis Gill	Health	Robert D. Muldoon
1978–81	James B. Bolger	Labour	Robert D. Muldoon

1880–1910: A White Dominion

The period from 1880 to 1910 was characterised by a consolidation of settler colonialism in New Zealand (Farmer 1985). As in Australia and Canada, New Zealand had been conceived as White and British in its establishment and government (Constantine 2002; Foks 2022) and 'many New Zealand residents shared the racial antipathy and sense of superiority that was common among the white races in North America and Australia' (Farmer 1985: 59). The veteran colonial administrator George Grey, who in total served seventeen years combined as Governor and Premier of New Zealand and later retired there, provided a quintessential expression of this Anglo-Saxonism in Parliament in July 1879 (New Zealand Herald 1879: 5):

> *The first migrants to New Zealand were selected with extreme care.*
> *... Thus, the foundations for the future nation were here most wisely*
> *laid. It would hardly be an exaggeration to say that the future of the*
> *islands of the Pacific Ocean depends upon the inhabitants of New*
> *Zealand being true to themselves, and preserving uninjured and*
> *unmixed that Anglo-Saxon population which now inhabits it.*

By the 1880s, the Māori population had been decimated by disease and war, numbering only 46,000 in 1881 and declining further to 42,000 by 1896. By 1901, non-Māori, overwhelmingly British and Irish, outnumbered the Indigenous population by sixteen to one. Moreover, by this time only one third of the New Zealand population was born abroad and much greater attention was being paid to the character of existing residents and the risks brought by new arrivals (Figure 1.5). Having usurped Māori authority and demographic dominance, public and political attention shifted more expressly towards the achievement of a 'Brittanic' White identity for New Zealand (Darwin 2009), a settler colonial endeavour that would focus intensively on restricting Chinese.

Racist immigration controls represented some early examples of government initiatives in New Zealand that were developed more independently of Great Britain (Farmer 1985). In 1881, New Zealand echoed Canadian and Australian moves to enact the Chinese Immigrants Act, which imposed a £10 poll tax on each Chinese immigrant, and limited arriving ships to one Chinese passenger per 10 tonnes of cargo. In 1898, restrictions on Chinese immigrants were increased so that only one Chinese migrant could enter per 200 tonnes of cargo; the poll tax on each Chinese immigrant was raised to £100. In 1894, the Undesirable Immigrants Act was passed, aimed specifically at Asian immigration (Spoonley & Bedford 2012: 102). In 1899, the Immigration Restriction Act prohibited any migrant (except British and Irish) who could not fill out an application form in 'any European language'. It became routine to ask non-White would-be immigrants to sit the test in obscure European languages which they would have no realistic chance of knowing. In 1907, the Chinese Immigrants Amendment Act required would-be Chinese entrants to sit an additional English-language test, which involved reading one hundred words of English in front of officials. The following year (1908) saw the introduction of a requirement for Chinese immigrants to place a thumbprint on their certificate of registration, as part of the Immigration Restriction Amendment Act. Meanwhile, naturalisation of Chinese immigrants came to a halt (and only resumed in 1952).

Chinese immigrants were not the only perceived threats to the racial purity of the colony. While Irish did not face explicit immigration restrictions, Irish Catholics were always at the margins of the Britannic identity in ascendency in the late nineteenth and early twentieth centuries. Political rhetoric problematised the presence and questioned the loyalty of Irish Catholics, and in day-to-day life they 'were subjected to both attitudinal sectarianism (such as name calling) and labour-market discrimination, that sought to prevent them from obtaining jobs or achieving positions of prominence in the workplace' (McCarthy 2022: 13). Indian migrants from the Punjab and Gujarat provinces had migrated to New Zealand as British subjects, although this was curtailed by the 1899 Immigration Restriction Act and more so by the 1920 amendment that limited Indian arrivals to those with existing family (Leckie 2022). There was also widespread hostility towards Dalmatian immigrants arriving to work as pickers and diggers of kauri tree gum since the 1890s (Farmer 1985). The Kauri Gum Industry Act of 1898 restricted the number of Dalmatians who could work on the gum fields, in order to reserve more places for British subjects (Jones 2012). And amid discussions of imperialism and racial purity and superiority there were also restrictions on people classed as 'idiot', 'insane', or suffering from contagious diseases, formalised in 1882 under the Imbecile Passengers Act (McCarthy 2015).

A key foundation for the systematic development of new immigration laws and regulations in the late nineteenth and early twentieth centuries was the emergence of political parties. The 1890s saw the rise of the New Zealand Liberal Party, the country's first real political party, which maintained power under a series of leaders between 1891 and 1912, during which time it built the foundations of both a welfare state and a government apparatus for immigration control. The party's founder, John Ballance was himself immigration minister from 1883 to 1887, before becoming leader of the new party and Premier in 1891. After dying in office, Ballance was succeeded as Premier by Liberal leader Richard Seddon (1893–1906), New Zealand's longest-serving Premier or Prime Minister. After Seddon's death in 1906, the premiership remained with the Liberals, passing briefly to William Hall-Jones, then to Joseph Ward (1906–1912), and finally to Thomas Mackenzie, who was quickly defeated in a vote of no confidence led by William Massey of the newly formed conservative Reform Party.

The Liberals left a lasting imprint on New Zealand's immigration system during their two decades in office, including the consolidation of the government's grip on land for settler colonisation. Their first immigration minister was John McKenzie, who served in the role from 1891 to 1896 under Ballance and then Seddon, and was for much of this period also Minister of Lands (1891–1900), Minister of Agriculture (1891–1900), and Commissioner of Forests (1893–1900). He was succeeded as immigration minister by William Walker (1896–1903), also an appointee of Richard Seddon. However, Seddon eventually took the role of Minister of Immigration for himself in his final years of office, from 1903 to 1906. The immigration portfolio in this

Figure 1.4. *Net Migration as a Percentage of Total Population in New Zealand, 1901–2023*
(**Sources:** Gamlen & Sherrell 2022; Statistics New Zealand)

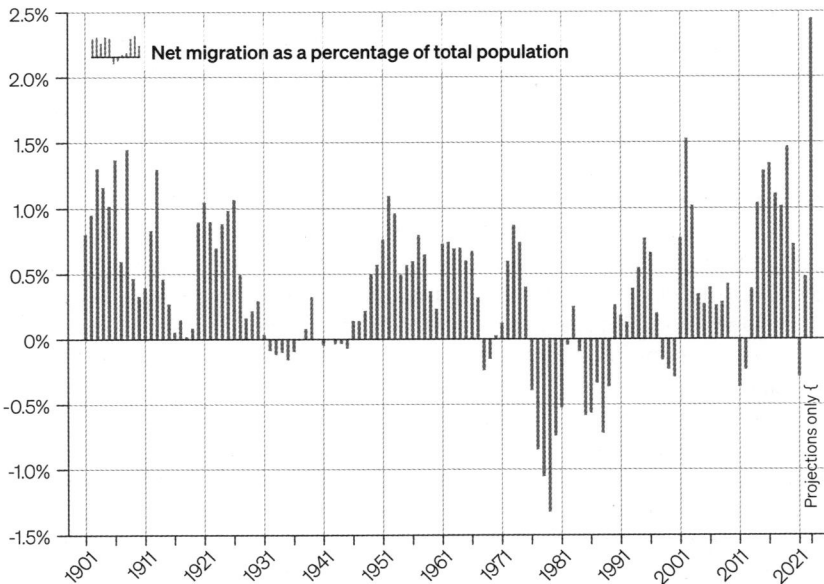

period was therefore dominated by Seddon, an avid racist (Farmer 1985), who in his first speech as a local candidate in the West Coast advocated to 'wage war with locomotives' in suppressing Māori resistance to colonialism, and likened the Chinese to monkeys. Seddon warned against New Zealand being 'deluged with Asiatic Tartars', and said, 'I would sooner address white men than these Chinese. You can't talk to them, you can't reason with them. All you can get from them is "No savvy"' (Hastings Standard 1906).

With Māori resistance to land confiscation now under control, the government could adopt new priorities in its efforts to attract settlers and build the colony. Seddon's racist approach to immigration continued to shape New Zealand politics after his death in 1906. The firm focus on attracting White immigrants and controlling other inflows remained consistent under his Liberal successors, including immigration ministers Charles H. Mills and James McGowan (1906–9), George Fowlds (1906–11), and George Warren Russell (1912) (Drummond 2013). But in contrast to their predecessors in the nineteenth century, immigration ministers from the early twentieth century onwards did not hold responsibility for the Lands

Figure 1.5. *Foreign-Born as a Percentage of Population in New Zealand, 1886–2019*
(**Source:** Gamlen & Sherrell 2022) (Note: As population figures are from censuses at 5–10-year intervals, other years are interpolated)

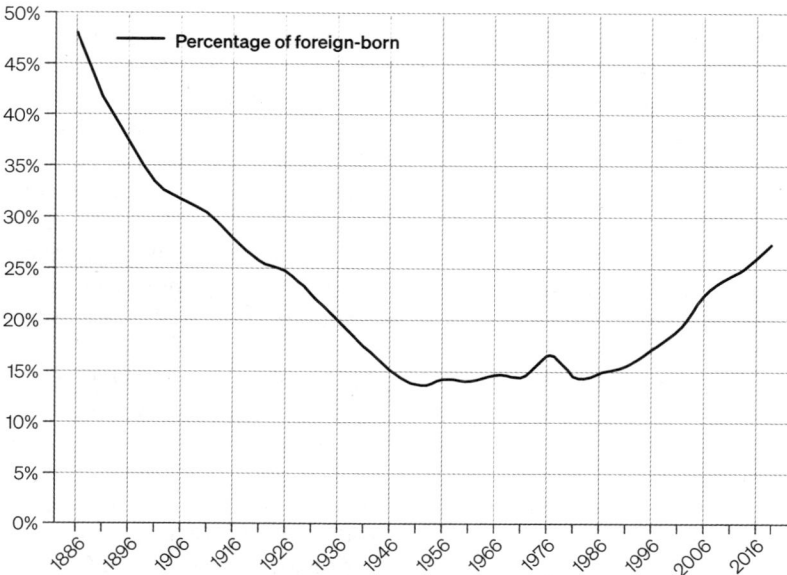

portfolio. Instead, they more commonly held joint responsibility for internal or external affairs, and later in the century were often simultaneously Minister of Labour and/or Employment (see Table 1.1).

1911–1928: The Great War and Its Aftermath

The colony of New Zealand was, at a superficial political level, growing in independence in the early twentieth century. But with growing independence came the potential for growing isolation: New Zealand was a far-flung outpost of a still-European-centred global system, and when the global tide receded it was left high and dry at the bottom of the world (Ballantyne 2012). With consistently lower levels of immigration and increasing natural increase in population, the foreign-born share of New Zealand's population shrank from around half in the 1880s to 30 per cent in 1911 (Pool 2015; also see Figure 1.5). Among a total population of 1,058,313, there were 305,689 immigrants in New Zealand in 1911; 75 per cent were from Britain and Ireland, and only 2611 were Chinese-born (a reduction from 2902 in 1901).

Immigration remained relatively low in the second decade of the twentieth century, running at below 5000 annual net migration in all years except 1912 (8922) and 1913 (14,219). An increasingly important group of immigrants were the Australian-born, who numbered 27,000 in 1901. Trans-Tasman flows had increased in the first decade of the century, and by 1911 there were 50,029 Australian-born immigrants in New Zealand – an increase of 23,000 over the decade. While it is common in the twenty-first century for New Zealand politicians and commentators to bemoan the uneven emigration loss of New Zealanders to Australia (Fraser 2019), in the relatively early years of both colonies, trans-Tasman migration was much more balanced and often flowed in New Zealand's favour (Poot 2010). However, the competition between the two colonies for dwindling flows of European immigrants led to the revival of government-assisted migration to New Zealand in 1904, supporting the passage of 36,500 immigrants to New Zealand between 1904 and 1915. The net migration uptick of 1913 included 12,000 from Britain and Ireland.

These early twentieth-century efforts to keep the colony growing, to populate or perish, withered in the face of looming world war. In 1916, the War Regulations Act dictated that no person over the age of fifteen could land in New Zealand without a passport or ID, the first such restriction and one that would be extended and developed throughout the following century. Risk and restrictions kept migration of all but soldiers to a minimum during the war itself: net migration from 1916 to 1919 was under 3000. There was a spurt of inflows after the end of World War I, in 1919 – some 3000 adults and 600 children – consisting of the foreign-born families that foreign-posted New Zealand soldiers had started while abroad. Assisted immigration was revived from 1919 to 1930, resulting in almost 72,000 assisted migrants from the UK (Belich 2002c). The government enticed migrants by reinforcing claims about New Zealand being 'The Great Britain of the South Seas', filled with promising opportunities for White settlers.

Despite the opening up after World War I and in contrast to the free-wheeling frontier days of the 1860s and 1870s, the post-World War I period was characterised by increasingly strong, centrally imposed immigration controls. In 1919, the Undesirable Immigrants Exclusion Act granted the Attorney-General power to prohibit the landing of any persons in New Zealand and to order 'undesirables' to leave the country (Henry 2008). It prohibited the arrival of immigrants and exiles from Britain's defeated World War I enemies, the former German and Austro-Hungarian empires. The 1920 Immigration Restriction Amendment Act aimed, much like the more explicit 'White Australia Policy', to keep New Zealand '98% British' (Spoonley & Bedford 2012: 37). It guaranteed the free entry of British and Irish migrants, while other migrants had to apply for permits, and 'Aboriginal natives' of any British colony did not qualify as British (Farmer 1985). Restrictions were imposed on Dalmatian migrants that limited them to 3500, although by 1921 there were only 1585 Dalmatian immigrants in New Zealand (Jones 2012). The language and thumbprint restrictions on Chinese migrants were removed, but the immigration of Chinese women was banned, effectively preventing the largely male population from reproducing, let alone growing (Spoonley & Bedford 2012: 103). From 1923, a non-British or non-Irish immigrant could apply to the Minister of Internal Affairs for naturalisation after three years of residence, but in 1926, Chinese were denied access to this pathway.

Indicative of the shifting balance of population, the first immigration minister in William Massey's Reform Party Government was the New Zealand-born Francis Bell, who held the portfolio from 1912 to 1915. Once war took hold in Europe in 1914, Massey reluctantly formed a bipartisan wartime Cabinet with the Liberals, led by Joseph Ward in 1915, resulting in the brief appointment of Liberal Josiah Alfred Hanan to the immigration role in August 1915. Bell was returned to the Minister of Immigration role a few weeks later and remained there till May 1920. However, it was Massey who commanded the terms of immigration policy, and he was driven by 'a deep-seated sentiment on the part of a huge majority of the people of this country that this Dominion shall be what is often called a "white" New

Zealand' (New Zealand Herald 1920). It was this sentiment that manifested in the Immigration Restriction Amendment Act of 1920, which was executed by William Nosworthy, Minister of Immigration from 1920 to 1928. After Massey's death in office in 1925, Nosworthy retained the portfolio and extended his power to claim the role of finance minister under Bell's 'caretaker' prime ministership, and retained the immigration portfolio under Joseph Gordon Coates, who held the Prime Minister's office in the final years of the Reform era. Although Bell was only Prime Minister for two weeks, he was the first New Zealand-born person to hold the role, and his successor Coates was the second.

Alongside the centralisation of immigration controls, the post-World War I period also saw a restructuring of British imperial immigration influence over its colonies. The New Zealand Government's dependence on and subservience to Britain markedly increased. During the period of mid-nineteenth-century explosive colonisation (or as historian James Belich (2002c) calls it, 'progressive colonisation'), New Zealand was a distant outpost for imperial exploration; a disorganised frontier post established to enable the opening and exploitation of wilderness areas by imperial outlaws. Accessible only by epic, months-long sailing journeys, it maintained a high degree of autonomy. However, in 1882, when the first shipment of frozen New Zealand meat had successfully reached Britain, the stage was set for closer economic ties between the imperial metropole and its distant colony in the South Pacific – as part of processes Belich (2002c) calls 'recolonisation' and 'dominionism'. By the early twentieth century, refrigerated container shipping on motorised vessels had created a veritable bridge of meat and butter between Britain and its antipodean hinterland; a link upon which New Zealand depended exclusively for its survival, as this protein industry provided its primary source of export income (Woods 2015). In this context of recolonisation, New Zealand's in-built dependence on settlers to feed and grow the colony became increasingly apparent.

An overriding concern of the colony in the 1910s and 1920s was therefore the stagnation of growth, through a combination of economic plateauing, an increasingly risky international environment, restrictionist tendencies concerning non-British migrants, and – importantly – the spectre of demographic decline (Farmer 1985). During the explosive period of colonisation, most immigrants were young, single men – often seeking escape from the confines and responsibilities of the old world and society in general. As the pioneers aged and enriched themselves on colonisation's spoils, they were not replaced by children, and the population of the colony ceased growing at the explosive rate upon which colonial planners and investors depended (Pool 2015). One response came in the Empire

Settlement Act 1922, which was an agreement between the British Crown and its colonies to facilitate settlement of farmers, domestic labourers, and children throughout the Empire (Constantine 2003; Foks 2022). The scheme granted free passage to single women of childbearing age (between eighteen and forty), leading to the migration of 4504 women to New Zealand as domestics in the interwar period (Pickles 2001).

1929–1945: Global Depression and World War II

In 1928, a change of government finally came, and it was to a new political force – the United Party of New Zealand, which had formed from the fragments of the Liberal Party. Their first term from 1928 to 1931 saw Joseph Ward, formerly Prime Minister for the Reform Party, returned to the top job. Ward appointed John George Cobbe as Minister of Immigration. Cobbe held the role from 1928 to 1930 alongside portfolio responsibility for Marine, Industries and Commerce and, after his time in Immigration, Defence and Finance. In 1930, Ward retired and the prime ministership passed to George Forbes, who took the reins during the Great Depression. He appointed Sydney George Smith as Minister of Immigration for one year before passing it to James Alexander Young from 1931 to 1935. In 1931, the Immigration Restriction Amendment Act prevented Europeans from immigrating (except British and Irish), with some exceptions, including those who had employment, capital, or skills 'without detriment to any resident of New Zealand'. However, in 1932, the Department of Immigration was formally shut down due to the massive downturn in immigration numbers resulting from the Great Depression (Spoonley & Bedford 2012: 33) and its administrative functions were given to the Department of Labour (Farmer 1985).

The United Party was ousted by New Zealand's first Labour Government in 1935 and then promptly merged with the Reform Party to form the National Party in opposition to Labour. These two parties – Labour and National – continue to dominate New Zealand politics today. When the Labour Government took office in 1935, they ceased assisted migration, against a Depression-era background of fears that immigrants would take jobs from working-class 'New Zealanders' (Farmer 1985). The emphasis on 'New Zealanders' (a term that in the early-to-mid-nineteenth century referred to Māori), and questions about the impacts of immigration on the employment of residents, reflect the beginnings of important shifts in identity – from imperial Britannic towards nationally centred – alongside the emerging political power of the descendants of colonists (Gentry 2015). Geopolitical shifts were afoot too. Japanese expansion in the Pacific, and its growing enmity with China, began to soften New Zealand's stance on Chinese immigration (Ip 2013). In 1934, the poll tax on Chinese migrants was waived (although it was not formally repealed until 1944), and in 1939, temporary permits for the wives and families of Chinese migrants were introduced after the Japanese occupation of Southern China. They were, however, required to pay a bond of £500, the equivalent of $60,000 in 2023.

The first Labour Government was led by the Australian-born Michael Joseph Savage and succeeded in the election with two seats secured by the Māori Rātana movement. Alongside Savage, the two other major figures in the first Labour Cabinet were Peter Fraser and Walter Nash, both of whom subsequently went on to serve as prime ministers. The new government was informed by Marxian thinking about capitalism and Keynesian approaches to state intervention, and they introduced a raft of progressive changes including the establishment of a welfare state (Franks & McAloon 2016). Labour's approach was indicative of progressive ideals around the British settler colonies, perhaps most famously in Franklin Roosevelt's 'New Deal' in the US; they sought to address inequality and make a better world for children to grow up in. Labour's first Minister of Immigration was Thomas Armstrong, who was simultaneously Minister of Labour, a dual role that almost all subsequent Ministers of Immigration would hold (see Table 1.1). Armstrong introduced pioneering labour laws including the establishment of a minimum wage, a 40-hour week, and compulsory union membership. David Wilson took over immigration in 1940 and held it until 1944, when he was replaced by two prominent former mining union organisers: Paddy Webb (till 1946), and Angus McLagan (till the end of Labour's term in 1949). Labour's term coincided with what may be regarded as the absolute nadir of immigration in New Zealand, at the end of almost two decades of extremely low inflows and net migration losses due to economic instability and war. The foreign-born population declined to 14 per cent in 1951, the lowest figure for over a century (see Figure 1.5).

1946–1971: End of Empire and Push to Populate

The end of World War II in 1945 also signalled the disintegration of several European empires (Bayly & Harper 2008). Anti-colonial and independence movements surged and the British Empire, which had once claimed authority over one quarter of the planet, was unable to maintain meaningful control. Australia had enacted the Statute of Westminster in 1942, which established full legislative independence and separate national citizenship, and Canada established its own citizenship in 1946.

India declared independence in 1947, Burma (now Myanmar) and Ceylon (now Sri Lanka) followed suit in early 1948, and in the subsequent three decades almost all former colonies exited Britain's rule. New Zealand enacted the Statute of Westminster in 1948, providing for its independent government and citizenship.

Up until this point, the status of national citizenship did not exist, either in Britain or in New Zealand. Its closest approximation derived from the 1928 British Nationality and Status of Aliens Act, which dictated that anyone naturalised anywhere in the British Empire obtained the status of British Subject, which applied across the realm (Hansen 2000). Any naturalised British Subject could therefore immigrate to New Zealand, and conversely anyone naturalised in New Zealand could move anywhere else in the Empire. To maintain connection with its former colonies after their independence, post-war Britain allowed for the status of Citizenship of the United Kingdom and Colonies in the 1948 British Nationality Act (Hansen 1999). The legislation was intended to protect the right to mobility of White British people moving among the English-speaking 'Old Commonwealth' countries of Canada, Australia, and New Zealand and their collective colonial motherland. But only between New Zealand and Australia would there remain the kind of open border that had previously characterised the whole Empire. During this epochal change, the Labour Party's fourteen-year spell in government came to an end in 1949 with defeat by the National Party, led by Sidney Holland, whose immigration ministers were Bill Sullivan (1949–54) then Ralph Hanan (1954–57).

Even as the Empire continued to decline, Britain remained influential in New Zealand's domestic politics and engagement with the wider world. Under Holland and Sullivan, the British Government continued sending 'deprived' children to its White settler colonies as part of 'social improvement' efforts. Around 500 such children arrived in New Zealand between 1949 and 1954 (Constantine 2002). New Zealand also participated, to a limited degree, in accepting refugees from the war in Europe – which led to the expansion and institutionalisation of a permanent humanitarian entry pathway. In 1944, New Zealand accepted eighty-two adults and 755 children as refugees from Poland (Bellamy 2018). Between 1949 and 1952, the country took in a further 4500 European refugees, including 300 Yugoslavs, 1000 Greeks, and 800 Poles (Beaglehole n.d.; Beaglehole 2013). In 1956, New Zealand received 1000 refugees from the Hungarian Revolution, and in 1959, New Zealand became one of the first countries to accept 'handicapped' refugees (Bellamy 2018), including those with ill health, disability, advanced age, or large numbers of dependent children. The humanitarian impulse was also expressed in provisions of the 1955

Adoption Act, which allowed any child adopted by a New Zealand citizen to receive New Zealand citizenship (Spoonley & Bedford 2012: 47). However, New Zealand acceded to the 1951 Refugee Convention only later, in 1960 (and signed the related 1967 Protocol only in 1973).

The commitment to White immigration was bipartisan in this period, and continued when Labour was elected in 1957 under the leadership of Walter Nash, who had explicitly resisted the immigration of Jewish refugees on the claim that he didn't want European-style anti-Semitism to emerge in New Zealand (Beaglehole n.d.). Nash's immigration minister was Fred Hackett (1957–1960), who was faced with challenges around decreasing immigration because of an economic rebound in Europe. However, the UK-centred imperial migration regime was not delivering enough British migrants to maintain the population growth that was believed necessary for national defence and economic recovery in the aftermath of the war. In moving towards independence from the UK, New Zealand and the other White settler colonies needed to address these matters on their own terms.

To address these concerns about the need for population growth, in 1945, under wartime Prime Minister Peter Fraser, the New Zealand Government had set up the Dominion Population Committee to study ways of increasing the country's population as a prerequisite for economic growth and military defence (Thorn 1946). This was mirrored across the Tasman in Australia's push to 'populate or perish', led by Australia's inaugural immigration minister, Arthur Calwell. In contrast to the Australian approach of aggressively recruiting immigrants from a broader range of European countries, the 1946 New Zealand report was cautious about opening the floodgates after the long wartime years of isolation. Planners feared a housing crisis if population growth were to outstrip infrastructure growth, and the report therefore favoured increasing births rather than immigration. However, the European settler population was not reproducing at a rate sufficient to address ongoing shortages. And the Māori population, which reached 99,007 in 1945 and was growing at a rate of 2 per cent annually, still only constituted 5 per cent of the total population (although that figure was minimised by the racist blood quantum mechanisms in the census – see Kukutai & Broman 2016).

The Population Committee's report assumed without question the preference for White European migrants, particularly immigrants from the UK. This was translated into policy in 1947 with the introduction of a new assisted migration scheme, which prioritised single persons over families, due to housing shortages, and focused on those with industrial skills, with preference given to British ex-servicemen. Applicants for assisted migration were interviewed by the New Zealand High Commission in London, and over the next thirty years 77,000 arrived in New Zealand (Hutching 1999). There were limits on the number of potential immigrants from the UK, however, which was now facing its own population and immigration challenges (Foks 2022). Indicative of the strong emphasis on assimilation into an Anglo-White settler identity, the report placed emphasis on the 'character' of different 'European types' in terms of their suitability for settlement. It advocated for Northern Europeans while describing 'southern European types' as itinerant, with a tendency to self-segregate and thus an inability to be 'completely absorbed into New Zealand's population' (Thorn 1946: 99). In 1950, an assisted migration scheme was set up with the Netherlands, leading to the arrival of 2700 Dutch immigrants in 1952 (Ongley & Pearson 1995). Within a further two years, more than 10,000 Dutch had arrived, and by 1971 there were over 20,000 Dutch people in New Zealand (Hartog & Winkelmann 2004). The ongoing proactive recruitment of assisted immigrants from Northern Europe reflected the still-dominant White settler philosophy, articulated in a Department of External Affairs memorandum in 1953 (Murphy 2003: 50):

> Our immigration is based firmly on the principle that we are and intend to remain a country of European development. It is inevitably discriminatory against Asians – indeed against all persons who are not wholly of European race and colour. Whereas we have done much to encourage immigration from Europe, we do everything to discourage it from Asia.

However, even broadening the scope of 'Whiteness' to non-British Europeans was not enough to satisfy the demand for population. There were simply more job vacancies than people to fill them. To broaden the net, New Zealand, like many post-war industrialised countries, began experimenting with recruitment from non-White countries through 'guest-worker' schemes, student migration, and other international agreements. In 1950, the Colombo Plan for Co-operative Economic Development in South and South-East Asia was introduced, signed initially by New Zealand, Australia, Britain, Canada, Ceylon (Sri Lanka), India, and Pakistan (Collins 2012). In its first decade, the plan brought 900 trainees – mainly from Malaysia, Thailand, and Indonesia – to New Zealand, primarily to study engineering, agriculture, and health science. The Colombo Plan resonated with a shifting emphasis of colonial and imperial discourse, which increasingly asserted the obligations of Britain and its settler colonies to support economic and social development in Asia, Africa, and the Pacific, while simultaneously establishing bulwarks against the potential incursion of communism (Oakman 2010).

The relative peace and prosperity of this period saw industrialised countries rebuild their economies and enter a long post-war economic boom. This geopolitical context enabled New Zealand to significantly broaden its economic, social, cultural, and political engagement with the world beyond Britain. The National Party was elected in 1960 under the leadership of Keith Holyoake, who held the prime ministership all the way until 1972, during which time Tom Shand and Jack Marshall served as immigration ministers. Shand, who served in the role from 1960 to 1969, was part of a growing cohort of politicians to address international economic developments, including Britain's forthcoming membership of the European Economic Community and the development of the International Monetary Fund and the World Bank (Templeton 2000). Jack Marshall was next to serve in the role, which he passed to David Spence Thomson when he went on to lead the party's final months in government in 1972.

It was in this context that, like most booming post-war industrialised countries, New Zealand began experimenting with non-White guestworker migration as a solution to pressing labour shortages. The Great Depression and World War II had led to industrial development in New Zealand, but by 1945 there were far too few workers to sustain the growing industries. The Population Committee report had proposed that short-term immigration would be needed and that 'steps should be taken straight away to make preparations, so that when it is possible in this country to house immigrants they can be immediately brought here' (Thorn 1946: 98). In many ways, this suggestion anticipated the vast increase in short-term migrant work schemes, especially from the Pacific Islands from the 1960s onwards. The focus on labour needs, and more independent rather than imperial migration controls, became manifest in the 1961 Immigration Restriction Amendment Act, which laid the groundwork for a less discriminatory migration policy, or at least one that more equally applied restrictions on entry. This Act introduced the need for all immigrants to have a permit prior to entering New Zealand, extended in the 1964 Immigration Act, although British and Irish migrants were exempt until 1974 (Bellamy 2008). The Statute of Westminster had already added another layer of distinction, dictating that non-citizen immigrant 'aliens' to New Zealand could not vote in general elections, stand for Parliament, own shares, become members of some associations, or take up some occupations (Spoonley & Bedford 2012: 47).

The 1960s saw a vast rise in Pacific immigration to fill domestic labour shortages. This came especially from Pacific Island countries, creating the first major diversification of migrant national origins since Chinese arrivals during the gold-rush. New Zealand's Treaty of Friendship with Samoa in 1962 established an annual quota of 1100 Samoan migrants who would enter on short-term permits, if they could guarantee accommodation and employment (Ongley & Pearson 1995; Thomsen et al. 2022). Bedford (2005a: 132) views this treaty as a 'defining moment in the history of the globalisation of New Zealand's international migration system', one which ensured the presence of Samoans in New Zealand and their visibility within New Zealand's late-twentieth-century social transformation. The Samoan Quota Scheme only came into practice in 1970, but other Pacific-based work permit schemes – such as the Fiji Rural Work Scheme in 1969 and Hutt Valley Scheme in 1971, aimed at Tongan workers – maintained a steady supply of Pacific migrants entering New Zealand, which in the short term kept the economy afloat (Friesen 2018; Levick 1988). Various church schemes were also set up around the same time, by Catholic and Methodist churches sponsoring unskilled Tongan workers to enter on temporary visas, largely for the purposes of seasonal work (Levick 1988: 60).

The new influx of Pacific migrants to New Zealand (and Australia) had deep colonial roots: in previous eras, Pacific people had often been forced into service on colonial ships and had become central to the British Empire's seafaring labour force of the nineteenth century (Bedford 2019; Mallon 2012). Like other people from outside Britain and Ireland, Pacific people had been prevented from moving to New Zealand under the Immigration Restriction Act of 1908 and its various amendments. However, those policies had been most vociferously applied to Chinese. The Pacific population in New Zealand had thus increased incrementally in the first half of the twentieth century, growing to nearly 3000 by 1945 (Bedford 2019: 316; New Zealand Census 1945). In this respect, New Zealand differed from Australia, which introduced measures to restrict Pacific migration with the 1901 Pacific Island Labourers Act. The Act also prevented Pacific people living in New Zealand from entering Australia (Bedford 2019: 316; Hamer 2014: 93). By the second half of the twentieth century, as restrictions on the source countries of migrants shifted and eventually receded, Pacific migration became increasingly central to New Zealand's economic survival.

The post-war period also saw major changes to the dynamics of internal migration within New Zealand and trans-Tasman migration across the open border with Australia. At the same time as increased Pacific immigration was changing the face of the New Zealand labour force, growing rural-to-urban Māori migration was contributing to rapid ethno-cultural diversification in New Zealand's British-dominated cities. As the Māori population grew at much higher rates than the New Zealand

Table 1.2. *Rural and Urban New Zealand Māori Population, 1936–1966*
(Source: *New Zealand Official Yearbook 1971*: https://www3.stats.govt.nz/New_Zealand_Official_Yearbooks/1971/NZOYB_1971.html#idchapter_1_8890)

Census year	Urban Māori		Rural Māori	
	Number	%	Number	%
1936	10,909	13.3	71,390	86.7
1945	20,317	20.6	78,407	79.4
1951	29,115	25.2	86,468	74.8
1956	41,897	30.6	95,185	69.4
1961	71,499	42.8	95,533	57.2
1966	118,228	58.7	82,867	41.3

European population, and rural economic growth had slowed, there was a marked movement of young Māori to urban centres. In 1945, only a fifth of Māori lived in towns and cities but this grew to almost a third in 1956 and 59 per cent in 1966 (Table 1.2).

The so-called 'silent migration' of Māori to cities (Grace et al. 2001) and the simultaneous growth of Pacific migration were also intertwined with growing net migration losses to Australia. A growing number of Māori began migrating across the Tasman, pulled by better weather and wages, and pushed by persistent racism and exclusion from an economic and political system still heavily dominated by the British (Hamer 2008). Māori in Australia were joined by a growing trickle of Pacific New Zealanders, and a broad cross-section of others who were taking advantage of more-accessible air travel to escape worsening economic recession at home and participate in the growing global economy (Bedford 2005b; Carmichael 1993; Poot et al. 2009; Poot 2010). Regular net losses to Australia became a recurrent pattern (Carmichael 1993), and by the 1980s, fears of a 'brain drain' became a regular feature of New Zealand political debate, and persist to this day (Gamlen 2013a; Reserve Bank 1986: 334; Walker 2021). Meanwhile, Australian commentators began grumbling about the growing number of (particularly Māori and Pacific) New Zealanders who were supposedly using the open border as a 'back door' into Australia, where they became stereotyped as 'Bondi Beach dole bludgers'. The fears on both sides of the Tasman were rebuffed rather than redressed by then-Prime Minister Robert Muldoon, who quipped – arguably with racist undertones – that the trans-Tasman migration trends improved the average IQ of both countries (Gamlen 2013a; Gamlen and Sherell 2022).

Table 1.3. *Country of Birth of New Zealand Population in 1956, 1961 and 1966*
(Source: https://www3.stats.govt.nz/New_Zealand_Official_Yearbooks/1971/NZOYB_1971.html#idchapter_1_8890)

Country of birth of New Zealand population	Census years					
	1956		1961		1966	
	Number	%	Number	%	Number	%
New Zealand (excl. Cook Islands & Niue)	1,863,344	85.7%	2,074,509	85.9%	2,279,994	85.2%
UK	206,181	9.5%	218,649	9.1%	244,601	9.1%
Australia	35,916	1.7%	35,412	1.5%	43,374	1.6%
Netherlands	12,544	0.6%	17,844	0.7%	20,461	0.8%
Ireland (excl. Northern Ireland)	8,423	0.4%	8,810	0.4%	8,448	0.3%
Pacific Islands:		0.0%		0.0%		0.0%
Cook Islands and Niue	2,745	0.1%	4,788	0.2%	7,852	0.3%
Fiji	2,273	0.1%	3,038	0.1%	5,384	0.2%
Tonga	768	0.0%	777	0.0%	1,005	0.0%
Western Samoa	2,995	0.1%	4,450	0.2%	7,447	0.3%
India	4,468	0.2%	4,753	0.2%	5,368	0.2%
China	3,883	0.2%	4,194	0.2%	4,218	0.2%
Other countries, and born at sea	30,522	1.4%	37,760	1.6%	48,767	1.8%
Totals	**2,174,062**	**100%**	**2,414,984**	**100%**	**2,676,919**	**100%**

Despite emerging interest in temporary Pacific labour migration and tentative engagement with Asia through the Colombo Plan, throughout the 1960s New Zealand's immigration system remained primarily oriented towards permanent settler immigration, population growth, and the maintenance of the country's British imperial heritage. The vast majority of New Zealand's foreign-born population came from the UK, Australia, the Netherlands, and Ireland (Table 1.3). In 1971, there were around 66,000 English-born people in New Zealand, representing 2.3 per cent of the country's total population, with under 4000 Irish- and Scottish-born and even fewer born beyond (New Zealand Census 1971). At the end of the 1960s, New Zealand was still demographically and politically asserting Whiteness.

However, against the background of the civil rights movement and the broad range of liberal 1960s social movements in the US and Europe – which New Zealanders watched intently – there were growing signs of

Table 1.4. *Ethnic Composition of New Zealand's Population in 1956, 1961 and 1966*
(Source: https://www3.stats.govt.nz/New_Zealand_Official_Yearbooks/1971/NZOYB_1971.html#idchapter_1_8890)

Ethnic groups	Census					
	1956		1961		1966	
	Number	%	Number	%	Number	%
Non-Māori	2,016,287	92.7%	2,216,886	91.8%	2,426,352	90.6%
Māori	137,151	6.3%	167,086	6.9%	201,159	7.5%
Other origins:						
Pacific peoples: Cook Island Māori	2,320	0.1%	4,499	0.2%	8,663	0.3%
Samoan	3,740	0.2%	6,481	0.3%	11,842	0.4%
Niuean	848	0.0%	1,728	0.1%	2,846	0.1%
Tongan	917	0.0%	1,043	0.0%	1,389	0.1%
Other	278	0.0%	589	0.0%	1,531	0.1%
Sub-totals, Pacific peoples	8,103	0.4%	14,340	0.6%	26,271	1.0%
Chinese	6,667	0.3%	8,333	0.3%	9,982	0.4%
Indian	3,087	0.1%	4,027	0.2%	6,655	0.2%
Syrian, Lebanese, and Arab	1,055	0.0%	1,057	0.0%	1,049	0.0%
Fijian	479	0.0%	746	0.0%	1,323	0.0%
Other races	1,233	0.1%	2,509	0.1%	4,128	0.2%
Sub-totals, others	12,521	0.6%	16,672	0.7%	23,137	0.9%
Totals	**2,174,062**	**100.0%**	**2,414,984**	**100.0%**	**2,676,919**	**100.0%**

migration-driven ethno-cultural change in the South Pacific. The growing Māori population had reached 232,022, representing over 8 per cent of the total population, and the majority were now living in towns and cities, where a Māori middle class had begun to emerge (Grace et al. 2001). By the 1960s and 1970s, The Treaty of Waitangi was once again the focus of Māori activism, which eventually achieved recognition through the 1975 Treaty of Waitangi Act, which would transform the country's social, cultural, economic, and political DNA in the coming decades. Meanwhile, Pacific peoples, Chinese, Indian, Middle Eastern, and other ethnic groups formed a small but growing percentage of the population (Table 1.4). Bicultural political shifts were well underway, and signs of an impending migration-led ethno-demographic diversification were on the horizon.

1972–1981: The Disintegration of the Imperial Migration Regime

The untethering of New Zealand's imperial linkages accelerated significantly in 1973 when the UK cut its preferential trading ties to the Commonwealth and joined the European Economic Community (EEC). From 1973 onwards, New Zealand began developing a more independent path in foreign relations, at times defying Anglo-American doctrine (as in the case of banning nuclear weapons), and incrementally shifted its focus towards the Asia-Pacific region. Some signs of this shift had already occurred in the withdrawal of New Zealand troops from the Vietnam War in 1971 and the establishment of diplomatic ties with the People's Republic of China in 1972. Prime Minister Norman Kirk (1972–74) declared something of this newly emerging independence in a speech in 1974: 'New Zealand has, in many ways, reached full nationhood. It stands on its own feet, it makes its own judgements, it charts its own course of action . . . [as] a country of the Asian and Pacific region' (Gamlen & Sherell 2022).

Before the UK's entry into the EEC, New Zealand had also signed a reciprocal waiver agreement regarding visas and visa fees with Japan in 1970 (Spoonley & Bedford 2012: 60). Later, in 1977, New Zealand accepted 412 Vietnamese refugees – often referred to as 'boat people' – the first group of refugees from outside Europe the country had officially accepted (Bellamy 2018). Imperial legacies were retained but also reworked in the formalisation of permit-free movement between Australia and New Zealand in the 1973 Trans-Tasman Travel Arrangement (TTTA) – one of the last remaining fragments of the globe-spanning free-mobility zone of the British Empire. The TTTA was an express acknowledgement of settler colonial affinity, established in a context where both countries' populations were overwhelmingly White and Anglo-Saxon (Hamer 2014).

The Labour Government returned to office in 1972, first under Norman Kirk (1972–74), then under Bill Rowling (1974–75). Globally, this was a period of economic downturn associated with the rising price of oil due to war in the Middle East – and the resulting contraction of demand for immigrant labour saw European and North American governments bring their post-war guestworker programmes to an end. In 1974, Rowling's immigration minister, Fraser Colman, oversaw an immigration policy review to address declining economic conditions and public anxiety about immigration levels (Ongley & Pearson 1995). The review placed particular emphasis on distinguishing between people in New Zealand with residence permits, the legal right to remain and be resident, and people who had entered on temporary permits that had expired. The review led to the end of unrestricted right of entry for British and Irish migrants (Bellamy 2018; Spoonley & Bedford 2012: 56), and the reaffirmation of free entry to citizens of Australia, the Cook Islands, Niue, and Tokelau (Bellamy 2018), the latter three countries constitutionally part of the Realm of New Zealand. All other migrants had to apply on family, humanitarian, refugee, or general grounds. The English-language requirements were eased, and there was a shift in focus towards skills and qualifications, although ministerial discretion on source countries remained (Ongley & Pearson 1995).

In a climate of growing hostility to 'guestworkers' across the industrialised world, the Kirk–Rowling Labour Government also initiated the infamous 'Dawn Raids' deportation campaign in 1973, a crackdown on people from Pacific countries whose visas had expired. The Dawn Raids involved police raiding the homes and workplaces of suspected 'overstayers' and prosecuting and/or deporting them and their families (Smith 2021: 32). Robert Muldoon's National Government, which succeeded Labour in 1975, significantly ramped up the Dawn Raids. Muldoon had campaigned by talking tough on immigration, which he claimed had – under the Labour Government – contributed to a recession and a housing shortage that threatened 'the New Zealand way of life' ('The Cities' election campaign advertisement). The 1975 election campaign was especially racist, with animated television advertisements for the National Party decrying immigration and depicting violent Pacific people drinking excessively and stealing jobs. Pacific people comprised a minority of overstayers but formed the vast majority of those prosecuted with overstaying, with people from Europe and North America without visas facing little scrutiny (Friesen 2018: 114; Spoonley & Bedford 2012: 130). The Dawn Raids mobilised fierce opposition across a range of groups in New Zealand, increasing support for the then-new notion of 'multiculturalism', which was gaining influence in Australia and Canada (Hjerm 2000). The home of Muldoon's first Minister of Immigration, Frank Gill, was picketed in 'counter raids' led by a protest group called the Polynesian Panthers (Anae 2020).

The deportations of the Dawn Raids represented the harshest form of immigration control at the time. A limited two-month amnesty for overstayers was offered in 1976, allowing regularisation of status by signing a register, which would give migrants a two-month visa extension (Smith 2021: 32). There was some softening of rules around family reunion, including adopted children, which 'allowed for a more culturally sensitive approach to Polynesian family migration' (Bedford et al. 2000: 18). A more regulated approach to managing labour migration was also introduced in 1975 through the South Pacific Work Permit Scheme (Levick & Bedford

1988). It provided work permits for up to a year to Fijians, Tongans, and Samoans in sectors with specific labour shortages, especially in seasonal occupations in rural areas. The most prolific users of the scheme were Fijians, until they were suspended after the 1987 political coups in that country (Ongley & Pearson 1995). The growing bureaucratic requirements of the scheme led to a reduction in the number of Tongan workers, while Samoans already had an entry quota and thus largely ignored the scheme anyway (Friesen 2018). However, by the 1980s, the scheme began to expand beyond rural occupations into urban workplaces, such as freezing works and market gardens (Friesen 2018).

In 1978, future National Party Prime Minister Jim Bolger succeeded Gill as the Minister of Immigration. However, in late 1980, while Muldoon was out of the country, Bolger took part in an unsuccessful leadership coup by a group of more liberal-leaning party members (Templeton 1995). As a result, Bolger fell out of favour and was replaced by Anthony George 'Aussie' Malcolm, who served as New Zealand's Minister of Immigration from 12 February 1981 to 26 July 1984 (and whose account we discuss in the next chapter). The Dawn Raids came to an end in 1979, but the broad policy shift, crystallised in the 1974 review of immigration policy, was by that time unstoppable: it had brought 'a further tightening of controls . . . linking immigration levels even more closely to the availability of employment, housing, and other resources in New Zealand' (Ongley & Pearson 1995: 769). By 1978, the immigration system was already markedly different than it had been at the height of the imperial regime. Assisted immigration schemes had come to an end (Bellamy 2018), and temporary visitors were unable to work without special permission. In place of the free and open but decidedly racist imperial immigration regime, New Zealand's immigration policy now recognised three main categories of permanent immigration: occupational, family reunion, and humanitarian (Farmer 1996a: 56).

Conclusion

The imperial migration regime that we have traced in this chapter transformed Aotearoa New Zealand into a White-settler-dominated colony by the late nineteenth century, a political demography that was cemented into the middle of the twentieth century. From little more than 2 per cent of the population at the signing of Te Tiriti o Waitangi in 1840, White settlers increased to 95 per cent of the population by the beginning of the twentieth century, with Māori comprising only 5 per cent. The usurping of Māori demographic dominance and sovereignty went hand in hand with the exclusion of almost all migrants who were not British and Irish, and especially those who were not seen as White. New Zealand was also linked into a globe-spanning British Empire that sustained the political authority of White settlers, provided economic-development opportunities, and centred a network of culture and identity with other settler colonies and the colonial metropole (Foks 2022).

Immigration policy was a central plank of the earliest expressions of government in New Zealand. Te Tiriti o Waitangi was arguably its first immigration policy document (Turia 2007), laying out consent for sovereignty and governance responsibilities specifically in relation to the growing arrival of British migrants. However, neither the Māori nor the English version of Te Tiriti / The Treaty was upheld; colonial and dominion governments held immigration policy as central to emergent state sovereignty. Ministers of Immigration were senior members of government from the earliest days of the colony, and a number had been or went on to become premiers or prime ministers. Immigration was also expressly linked to the coercive acquisition of Māori land, and thus population arrivals were woven into the remaking of territory that is so central to the achievement of settler colonialism.

The transformation of New Zealand was thus not incidental but a result of the direct efforts to make New Zealand a 'Britain of the South Seas' where Anglo-Saxonism would dominate. The institutions of New Zealand today – the Crown, the Westminster parliamentary system, the judiciary, the language, the education and health systems, the planning regime, and much more beyond – all speak to the imperial and colonial legacy established from this time onward. British- and Irish-derived communities made New Zealand a place of similar culture, politics, and economy, which then had the effect of easing the process of arrival and assimilation of later settlers from the British Isles and Ireland throughout the twentieth century and into the twenty-first century (Constantine 2003).

The imperial migration regime would not last, however, not least because the British Empire itself disintegrated rapidly from the middle of the twentieth century onwards. Growing independence from British rule expressed itself in national concerns over current and future population, as demonstrated in the Dominion Population Committee's concerns in the immediate post-World War II years. White dominance remained central to emerging expressions of New Zealand national rather than imperial identity, but immigration policy started to incrementally open opportunities for arrivals from other parts of Europe and then, through labour migration schemes, countries in the South Pacific. By the late twentieth century, the Māori population had also grown to represent around 12 per cent of the population (1981) – and political movements reasserting Indigenous sovereignty were well underway. The signs of a more ethnically diverse New Zealand population were becoming apparent as the foundations upon which White settler colonialism depended were being questioned.

Our task in the remainder of this book is to examine in depth the four decades that followed the long period of the imperial migration regime in New Zealand. The emergence of ethnic diversity represents one important feature of the trends that would come to shape immigration policy in the years that followed. The other was a growing emphasis on economic dimensions of immigration policy. These were evident from the mid-twentieth century in the frequent linking of the Immigration and Labour portfolios and in a focus on labour shortages. The economic dimensions of immigration policy took a new turn in the years that followed, however, as theories of neoliberalism ripped through New Zealand politics and fundamentally transformed the country's economy and society and its linkages with the world. Immigration policy, once designed to encourage, manage, and maintain White settler population growth and dominance, would become increasingly driven by assessments of the economic value of migrants and their potential contribution to the making of a global, economically successful nation centred in the Asia-Pacific region.

CHAPTER 2

The Neoliberal Revolution and the Rise of Economic Multiculturalism, 1981–1988

The 1980s witnessed unprecedented transformations in migration policy in New Zealand. The changes, most notably the introduction of the 1987 Immigration Act and the movement towards a skills-based points system by the late 1980s, led to both an increased volume of migration and a diversification in the national origins of migrants. Having drawn principally from the UK, Ireland, and some parts of Northern Europe through the mid-to-late twentieth century, and following the tentative opening of labour migration connections in the Pacific, New Zealand governments increasingly permitted arrivals from East and Southeast Asia. New techniques were established or proposed for assessing skills, and business immigration programmes were devised to attract and retain investors and entrepreneurs who might contribute to economic growth and transformation.

In a.clear departure from the imperial migration regime outlined in the previous chapter, the migration regime of the 1980s emerged during what is often called the neoliberal 'revolution' (Kelsey 1995). Meanwhile, in other former British colonies, migration policy was also being re-conceived to prioritise new visions of ethnic diversity and national identity. In particular, Canada and Australia were embracing a rhetoric of 'multiculturalism', which nominally aimed to recognise and celebrate cultural differences rather than expecting immigrants to assimilate into the Anglo-centric mainstream culture. As we trace in this chapter, New Zealand's immigration policy in the 1980s was crafted in an effort to move beyond the imperial migration regime, and to accommodate these emerging ideas of multiculturalism and neoliberalism, in the context of rapidly shifting geopolitical configurations arising from the disintegration of the British Empire. In this context, population and labour-market concerns underpinned a drive towards new notions of 'fairness' in deciding who could be admitted. Implementing these new ideas of fairness became intertwined with a growing obsession with assessing, measuring, and managing the economic value of migrants.

Having reviewed the long history of New Zealand immigration policy up to this point in Chapter 1, this chapter is where our own story of New Zealand's immigration policy development begins, based primarily on our in-depth interviews with former immigration ministers, supplemented by secondary research. Based on these sources, the chapter explores the transformation in migration policymaking and the emergence of what we call 'economic multiculturalism' that occurred in the tumultuous 1980s, foregrounding the accounts of Anthony 'Aussie' Malcolm, the final Minister of Immigration in Robert Muldoon's Third National Government (1975–84), and two of the Ministers who succeeded Malcolm in the Fourth Labour Government (1984–90): Kerry Burke and Stan Rodger. Following an overview of the key changes and influences in this period, we focus on the diverse imperatives and influences that came to shape migration policymaking in this era.

In particular, we address the recrafting of migration policy in line with two interwoven political framings that underpinned many of the early neoliberal reforms implemented in this fifteen-year period. The first was a traditional, socially liberal Labour Party focus on fairness, equality, and diversity, which called for an end to the informality and discrimination of the kin-based imperial migration regime. The second was a new – and increasingly powerful – economically liberal argument about the market value of migration. Many accounts of the 1980s focus on reforms in finance and commerce and conflate the neoliberal revolution of this period with purely economic ideas. However, a study of issues such as immigration shows that the success of neoliberal reforms in this period depended on an amalgam of both economically *and* socially liberal ideas.

Migration policy had, as we have outlined in the previous chapter, been central in the settler colonisation of New Zealand, but it had seemingly become more diffuse as the imperial migration regime disintegrated. The 1980s saw the reconfiguration of migration policy as a focus of state attention, firstly in a formal shift towards more ethnically open selection processes and then incrementally, over the following decades, in an increasing concern for the knowledge and techniques needed to make migration able to be acted upon in the national interest. We observe growing interest in managing migration that manifests in new approaches to and rationales for migrant selection, a theme that continues and intensifies in the decades that follow. We also pay attention to the political influences, relationships, and work that was involved in the reconstitution of migration policy. Our account highlights different influences on migration policymaking, including international relationships with Australia and Canada, as well as other geopolitical and geoeconomic concerns. We also touch on the relationship between migration policy and Te Tiriti o Waitangi and Māori during the period in question, which is open to differing interpretations. One analysis highlights the ways in which the reconfiguration of migration policy in the 1980s occurred without significant input from Māori in a way that reflected and reinforced elements of the coloniality of migration policymaking. Another view suggests that, while the above argument conforms to current-day orthodoxy, it extrapolates too far beyond the research evidence available to us in this study, and is at odds with lived experiences of Māoridom during and since the period in question. This discussion sets the scene for later chapters, wherein we address the rising tensions between values of biculturalism, multiculturalism, and neoliberal economics, globalisation, national identity, the management of migration, and new concerns around security and border control.

Beyond the Imperial Migration Regime

The revolution in New Zealand migration policy of the 1980s had been brewing since the end of World War II, with the final disintegration of the British Empire and its former colonies' adoption of national independence. By the early 1970s, the imperial migration regime, in place since the mid-nineteenth century, was already on the verge of collapse. The perceived post-war need to 'populate or perish' had forced New Zealand to widen its settler recruitment efforts to include people from Northern Europe. And governments had begun to systematically encourage non-permanent immigration from the Pacific Islands to fill labour shortages, echoing older practices of colonial indentured labour, and mirroring the post-war European and North American 'guestworker' schemes. In step with the closing of those schemes during and after the oil shocks, New Zealand also turned sour on Pacific labour immigration during the mid-1970s. Pacific people in New Zealand were now cast as scapegoats for the global economic downturn and rising local unemployment, leading to an infamous deportation programme known as the 'Dawn Raids' (see Chapter 1).

An increasingly intractable problem with the imperial migration regime was that explicitly racist immigrant selection was no longer tenable either economically or politically. If migrants could only be acquired from a single, homogenous pool of recruits on the far side of the planet, New Zealand could not get the quantity of them it needed to offset population ageing, nor the quality it needed to fill skills gaps in its increasingly diverse economy. Meanwhile, New Zealand's largest export market was drying up: imperial-era trading ties with Britain had guaranteed a market for most of New Zealand's exports – but these ended in 1973. And New Zealand's emergence from the protective cocoon of the Empire exposed it to the turbulent global economic and geopolitical transformations of the 1970s, which involved the rise of global finance – and with it new levels of financial volatility that were catastrophic for small, export-commodity-based economies like New Zealand (Garten 2021). As economic conditions worsened, New Zealand began to experience sustained, year-on-year net migration losses, especially to Australia. There was a growing feeling that something drastic must be done to revive the country's performance. New sources of population, labour, and export income had to be found – preferably closer to home, in Asia and the Pacific.

These harsh global conditions were the background to economically liberal arguments for opening the New Zealand economy, which grew louder as the 1970s progressed. These ideas, which we now generally understand as 'neoliberal', had been in seed since the end of World War I, when a group of Austrian economists, most notably Ludwig von Mises and Friedrich Hayek, plotted an alternative vision of a market society against the rising tide of socialism (Slobodian 2018). In 1938, with fascism underway, several proponents of this alternative market society met at the Walter Lippman Colloquium in Paris, where the term 'neoliberalism' first emerged as a coherent concept (Denord 2009; Dardot & Laval 2014; Reinhoudt & Audier 2018). Against the *laissez-faire* (in French, literally 'allow to do') market economy of nineteenth-century classical liberalism, in which the state did not intervene in the market, the neoliberals argued for the necessity of strong state infrastructures and institutions to oversee and encase the market economy. A neoliberal market economy thus entailed, as Jamie Peck notes, the 'roll back' of the state in terms of deregulation, privatisation, and cuts to social spending, alongside the equally important 'roll out' of the state through institutions, policies, and governance that determined the ways that people could act within the market (Peck 2010).

In the post-war period, a growing number of followers of the neoliberal creed – at this point channelled through think-tanks and institutions such as the Mont Pèlerin Society (Mirowski & Plehwe 2009) and the Chicago School of Economics (Stedman Jones 2012) – began a decades-long struggle against the Keynesian orthodoxy of the time, demanding lower taxes, weaker labour unions, stronger employers and entrepreneurs, and a larger share of GDP relative to that of the state sector. These global economic changes created the impetus for New Zealand to reorient politically and economically away from Britain and Europe and towards Asia and the Pacific, especially after Britain joined the European Economic Community (EEC) in 1973. New Zealand's shift away from its imperial pole entailed the assembly of new geopolitical and economic relationships, including through immigration. For example, financialisation was partly reflected through the introduction of more business and entrepreneurial migration categories, including the 1970 Entrepreneur Investor Policy aimed at European investors, and the Business Immigration Programme from 1986, which focused primarily on Asian entrepreneurs (Bedford et al. 2002a). These trends would eventually coalesce with an emergent multicultural rhetoric and the drive towards wholesale neoliberal political reform in the 1980s and 1990s (Le Heron & Pawson 1996).

By the late 1970s, neoliberal economic thinking had already gathered a following in New Zealand, and it began seeping into the mainstream of New Zealand politics and policy in the years leading up to the election of the Fourth Labour Government in 1984 (Kelsey 1995; Leay 1999; Le Heron & Pawson 1996). The Treasury, with its growing cohort of neo-classically trained economists, was a key conduit through which the new economic thinking gained a foothold. The 1983 Closer Economic Relations (CER) Agreement with Australia had been implemented under the Third National Government (1975–84), one of two or three 'small steps' towards deregulation that adherents of the new approach were able to push past then-Prime Minister Muldoon, a devoted state-centric Keynesian who openly scorned the 'voodoo economics' of Milton Friedman (Alchin 1990; Belich 2002c; Leay 1999; Muldoon 1984; Scollay et al. 2010).[7] The CER agreement promised to end all tariffs on products moving between the two countries – a goal that was reached by 1990. It also complemented the free movement of people between the two countries, which had been allowed since the inception of both colonies and was formalised in 1973. These trans-Tasman connections would also come to indirectly influence migration policy, both through inter-governmental policy sharing and emulation, and through the impact of emigration losses to Australia.

Alongside these economic currents, the social and political transformations of the 1970s also introduced a more globalist and activist outlook in New Zealand (Johnson 2016). As Ranginui Walker (1994: 86)

---

7   These changes were adamantly resisted by the domineering Prime Minister and Minister of Finance of that time, Robert Muldoon, who had a strong authoritarian streak and regarded himself not only as the singular authority on all matters regarding the New Zealand economy, but as one of the great architects and planners of the imperially bequeathed global economic system. Muldoon was the opposite of a neoliberal: he was 'a devout and determined Keynesian' and moreover 'a committed "centralist" who believed in and practised big government and high taxes … saw nothing wrong in massive redistribution of income and subsidies from everyone's taxes' (Leay 1999: 123). Muldoon's state-centric Keynesianism could not even be dispelled by the luminaries of neoliberalism: Margaret Thatcher's visit in 1976 made no impression on his economic views; Muldoon refused to see the visiting Milton and Rose Friedman in 1980, describing their arguments as 'voodoo' economics; and he rejected US Trade Representative Bill Brock's encouragement to engage with Reaganomics (Leay 1999). Muldoon was by no means alone in Cabinet in his rejection of the new economics, which even Muldoon's reform-minded Minister of Immigration Anthony 'Aussie' Malcolm later referred to as 'Friedmanite bullshit'.

has illustrated, the 1970s in New Zealand were 'characterised by the rise of urban activism which crystallized into a Maori land rights movement'. Groups like Ngā Tamatoa, an activist organisation led by young, educated, urban Māori, brought new challenges to the White-settler-dominated New Zealand state (Harris 2004). Taking up the long-established challenge of land confiscation, language loss, and cultural degradation, Ngā Tamatoa – and other protest groups that emerged from it – also gained inspiration from the international civil rights movement emanating from North America. The state responded to these challenges in part with the establishment of the Waitangi Tribunal in 1975, a permanent commission of inquiry which has shaped key elements of New Zealand policy and colonial redress. Movements and coalitions also emerged around a new awareness of New Zealand's role in global social issues, symbolised prominently by the nuclear-free movement and the widespread protests against the South African rugby tour of New Zealand in 1981.

Together, the economic liberals and the social liberals formed a powerful coalition against the fraying status quo. Just as economic neoliberals were calling for labour-market deregulation and greater 'flexibility' to recruit workers from abroad, social liberals were railing against race-based immigration policies. The 'Dawn Raids' campaigns of the late 1970s and early 1980s (see Chapter 1) prompted community-led protest movements that brought organised protesters like Ngā Tamatoa, trade unions, and other socially liberal groups into coalition with the Polynesian Panthers, to campaign against deportation and racism (Anae et al. 2015). While changes to migration policy were not the top priority for most of the new social movements, their claims of solidarity with various minority groups and causes excluded by and opposed to the White settler establishment made them natural allies with those seeking a more liberal approach to immigration. The imperial migration regime was thus being questioned not just in economic terms, but in relation to the politics and identity of New Zealand as a modern and independent nation-state within the Asia-Pacific region.

Indeed, as numerous scholars have pointed out (Boltanski & Chiapello 2005; Dean 2009; Harvey 2005; Vallelly 2021), the economic neoliberals and the social liberals were often sides of the same coin: emergent among the White middle classes, formed by the same schools and universities, in the same industrialised countries, they generated their revolutionary liberal manifestos in the same cafés in major Western cities during the same decades of the mid-to-late twentieth century. As David Harvey (2005: 41–42) puts it, in the context of the May 1968 movement, 'for almost everyone involved in the movement of '68, the intrusive state was the enemy and it had to be reformed. And on that, the neoliberals could easily agree'. Neoliberal economic activists were arguing that innovators, entrepreneurs, and over-achievers were governed, regulated, and flattened into mediocrity by the tyranny of the majority. Their views blended at times with those of the new social movements, which were simultaneously railing against the tyranny of patriarchal and ethnically homogenous majorities.

This alliance between social and economic neoliberalism is clearly expressed in the merging of multicultural political philosophy with neoliberal economic ideas about immigration, which came to dominate immigration policy from the 1980s onwards. This approach, which stresses the need for high rates of immigration and ethnic diversity as a function of a global market society, is at the core of what we call 'economic multiculturalism'. As we conceive it, economic multiculturalism is a central dynamic within the wave of economic and social liberalisation and globalisation that began after World War II and accelerated from the 1970s (Kymlicka 2013). This wider wave of neoliberal globalisation began with the decolonisation of European empires, and in post-colonial nation-state-building projects around the world. On the one hand, this transformation involved a commitment to ending racist imperial-era immigration controls in former settler colonial societies and accommodating a new range of ethnic minorities more fully into the mainstream in countries like New Zealand, Australia, and Canada. On the other hand, it was about deregulating national labour markets and limiting the power of unions, so that employers could recruit skills and talent from a wider range of source countries at cheaper prices. The two strands of economic multiculturalism would drive significant liberalisation in New Zealand's migration controls in the coming decades.

Towards a Neoliberal Migration Regime

The trigger for the coming overhaul of New Zealand's migration regime was the election of the Fourth Labour Government and the neoliberal revolution it sparked. But the tinder for this spark was put in place in the waning years of Muldoonism. In a climate of global economic crisis and the economic withdrawal of Britain from its empire, the New Zealand economy had severely contracted in the 1970s, and unemployment was extremely high. In response, Prime Minister Robert Muldoon had introduced the Keynesian, pump-priming 'Think Big' programme, which aimed at large-scale infrastructure investment, backed by extensive government borrowing from overseas – in a direct emulation of the debt-financed 'Great Immigration and Public Works Scheme' that Julius Vogel had spearheaded one hundred years earlier (Boshier 2023). In 1983, the Muldoon Government introduced a new immigration Bill to Parliament that would facilitate the Think Big strategy – but it was never translated into policy, as Parliament was prorogued in early 1984 before Muldoon called a snap election for July of that year.

By this point, migration policy had come to broadly recognise three categories of permits: occupational, family reunion, and humanitarian (Farmer 1996a). This categorisation prefigured the later shift away from race-based migration controls towards an economistic approach of attracting 'human capital' (Schultz 1972), which was becoming more common internationally through the 1970s and 1980s (Koslowski 2014). The Dominion Population Committee Report in 1946 had hinted at such a future, but it had concerned itself largely with the potential ethnicity of New Zealand's future population with respect to migration policy. However, by the 1970s, the 'traditional source country preferences' were widely considered an obstacle to an immigration policy that was both fair (in terms of not discriminating by race) and effective (in terms of attracting the right mix of skills in sufficient quantity). Indeed, during the Muldoon years (1975–84), pressure mounted for more openness in the migration regime, especially among ethnic communities who were unable to grow under the race-based controls.

The emergence of neoliberal reforms to immigration under Muldoon was explained to us by Muldoon's Minister of Immigration Anthony George 'Aussie' Malcolm. While National was still in power, it was Malcolm who introduced a key immigration Bill that later developed into legislation passed by the Fourth Labour Government. In Malcolm's telling, his objective as Minister was to soften the sharp edges of a racist immigration policy until formal legislative change could be achieved:

> At that time, I believed I had been appointed to do a job and I believed – and so did those around me – that as Minister of Immigration my job was to run the immigration process. So, as pressure developed, I would use my discretion to constantly soften the sharp edges, moving towards formal change of policy, which we finally achieved in 1984 in a Bill which was to be introduced into the House, wait for it, on the night Muldoon threw a surprise election. So, that Bill emerged a year later as a Labour Bill but in fact I wrote it, and I ran the select committee, and that took away that racism. When I was there, it was a question of softening, easing the edges. . . . My policy was to bend the rules as an exception to policy, allow that family to bring an unskilled family member from China to continue to keep the farm

and the process going. All sorts of people would be coming in from China without any qualifications; even though that appeared not to be policy, there was in fact an Asianisation going on quietly.

Malcolm's account highlights that key decision-makers were already aware that racist immigration controls were not sustainable and needed to be worked around and eventually changed. It also draws attention to the importance of making changes that would simultaneously address the informality and inefficiency of the outdated selection methods. Race was no longer considered a rational basis for a formal migration policy, and so formalising required focusing on the economic capacity of migrants, matching them with 'objective' measurements of demand and supply for particular kinds of labour (Ongley & Pearson 1995). It required ending unrestricted entry rights for immigrants from the UK and Ireland, regardless of their perceived economic worthiness (which had already occurred in 1974 – Farmer 1985). And it required actively opening the door to immigrants from a wider range of countries. This was initially pursued by 'softening the edges' of the outdated race-based policy, and eventually achieved by formally changing the policy through new legislation, which was drafted as Malcolm was on the way out of office, and passed when the new Labour Government came in.

The shift from discriminatory towards economistic migration policy gathered even more momentum once David Lange's Labour Party won the election and formed a new government. A review of immigration policy was part of the Labour Party's policy platform going into the 1984 snap election (Farmer 1996a; New Zealand Labour Party 1984). Once in office, they implemented the Immigration Policy Review of 1986 and the 1987 Immigration Act – a watershed moment, marking the transition from imperial migration controls to a new regime prioritising economic contribution and diversity (Gamlen & Sherell 2022). In the words of then-Minister of Immigration Kerry Burke (1986: 10), the aim was to 'enrich the multicultural social fabric of New Zealand society through the selection of new settlers principally on the strength of their potential personal contribution to the future well-being of New Zealand'. With the UK now ensconced in the EEC, and after a decade of slow economic growth, New Zealand's economic dependence on British and Irish migration had receded. Meanwhile, New Zealand's net migration losses to Australia reached a nadir of 41,791 in 1979 and did not recover to consistent net migration gains until 1990 (Statistics New Zealand 2022). Taking this changed reality into account, the Immigration Policy Review of 1986 and subsequent legislation in 1987 initiated a migration policy 'more consistent with the shift towards an open, market-led economy' (Bedford 1994: 191). This approach was determined less by the source country of immigrants, and more by the skills and capital that migrants could bring to the economy (Trlin et al. 1997). The review placed emphasis on 'benefits' to New Zealand and stated that 'the selection of new immigrants will be based on criteria of personal merit without discrimination on grounds of race, national or ethnic origin, colour, sex or marital status, religion or ethical belief' (Burke 1986: 1.3.2). New Zealand migration policy, in theory, was stripped of its discriminatory basis and became more focused on the individual distinctions and economic potential of each applicant, irrespective of their cultural background. It promised a new meritocratic and 'multiracial' future for New Zealand society. Kerry Burke, Minister of Immigration from 1984 to 1987, neatly summarises the emergence of economic multiculturalism under the Fourth Labour Government:

> *The immigration structure which I had inherited was . . . a racist structure that was built on a traditional source of migration flow and that happened to be White Western Europe, North America and Australia. . . . The bigger picture [was] that in the modern world as we could see it then, we ought to be able to draw talent from wherever. . . . [B]y the time we got into government in 1984, the country was in real trouble and so major surgery was needed and immigration became part of that. But the main driving force behind the immigration change was simply to put everybody across the world on a level playing field so that if they met our criteria, it didn't matter which country they came from, they would be able to settle here.*

The economic multiculturalism articulated here by Burke was also stretched into tertiary education policy by the end of the decade, with the 1989 Education Act reducing funding to universities. This legislation forced universities to offset their deficits by charging a standard fee across all courses, which was amended in 1991 to allow universities to set their own fees and permitted and encouraged marketing to full-fee-paying international students (Tarling 2004). The global marketisation of university education has been well documented (Collins & Park 2016), and in the case of New Zealand, it led to universities aggressively competing against one another for lucrative international students (Collins & Lewis 2016). The New Zealand international student market entered a boom period and by the turn of the century accounted for over 70 per cent of temporary migration (Gamlen & Sherrell 2022). While initially conceived in distinction from migration policy, we observe in Chapters 5 and 6 how education and migration enter into a political-economic nexus that centres on notions of global competitiveness and the extraction of value (Robertson 2013).

Humanitarian concerns also influenced policy at this time, and New Zealand temporarily loosened its policies in 1987 to allow Fijian Indians to enter New Zealand in the wake of two coups in Fiji (Bedford 1994). New Zealand also introduced an annual refugee quota of 800 in 1987, which was proportionally much lower than Canada and Australia (Ongley & Pearson 1995), and in 1989 committed to accepting 1100 Indo-Chinese refugees over the next three years (Bellamy 2008). But, despite these gestures towards humanitarianism, it was clear that economics and population growth were the driving force of migration policy. What was distinct from the earlier imperial migration regime was that populating through migration was being more explicitly framed in terms of the availability of labour and investment capital and in a way that would broaden the potential source countries of immigrants.

The effects of immigration policy change were rapid and far-reaching in terms of the volume and nationality-composition of migration flows (Bedford et al. 2002a). The net gain of permanent and long-term non-citizens increased from 40,718 in the five years from 1982 to 1986 to 66,462 in the five years from the implementation of the Immigration Act in 1987. New Zealand citizens were still leaving in high numbers, with net losses of 72,159 and 113,466 over these two five-year periods respectively. Perhaps more notably in terms of the operation of the Act's new selection criteria, the number of approvals for residence more than doubled between these periods, from 49,396 (1982–86) to 112,295 (1987–91). Regarding both net migration of non-citizens and approvals for residence, there was also a significant diversification in the national origins of migrants that reflected the new openness aspired to in the 1987 Immigration Act. As Table 2.1 shows, as migration increased in volume, the proportion of people coming from 'traditional' source countries (UK/Ireland, Australia, North and Western Europe) declined while those from non-traditional sources, especially Asia, increased. Similarly, in relation to approvals for residence, people from the UK, Europe, and North America made up a declining proportion, while those from Asia and other parts of the world increased. Particularly notable for our discussion later in this book, both net migration and residence approvals increased markedly for Southeast and Northeast Asia. As we discuss in Chapter 3, the ethno-national makeup of population changes led to one of the first significant challenges to New Zealand's newly claimed openness to the world, in the form of resurgent public expressions of racism and anti-immigrationism (Parr 2000).

Table 2.1. *Net Permanent and Long-Term Migration, 1982–1991*
(**Source:** Bedford et al. 2002a)

	Net Permanent and Long-Term Migration		Approvals for Residence	
	1982–1986	1987–1991	1982–1986	1987–1991
New Zealand Citizens	-72,159	-113,466	N/A	N/A
Total (non-citizens)	40,718	66,462	49,396	112,295
Australia	15.4%	8.8%	N/A	N/A
Pacific Islands	16.9%	15.9%	23.0%	23.4%
UK/Ireland	28.8%	15.8%	35.9%	23.3%
North and Western Europe	11.8%	5.3%	11.9%	5.7%
South and East Europe	1.6%	2.8%	1.8%	1.1%
North America	5.5%	4.0%	7.7%	4.1%
South and Central America	0.4%	0.6%	0.4%	0.6%
Southeast Asia	12.8%	16.0%	11.7%	14.9%
Northeast Asia	3.4%	25.7%	3.1%	23.6%
South Asia	0.9%	2.1%	1.7%	3.9%
Middle East	0.5%	1.4%	0.5%	1.3%
Africa	1.3%	1.7%	1.4%	1.6%

The Value(s) of Immigration

The emergence of what we call economic multiculturalism in the 1980s was part of the neoliberal revolution of that period, which brought together a coalition of two major political positions opposing the status quo. On one side was neoliberal economics – with its focus on deregulation, opening of foreign investment, and privatisation of the public sphere – which seemed to promise both improved economic growth and a rolling back of the kinds of state interventions administered under the Keynesian economic consensus that had dominated since World War II and were seen as restrictive towards entrepreneurship, private enterprise, efficiency, and wealth creation. On the other side, building on the legacy of 1960s–70s social movements, the state had come to be seen as repressive and conformist, quelling individual autonomy and creativity. The 1986 Immigration Review appeared to point towards an approach to immigration policy that might satisfy both these neoliberal factions. By opening the New Zealand border to foreign capital, migration policy could aid economic growth, free up trade, and create new investment possibilities. And by attracting non-European migrants, New Zealand would become more diverse, cosmopolitan, socially liberal, and aligned with neoliberal cultural values of individual freedom and respect for human rights.

In 1980s New Zealand, the economic and social elements of the neoliberal coalition were represented by competing factions within the Fourth Labour Government. On one hand, Prime Minister David Lange led the traditional, union-backed socially liberal establishment of Labour. On the other, Finance Minister Roger Douglas led an anti-establishment ginger group of reformist economic liberals who wanted to break away from the unions.

The first challenge facing immigration reformers was to win over economic conservatives within the Labour Party's traditional union establishment, which harboured long-standing fears that mass immigration would undermine hard-won minimum standards for wages and working conditions. To overcome such objections, the party's election campaign platform placed primary emphasis on the less-contentious socially liberal aspects of immigration reform, by proposing reforms focused on fairness and liberty: 'Labour will review the Immigration Act to ensure that immigration procedures are fair and that the civil liberties of the people are properly protected' (McCluskey 2008; New Zealand Labour Party 1984: 43). However, once Labour entered office in the face of an economic crisis, it became increasingly necessary to couch proposals in terms favourable to Finance Minister Roger Douglas and his neoliberal economist allies in the Treasury. By the time the review took place in 1986, a new landmark Commerce Act was passing through Parliament, which deregulated price controls and removed preventive measures against exploitative profiteering that had been in place throughout the history of the New Zealand economy (Berry 2013). Against this background, reformers were beginning to flesh out how the immigration review connected to the government's wider economic agenda, noting that 'the whole economic environment within which previous policy guidelines were framed has been changed as a consequence of the restructuring and deregulation embarked upon by this Government' (Burke 1986: 20). Part of this economic case for immigration reform was the need for more labour-market 'flexibility' than was possible under race-based imperial controls. As Burke explained to us, 'we started with the view that we should draw our migrants on the basis of their talents . . . from anywhere in the world'.

As well as bridging intra-party-political divides, Burke's immigration reforms would first have to overcome the arguably even more fundamental challenge of convincing the Labour Party that immigration mattered much. In this period, at least across the English-speaking world, immigration was generally considered an issue of second-order political priority; unlike matters of security, diplomacy, trade, and investment, it was not considered part of the realm of 'high-politics' (Hollifield 2004). In 1980s New Zealand, immigration was rather low on the Labour Party's political agenda (Farmer 1996a; McCluskey 2008) – as attested by several former immigration ministers from this time. According to Burke's successor, Stan Rodger (1987–89), immigration was 'tangential to the government's agenda' and only 'by coincidence accorded with the drive to open up the economy'. For Annette King (1990), immigration 'wasn't high profile' as an issue. Indeed, even Roger Douglas himself, who was Minister of Immigration from 1989 to 1990, described immigration as 'an isolated area', the political importance of which was not widely recognised. In his telling, immigration was obviously important to a wide range of government priorities, but it did not seem to matter much 'in a political sense', and the 'Minister of Immigration tended to be isolated' from the very centre of power. It would require a significant amount of political work for Burke to gain approval from a sharply divided party for a programme of reforms in a low-priority area, based on policy designs inherited from the Muldoon-led National Government.

In this context, Burke described an approach whereby the values-based case for non-discriminatory immigration policy would unite the Labour Party around its core values, while the economic argument would divide the party along factional lines, placing the traditional union-backed faction on one side of the issue and the economic reformists on the other. As Kerry Burke explained to us:

> We wanted unanimity among the parliament, not to have it seen as a divisive issue [. . .] I think we covered all the bases on the political spectrum, of the left obviously. In the end the whole parliament was happy with it. But the formation, I think we were pretty inclusive . . . Some people might have seen this not on its own merits but as part of the dramatic changes which are taking place and there were some tensions within the government. . . . It was concurrent with the neoliberal reforms but how could anybody with Labour values oppose a policy which treated everybody as equal? Pretty hard. I think in terms of trade union representatives, people on the left of the caucus, they couldn't oppose that. You can't be for human rights, against structural inequalities and not support a policy like that. It kind of got all sides involved.

Our description of Labour's immigration reforms differs somewhat from other key accounts of the period. For example, Paul Spoonley (2015a: 177) writes that: 'The new imperatives were defined by neo-liberal ambitions to internationalise the economy, to shift the nature of labour recruitment to skilled, relatively well-funded migrants to meet an expanding service economy, and to establish new geo-political linkages with the Asian economies of the Pacific Rim.' We add some nuance to this argument. It is certainly true that the values-based case for a more open, non-discriminatory immigration policy resonated naturally with the neoliberal economic case for a more open economy – and this helped cement Labour Party unity on the issue. However, the accounts of immigration ministers make it clear that the Fourth Labour Government emphasised the values-based case for immigration reform, not the economic case. As Anthony 'Aussie' Malcolm puts it:

> The real shift to economics actually came a little bit later. The real shift to economics came from Bill Birch, I'm thinking [19]91 maybe, I'm not sure, when in an act of total Friedmanite bullshit, Birch as Minister of Immigration provided for quotas. Now, I thought then, and I still think now, that that is absolutely insane. That isn't an immigration policy, that's a population policy. Whilst free marketeers and Friedmanites might be enamoured by numbers, my view is the numbers don't provide for equity or justice or common sense; they're simply numbers.

Thus, the radical transformation of migration policy in the mid-1980s did become symbiotic with New Zealand's neoliberal economic revolution (Simon-Kumar 2015). However, it initially emerged from the social strand of neoliberal thinking, rather than the economic strand. By uniting socially liberal and economically liberal factions, the Fourth Labour Government was able to pass the Immigration Act 1987, thus changing migrant selection in a way that opened the doors for population diversification and competition in the labour market in the years and decades that followed.

Operationalising Neo-liberal Immigration Policy

It is in the operationalisation of the Immigration Act 1987 that the connections between these transformations and the political rationalities underpinning neoliberalisation became much more apparent. With the size and diversity of the migration programme having increased, there was a need to establish new modes of management. The increase in net migration of non-citizens and the growth in approvals for residence permits from the early to late 1980s required the establishment of new programmes for attracting and processing migrants, along with techniques to align migrants with selection criteria. Consider, for example, the process by which migrants were selected from traditional source countries in the dying days of the imperial migration regime. As Anthony Malcolm stated:

> In those days, remember, the policy wasn't a set public policy. The policy was not widely publicised. It was expressed in terms of immigration officers may approve cases that represent a value to New Zealand or something, I'm paraphrasing. But the point is the word was 'may', not 'shall'. The immigration policy was actually a set of guidelines. In the case of our major source of migrants, which was Great Britain, and to a lesser extent, Europe, the final decision was not made according to policy. The final decision was made according to an interview with an immigration officer at New Zealand House [in London]. People would file their application and would have little knowledge of what the real policy was but would feel they were probably qualified because they were British and a plumber and they had a job, and they would answer Immigration's questions and then they would turn up for an interview at New Zealand House. At the end of the interview the immigration officer would say, 'Righto, you're in.' It was a very different world.

Such an approach was untenable under the new regime, which had led to a much higher volume of applications for migrant status from a wider range of source countries, and had placed a sharper emphasis on accurately assessing the 'the strength of [migrants'] potential personal contribution to the future well-being of New Zealand' (Burke 1986: 10). Immigration procedures needed to become more formal, professional, systematic, and focused on the measurement of immigrants' economic value.

The 1986 Review reiterated that migration should remain an 'instrument of labour market policy rather than a means to promote economic growth' (Ongley & Pearson 1995: 770). For those applying for longer-term work visas, the two main eligibility criteria were a skill or qualification that was included on the Occupational Priority List – which outlined the job areas with identified labour shortages in New Zealand – and a concrete job offer. Greater employment flexibility was afforded to those on visitor permits, who, until the Immigration Act 1987, were unable to be employed officially, a policy that was policed more heavily in the preceding ten years due to high levels of unemployment in New Zealand (Bedford et al. 1987). The new policy enabled those in New Zealand on visitor visas to be issued with a work permit if they had a job offer for seasonal work that could not be fulfilled by a New Zealand citizen (Ongley & Pearson 1995). And, with the extension of the South Pacific Worker Permit Scheme to include Kiribati and Tuvalu, albeit in very small numbers, it was clear that flexible, short-term migrant labour was viewed as a feature of immigration, an orientation that complemented other developments in the new market-led economy.

Once implemented, these new procedures were not as blind to cultural background as the wording of the original 1986 Review might have suggested. Instead, they mixed assessments of 'economic value' with long-standing, implicitly racial selection criteria, through language requirements, interviewing procedures, and the intricacies of a points system (eventually introduced in 1991) that inherently favoured some nationalities over others (Simon-Kumar 2015). In many ways, this continued a key dimension of policy from the mid-1970s, in which immigration procedures were designed to 'include examination of the capacity of the individual immigrant and family to adapt to New Zealand society' (New Zealand National Party 1975). In fact, it has been argued that, through these screening measures, 'New Zealand could be seen to be exercising, albeit in a more subtle and covert manner, a *modified* source country preference' (Bedford et al. 1987: 52; emphasis in orginal). As we will discuss in later chapters, the implementation of such criteria and requirements in the mid-1980s anticipates a much more targeted focus on the characteristics of migrants that came to typify migration policy in the following decades, and especially in the twenty-first century (Collins 2020). In particular, the 1986 Review's emphasis that the English-language skills of the applicant and their immediate family 'should be a significant element in the assessment of occupational immigrants' (Burke 1986: 3.2.9) gives an important insight into the ongoing importance of maintaining English language as a key criteria of migration-led population growth. Burke explained language as a key limiting criterion of the government's liberalisation of immigration policy:

> I'm pretty sure we didn't start by thinking let's get a multicultural society. I think we started with the view that we should draw our migrants on the basis of their talents, and, of course, some knowledge of English, but from anywhere in the world. The Americans, the United States, their policy was that you only needed to be literate in your own language. I don't think even now they have an English language test in the United States but you must be able to read and write in your own language. But we didn't go that far.

While the review prioritised 'the retention by ethnic minorities of their cultural heritage' (Burke 1986: 48), this was only possible within the precondition of economic multiculturalism that new migrants were able to adapt to and integrate into the Anglophone and British-inflected society that had been established in New Zealand since 1840. As Simon-Kumar puts it, within the 'overt frame of race-free neoliberalism' (Simon-Kumar 2015: 1186), the notion of the desirable migrant is one in which 'race is inextricably tied in with class and class mobility'.

A new Business Immigration Policy, introduced in the same year as the Commerce Act (1986), suggested that the government was aware of the capacity of immigration to contribute to economic growth alongside providing labour-market supply, a capacity that subsequent New Zealand governments prioritised more determinedly. The Business Immigration Policy, which mirrored schemes introduced in Australia in 1976 (Collins 2012) and Canada in 1978 (Ley 2003), targeted investment capital programmes and overseas investors (Ongley and Pearson 1995; Bedford et al. 2002a). More so than the focus on labour-market policy, such policies carry a particularly neoliberal flavour. As David Ley (2003: 437) explains, 'In seeking to lure *homo economicus* with the prize of citizenship in return for entrepreneurial activity, the state is engaging the heart of the enterprise culture, the very figment of the imagination of neoliberal globalization theory.' In New Zealand, the Business Immigration Policy brought in 10,500 immigrants in the first four years, primarily from Asian countries, such as Hong Kong and Taiwan (Trlin & Kang 1992). Furthermore, visitor visa waivers were introduced with Singapore, Malaysia, Indonesia, and Thailand (Spoonley & Bedford 2012), which 'promoted a broader agenda of tapping into dynamic Asian economies as markets for commodities and sources of investment capital, tourists, and skilled migrants' (Bedford 2005a: 136).

The Mobility of Migration Policy in the Post-colonial Commonwealth

New Zealand was not the only British settler colony wrestling with its future as British imperial connections crumbled and neoliberal policymaking gained ascendency. Indeed, New Zealand's changes can be further contextualised and understood in relation to migration policy changes that had been undertaken in Australia and Canada. Where New Zealand's Dominion Population Committee had been tentative on the role of immigration in shaping New Zealand's future in the aftermath of World War II, Australia's post-war planners had been much more strident in calling for the country to 'populate or perish', and more proactive in increasing post-war immigration to increase population growth. A target of a 1 per cent growth in population through immigration had been introduced in 1945 and an 'expansive immigration population building policy was pursued until the early 1970s' (Ongley & Pearson 1995: 766). When suffering from similar economic problems to New Zealand, because of the oil crisis, a new Labor Government in Australia in 1972 restricted immigration, and by 1976 Australia had encountered its first net migration loss in the post-war period. The White Australia policy – which was a more explicitly racist version of the policy change Massey introduced to New Zealand in the 1920s – was formally ended in 1973, leading to a vast revamp of Australian migration policy towards a new multiculturalism (Gamlen & Sherrell 2022). Like the later reforms in New Zealand, this multicultural turn in Australian policy was tied up with economic interests, as migrants were now selected in terms of their economic potential rather than socio-cultural heritage, especially once a points-based system was introduced in 1979 (Gamlen & Sherrell 2022). In 1988, Australia undertook a similar review of migration policy as New Zealand had done in 1986, with the FitzGerald Report on Immigration Policy, which, even more so than the New Zealand review, advocated for a 'sharper economic focus' targeting 'skilled, entrepreneurial and youthful immigrants, with English and other language skills' (Encel 1988). Much like in New Zealand, these policies were enacted by a centre-left Labor government, confirming the extent to which transformation in migration policy entailed both an emphasis on multicultural openness and an articulation of neoliberal rationality that would come to dominate the entire political spectrum (Humphrys 2018).

Canada also pursued immigration in the post-war period, but less to boost population and more as a response to changing labour-market conditions (Ongley & Pearson 1995). As a result, Canadian levels of immigration fluctuated much more than those in Australia and New Zealand. Canadian migration policy had similarly been concerned with the ethnicity of migrants since the Immigration Act in 1910, which established a strict preference for European migrants (Hawkins 1988). In fact, up until the 1960s, Canadian immigration policy 'showed an explicit anti-Asiatic bias and a preference for migrants fitting an Anglocentric and Gallic norm' (Ongley & Pearson 1995: 770). Canada moved to end its ethnocentric migration policy earlier than Australia and New Zealand, with a new Immigration Act in 1962 that removed origin country restrictions and the introduction of a points system in 1967. While the global economic problems of the 1970s did not impact Canada as severely as Australia or New Zealand, it similarly introduced new, tighter immigration measures in the 1970s. At the same time, however, Canada expanded its *business* migration categories in the late 1970s, leading to a vast increase in Asian migration over the coming decade (Ley 2011). Again, like Australia and New Zealand, the shifts of the 1980s also moved the focus of Canadian migration policy towards a new 'expansionary' and multicultural society.

The similar shifts towards liberalising migration policy across these three settler colonial societies is significant for understanding policy change in New Zealand in both general and specific ways. Generally, as Kerry Burke recalled in his interview for this book, the similarities in the process and outcomes of changes in Australia, Canada, and New Zealand revealed 'a concept whose time had come'. Having established themselves as unabashedly White-settler-dominated colonies throughout the nineteenth and early-to-mid-twentieth centuries, all three countries were facing challenges to the dominant social and cultural order from Indigenous, civil rights, and counter-cultural movements alongside shifting demographics that had the potential to undermine future prosperity (Johnson 2016). Multiculturalism, either explicitly (in Canada and Australia) or more implicitly (in New Zealand), provided a political basis for reframing national identity and national development. In the realm of migration and migrant inclusion, multiculturalism made space for expressions of cultural liberalism that centred on freedom of choice for the individual and the constitution of a unified, tolerant, and coherent nation in and through population diversity (Mitchell 2004). As Mitchell (2004: 122) has argued in the Canadian context, 'multiculturalism also operated as a fundamental institutional and conceptual tool that gave the state enhanced ability to *control* difference' (emphasis in original), to set parameters for acceptable diversity that were often made manifest in forms of migrant selection that emphasised education, income, and wealth as the trade-off for non-discriminatory regulation (Simon-Kumar 2015).

The similarities between the reports, policies, and governmental technologies deployed by governments in Australia, Canada, and New Zealand speak to both intentional policy learning and best-practice emulation. While Burke remained uncertain about specific inter-governmental communication and policy learning among New Zealand, Australian, and Canadian officials and experts during his tenure, he described 'being aware of changes that were taking place elsewhere', and noted the involvement of the New Zealand Minister of Immigration as an invited attendee at the Federal and State Immigration and Ethnic Affairs Ministers meeting in Australia. Stan Rodger went further, suggesting that a direct adaptation of Canadian policy had occurred in 1987:

I wasn't involved in the policy formulation but they drew down as best I understand on what the Canadians were doing. That would have had a lot of appeal to me had I been consulted, because I have a great deal of time for the Canadians, as I do for the Scandinavians interestingly enough, because I think they think like New Zealanders and it might be its big brother beside smaller brother phenomenon, I don't know but they come to policy positions which in my view are broadly sensible. So we went down the Canadian track which was of course a skills based driver. It didn't matter where you came from. Essentially, if you had the appropriate bunch of skills you were rendered of being capable of being considered for admission into New Zealand.

This was not an isolated occurrence but rather reflects the deep inter-connections across these settler colonial contexts in the formation of migration policy as well as emergent global migration policy mobilities (Gamlen 2019; Prince 2020). As Bedford & Spoonley (2014: 891) have noted, such iterative policy development has been commonplace between Australia, Canada, and New Zealand, and has arguably increased over the subsequent decades: 'When one country changes immigration policy, either to improve the operation of its selection system, or to ensure better employment outcomes for migrants approved for permanent entry, the other two countries monitor the new initiatives closely.' Policy mobility of this kind, emulating best practice from other contexts, is fundamental to the experimental statecraft that underpins neoliberalism because it allows for rapid acquisition of pragmatic lessons and policy responses in creating and managing market rule (Brown 2015; Peck & Theodore 2015).

Geopolitical Reconfiguration and Colonial Continuity

The 1980s changes to immigration policy in New Zealand reflected geopolitical reconfigurations that have some alignment with the concurrent experiences of Canada and Australia, while also reflecting particularities of New Zealand's position in the last decades of the twentieth century. By the 1980s, countries like Canada, Australia and New Zealand – having separated from the British Empire – were beginning to recognise and engage tentatively with emerging Asian geoeconomic and geopolitical powers (Ley 2011; Mitchell 2004; Rizvi 1997). The 1986 Review in New Zealand occurred in the context of a wholesale shift in orientation towards Asia and the Pacific and the Third Labour Government's efforts to end racism and initiate a new era of partnership with Māori (Bedford 2005a; Parr 2000), outlined earlier and in Chapter 1, which had been underway since at least the 1970s. As Prime Minister Norman Kirk put it during a 1973 state dinner in Singapore:

There is a new spirit – almost I would say a pioneering one – now guiding New Zealand's relations with other countries. For too long New Zealanders were content to look at the world and particularly this part of the world, through the eyes of others. That is no longer so. We are, at last, attuned to the reality of our geographical situation. We are, belatedly, but with all the energy and imagination we can draw upon, moving to associate ourselves with the region – Asia and the Pacific – in which our destiny lies.

Schemes like the Colombo Plan in the 1960s and 1970s brought hundreds of students from Asian countries to New Zealand universities, mostly from Malaysia, and New Zealand's involvement in Cold War proxy wars in Southeast Asia indicated a new engagement with the Asian region (Tarling 2004). In the mid-1970s, recognition and engagement with Asia occurred in other ways. As one of its first acts, the Kirk Government campaigned on and formally recognised the People's Republic of China in 1972. Later, parts of the New Zealand Government even turned to Rewi Alley – a Canterbury-born World War I veteran who had become a member of the Chinese Communist Party and had set up the Chinese Industrial Cooperatives – to help with diplomatic relations with China (Brady 2002). In 1975, the New Zealand ambassador to China, Bryce Harland, attempted to convince Prime Minister Muldoon that Alley could be an asset in developing New Zealand's relationship with China because, 'in learning to live with our neighbours, it is essential for us New Zealanders – or at least some of us – to acquire an understanding of countries like China as they are today' (Brady 2002: 132–33). While Muldoon remained sceptical of Alley, the episode reveals a realisation within parts of the government that relations with Asian countries would be critical to New Zealand's political and economic future.

The 1986 Review and 1987 Immigration Act formalised this turn towards Asia, which had been prefigured by the introduction of a working holiday scheme with Japan in 1985 (Bellamy 2008). Kerry Burke explained this in terms of the link between trading relationships, geopolitical position, and immigration policy:

When I was a child, 95% of our trade was with Britain. I think it's 4 or 5% now, so we have transformed our trading relationships and our geopolitical position and I think it's perfectly fair to put the

*immigration policy in that context as well. I don't know that it was
conscious but it was just, this is the path we're on now, this is the way
it's going to be. . . . There was a reorientation, and Norman Kirk led
this, there was a reorientation to Asia, Southeast Asia, recognising
China was part of that.*

The ethno-demographic effects of this reorientation were substantial and
have continued in the shifting population makeup of New Zealand in the
twenty-first century. In the ten years following the 1986 Review, the Asian
percentage of the New Zealand population grew from 1.66 per cent to 4.8
per cent (Spoonley & Bedford 2012), and the percentage of immigrants
to New Zealand born in Asian countries (47 per cent) had quadrupled
from the number in the mid-1980s (Bedford 2005a). Alongside this
shift, New Zealand through the 1990s built a much stronger set of trade
relationships with countries in Asia that have often been tied to the
economic activities of a much larger Asian population (Larner 1998), a
point we discuss further in the next chapter.

New Zealand's migration policy development also occurred in
the context of sometimes challenging trans-Tasman relationships and
migration patterns. Whether planned or not, immigration policy has also
operated in connection with patterns of emigration. There had been
net migration losses in every year between 1976 and 1982, cumulatively
amounting to a net migration loss of over 100,000 (Farmer 1985), with
particularly significant flows towards Australia (Carmichael 1993). In 1979,
Kerry Burke made the connection between emigration and immigration
policy explicit, criticising the Muldoon Government in parliamentary
debates for seeking to cut immigration numbers and connecting
this to ongoing net migration losses (Burke 1979). Net losses of New
Zealand citizens continued through the 1980s and beyond, meaning
that immigration policy was increasingly seen as a means of replacing
emigrants with non-citizen arrivals in order to sustain population growth
(Bedford et al. 2002a).

Outflows of citizens to Australia is a particularly well-established
pattern from this era (Poot 2010), and ministers noted both awareness of
the loss of New Zealand citizens and patterns of onward migration from
New Zealand to Australia. Stan Rodger recalled discussing the onward
migration of people from Vietnam, Laos, and Cambodia to Sydney with
Robert Ray (Australian Minister for Immigration, 1988–90), who responded
with a commentary that highlighted New Zealand's secondary geopolitical
and geoeconomic place in trans-Tasman relationships:

> [Robert said] 'It doesn't matter, Stan. The New Zealand taxpayers are paying for all of their settlement. You're getting their health right, you're getting their education, getting their English language up, building their skills levels up and then you shoot them off to Australia, it doesn't matter. In any case, if you look at the statistics the most economically active proportion of the total workforce of Australia are New Zealanders.'

While the movement of White New Zealand citizens and newly valorised Asian migrants was deemed desirable from the Australian Government's perspective, Māori migration and onward movement of Pacific people to Australia has been viewed much more ambivalently (Hamer 2008). The formalisation of free movement across the Tasman was not without limits: indeed, rather than initiating free movement, the 1973 Trans-Tasman Travel Arrangement was intended to preserve, but also to formalise and more tightly control, what had previously been informal – and by default unrestricted – migration between New Zealand and Australia. Since then, Australian governments have looked to incrementally restrict movement (Hamer 2008). Notable during this era was the imposition of passport requirements in 1981, a move that Anthony 'Aussie' Malcolm saw as a direct attempt to stop the migration of non-citizen Pacific people in New Zealand to Australia:

> No one consulted us. . . . It was pure simple overt racism, and that leads today to all the hassles that we have today, all because Australia was happy to accept Kiwis when they were White. But when air travel between the Islands and the Pacific, the whole impact of what we were talking about before about Polynesian migration to New Zealand, the urban migration of Māori leading people away from marae and into the cities, produced a stream of people at Australian airports who had brown skins and the Aussies couldn't take it.

In addition to acting unilaterally in relation to trans-Tasman migration arrangements, Australian politicians also pressured New Zealand Ministers of Immigration and others to increase controls on migration from the Pacific. As Stan Rodger stated:

> Oh yes, and they've always been twitchy about the Pacific Island intake. They think it's a soft entry point to Australia. And they used to raise that with me and I just had to grin and bear it. They would raise

that. They're even more intense about it now, but they did see that as
a soft entry point because of the automatic rights, more especially
Cook Islanders to come down here but there's a fairly big quota
for Samoa every year as well. Many hundreds. I forget how many
hundred a year it is but it's quite a number. They saw that as a soft
entry point as well. They were getting a bit restive about that so they
used to take me aside and chew my ear.

While Rodger and others did not indicate that such inter-governmental encounters directly influenced policy decisions in New Zealand, it does clearly establish the power relations in the relationship between Australia and New Zealand, and more broadly in the Pacific region, and the ways in which an emphasis on migration control is maintained by multiple forces. Claims are often made about settler colonial affinity between Australia and New Zealand, especially in the context of histories of military activity and sporting rivalry, but the unilateral border actions and migration policy interventions of the Australian Government speak to power asymmetry in this regional geopolitical arrangement.

While New Zealand ministers were subject to or pressured by the Australian Government's impositions, they each discussed the emphasis in the 1980s on the imperative to control immigration from the Pacific. In relation to the racist 'Dawn Raids' deportation campaigns, for example, Anthony 'Aussie' Malcolm spoke about the question of 'how you managed Pacific Island labour in the context of a tightening workforce'. He described the need to have 'an enforcement policy' in order 'to move people on', and he noted that the issue needed to be addressed, saying 'the whole area . . . needed to be cleaned up, because it was absolutely improper'. Anxieties had been heightened across the political spectrum in 1982 when the Privy Council ruled that all Samoans born between 1924 and 1948 were British subjects and therefore had automatically – because of New Zealand's colonial rule over Samoa – become citizens of New Zealand in 1949, along with all of their descendants. The response of the New Zealand Government was rapid, with then-Opposition Deputy Leader David Lange accompanying then-Attorney-General Jim McLay to Samoa to negotiate an amendment to the Treaty of Friendship and a form of amnesty for Samoans in New Zealand (Palmer 2013). By September 1982, legislation had been passed to limit access to citizenship for Samoans already living in New Zealand. According to Stan Rodger:

Now [the Privy Council ruling] put the cat among the canaries, and [Lange] and [McClay] flew off to Samoa to get a deal,[8] and they got a partial amnesty too: if you're here you're okay but you weren't allowed otherwise. Otherwise there wouldn't be anybody living in Samoa today, they'd all be here. Look at the Cook Islands, look at Niue. My wife and I go to Niue every year for a holiday. They're lovely people but there's hardly anyone who lives there, 1,600 now I think. They're good people here but they've so denuded the population in the home base they've nearly ruined their societies.

The Samoan citizenship episode speaks to the continuity of colonial relations between New Zealand and countries in the Pacific (Tagupa 1994), as does Stan Rodger's framing of Pacific peoples as being 'lovely', 'good' and in need of immigration control for their own societal wellbeing. While New Zealand ministers found themselves pressured by their Australian counterparts about the relationship between immigration and emigration, they in turn looked to control movement in the Pacific because it was 'our sphere of influence', as Annette King put it. This ongoing colonial attitude continued under the Fourth Labour Government, even as it was implementing major policy reforms that were framed by a multicultural rhetoric of non-discriminatory migration policy. Kerry Burke recalled negotiating visa-free arrangements with Fiji, Tonga, and Samoa but facing unease in Cabinet: 'they were very unhappy about the prospect of anybody of Pacific Islands just being able to come on down and live here'. As it happened, there was only short-lived visa-free status for these countries, which was suspended in February 1987 because 'officials were becoming increasingly concerned that many Pacific Island residents may have had no intention of returning' (Bedford 2005a: 140). Set in the context of the skills-focused 1987 Immigration Act, its embeddedness in a geopolitical shift to Asia and relationship to trans-Tasman affairs, the desire to control Pacific immigration that was articulated in the 1980s showed the boundaries and discrimination at work in even seemingly open multicultural approaches to migration policy.

8   While Stan Rodger referred in his interview to Labour MPs Geoffrey Palmer and David Caygill being part of this mission to Western Samoa, this does not align with the year, which was 1982 when National was in office. Geoffrey Palmer's (2013) memoir states that it was a bipartisan response and that David Lange joined Jim McClay to negotiate with the Samoan Government.

Te Tiriti o Waitangi and Immigration

As outlined in the Introduction, there are parts of the story of migration policymaking in New Zealand where we as co-authors differ in our interpretation of the material at hand. One of the key areas is the way in which Te Tiriti o Waitangi has been taken into account in the development of immigration policy and the significance this has for understanding the governing of migration in New Zealand.

One argument is that the transformation of migration policy in the 1980s occurred almost completely separately from landmark developments in Māori politics and the increasing significance of Te Tiriti o Waitangi / The Treaty of Waitangi and the Waitangi Tribunal (Walker 1994; Kukutai & Rata 2017). According to this view, the 1980s marked the tentative beginnings of what evolved, decades later, into 'partnership' between the Crown and Māori over some domestic policy issues – and it is worthy of note that, in retrospect, Māori perspectives were omitted from the formation of major migration policy changes. Such omissions, this argument goes, show how legacies of settler colonialism continued to characterise this period of immigration policy transformation.

Another argument suggests that immigration was not a priority for Māori in this period, compared to issues such as land, nor did the government have the same Te Tiriti obligations as it has today. It is therefore no surprise that 1980s Māori were not consulted on migration policy in the way we now consider to be normal, because the norms themselves have radically changed. This argument, therefore, suggests that to situate migration policy transformation in the 1980s within a wider critique of settler colonialism is over-determined, and what is at play might be more to do with the pragmatics of politics and policymaking in this period. Of course, the answer might lie somewhere between these two poles, and we leave it to the reader to decide where they stand.

In what follows, we have tried to synthesise the two arguments to a certain extent, while allowing their different emphases to co-exist. Our interviews included only a limited line of questions with some former ministers about the involvement of Māori in migration policy, so it is not a huge surprise that the ministers had little to say about what sorts of engagement with Māori had occurred, or whether the relationship between Te Tiriti and immigration policy had been considered at all. Kerry Burke didn't 'recall any controversy among Māori about the broadening of the immigration arrangements'. Annette King identified New Zealand as 'predominantly a bicultural nation', setting that apart from and prior to multiculturalism driven by migration: 'I think we're still on that journey and I think we've got a long way to go in multiculturalism.' Stan Rodger retrospectively acknowledged the omission of Te Tiriti and Māori as a significant shortfall of the Labour Government's approach:

> As I look back, one of the things I do regret is that we didn't have a broad debate within society on population policy. And I'm sort of sensitive to the fact that we didn't embrace Māori in that debate. I mean, a whole drive of that Act was skills based regardless of where you're from, and I don't think we necessarily recognised as ministers at the time that that meant we were opening the door to areas of the world's population which had not traditionally come here and probably there should have been a debate about that.

Moreover, Rodger acknowledged Ranginui Walker's subsequent critique in the early 1990s that highlighted how migration policy change breached the Treaty relationship between Māori and the Crown and was an extension of colonialism (Walker 1994): 'I think it was a legitimate complaint. I mean it's all very well conceding 30 years afterwards, but I think that's true.' We address Walker's critique in the next chapter alongside related commentary from that time, including the Population Monitoring Group's account of immigration policy changes.

Of course, governments in the 1980s did not have the same legal and ethical obligations 'to engage with Māori and to understand Māori perspectives' as governments do today, and we cannot expect governments of the past to conform to norms and values of the present. When former ministers expressed regret at not engaging more with Māori or hope that future governments would engage more, they were not describing what happened in the 1980s but endorsing and aligning themselves with a particular moral and political view that has come into existence subsequently. Rodger's acknowledgement, for instance, comes with a high degree of hindsight, as well as a recognition that ministers *could* and perhaps *should* have acted differently. It should also be noted that Rodger subsequently admitted that, 'It's only a guess because my contact with Māoridom is comparatively limited.' What this implies most of all is that Rodger himself was not thinking too much about Māori consultation on migration policy in this period. However, it does also raise questions about why someone such as Rodger, without much discernible understanding of Māoridom, was appointed to the role of immigration minister. One explanation might be that the government of the day considered knowledge of Māori issues irrelevant to the immigration portfolio.

At the same time, this is not to say that the Labour Party in the period was ignoring Māori and issues of race and colonisation – far from it. As Burke explained, the policy changes that resulted in the 1987 Immigration Act had been mushrooming since the early 1970s. Norman Kirk's Third Labour Government had won a landslide victory in 1972 on the campaign slogan 'It's time for change', and had set in motion a series of radical reforms to promote equal opportunity, end colonial-era racism, and instigate 'a new era of racial partnership' between Māori and Pākehā (Bassett 2000). The anti-racist agenda was expressed internationally in diplomatic overtures to China and a range of non-White Commonwealth countries. Domestically, it was expressed in symbolic gestures such as Kirk being photographed holding the hand of a small Māori boy at the 1973 Waitangi celebrations, and in generation-defining actions such as refusing visas for the South African rugby team because it was racially segregated. Amid these progressive moves, Kirk also sought to address public anxieties about racism through new restrictive approaches to Pacific people, cancelling visa programmes, and initiating the 'Dawn Raids' deportation campaign (as discussed above and in detail in Chapter 1), which disproportionately targeted Pacific peoples (Anae 2020; Spoonley & Bedford 2012). The Third Labour Government's core achievements included reforming Māori land law, accelerating settlement of Māori land claims, and passing the Treaty of Waitangi Act, leading to the establishment of the Waitangi Tribunal. As Burke explained in his interview, the Fourth Labour Government's immigration reforms were built on this progressive agenda:

> That Bill from what happened in 1974, that really is representative of the Labour approach of equality, human equality. . . . Fraser Colman was minister in the Kirk–Rowling government and I remember him briefing the caucus on the policy. . . . By 1984, Labour actually had developed a policy to move towards the white paper contents. It took a while with Richard Northey chairing the caucus group and, of course, with me and some other officials involved it took a while to work through all of the ramifications of that as it appeared finally a couple of years after we were elected.

We do not know first-hand exactly what consultations with Māori occurred in the 1970s during the development of Labour's revolutionary immigration Bill, as we did not interview former Ministers of Immigration prior to Aussie Malcolm. Within the scope of our research we did not find government records or press releases from this period that directly suggest Māori consultation on immigration policy development. But we do know that the

Kirk Government placed a new era of partnership with Māori at the centre of its agenda, so much so that Kirk himself was often assumed (probably wrongly) to be Māori himself.

Burke was the one who eventually got the new immigration legislation across the line. He suggested in our interviews that he didn't 'recall any controversy among Māori about the broadening of the immigration arrangements' without elaborating on how such consultation might have taken place (and he was not asked to elaborate). However, we know from Burke's other statements in the interview and from the public record that he did in fact demonstrate engagement with Māori and understanding of their perspectives during his tenure as a cabinet minister. He sat alongside Peter Tapsell and Koro Wetere in Cabinet, and he engaged extensively with Māori in his role as Minister of Employment, which he held concurrently with the immigration portfolio, in reflection of the fact that immigration was seen in this period as an aspect of the labour market (rather than, say, as an aspect of justice and security, or internal affairs). In our interview Burke noted:

> Burke: [A]s Minister of Employment, I was conscious of the strong Māori component in looking for employment policy and I think I was possibly [first] at the Cabinet to use the term 'Māori Renaissance', because it was most evident in their interest in employment programmes and skills training and that sort of thing. [For example,] Tariana Turia was very active in running employment programmes in her area. . . . But I don't recall any controversy among Māori about the broadening of the immigration arrangements. In fact, I think they were probably supportive because it diluted in some ways the White Western European versus Māori dynamic that had been [going] on in New Zealand, and you had this broadening. So Māori – in my understanding of [how] things opened over years since then – have been very supportive of some of these local [immigrant] groups.

> Interviewer: . . . It sounds like you're characterising this period as one where Māori were essentially allies with other minorities . . .

> Burke: Yeah, I think that's a fair way to describe it.

It is clear in the above statement that Burke was certainly aware of wider developments of Māori politics in the 1980s, and that such politics were discussed at cabinet meetings and in the Labour caucus (and had been at least since Kirk became Labour leader in 1965). Burke's comments also reveal he understood where key Māori positioned themselves politically on the labour market, for which he was responsible as Minister of Employment and Immigration. His responsibility was to ensure the supply of workers for the economy; he could either grow local labour by training and upskilling Māori, as advocated by Turia. Or he could import skilled labour through immigration. These issues were deeply intertwined within his portfolio, and that portfolio was embedded in an anti-racist, pro-Māori Labour policy agenda that had been developing over the previous twenty years.

It is important to note, as we do in the Introduction, that the interviews are not the only sources we analysed for this book. We also drew on parliamentary records, government press releases and reports on migration policy, and academic literature on migration policy. Alongside the interviews, these sources reveal silences on the role of Te Tiriti in immigration policy, which echo elements of early settler colonisation and state sovereignty over borders and migration. This is not to suggest that such silences, especially on the part of the ministers, were necessarily conscious or vindictive. Instead, it is to raise the idea that such silences suggest a deeper-seated entanglement between migration policy and state sovereignty, which are complicated, like they are in other settler colonies, by the history of settler colonialism in New Zealand.

In their analysis of the omission of Māori from migration policy, Tahu Kukutai and Arama Rata argue that such omissions continue to the present day and have 'erased Māori from national conversations on immigration' (Kukutai & Rata 2017: 27). Decisions about who could or could not enter the territory of New Zealand have remained steadfastly at the behest of the Crown, as Walker (1994) also noted in his critique. Moreover, government records and press releases from the 1980s indicate that the impact of these policy changes on Māori, especially in terms of housing and the labour market, were never seriously considered (Kukutai & Rata 2017). Again, this is not to say that there was some kind of concerted effort on the part of the ministers to sideline such considerations, but it does reflect a current-day view that, in the 1980s, these issues were perhaps less connected or connected differently from how they are today. One reason for this might be that emergent Māori political movements did not explicitly identify these migration policies as top priorities, and/ or policymakers were not as cognisant of the impact of such policies on Māori as they might be today.

The tentative introduction of multiculturalism and migration-led diversification during the 1980s did not lead to the immediate abandonment of pre-1980s norms of New Zealand nationhood. Certainly, the changes in the 1980s led to a significant increase in the number of migrants from outside of traditional source countries. The huge increase in the number of Asian immigrants specifically, however, pushed the sociologist Arnold Parr (2000) to question whether migration policy had really made New Zealand a more globally multicultural society. Drawing on a series of national and local surveys, he argued that not only did the majority of immigrants come from a handful of source countries in Asia, reflecting the geopolitical pivot at work in migration policy, but the surveys also reflected a chasm between the data on migration flows and cultural attitudes towards globalisation. As Parr notes: 'Even if there is a high number of applicants from a diverse range of countries, the views of New Zealanders are not conducive to the population of New Zealand becoming more diversified globally' (Parr 2000: 329).

We address the xenophobia that Parr points to here in more detail in subsequent chapters. For the time being, though, it is worth highlighting that while transformations of immigration policy attempted to appease the needs of economic and culturally liberal attitudes, as discussed above, it was clear that economic liberalisation leading to population change did not necessarily constitute cultural liberalisation, as was also evident with the anti-immigrant politics that developed under Winston Peters in the 1990s.

It is also noteworthy that among the Ministers of Immigration throughout the four decades covered by this book, only Tuariki Delamere (1998–99) is Māori and all other ministers would be deemed 'New Zealand European' (although subsequent to our interviews Kris Faafoi, whose parents are from Tokelau, became Minister of Immigration in 2020). The positionality of ministers is indicative of the people for whom they are imagined to represent. This point was made explicit by both Kerry Burke and Stan Rodger when they expressed the importance of having a minister who was in an electoral seat that was *not* ethnically diverse:

> I was MP for West Coast, and MPs from Auckland for example who were in Cabinet would almost inevitably be conflicted on immigration matters because it's where all the big immigration issues were at work. So I became Minister of Immigration, at least in part because there were no major immigration issues at all on the West Coast, so I didn't have any constituency conflicts. I didn't have queues of migrant families at my constituency office like I would have had if I'd been a minister representing an Auckland constituency. I think Aussie Malcolm who came before me, I think he had Tongans camping on his front lawn or something at one stage.

— Kerry Burke

I thought that it was a good thing not to have an Auckland-based minister because there was all sorts of pressures on a Minister of Immigration from the ethnic communities in Auckland, and here in Dunedin it was a fairly placid place in terms of interests of that sort and so I didn't bring a particular agenda to bear, I didn't have personal baggage in terms of people I'd advocated for, that sort of thing.

— Stan Rodger

Entering the role of Minister of Immigration without 'personal baggage' associated with migration, away from areas where immigration was significant, and references to 'queues of migrant families' or Tongans camping on the front lawn, all speak to positioning migrants as non-New Zealanders. Such assertions highlight the position of migrants, and 'ethnic communities' more generally, as being apart from the broader New Zealand electorate that ministers were deemed to represent.

Significant transformations in migration policy undoubtedly took place in the 1980s. In light of these transformations, we might argue that the framing of power relations within New Zealand society remained at least partly continuous with its settler colonial past, rather than fully ruptured. The absence of Te Tiriti from immigration policy discussions, anxieties about the migration of Pacific people to New Zealand, xenophobic responses to Asian migration, and the continuing importance given to White settler populations in policymaking highlight how the foundations of the imperial migration regime were not totally upended even as the methods and social consequences of migration were radically transformed. To make such an argument, however, is not to suggest that the ministers or migration policymakers more generally were consciously reinforcing legacies of settler colonialism or setting out to actively sideline Māori perspectives in policy discussions. The expectations around Māori consultation were not the same as they are today, nor was immigration a hot topic for the emergent Māori politics in this period. These policy changes in the 1980s therefore reflected the settler colonial foundations of state sovereignty in New Zealand, of which migration policy was an important part, but also the extent to which Māori were more concerned in this period with issues within the state, such as land and economic redistribution, than with debates about who could and could not enter the country.

Conclusion

The Immigration Act 1987 represented a formative moment in New Zealand immigration policy: an attempt to close the door on the imperial migration regime that had dominated the country for over a century, and an effort to formalise economic multiculturalism as the basis for planning and operating migration controls for the future. While these changes are often associated with the overt neoliberal agenda of the Fourth Labour Government, our analysis in this chapter has shown how this significant transformation in immigration policy was introduced in earlier political moves initiated by the socially progressive Third Labour Government, and only became part of the neoliberal economic project after its enactment. In the early-to-mid-1970s, the Kirk Government had taken steps to transform New Zealand's racist attitudes towards Māori in the domestic sphere, and towards Asia-Pacific nations in the international sphere, and had forged the progressive, socially liberal policy framework out of which the revolutionary 1987 Immigration Act later emerged. In the late 1970s and early 1980s, Anthony 'Aussie' Malcolm and the National Party began working with the public service to develop immigration policy reforms that were implicitly less racist and explicitly more modern and efficient. Within the Fourth Labour Government, Kerry Burke again took up the baton and eventually delivered what became a bipartisan consensus on migration policy: that it should be outwardly fair and free of nationality discrimination and that migrants should make positive contributions to New Zealand society. As Burke recalled in his interview for this book over three decades later, 'I don't think any government would try to dismantle the framework which has been there now for over 30 years.'

There were multiple dimensions to the way in which economic multiculturalism shaped these transformations in immigration policy. While immigration was on the margins of the Fourth Labour Government's neoliberal policy drive, it did articulate political rationalities that had important affinities with forms of economic and social liberalisation that were central influences in the enactment of neoliberalism. New Zealand politics and society were undergoing substantial changes during this period, not least those emerging from Māori political movements to honour Te Tiriti o Waitangi; campaigns against the Dawn Raids, the Vietnam War, racism, and nuclear weapons; and other progressive social movements. The political discourse of accepting greater ethnic diversity aligned with these movements. It also made sense in a geopolitical and geoeconomic pivot towards Asia that had been necessitated by the untethering of New

Zealand's relationship with the British colonial metropole. Engaging Asia politically and economically became tied to providing space for migration from Asian countries, a link that was strengthened in the following decade.

As we have shown, however, the politics of change that we have traced here were not simply a departure from the imperial migration regime but rather entailed a reconfiguration of nationhood in a way that carried legacies of settler colonialism into a diversified and increasingly neoliberal era. New Zealand's immigration policy development followed the arc established by first Canadian and then Australian governments and reflected a set of claims about the inclusion of economically valuable ethnic diversity within still White-settler-dominated societies. In contrast, New Zealand's relationship with the Pacific remained characterised by colonialism. The New Zealand Government sought to restrict arrivals from Pacific countries and rapidly respond to risks of opening borders while the Australian Government pressured New Zealand towards even greater restrictions in the name of settler colonial affinity and free movement.

Many of the themes we have highlighted in this chapter continue through the stories and histories presented in the chapters that follow. These include: the growing economisation of migration, the tension between economic and cultural implications of migration, the multiple forces involved in migration policymaking, and the legacies of settler colonialism in governing migration at the edges of empire. The next chapter turns to the period that follows these initial transformations, as immigration policy starts to take on a much more overtly neoliberal character.

CHAPTER 3

Globalisation and the New Migration Orthodoxy, 1989–1996

I f the early-to-mid-1980s constituted a transformation of New Zealand migration policy within the context of the neoliberal restructuring, then the following decade entailed the consolidation and institutionalisation of migration policy along neoliberal lines, in a way that increasingly emphasised the importance of globalisation. The changes established in the 1987 Immigration Act had heralded the way for a quite different approach to immigration, and opened possibilities for a much larger number of migrants from a much wider range of nationalities to enter New Zealand. As we detail in this chapter, however, the roll-back of the imperial migration regime did not come hand in hand with a fully developed new approach to managing migration. Rather, it was *after* the 1987 Act, in the last years of the Fourth Labour Government and the first two terms of the Fourth National Government (1990–99), that the economic multiculturalism of the 1980s would be recalibrated into a more targeted economic immigration regime. Immigration policy and regulation started to acquire a technocratic character in this period as mechanisms for selecting the 'best' immigrants were established and refined, while political work shifted to crafting and circulating discourses of globalisation and cosmopolitanism that could reconfigure New Zealand and New Zealanders as multicultural. Put differently, the Labour Government introduced economic multiculturalism in the 1980s – with an emphasis on the 'multicultural' part of the equation; then in the late 1980s and 1990s, the National Government fleshed out and refined this approach to immigration, emphasising the 'economic' part.

This chapter traces the way in which migration policy became explicitly articulated and institutionalised as part of deepening neoliberal economic reforms from the late 1980s until the mid-1990s. Traversing the tenure and accounts of four former Ministers of Immigration – Roger Douglas, Annette King, Bill Birch, and Roger Maxwell – the chapter traces two key shifts in migration policy: (1) the formulation and eventual development of the Immigration Amendment Act 1991, which introduced the points system for assessing migrants; and (2) the explicit articulation of migration as part of New Zealand's globalisation agenda and in particular its turn to Asia. As we illustrate, the combined effect of these developments was an even greater shift in the volume and ethno-demographic makeup of migrants entering New Zealand in the 1990s. Growth in immigration and its impacts laid a foundation for significant critiques of immigration policy to emerge, especially anti-Asian racist attacks led by the prominent anti-immigration politician Winston Peters. The government response to such criticisms was to advance even more forthrightly a vision for New Zealand as a twenty-first-century multicultural society where skills rather than ethnicity mattered. While the success of that discourse in overcoming racism and anti-immigrationism was limited, its effect was also, arguably, to further sideline Māori and Te Tiriti o Waitangi from being central concerns in the design, development, and decision-making around immigration policy. By the end of this period, immigration had shifted from a relatively less-significant portfolio to a highly politicised sphere where contestations over value, identity, and nation were central.

Neoliberal Revolution to Neoliberal Orthodoxy

The Fourth Labour Government had started to fracture as it entered its second term and was resoundingly defeated by the National Party in the 1990 General Election, with National winning sixty-seven seats, more than any party in the history of the New Zealand Parliament. The Labour Party held on to only twenty-nine seats, nearly halving their representation in Parliament, and the NewLabour Party, led by ex-Labour MP Jim Anderton, secured one seat. An important factor in this defeat was the earlier collapse of the stock exchange on 'Black Monday', 19 October 1987, which was followed by a severe recession. While the economic impact of the stock-market crash was short-lived for many wealthy economies in the Global North, New Zealand arguably suffered worse damage than any other country in the world (Dann 2017). By early 1988, the New Zealand stock market had shrunk by almost 60 per cent and a 'generation of investors . . . turned away from capital markets and put their savings into property and property focused finance companies' (Dann 2017). In many ways, the 1987 stock-market crash paved the way for the housing crisis that hit New Zealand in the twenty-first century, which we shall discuss in the context of migration in later chapters.

Black Monday was not the sole cause of Labour's demise. The latter years of the Fourth Labour Government were also characterised by antagonism within Cabinet that would help assure the party's defeat in 1990 (Vowles & Aimer 1993). Divisions had emerged following Labour's re-election in 1987. Prime Minister David Lange began expressing concern about the extent and effects of radical economic restructuring, especially in the aftermath of the stock-market crash. However, Finance Minister Roger Douglas continued to insist that the government must press on with reforms, including proposals for a flat tax. This divergence in the political agenda at the top of the party led to Douglas's replacement as Minister of Finance by David Caygill (one of Douglas's associate ministers) – who also insisted on a continuation of what had by that time become known as 'Rogernomics'. In 1989, a split occurred, with high-profile MP and former party president Jim Anderton leaving Labour and establishing NewLabour as a party representing traditional left-wing political values.[9] Douglas was re-elected to Cabinet in August 1989 and allocated the immigration portfolio. Lange subsequently resigned, with the role of leader passing first to his deputy, Geoffrey Palmer, and subsequently to Mike Moore (then-Minister of Foreign Affairs and Trade, and an opponent of Lange), a matter of months before the 1990 election. Douglas held the Immigration portfolio for a period of only seven months from August 1989 to February 1990, although, as we will show, during this time some significant developments in policy thinking occurred. He handed the role to Annette King, who was first elected to Cabinet in 1989 and held the role of Minister of Immigration in the months leading up to Labour's massive election defeat in November 1990.

A major factor in Labour's defeat was the severity of market reforms they had pursued in office, which many on the left saw as a betrayal of the party's traditional working-class base (Vowles & Aimer 1993). The National Party, under the leadership of Jim Bolger, capitalised on these economic conditions and the political turmoil within Labour leading up to the 1990 General Election, and promised to 'start cleaning up the mess that Labour will leave behind' (New Zealand National Party 1990: 1). While castigating Labour for the economic recession, once in office, 'the National Government imposed yet more dramatic change [that] continued along the path of Labour's economic policies . . . despite the severity of Labour's electoral defeat on the basis of the same policies' (Vowles & Aimer 1993: 8). If the second half of the 1980s was dominated by 'Rogernomics', the first half of the 1990s was the period of 'Ruthanasia', named after the new Minister of Finance, Ruth Richardson. In 1991, Richardson introduced what

9   The policy agenda of New Zealand's NewLabour Party in this period is not to be confused with that of Great Britain's 'New Labour', led by Tony Blair, which was elected in 1997. Both parties articulated a desire to reinvent left-wing politics, but they reflect different approaches to the task. Anderton's approach was to shore up alliances with unions and return to traditional, protectionist Labour strategies. Blair's approach was to do the opposite, reinventing Labour as the party of 'The Third Way', which involved the embrace of free-market reforms while maintaining a social safety net.

she nicknamed the 'Mother of all Budgets', which had been drafted in close collaboration with the Minister of Social Welfare, Jenny Shipley, who went on to replace Bolger as Prime Minister in late 1997. The new budget introduced user-pay models to hospitals and schools, and public services such as state housing were privatised (Johansson 2006). Richardson and Shipley also scythed welfare spending – with the unemployment, sickness, and family benefits radically cut – and laid the groundwork for decades of neoliberal welfare policies that would increase poverty while policing and stigmatising beneficiaries.

These drastic changes, and the subsequent policy developments in restructuring welfare, anticipated further shifts in migration policy that began about ten years later. Labour-market deregulation, legislated in the Employment Contracts Act 1991, which would neuter trade unions, set the stage for declining real wages and conditions across a range of industries throughout the 1990s and 2000s. Greater targeting of migrants' economic value was introduced in the early 2000s (Bedford 2004; Collins 2020; discussed in Chapter 4), echoing the regulation of all aspects of beneficiaries' lives that had become commonplace in the 1990s. Immigration was increasingly seen as a response to labour-market shortages that started to emerge alongside the flexibilisation of work under the Fourth National Government.

The budget and the early work of policy change alienated the Keynesian old guard of the National Party, contributing to the resignation of former Prime Minister Robert Muldoon in December 1991 (Wolfe 2005: 209). The divergence of National from traditional conservative economic policies also contributed to the 1993 resignation of Muldoon's protégé Winston Peters, who would go on to form the populist New Zealand First party, via which he would remain in Parliament almost continuously for the next three decades (including through four stints as a senior cabinet minister), and become the most prominent anti-immigrationist in New Zealand politics. By 1992, all price controls that had remained after the neoliberal restructuring of the 1980s had been eliminated by the National Government (Dalziel & Lattimore 2001: 80; McCluskey 2008: 354), in the name of promoting competition – a central tenet of neoliberal thought. By the early 1990s, under the guidance of Richardson, the neoliberal revolution that had started in the 1980s was no longer revolutionary but simply orthodoxy.

Embedding the Neoliberal Migration Regime

The 1987 Immigration Act was significant for the way in which it explicitly removed source country criteria and derided discriminatory approaches to immigration selection as unfit for a modern globalising nation-state. Having passed such landmark legislation, the immediate role for immigration ministers, as Stan Rodger put it in his interview, was 'mainly just making sure that the bureaucracy was sensitised to it'. This was a task for Kerry Burke's successors, since, following the Act's passage into legislation, Stan Rodger became Acting Minister of Immigration as Burke took leave to care for his wife, Helen Paske, who had been diagnosed with cancer. Following Labour's re-election in August 1987, Burke was elected Speaker of Parliament, removing him from any further role in immigration or other policymaking matters. The transition from political work to administrative embeddedness emerged as the central challenge in the latter years of the Fourth Labour Government. All three of Burke's Labour Party successors (Rodger, Douglas, and King) placed emphasis on the role of the bureaucracy. Stan Rodger, for example, emphasised his relationship with Gordon Shroff, Assistant Secretary of Labour (Immigration), who headed the New Zealand Immigration Service in the mid-1980s: 'he oversaw the admin side of it and I oversaw the political side, *just smooth introduction of the legislation*' (interview, Stan Rodger, emphasis added).

The administrative side of implementing the new legislation was hardly smooth, however, with the Immigration Service experiencing increasing delays in processing times through 1987 and 1988, as the new legislation was bedded in, and record numbers of migrants in New Zealand applying for residence status. The number of people resident in New Zealand without a visa or permit increased steadily from 10,034 in 1984 to 17,833 in March 1988 (Rodger 1988), and exceeded 18,000 in mid-1990 (Birch 1990a). Opposition politicians regularly raised questions about the procedures under which immigration decisions were being made, including through delegated and discretionary approval by immigration officers. In many respects, the Act continued operational approaches to selection that pre-dated its implementation in 1987. The Occupational Priority List, for example, reflected a focus on labour-market needs that had been in place since the 1970s, although it now operated through a published list of skills needed in New Zealand. The 1987 Act had opened possibilities for a much wider range of applications for immigration status, now no longer limited by nationality, but did not yet operate through governmental technologies capable of managing the increased volume of applications that it had generated. Similarly, the Business Immigration Programme reportedly had wait times of over nine months for decisions, in stark contrast to Australia's purported forty-five-day turnaround, and opposition politicians criticised its inability to lead to new business start-ups (McCully 1989). According to the opposition, New Zealand was being 'denied the cream of the potential migrants', as Murray McCully (1989) stated:

> The bureaucratic bungling of the New Zealand Immigration Service both here and overseas is ensuring that we are denied the cream of the potential migrants, who have their applications processed more promptly, more courteously, and with greater competence by the immigration authorities of countries such as Australia.

Amid these problems, Roger Douglas was appointed the role of Minister of Immigration when he was re-elected to Cabinet in August 1989. He was allocated the role because, according to Stan Rodger, it was untenable for Douglas to return to a major cabinet portfolio such as Minister of Finance, since his public spat with Lange had damaged both his own image and that of the party. The Minister of Immigration was perceived as having a relatively light workload and 'not the most cherished post in government' (interview, Stan Rodger). Nonetheless, Douglas was quick to focus on reform, as Stan Rodger explained:

> He made a notable speech to the employers, I think. And he was signalling all sorts of opening up, as you might have expected from him. He brought his by-then-refined economic-reform views to the portfolio. There was one notable speech where he signalled all sorts of change. I don't think he had the chance to implement it but he made the speech.

For Douglas, the role had created an opportunity to engage with 'basic questions' of reconceiving the role of immigration in the economy, in a portfolio he acknowledged that he had previously not seen as particularly significant. Douglas reflected on engaging with Jas McKenzie, Secretary of Labour between 1986 and 1994, and together shifting the focus towards an understanding of the benefits of immigration:

> I met largely with Jas and we just asked some basic questions. . . . If you're going to have immigration who is most likely to benefit, and that drove us to, it was skills. Largely, if you get people with skills

then on average they're going to deliver more than the average New Zealander's currently doing it, and so you lift the bar. So, we worked on that a bit. It doesn't sound long, but that's the way we went and that's where the department went under Jas to work on.

Douglas's comments, and those of Stan Rodger that emphasised the sensitising of the bureaucracy to new policy settings, speak to the processes of embedding neoliberalism (Cahill 2018). As Cahill (2018) argues, neoliberal projects often take shape as policy becomes embedded within institutions and social norms, which is why bureaucrats respond to the challenges created by policies like the liberalisation of migration with more neoliberal policies. The shift from the political work of crafting and passing legislation to the administrative bedding in and the establishment of what kinds of measures are needed to manage immigration opens the door to more economistic assessments of migration and migrant selection. Such assessments have over time become constitutive of the neoliberal governmentality that characterises contemporary migration policy: the measurement of migrants in terms of their economic value to the nation (Simon-Kumar 2015).

Having expanded the routes for entry and set new ambitions for immigration policy, the task of government shifted to determining exactly who is likely to be of most benefit to the nation, according to the new underlying values. The imperial regime had developed many measures and proxies for the Whiteness it sought in migrants – but the new legislation shifted the underlying values of immigrant selection away from Whiteness and towards economic benefit. The task became one of making the economic benefits of migrants clear to policymakers, by establishing measures, databases, standards, and assessment procedures as the basis of a system for controlling for whom the border gate would open and to whom it would remain closed (Walters 2015). Such techniques and technologies were only embryonic in the late 1980s in the immediate wake of the passage of the new Immigration Act. There were expressed desires for the capacity to govern in line with neoliberal social and economic values, but many of these were sweeping feel-good platitudes that few could disagree with. They were not given detailed regulatory effect until the first years of the Fourth National Government.

Nonetheless, the task of operationalising the new legislation began prior to this, under Labour. Douglas, for example, framed the problem as one of assessment:

It started by saying what is most likely to deliver for New Zealand, immigrants who have skills. And therefore the issue then becomes how do you assess, how do you do the trade-offs; a whole lot of questions. Yeah, you've got skills and part comes down to, skills in what area do you need. . . . And so the points system, I guess, I was responsible for [determining that]. I did a trip to Australia, met with, I think it was Richardson, who had been minister over there, a fairly smart guy, and talked through why they had a points system and I guess that's why we ended up with the points system. We'd already determined what our approach was, it had to benefit New Zealand, and skills and a points system seemed to fit that.

The points system, for assessing immigrants for residence permits, was not implemented until 1991 under National (as discussed in the next section). But the reconceptualisation of immigrant-selection processes that was emerging in the late 1980s was clearly headed in that direction. Through ever more policy emulation and 'benchmarking loops' (Gamlen 2019), New Zealand immigration policy converged and moved in tandem with similar developments in Australia and Canada, setting in place an economistic language of immigration's benefits that remained pervasive in the subsequent decades covered by this book.

A points-based system had been in operation in Canada since 1967 and in Australia since 1979. The Canadian model had effectively removed any official discrimination against the source countries of migrants, and it closely aligned Canadian migration policy with labour demands (Richmond 1975). The Numerical Multifactor Assessment System in Australia was broadly modelled on the Canadian precedent, with its focus on the economic characteristics of migrants over socio-cultural traits (Gamlen & Sherrell 2022). It is important to note that, despite this shift, the Australian system initially maintained a focus on character assessments and strict language provisions, which favoured migration from European countries (Ongley & Pearson 1995: 772). During the Indochina Refugee Crisis of the 1970s, growing humanitarian immigration sped up the process of diversification. And by the end of the 1980s, the Australian points system was facilitating migration from other parts of the world, especially Asia, as a commitment to multiculturalism was symbolised by the establishment of the Office of Multicultural Affairs in 1987. By the mid-1990s, the Australian points-based system was deeply embedded within an economic rationality, and a commitment to multiculturalism in the source regions of migrants was more closely aligned to the economic benefits of migration (Gamlen & Sherrell 2022).

Where the Occupational Priority List had tied immigration to job vacancies in specific fields of occupation, the new points system would aim to realign immigration policy within the schema of 'human capital'. The OECD defines human capital as 'the knowledge, skills, competencies and attributes embodied in individuals that facilitate the creation of person, social and economy wellbeing' (Keeley 2007: 29). The idea was indebted to a long history of liberal thought going back at least to Adam Smith, who – although he did not use the term itself – noted that part of the fixed capital of any society consisted in 'the acquired and useful abilities of all the inhabitants or members of the society' (Smith 1811: 10). It began to gather momentum in the work of the neoliberal economists at the Chicago School of Economics in the mid-twentieth century, most notably in the work of Jacob Mincer (1958) and Gary Becker (1964), who developed human capital into a theory of human life (Brown 2015; Vallelly 2021).

In the context of immigration policy, a human capital framework judged applicants on both their current stocks of human capital and their capacity to invest in their future human capital, by undertaking further education, developing new skills, or exercising their entrepreneurial potential. The new system allocated points to each applicant, based on qualifications, skills, assets, work experience, and age, with the greatest weighting given to skills and qualifications (New Zealand Productivity Commission 2021: 21). In this sense, migration became more focused on potential than on need, less concerned with identifying present problems and adjusting migration settings to tackle these problems, and more concerned with the capacity of migrants to generate future economic growth (Skilling 2012: 369). Such an approach was in keeping with the broader development of neoliberal governmental technologies emerging internationally in the early 1990s. As Rose and Miller (1992: 175) noted, such technologies centred on 'knowledge' as 'central to these activities of government and to the very formation of its objects, for government is a domain of cognition, calculation, experimentation and evaluation'. Gaining benefit from the human capital potential of immigration required the establishment of techniques of assessment that would make that benefit visible and calculable and thus amenable to ongoing government intervention (Power 1997). The points system embedded in the Immigration Amendment Act 1991 was essential to such a focus of modern government.

Douglas made clear to the public, in 1989, that a points system in New Zealand was about valuing migrants for their 'human capital'. This differed markedly from the approach to managing the labour market that had characterised the end of the imperial migration regime. In media reports in November 1989, Douglas described a focus on selecting 'the best of all migrants', 'effectively assuming that skilled people will find jobs on their own initiative', rather than specifying priority occupations (New Zealand Herald 1989). As he did in his interview for this book, Douglas explicitly referred to the Australian model as the basis from which this approach had been developed – but whereas the Australian approach was reactive, New Zealand would be 'proactive', promoting immigration from a range of source countries: 'what you are actually looking for is a blend'. Annette King oversaw the continuation of this policy work during her brief tenure in the final months of the Fourth Labour Government, describing in February 1990 the need for a 'straightforward, transparent and decisive' process to get the best outcome: 'New Zealand was entering the world market for skills. We are wanting the best people' (New Zealand Herald 1990). However, with the landslide defeat of the Fourth Labour Government in 1990, it was left to the newly elected National Party, and Bill Birch and Roger Maxwell as Ministers of Immigration, to see these changes through to legislation and bureaucratic operation.

The Immigration Amendment Act 1991

Immigration policy was largely absent from the National Party's 1990 election manifesto, which merely asserted that 'We will increase New Zealand's skill levels by developing an active immigration programme' (New Zealand National Party 1990). Their political framing of immigration and policy responses in office, however, undoubtedly became central to the consolidation of the new neoliberal orthodoxy of the 1990s. By the end of the 1980s, there was no going back to the old ethnicity-based system, as the synergy between migration and economic policies was becoming firmly embedded (Ongley & Pearson 1995: 770). As we noted in the previous chapter, there had been widespread parliamentary support for the Immigration Act 1987. Parliamentary debate over the subsequent three years focused primarily on questions about the effectiveness of the Immigration Service's systems and procedures, its delays and backlogs in visa processing, and the growing number of people on visas or permits that had expired. The National Party, for the most part, endorsed the direction of policy travel under Douglas and King, particularly in terms of introducing a points system: 'We certainly hope that the occupational priority list will be scrapped in favour of a more broadly based skills-orientated system similar to the points system that operates in Australia' (Murray McCully, 22 November 1989).

By the time the National Party was elected to office in November 1990, a potential points system had already been discussed publicly and in Parliament for over a year. In his speech from the throne on 29 November

1990, then Governor-General Paul Reeves signalled the new National Government's intention to continue focusing on the economic value of immigration in general terms: 'HONOURABLE MEMBERS, immigration also contributes to the economic prosperity and social development of our nation. My Government will encourage more skilled migrants from a wider variety of countries to come to New Zealand.'

Bill Birch, the first Minister of Immigration in the new government, was himself already convinced of the value of a points system by this time. He recalled, as opposition spokesperson, being 'persuaded that the points system was a change that needed to be made'. Birch also recalled that Jas McKenzie had insisted he would only remain as Secretary of Labour if the new government continued with the current policy direction:

> It made a lot of sense. I actually think Australia went before us and I think that seemed to work pretty well. It was essentially to put some principles around how you decide on a person who wanted to migrate to New Zealand. This is really what drove those policy changes to introduce a points-based system, so if you qualified with enough points you got in and that's what was developed and passed into law.

In other words, the agenda for a new immigration governing regime had already been set, and by 12 December 1990 (a mere fifteen days after being elected), Birch was articulating an approach that was nearly identical to that proposed by Douglas and King over the previous twelve months: 'It is intended that the occupational priority list should be abolished. A ministerial working group is being established to make recommendations on a points system and other aspects of the new Government's immig-ration policy' (Birch 1990b).

The ministerial working party recommended that the Occupational Priority List be replaced with a points system, developed by the Business Immigration Programme, which would implement new approaches to assessing applicants' ability to promote economic development. It also recommended that the Immigration Service develop a marketing plan to attract 'quality migrants' (Population Monitoring Group 1991). The ideas underpinning new policy developments in immigration selection and management were also circulating in other spaces around the new government. The libertarian New Zealand Business Roundtable, an influential big-business lobby group in the 1980s and 1990s, published economist Wolfgang Kasper's *Populate or Languish? Rethinking New Zealand's Immigration Policy* in 1990. The book explicitly developed a neoliberal view of immigration, asserting that policy ought to 'shift to a more open, growth-oriented, long-term approach'. Kasper (1990: 72) expressed a dim view of any kind of bureaucratic procedures to select immigrants, affording only that minimal guidelines would be tolerable:

> All that one can try to achieve within the general framework of an administered rationing mechanism is to lay down some general policy guidelines about expected positive net contributions to national productivity growth and to screen out anti-social elements and free riders. This is, arguably, the objective of New Zealand's new, simplified points system for selecting immigrants.

Kasper's vision of immigration almost unfettered by administrative selection processes was never going to satisfy the 'proactive' approach articulated by Douglas, King, and Birch. But it indicated a general atmosphere of enthusiasm for a larger and more open immigration programme, which chimed with and reinforced the thinking in government. Indeed, Birch described consulting Roger Kerr, then Executive Director of the Business Roundtable, on immigration and labour-market reform:

> Roger was brilliant at labour-market policies. In terms of doing what's best for the market, he was extremely good. I liked Roger, he was very clear. He was a major contributor to the Employment Contracts Act. Again, I would have looked to him on immigration; I'm sure I had several talks to him. Because what you do, you consult a lot, all the people involved.

The New Zealand Treasury (where Kerr had previously been Director of Economics) had been a major channel through which neoliberal economic theory and policy entered New Zealand during the 1970s and 1980s. During the 1990s, Treasury continued to be a major think-tank for policy reforms based on the thinking of the dominant neoliberal economics of the period. Reflecting on her experience as a Treasury analyst in the early 1990s, prominent immigration economist Julie Fry[10] described the singular focus on the positive benefits of immigration:

---

10   Julie Fry, discussion during seminar on 'exploring immigration settings and outcomes', Motu Economic and Public Policy Seminar Series. Available online: https://www.motu.nz/about-us/public-policy-seminars/events/exploring-immigration-settings-effects-and-outcomes/

We were looking at things coming out of the US like Anna Saxenian's research about [immigration] impacts in Silicon Valley. . . . Immigration looked like it was a one-way bet, it looked like it had potential to do amazing things in terms of productivity without any downsides for locals.

The points system for immigrant selection, with its new emphasis on human capital, was established in a new Immigration Amendment Act, which was given Royal Assent on 7 November 1991. The new Act also introduced a much more stringent approach to people's ability to apply for migrant status in New Zealand, broadening the general criteria for identifying desirable migrants, while enhancing the powers of government to enforce border controls. At the time, Bill Birch stated that the new system was an attempt to change the 'border guard approach' of New Zealand migration policy (quoted in Farmer 1996b: 2), replacing a singular decision on immigration selection at the border with more distributed and diverse pathways to immigration that also increased the potential to manage migration. Whereas the border-guard approach privileged the government's sovereign authority to decide who entered the territory, the new approach sought to reduce centralised control, enabling employers to recruit labour from abroad according to a set of clear criteria. The border-guard approach had effectively been discarded in the aftermath of the 1986 Review, but, without a clear mechanism for managing immigrant selection, the 1987 Act 'was seen to not be operating fairly; too many decisions were just made arbitrarily' (Bill Birch, interview). Under the new approach, immigration policy would become more 'transparent' and 'accountable', in the neoliberal public-sector jargon of that period. Through the introduction of the points system, decision procedures would be strictly defined according to supposedly objective economic criteria. And decisions would be open to audit, so that responsibility for failures or poor decisions could be pinpointed, and where appropriate, challenged by a newly established Residence Appeal Authority. The aim, as Birch made clear at the time, was to attract highly skilled migrants who would 'bring skills, capital and energy which will increase domestic demand and provide employment opportunities' (Birch 1991). Table 3.1 outlines the 1991 points system for the general category.

The Immigration Amendment Act introduced four residency categories: 'General' (which became 'General Skills' in 1995); Business Investment' (which became 'Business Investor' in 1995); 'Family'; and 'Humanitarian'. It also established an annual 'target' of 25,000 migrants to be granted residence, excluding refugees – not quite the 40,000 advocated by Kasper but certainly an ambitious growth target. Initially,

Table 3.1. *The 1991 Points System – General Category*
(**Source:** Farmer 1996b)

Employability	Points allocation
1. Qualifications	1
Postgraduate degree, or bachelor's degree in science, technical or engineering areas	15
Other bachelor's degree, trade certificate or advanced trade qualification (minimum 3 years full-time study)	12
Diploma or certificate (2 or 3 years full-time study)	8
Attended school for 12 years	2
2. Approved work experience	1 point for every 2 years (maximum 10 points)
Age	
12–24	8
25–29	10
30–34	8
35–39	6
40–44	4
45–49	2
55+	ineligible
Settlement factors	
A maximum of 5 points for any combination of the following:	
The equivalent of NZ$100,000 to be used as settlement funds	2
Sponsorship by an immediate family member	2
Sponsorship by an established community organisation	3
Investment funds	1 point for each NZ$100,000 (maximum 3 points)
Offer of skilled employment	3

the economic recession of the early 1990s meant that New Zealand was not such an attractive destination for potential migrants, with a headline in the *New Zealand Herald* in February 1992 reading 'Migrant Scheme fails as lure' (Farmer 1996b: 3). A $100,000 marketing programme was introduced in Britain – with undoubted echoes of the assisted migration schemes of the imperial migration era – but similar schemes were also introduced in Asia (Farmer 1996b: 3). The 25,000 'target' was a 'goal' rather than a 'limit', and by 1993 immigration numbers far exceeded the annual target, peaking in 1995 at 56,000 residency approvals (Farmer 1996b: 1; Winkelmann 1999: 12). As Ongley and Pearson (1995: 770) noted at the time, the 'liberalisation of [migration] policy at a time of high unemployment represents a marked departure from the former labour market-oriented approach'. An auto-pass policy was initially introduced for the general and business investment categories, with lowered English-language requirements, where applicants who met the points threshold were granted approval if they also passed a police and health check (Bedford & Lidgard 1997; Farmer 1996b: 2; Simon-Kumar 2015: 1176; Spoonley & Bedford 2012: 87; Trlin 1997). As Birch described, there was a focus on managing flows:

> Interviewer: It sounds like this was about creating a reliable mechanism for filtering the inflow.
>
> Birch: Exactly, that's exactly what it was. It was to enable some sort of I suppose pathway for highly qualified people who are big assets from our point of view. If you get engineers that are trained overseas and they've got good qualifications, that's worth a lot to the country. But you don't want too many of them because if you open it up too wide and they have a right under the policy to come in, it's very hard to stop it quickly.

Globalisation and Immigration

As we outlined in the previous chapter, the 1986 Review and subsequent legislation had precipitated a vast demographic shift in migration to New Zealand, with approvals from Asian countries between 1987 and 1991 matching those from the UK, Ireland, and Pacific nations (Bedford 2005a: 137). The new points system accelerated these changes, especially under the General and Business Investor categories (Li 2014: 231). The period between April 1991 and March 1996 saw New Zealand's highest net migration since the late nineteenth century (130,273), which was almost double the net migration rate of the previous five years (66,462). This growth in net migration was marked by notable shifts in the national origin of immigrants, with the percentage of those coming from non-traditional source countries increasing from 33.5 per cent to 58.8 per cent by the end of that period (excluding returning New Zealanders). In the same period, the number of residence approvals from non-traditional source countries increased from 47.2 per cent to 71.6 per cent, with 55 per cent from Asia (Bedford et al. 2002a: 75–79).

Table 3.2 provides more detailed information on net migration and residence approvals during the early-to-mid-1990s by world region. Particularly notable here was the threefold increase in net migration from Northeast Asia, from 17,088 between 1987 and 1991 to 51,668 between 1992 and 1996, with considerable growth in South Asian immigration (from 1369 to 9263) and a modest increase from Southeast Asia (from 10,663 to 13,348). While Asia became the dominant source within the new migration orthodoxy, there was also a sizeable increase from regions with little history of migration to New Zealand, including Southern and Eastern Europe (from 1893 to 8286), Africa (from 1174 to 7308), and the Middle East (from 932 to 4044). Similar geographical patterns can be observed in approvals for residence, which overall had grown from 112,295 to 196,215 because of the government's new proactive immigration policy. As noted by Roger Maxwell, Associate Minister of Immigration under Bill Birch before becoming Minister of Immigration in 1993, these shifts in the national composition of immigration were anticipated and consistent with the emergent geopolitical and geoeconomic aspirations of the National Government:

> Well, we wanted to do two things. One, increase the number of people in a managed way and get the so-called 'right people', the people we needed and that would fit into our society, and [two], also spread the source of the countries. Rather than UK, a dramatic change in the number of migrants from Asia for example. Now, that wasn't that popular at the time. Then Bolger got around to deciding, you know, when he made that one-liner which became quite important was, 'our future lies in Asia'. So, there was a whole lot of stuff going on before that and then we had the point system brought in, but how do you actually select the right people.

In contrast to an avowed focus on recruiting the 'right people' from Asian countries as part of a drive towards globalisation, net migration from Pacific Island countries decreased from 10,548 between 1987 and 1991, to a mere 3969 between 1992 and 1996. And while overall residence approvals increased by 75 per cent between these two periods, residence approvals for people from Pacific Island countries declined by over 31 per cent to only 18,092 between 1992 and 1996. As Bedford (1994) noted, Pacific migration was coming under closer scrutiny at the time that the points system was being developed in the late 1980s. The number of Western Samoans

Table 3.2. *Net Migration and Approvals for Residence, 1987–1996*
(Source: Bedford et al. 2002a)

	Net permanent and long-term migration (March years)		Approvals for residence (calendar years)	
	1987–91	**1992–96**	**1987–91**	**1992–96**
New Zealand citizens	-113,466	-52,022	N/A	N/A
Total (non-citizens)	66,462	130,273	112,295	196,215
Australia	5,880	8,911	N/A	N/A
Pacific Islands	10,548	3,969	26,326	18,092
UK/Ireland	10,513	16,006	21,341	26,120
North and Western Europe	3,547	3,702	6,381	5,514
Southern and Eastern Europe	1,893	8,286	1,288	9,987
North America	2,690	3,007	4,586	5,103
South and Central America	434	500	678	800
Southeast Asia	10,663	13,348	16,785	13,613
Northeast Asia	17,088	51,668	26,523	75,762
South Asia	1,369	9,263	4,399	18,402
Middle East	932	4,044	1,429	6,331
Africa	1,174	7,308	1,912	15,504

granted visas or permits had grown to 4355 in 1989 and, to encourage a return to 'traditional' levels of immigration, Prime Minister David Lange had mooted the termination of the 1100 annual quota of residence permits (Bedford & Larner 1992). Foreign Affairs Minister Russell Marshall led a delegation to Apia in June 1989 to review the agreement with the Samoan Government, which led to the retention of the annual migrant quota on the basis that immigration policies would eventually decrease the numbers of Samoan migrants in the future. The points system that Douglas had been conceiving with bureaucrats and that Birch delivered in legislation clearly disadvantaged Pacific migrants because prior migration of Pacific people to New Zealand had been into areas that were classed as 'unskilled' and therefore did not count for 'offers of skilled employment', or 'approved work experience.' Moreover, tertiary qualifications were the primary source of points and were uncommon in Pacific countries at the time; the availability of settlement or investment funds in excess of $100,000 was even rarer. The only exception were populations such as Indian Fijians, who were more likely to have recognised qualifications and capital assets (Bedford 1994).

Although the family reunion category remained open to such migrants if they already had family in New Zealand (Bedford 2005a: 138–39; Ongley & Pearson 1995: 775), this effectively positioned people from the Pacific as outside of the valorised economic core of the new neoliberal immigration regime. Many Pacific people who had become undocumented were unable to afford the fee for a residency application, mainly because the neoliberal restructuring of the New Zealand economy and its accompanying migration policy had led to widespread unemployment in Pacific communities (Farmer 1996b: 8). Visa-waiver arrangements played a role too: while waivers were rescinded for Fiji, Western Samoa, and Tonga in February 1987 (only three months after being introduced), new visa-waiver arrangements were introduced for Singapore (1986); Malaysia, Indonesia, and Thailand (1987); and South Korea and Brunei (1993). The government courted Taiwan (1994), but this was rebuked by the People's Republic of China (Bedford & Lidgard 1997). Moreover, Pacific people in New Zealand once again found themselves the target of a crackdown on overstayers, with a removal order for overstayers introduced in November 1991. In the context of the new neoliberal orthodoxy in migration governance, it was the Asian part of the Asia-Pacific region that became the core focus of government attention. Globalisation and multiculturalism were not simply discursive accompaniments to the neoliberal changes in immigration policy. They were co-constituted in terms of the uneven peopling of migration and the perceived value of different global connections.

While the population figures from the early 1990s show a substantial increase in migrants from Asia in general, the demographic shifts within these numbers provide a helpful picture of the evolving nature of Asian migration to New Zealand and the wider geopolitical context in which these migration flows took place. Hong Kong, for instance, had the highest proportion (12.9 per cent) of residence approvals of any country between April 1992 and March 1993. By March 1996, Hong Kong still accounted for 5 per cent of approvals (Farmer 1996b: 5). In this period, Hong Kong faced an uncertain future. The Sino-British Joint Declaration in 1984 had confirmed the handover of Hong Kong from the UK to China for 1997. For many who had fled China during the Civil War, especially entrepreneurs and businesspeople who were now deeply embedded in the capitalist state of Hong Kong, a return to a communist state was unthinkable (Skeldon 1990: 501). Likewise, the Tiananmen Square protests and massacre in 1989 led many Hong Kong nationals to consider migrating before the handover date (Siu-lun 1992; Skeldon 1990). In 1990, approximately 62,000 Hong Kong citizens emigrated – excluding those who left on student visas and those who migrated to mainland China or Taiwan – which constituted roughly 1 per cent of the population (Skeldon 1994: 30). Many went to the UK under the British National (Overseas) scheme, but the most popular destinations were Canada, Australia, and the US. Its relatively secure political situation, coupled with its reputable English-language education system, also made New Zealand an attractive destination (Ho et al. 2001: 26). Most immigrants from Hong Kong were approved under the business investment programme (Ho & Farmer 1994), and between 1992 and 1995, Hong Kong had the highest proportion of business investor approvals of any country, peaking at 54.7 per cent of total business investor approvals between April 1993 and March 1994 (Farmer 1996b: 6).

In the first half of the 1990s, geopolitical circumstances also increased migration from Taiwan to New Zealand, which rose from 9 per cent in 1992 to 25 per cent by 1996 (Farmer 1996b: 5). Like New Zealand, Taiwan went through a major neoliberal restructuring by transitioning towards a market-led economy in the 1980s, backed up by widescale privatisation (Clark & Clark 2016; Tsai 2001). The influx of international money and immigrants into Taiwan led many highly skilled and capital-holding Taiwanese to search for opportunities outside of the country, with New Zealand seen by some as the 'last utopia' (Ip 2003b). Likewise, the end of the apartheid era in South Africa, when the African National Congress won a landslide victory at the 1994 General Election under the leadership of Nelson Mandela, led to 400,000 White South Africans emigrating (Meares 2007: 11). In March 1993, South African migrants made up only 2 per cent of residence approvals granted in New Zealand over the previous twelve months, but by March 1994, that number had jumped to 11.8 per cent (Farmer 1996b: 5). The examples of Hong Kong, Taiwan, and South Africa illustrate that the introduction of a points system in migration policy made migration flows to New Zealand much more sensitive to economic and political shifts elsewhere. The previous ethnicity-based migration policies, especially before 1986, had only enabled migrants outside the traditional source countries to arrive on humanitarian permits (which were minimal) or short-term permits (to fill labour shortages). The new points systems made it possible for migrants from any part of the world to migrate to New Zealand, particularly if they were highly skilled and wealthy. This made New Zealand especially attractive to middle-class people caught up in geopolitical transformations who suddenly found that political, social, and economic circumstances in their home countries were to their detriment.

By the early-to-mid-1990s, the National Government was actively courting trading partnerships in Asia, seeing people-to-people links generated through migration as critical to enhancing trade and investment relationships and giving New Zealand firms access to global markets. Maxwell, in many respects, embodied the articulation of these links between immigration, economics, and diplomacy. He described travelling internationally on several occasions during his time in Parliament (1984–99), including being only the second New Zealand cabinet minister to go to China in 1992, to build relationships that subsequently influenced his own view of the significance of migration:

> Getting back to immigration, if there was ever any doubt I had about linking up with Chinese and China, there was no doubt that there was huge potential to develop this relationship and that we were a favoured treatment because of Rewi Alley and going back and the other things that had happened sequentially along the way. I suppose the issue was how do you actually control that in a positive way without saying 'well, we don't want you here but we want everything else you can offer'. So, it was a two-way street.

Maxwell's account points to the way that, by the mid-1990s, a deep commitment to the economic benefits of immigration was fully cemented: the government was now moving on to consider how immigration could be linked into broader geopolitical developments and their socio-cultural implications. Doing so entailed an orientation towards globalisation as integral to the political rationality of the 1990s (Larner 1998) alongside the development in public discourse of a moral argument for greater cultural diversity (Laffey 1999). Asia loomed large in New Zealand's globalisation agenda in the 1990s, with Prime Minister Bolger asserting in 1994 that New Zealand's future was unequivocally with Asia: 'Asia is defining the new reality in which we have to live and compete and earn our living. In the next period of world history there will be no prosperity for New Zealand that does not have an Asian dimension in it' (Barber 1994). As we noted in the previous chapter, and Maxwell alluded to in the above quote, these connections with Asia as part of New Zealand's future were hardly new in the 1990s. Indeed, ever since the formal recognition of China in 1972, New Zealand governments have tentatively engaged with the idea of relationships in Asia and seen them as having importance for geoeconomic and geopolitical reasons, particularly in the aftermath of the UK's increased integration into Europe. What distinguished the approach of the National Government of the 1990s, however, was the explicit and consistent naming of Asian partners and New Zealand's positioning in the Asia-Pacific region. Key shifts during this era included labour-market deregulation, the promotion of foreign investment, supporting the establishment of APEC, and launching the Asia 2000 Foundation to build awareness of Asia. These changes articulated with a realignment of New Zealand as a competitive small economy positioned in the Pacific Rim (Larner 1998) – and immigration policy was a key platform for this realignment. Now that immigration policy had become oriented towards human and financial capital through the Immigration Amendment Act, it could serve as a pathway to realising globalisation in New Zealand.

Globalisation Challenged: Racism and Anti-immigrationism

Realising globalisation also entailed another task for government that focused on the political work of making moral arguments for the value and importance of cultural diversity. While the Immigration Act 1987 had articulated a multicultural openness and could itself be seen as an earlier stage of the reorientation towards Asia, it did not necessarily reflect a widespread view among the public that the ethnic makeup of New Zealand should be reconfigured (Parr 2000). Maxwell played a significant role in making the case for diversity during his tenure as Minister of Immigration, arguing to the public in 1993 that new immigration policies were both righteous and beneficial (quoted in Beaglehole 2009: 113):

> Our new immigration and refugee policies are leading to a greater diversity in the ethnic groups which are settling in New Zealand ... Unlike some of our past immigration policies, national origin is no longer a consideration ... This change in direction reflects a new public opinion that discrimination related to accident of birth is no longer acceptable and an acknowledgement that diversity can enrich rather than weaken New Zealand society ... Over the years ethnic communities have made immeasurable contributions to economic, social, professional and cultural life in New Zealand. The diversity they have brought to our society has served to enrich and strengthen our country.

In his interview for this book, Maxwell recalled making many speeches advocating for a positive view of immigration and its diversity benefits, 'that with the people comes the cultural link, the trade link, all that sort of thing flows'. The claims responded to political debates and media discourse in the late 1980s and early 1990s, which often focused on fears about the number of Pacific and Asian people who might come to New Zealand, and criticised – with racist undertones – the unscrupulousness of migrants, immigration agents, and overseas investors. Maxwell's speeches sought to counter this growing racist anti-immigrationism that was highlighting challenges within the immigration regime in the 1990s.

There were also structural impediments to the inclusion of new migrants. The auto-pass policy for residence approval, for example, did not consider that international qualifications often did not meet the standards of New Zealand professional organisations. Highly skilled migrants thus arrived in New Zealand with an expectation that their qualification would make it easy to find work – but they had access to very few employment opportunities in their respective areas (Bedford 2005a: 141; Spoonley & Bedford 2012: 87–88; Fry & Wilson 2018: 61). Many Taiwanese immigrants, for instance, found the 'last utopia' of New Zealand to be anything but utopian, with high levels of unemployment and discrimination in workplaces (Boyer 1996; Ip 2003b). Likewise, anti-immigrant politics attached itself to the phenomenon of the 'astronaut' family, where migrant families lived in New Zealand, while one of the parents, usually the father, worked and spent most of their time in the source country (Ho et al. 1997; Ho 2002; Ip 2000; Bedford 2005a: 142–43). Other racist responses latched on to the wealth of immigrants from Asia, assertions about driving capability, and impacts on schooling.

A particularly notorious example was a two-article series published in Auckland community newspapers under the headline 'Inv-Asian' (Spoonley & Trlin 2004). Authored by Pat Booth and Yvonne Martin (*Eastern Courier*, 16 April 1993), the articles sensationalised migration in a racialised way that emphasised problems:

> Whichever way you look at it, New Zealand has had/has got/will have problems over Asian migration. . . . What lies beneath the image of crowds of Asian children coming out of the best schools, the buy-up of expensive homes, slow, erratic drivers in big Mercedes and migration figures which suggest Auckland is becoming the Taipei/ Hong Kong/Seoul of the South Pacific.

In many ways, the articles, which were subject to a complaint to the Press Council, characterised the tone of public debate on immigration for much of the next decade (Spoonley & Trlin 2004). Alongside other immigration reporting in the 1990s, they provided legitimacy for racism towards migrants and created space and energy for anti-immigrationism in the political sphere, most notably expressed in the rise of the New Zealand First party. Winston Peters, former National Party MP and the leader of New Zealand First, focused on harnessing anti-Asian sentiment in New Zealand, some of which echoed vehement anti-Chinese rhetoric from the late nineteenth and early twentieth centuries (McKinnon 1996; Bedford et al. 2002a; Simon-Kumar 2015).

By the middle of the decade, there was considerable public and political pressure to decrease Asian immigration (Ip & Friesen 2001: 215; Bedford 2005a: 141; Spoonley & Bedford 2012: 88; Simon-Kumar 2015: 1176). This resulted in changes to the points system in 1995. The original 1991 points system imposed relatively low English-language capability thresholds, which the 1995 amendments made much stricter. These requirements were applied not only to the principal applicant, but to accompanying family members over the age of sixteen (Farmer 1996b; Winkelmann 1999: 12; Trlin 1997; Ip & Friesen 2001). In a move reminiscent of the anti-Chinese poll taxes of the early twentieth century, the changes imposed a $20,000 bond on those who failed an English-language test. The bond would be fully refunded if they resat and passed within three months, partially refunded if passed within twelve months, and forfeited altogether if language requirements were not met within twelve months (Farmer 1996b: 11; Ip & Friesen 2001: 215). This bond was replaced in 1998 with pre-paid language training (Gilbertson & Meares 2013). The 1995 amendments also removed points for overseas qualifications that were not recognised by New Zealand professional bodies (Winkelmann 1999: 12; Ip & Friesen 2001: 215). After these changes, migration from Asia declined significantly for the rest of the decade, particularly after the Asian financial crisis in 1997 (Ip & Friesen 2001: 217–18; Liu 2017).

The tightening of measures in the 1995 amendments suggests a slight shift in focus in the philosophy of migration policy away from merely attracting highly qualified migrants, irrespective of source country, towards a greater emphasis on the management of migration (Farmer 1996b: 10). These changes also represent a reassertion of Anglo-cultural competence as a criteron of entry that had significant echoes of the imperial migration regime techniques for assuring immigration in the nineteenth and twentieth centuries was White and British (see Chapter 1). The points system had introduced a target for migration, but the auto-pass policy had led to the surpassing of that target year on year. The 1995 changes effectively implemented a limit on migration numbers, which would be decided annually by the government. The limits were managed by weekly changes to the required pass mark on the points system, overseen by the Immigration Service in line with their 'Operational Manual' composed in 1995 (Farmer 1996b: 11).

The shift towards stricter management and monitoring of migration from the mid-1990s is, at least in part, constitutive of the febrile political atmosphere that existed around immigration in the lead-up to the 1996 General Election. The New Zealand First party had been established in 1993, under the leadership of former National MP Winston Peters, who had left the National Party and Parliament acrimoniously that year. Initially, New Zealand First policy was relatively unclear, but focused on resistance to free-market ideas and nostalgia for the state-controlled economy of the Muldoon era (Hayward & Shaw 2016: 221). However, like many populist parties, New Zealand First only began to gather a major political following when it staked out an anti-immigrant position that was well to the right of any other party (Cooke 2018). Peters wanted to reduce immigration levels from a peak of 55,000 in 1995 down to just 10,000, and to restrict foreign ownership in New Zealand (Liu & Mills 2006: 88). The 1996 census had shown that migrants from Northeast Asia had the highest levels of unemployment, which helped ground Peters' argument that such migration was a drain on the country's resources (Bedford et al. 2005: 3). Ahead of the 1996 election, Peters made an inflammatory speech in Auckland in February, which targeted Asian immigrants, including stories of Vietnamese refugees stealing gold from jewellery shops, melting it down, and sending it back to Vietnam. In an extensive media analysis of Peters' speech, Liu and Mills (2006: 87) note that in January, New Zealand First was polling at 5 per cent, but after this speech, reached 30 per cent in April, eventually securing 13.35 per cent of the vote in the 1996 election. Furthermore, after this speech, media coverage of Peters increased fourfold, leading Liu and Mills (2006: 89) to conclude that they 'rose to prominence on the wings of racism and anti-Asian sentiment'. In the wake of this speech, Prime Minister Bolger had labelled Peters a 'despicable racist' (Liu & Mills 2006: 92). However, by November that year – after New Zealand First had won seventeen seats in the general election – Bolger was forming a coalition government with New Zealand First, in which Peters held the key positions of Deputy Prime Minister and Treasurer.

Maxwell and the National Government's attempts to construct a discourse of cosmopolitanism in response to such anti-immigrationism had both offshore and onshore audiences. On the one hand, there was a need to convince potential immigrants and investors, as well as Asian trading partners, that New Zealand was not a racist place, nor one still dominated by narratives of a White, European national identity (Laffey 1999). Maxwell's Asian travel, and his consistent messaging about the cultural and economic value of immigration, may well have achieved success in external messaging. Advancing a cosmopolitan view of immigration was also about promoting a more global outlook in New Zealand firms and communities, which had been very insular for much of the mid-twentieth century. As one scholar of the period puts it, the cosmopolitan rhetoric of this period aimed to 'explicitly renarrate New Zealand as multicultural and part of Asia, and thereby produce new subjects who will look to and actively engage with East Asia' (Laffey 1999: 235). Maxwell claimed in his interview that 'the whole thing was successful'. But some studies question whether a 'new public opinion' really developed, emphasising the persistence of entrenched anti-immigrant sentiments in New Zealand society (Simon-Kumar 2015: 1176). As Bedford et al. (2002a: 73) put it a decade later: 'Globalisation of flows is clearly not a good indicator of globalisation of minds!' Indeed, the growing popularity of Winston Peters' anti-immigrant New Zealand First party suggests that not all New Zealanders have been convinced by arguments about the benefits of multiculturalism.

Immigration without Indigeneity

During this period, an increasing number of Māori commentators were growing uncomfortable with the trajectory of New Zealand immigration policy. The 1991 Immigration Amendment Act reinforced New Zealand's commitment to neoliberal economic principles, with a migration policy that pursued economic globalisation and multiculturalism. But this process coincided with the peak of what was referred to as a period of 'Māori renaissance'. This involved cultural revitalisation and increased Māori assertiveness in all areas of national life, including through the promotion of *biculturalism*, based on the Treaty of Waitangi, as a framework for all areas of governance in New Zealand. It had begun much earlier, and must in some ways be seen only as the strengthening of a multigenerational struggle that began with colonisation. And it took large steps forward during the Third Labour Government under Norman Kirk. But it was during the 1980s and 1990s that these efforts bore fruit in a cascade of changes in awareness of, and attitudes towards, te ao Māori – the Māori world. As part of this wider movement, strong views were beginning to emerge around the rapid changes to New Zealand's immigration system.

At the time, Ranginui Walker (1994: 87) noted that the turn towards non-traditional source countries in the new immigration policy from the mid-1980s required consultation with Māori under the conditions of Te Tiriti o Waitangi, a claim that was backed up by the Human Rights Commission at the time (New Zealand Productivity Commission 2021). Walker (1994) made the point that, when the points system was in development, Birch consulted a limited number of Auckland and Wellington Māori leaders, who roundly criticised the proposals. But, in Parliament, Birch stated that the Māori leaders were 'broadly positive' about the introduction of the points system (Walker 1994: 87). The Population Monitoring Group (1991) led by Richard Bedford pointed out that the multiplicity and diversity of Māori voices on immigration policy had been ignored in policy debate and development. A claim was made to the Waitangi Tribunal in 1991 by the Auckland District Māori Council, which stated that the proposed points system conflicted with Te Tiriti o Waitangi, and that Māori had been inadequately consulted on policy changes (New Zealand Productivity Commission 2021: 5). While this claim did not make it to a hearing, the Crown rejected 'as a general principle that it has a formal duty to consult with the Māori people in matters where their rights under the Treaty of Waitangi are, or may be, involved' (Stevenson 1992: 6).

The Population Monitoring Group and the New Zealand Planning Council also identified that 'fundamental issues' remained in New Zealand's immigration policy and that the 'most important of these [was] the extent to which Māori concerns over acknowledgement of obligations under the Treaty of Waitangi [were] being met by those responsible for designing immigration policy' (Population Monitoring Group 1991: 53). Such an assertion does not suggest that there is a singular view on immigration among Māori, either then or since. Indeed, the report highlights contemporary public statements by Māori leaders and organisations, some of which advocated immigration in support of Māori social, economic, and political aspirations, and others of which raised concerns about the labour-market and economic impacts of increased immigration on Māori. As the report notes, drawing on the conclusions of a Royal Commission on Social Policy that had reported in 1988, 'the Treaty of Waitangi provide[s] the foundation for all aspects of policy concerning relationships between the tangata whenua and the tauiwi (later settlers)', including 'immigration policy – policy which has a direct impact on the size and composition of the tauiwi component and the balance between tangata whenua and tauiwi within New Zealand' (Population Monitoring Group 1991: 53, 55).

In interviews carried out for this book, Birch made no reference to Māori at all in his discussion of policy development or implementation in the early 1990s. In a speech before becoming Minister of Immigration, however, Birch did make it clear that he envisaged twenty-first-century New Zealand becoming a 'multi-cultural society' rather than merely a bicultural one:

As New Zealand moves towards a bi-cultural society, I am constantly reminded by my Pacific Island constituents that New Zealand should not stop there but embrace multiculturalism – ethnic pluralism if you like – as a positive boon to our society. The reality is that it must be faced. As we enter the 21st Century New Zealand will be a multi-cultural society. So the problem is not ethnicity. It is skills, the calibre of our immigrants, that should drive immigration policy. (Birch 1989: 13)

As has been noted by others (Spoonley & Bedford 2012), Birch was touching on an inherent tension between biculturalism and multiculturalism that was attracting a growing number of increasingly politically active Māori. Many of the socio-economic and political gains made by Māori, throughout their encounters with colonisation, had rested on assertions of an essential status of Indigenous people. In postcolonial scholarship, similar political activity has been described as 'strategic essentialism', 'a strategic use of positivist essentialism in a scrupulously visible political interest' (Spivak 1985: 214) – expressing a shared identity in the public sphere through temporary and tactical unity in order to struggle for equality. As New Zealand sociologist Avril Bell has argued, however, strategic essentialism only partially accounts for Māori claims to Indigenous identity because the identity aims of Māori political movements have not been temporary but rather entail a 'desire to maintain their different and autonomous existence' (Bell 2014: 121). By the late twentieth century, Māori had pursued almost two centuries of political mobilisation based on a colonial difference between 'Indigenous' and 'non-Indigenous' people, which had been deeply reinforced by The Treaty's framing as a partnership between Māori and the British Crown. In the nineteenth century, rangatira had strategically promoted essentialist notions of Māoritanga (Māori-ness) in their efforts to overcome intertribal conflict and oppose British domination, but also 'as a means of finding strength in numbers in a struggle for the survival of cultural frameworks' (Pihama 1993: 35, cited in Bell 2014).

It is perhaps unsurprising, therefore, that some Māori might have resented the implication that they were 'simply one of many immigrant groups' (Beaglehole 2009: 114). For example, the 1986 Review stated that 'Maori peoples established themselves as the tangata whenua after historic voyages of migration from countries in the Pacific' (Burke 1986: 8). The National Government's foreign minister, Don McKinnon (1990–99), put this even more bluntly, when reflecting on the new multicultural immigration policy, saying that 'an implicit contradiction between "immigrant" and "indigenous" is solved by a timeline' (quoted in Beaglehole 2009: 114). If Māori were seen as just one of many minorities in a multicultural society, there was a danger that the difference of Māori indigeneity would be reduced or even erased in the idea of the nation, especially in a context where the political realm was also opened up to identity assertions of new ethnically organised communities. The risk, as articulated by Ranginui Walker (1994), would be that the Pākehā government could potentially play divide and rule.

Despite the growing tensions between biculturalism and multi-culturalism, governments aimed to keep the two issues separate. Te Tiriti o Waitangi was deemed irrelevant to the process of immigration policy design and decision-making, and immigration was either asserted by politicians as a benefit to Māori (Population Monitoring Group 1991) or framed as outside of their concerns and sphere of life in New Zealand. Maxwell, for example, suggested that there had been no 'specific instance of where a group or representative Māori group were unhappy about migration'. While the historical record clearly shows that several prominent Māori, not least Ranginui Walker (1994), and groups, such as the Anglican Māori Church, exercised strong views on immigration policy changes, for Ministers of Immigration, at this time, these were considered separate issues. Roger Maxwell stated:

> In the end, most of the migration was happening in the bigger cities and so I suppose the silo-ing of migrants was limiting the impact they'd have in a particular area. I can't recall any instance where [Māori] people were saying, we're being displaced by migrants, people coming into our land. I didn't have that. And in terms of the policy that was being used, no great example of that and influence that I can recall.

Maxwell's reflection that Māori did not necessarily have a view on immigration policy echoes those statements made by Kerry Burke and Stan Rodger that were covered in the previous chapter. He also expresses a slightly different view here, one that focuses on the position of Māori in rural spaces and is thus principally concerned about displacement from land and the primary direction of immigration flows into cities, especially Auckland. Of course, by this stage, Māori movement to the cities had been underway for some time, and major centres including Auckland were already home to large populations of Māori. Even on these terms, however, the opening of New Zealand to a more diverse range of migrants, especially investors, in this period was coupled with the increasing enclosure of Māori land under the 1981 Public Works Act (Kukutai & Rata 2017). Alongside these enclosures, the pressures placed on the housing market by immigration, and over subsequent decades the exploitation of migrant labour, have disproportionately affected Māori, with rising unemployment and homelessness levels in the Māori community (Kukutai & Rata 2017). The emphasis of the day, however, was on the achievement of a multicultural society, which was framed as an extension beyond a bicultural one. In this imagined multicultural future, Māori did not hold any special place in the making of immigration policy.

Conclusion

The first half of the 1990s marks an important juncture in the evolution of a New Zealand migration policy that had begun in the early 1980s with the shift away from an ethnicity-based migration system towards a human capital–oriented approach. The National Party might have campaigned in the 1990 General Election against the Fourth Labour Government's neoliberal revolution, but once in office, it was clear that the neoliberal approach to policymaking became more deeply embedded within the state infrastructure, encapsulated in the 'Ruthanasia' years at the beginning of the decade. Moreover, in relation to immigration policy, both political debate and policy development speak to continuity rather than rupture. The introduction of the immigration points system in 1991 built on the work undertaken by Roger Douglas, which pointed towards a new way of managing migration according to free-market economic principles, where migrants were selected based on their economistic characteristics. The auto-pass system and the loosening of language and qualification requirements also suggested that the discriminatory aspects of migration policy that had remained in the neoliberal revolution were lessening, albeit only for those people who could demonstrate they qualified as valuable migrants because of their skills.

This period also saw the rise of public dissatisfaction with high levels of immigration and racism towards Asian immigrants, with that dissatisfaction given a voice through the establishment of the New Zealand First party. The 1995 amendments to the points system serve as a helpful reminder that while a purportedly post-racial neoliberal orthodoxy had become increasingly bureaucratised in this period, politics and questions of nation and identity still had a say in the direction of future migration policy. As language requirements became stricter and overseas qualifications less recognised by New Zealand professional bodies, migration numbers, especially from Asia, declined in the second half of the decade.

By the mid-1990s, a new managerial logic had come to shape migration policy, with the auto-pass policy eliminated and the Immigration Service more closely monitoring the points system and enforcing limits on annual migration numbers to manage both outcomes of immigration and potential political fallout. While this more targeted approach to immigration foreclosed some of the promise of openness in the economic multiculturalism of the 1980s, it served to lay the groundwork for the continued roll-out of neoliberal governmental technologies to manage migration. Indeed, as we discuss in the next chapter, once established as an orthodoxy, a targeted approach to immigration demanded a constant process of innovation in technologies to underpin the selection, surveillance, and management of immigration flows, migrant lives, and the impact of migrants in society.

CHAPTER 4

Managing Migration, 1997–2004

As the twentieth century drew to a close, New Zealand's migration policies had undergone a radical transformation from the ethnicity-based principles of the imperial migration regime to a human capital and market-based approach to migration. A key result of this shift, as we have noted in the previous chapter, was a substantial increase in the volume and diversification of the nationality of people immigrating to New Zealand, with a particularly marked growth in arrivals and settlement of people from countries in Asia. In the first two terms of the Fourth National Government (1990–96), migration policy had focused on two matters: firstly, establishing the points system for human capital selection of potential immigrants; and secondly, rationalising this publicly in New Zealand and internationally through a concerted globalisation agenda. While the New Zealand Government appeared to be wholeheartedly committed to maintaining high levels of immigration, there were also headwinds, not least the re-racialisation and politicisation of immigration issues in the media, particularly by Winston Peters, who led the rise of the populist-nationalist New Zealand First party in the mid-1990s.

The consequence of migration policy changes and the public and political reactions to heightened volumes of immigration was that immigration came to represent a problem for governments by the mid-1990s. On the one hand, there was a growing desire to optimise the benefits of immigration via identifying, testing, and implementing new techniques of selection and settlement. On the other hand, immigration ministers, especially Roger Maxwell, and the National Government more generally, were increasingly compelled to address recurrent anti-immigration political rhetoric and public opinion. From the mid-1990s until the mid-2000s (the period covered by this chapter), migration policy started to become focused on the type of migration into New Zealand, the outcomes of migration, and the best ways to manage the arrival and conditions of migrants. As we discuss in this chapter, settlement became a particularly important focus for ministers as stories of immigrants experiencing deskilling and underemployment surfaced and gained currency in political critiques of the immigration system. The central regulatory response to the perceived problem of uneven settlement was to alter selection criteria, by considering the number of residence permits granted as well as adding additional obstacles such as English-language tests and penalties for those who did not pass them. In the latter part of this period, especially under the tenure of Lianne Dalziel (1999–2004), migration policy was also reconfigured around the timing and geography of selection, with a shift from approving residence permits for offshore applicants towards a focus on granting temporary visas in the first instance and residence permits only to those temporary migrants who had already demonstrated the ability to settle successfully once onshore.

This tailoring of migration policy indicates an emerging public-sector interest in 'management science'. Across the 1990s, the shift towards neoliberal modes of governing and globalisation led to the introduction of management discourse into state practice. The so-called 'new public management' approach placed an emphasis on the use of business-management practices in government and a 'reliance on individual rationalities and market mechanisms in the restructuring and operation of the public sector' (Salskov-Iversen et al. 2000: 183–84). The effect would be to transform how state bureaucracies and decision-makers used data and knowledge in the development of policies (Knafo 2020). In contrast to early periods of 'roll-back neoliberalism', which entailed radical deregulation and cuts in state spending, the late 1990s and early 2000s saw an emphasis on the application of management theory to public-sector practice, giving ostensibly 'evidence-based' policies the imprimatur of scientific rigour, and turning the new economic approach – which had only recently been seen as revolutionary – into unquestionable common sense (Peck & Tickell 2002).

In the sphere of migration, similar trends were at play by the late 1990s, with international organisations promoting the idea of 'migration management' (Ghosh 2000), which would become orthodoxy among international and national migration policymakers around the world in the first two decades of the twenty-first century. In its boldest forms, migration management invoked imaginaries 'in which all forms of international mobility would be comprehensively managed in a coherent and efficient way on the basis of (primarily) economic criteria' (Georgi 2010: 56). More pragmatically, the focus on managing migration emerged in specific state discourses and practices, a more concerted focus on projecting and planning migration and population futures, targeted selection criteria, monitoring of outcomes, and increased 'responsibilisation' of migrants. These shifts were evident in the US, for example, in efforts to 'improve management of the immigration system' (Commission on Immigration Reform 1997) and a shift towards skills-based immigrant selection (Chishti & Yale-Loehr 2016). In Western Europe, immigration was becoming politicised around the free movement of EU workers (Boswell 2003: 621) and the number of people seeking asylum from former Eastern-bloc countries (Garson 2004). And, Australia had undertaken the Roach review of migration policy in 1995, which had recommended a more 'flexible immigration system' that allowed for attracting skills needed for a shift towards the new knowledge economy (Gamlen & Sherrell 2022). These and similar developments in several other countries speak to the growing interest in managing migration in more intricate ways in pursuit of more orderly and productive flows of people.

In this chapter we trace the emergence of this new managerialism in New Zealand's migration policy from 1996 to 2004, encompassing the final term of the Fourth National Government and most of the first two terms of the Fifth Labour Government (specifically 1999–2004). Covering the tenures of Max Bradford, Tuariki Delamere, and Lianne Dalziel, the chapter discusses the political turmoil of the coalition governments of the late 1990s, explores how migration policy was being rethought alongside efforts to project and plan for population futures, and examines the development of specific efforts to adapt and optimise migration systems and outcomes. While emergent across this period, managerialism became especially apparent during Lianne Dalziel's tenure as Minister of Immigration, which in many ways has laid the foundation for immigration policy over the subsequent two decades covered by this book. While major changes to immigration regulations were implemented in this period, there were no fundamental legislative changes comparable to the 1987 Immigration Act (which removed 'traditional source country preferences') or the 1991 Immigration Amendment Act (which introduced the points system for migrant selection). Rather, the period 1996–2004 is one of incremental but influential regulatory change, especially during the tenure of Dalziel, which Bedford (2004) described as 'a quiet revolution'.

Political Change and Turmoil

Immigration policy developments in the late 1990s took place in a context of significant political change and turmoil. In the 1996 General Election, New Zealand adopted a Mixed-Member Proportional (MMP) electoral system, following the outcome of a referendum on this issue at the 1993 General Election (Levine & Roberts 1994).[11] MMP in New Zealand resembles Germany's post-war electoral system, allocating legislature seats according to a formula that balances the results of two simultaneous national polls: one for the voter's local 'electorate' candidate (the electorate vote), and one for the voter's choice of political party (the party vote). Under the previous electoral system (First Past the Post), elections were reliably won by one of two major parties and minor political parties were under-represented if not completely shut out of Parliament. The introduction of MMP changed this by granting minor parties a number of legislature seats in proportion to their share of the party vote, so long as they won at least one electorate or gained at least 5 per cent of the party vote. MMP brought substantial political changes to New Zealand by facilitating the entry and growth of new political parties in Parliament, establishing coalition governments as the normal outcome of elections, and over time has facilitated greater ethnic, gender, and political representation in Parliament (McMillan 2020).

The 1996 General Election under the new MMP system led to the formation of a coalition government between the incumbent National Party and the New Zealand First party (the latter led by the prominent anti-immigrationist politician Winston Peters, as discussed in previous chapters). A focus on immigration and foreign ownership formed a substantial platform for New Zealand First, propelling them from around 8 per cent of the vote in the 1993 election to over 30 per cent in some polls in 1996, making them potentially the second-largest party ahead of the Labour Party and the leftist Alliance party (Vowles 1997). Peters leveraged the anti-Asian racism described in the previous chapter to his electoral advantage, amplifying an 'Asian invasion' rhetoric that had emerged in media commentary and making substantial policy promises around numerical limits on immigration and restrictions on overseas investment (Bedford et al. 2003; Boston et al. 1997). In a 'state of the nation' speech to party faithful that subsequently gained widespread media attention (Munshi 1998), Peters asserted a need for a radical reduction in migration (Pullman 1996):

11   This process of shifting electoral systems had been underway for some time (see Boston et al. 1997 for further detail). The Fourth Labour Government had initiated a Royal Commission on the Electoral System in 1985, which in its 1986 report evaluated a range of systems and recommended a mixed system with considerable similarities to the German model. A referendum was held in September 1992 to indicate appetite for system change and to select between four different electoral systems (MMP, preferential voting, supplementary member, and single-transferable voting). In the 1992 referendum, 84.7 per cent of voters indicated a preference for change and, among the options provided, MMP was selected by a majority of 70.5 per cent of voters. The 1993 referendum that led to electoral system change was much more tightly contested following an intense period of campaigning; 53.9 per cent of voters selected MMP over the existing FPP system (46.1 per cent).

It is time to call a halt to the madness. It is New Zealanders, not foreigners or intending immigrants, who must have first and full attention from the government we elect. . . . Given the problems facing us right now, particularly the ongoing and unrecognised crisis of unemployment, we say the time has come to cut immigration to the bone. We will cut it back to a criteria where we will have people we need coming to this country, not people who need this country. . . . Whose country is it? A country fit for the families of ordinary New Zealanders whose votes have placed the politicians in power, or a paradise for foreign takeover merchants posing as investors and other big money merchants looking for cheap gains at our expense?

While it was only Peters and New Zealand First that articulated such a stridently xenophobic campaign platform, immigration did become a much more significant component of the policy proposals of parties across Parliament in the 1996 election (Farmer 1996b). Seeking to unseat the incumbent centre-right National Party, the Labour Party proposed a detailed list of changes, including slashing General Skills visa grants from 35,000 to 15,000, and increasing settlement support through English-language training and funding for schools (instead of merely imposing a $20,000 bond on migrants who did not meet English-language requirements). The left-wing Alliance party committed to ending the business migration scheme and planning migration in relation to capacity. Meanwhile, the far-right, libertarian ACT party (founded by neoliberal architect and former Minister of Immigration Roger Douglas) sought to generate revenue from the business scheme by tendering places to the highest bidders.

The election-night results provided for a much more politically diverse Parliament than had previously been possible. The incumbent National Party secured forty-four seats followed by Labour (thirty-seven), New Zealand First (seventeen), Alliance (thirteen), ACT (eight) and United New Zealand (one). In addition to success in the party vote, New Zealand First also swept all five of the Māori electorate seats that had previously been held by the Labour Party – those elected included future Minister of Immigration Tuariki Delamere. After a relatively long (by New Zealand standards) period of negotiation, a government was formed by the National Party and New Zealand First, confirmed by Winston Peters on 10 December 1996 (nearly two months after election night). The reason for the drawn-out negotiation was straightforward: it was clear to everyone that Peters held the balance of votes, and that whomever he chose as coalition partner would form the next government. Peters used this high-leverage moment as 'kingmaker' to meet frequently with the leadership of both main parties, coaxing them to outbid each other. As a result, the final coalition agreement relied on extensive compromises by National, including the allocation of five cabinet positions to New Zealand First, the Deputy Prime Ministership to Winston Peters, and his appointment as Treasurer (with Tuariki Delamere appointed Associate Treasurer), a new senior economic position that relegated Bill Birch to a subordinate Minister of Finance role. New Zealand First also gained significant policy concessions that reversed some of National's key earlier health reforms, abolished the superannuation surcharge, increased spending in health and education, deferred tax cuts, prohibited the sale of large state assets, and strengthened the 'national interest' requirement for foreign investment. Additionally, New Zealand First secured the removal of financial limits on Treaty of Waitangi settlements (Boston et al. 1997; Vowles 1998).

Despite the strong anti-immigration emphasis in the election campaign, during the coalition negotiations, New Zealand First sought and achieved relatively few concessions related to immigration. Indeed, immigration occupied merely half a page of the seventy-three-page coalition agreement, which asserted that current immigration flows would be maintained, while offering unspecified initiatives about a 'four-year probationary period', limitations on amnesties, health screening, a 'clamp down on refugee scams', and increased resources to policing immigration policies. In contrast to their anti-Asian electioneering, New Zealand First agreed that New Zealand should 'strengthen our commitment to the Asia/Pacific region as our priority area in foreign relations'. The coalition agreement also committed to holding a Population Conference in 1997, as discussed in greater detail below (Coalition Agreement 1996).

New Zealand First's approach to immigration – at least since the 1996 coalition negotiations – has arguably been more focused on rhetorically mobilising the anti-immigrant vote than on seeking substantive changes to immigration policy. This textbook tactic became widespread across liberal democracies during the period of intensive globalisation from the 1980s to the 2000s (Castles 2004; Gamlen 2013b; Hollifield 2004; Joppke 2003). Political parties like New Zealand First often achieve their best electoral outcomes by deliberately failing in their migration policies. They talk tough to placate anti-immigration groups, but abandon their plans or pursue unworkable migration restrictions once in power, so as to please pro-immigration groups.

In this respect it is illustrative that, despite its campaign focus on immigration, New Zealand First did not demand the immigration portfolio. Instead, Peters and colleagues focused on accumulating the more powerful and central ministerial portfolios in charge of the economy. Immigration was, however, allocated to Max Bradford, who had been a key player in the coalition negotiations and who, by his own account, had gained the trust of New Zealand First. As he told us in his interview for this book, New Zealand First's relative lack of interest in immigration policy once elected to office became an established pattern over their involvement in this and subsequent governments:

> Their attitude towards immigration has pretty much characterised them all the way through their participation in governments. Winston Peters used to talk a lot about being anti-immigration but by the time he became a minister or the New Zealand First Party joined in government, they always toned down very substantially their anti-immigration stance. I suppose I was regarded by the Prime Minister, Jim Bolger, as a reasonably safe pair of hands on an issue like this, I never had much time for the New Zealand First approach to immigration. We just got on with the job. Wherever the rules were changed, it was to ensure that we got the people into the country that we needed.

Notwithstanding these comments, it is unlikely that Peters' and New Zealand First's commitment to reducing migration was merely symbolic. Although they tactically de-emphasised migration in the coalition agreement, the appointment of Bradford, whom the coalition negotiations had revealed to be an ally, proved instrumental. At the time, there were concerns that the new points system was enabling an uncontrolled surge in immigration, particularly from 'non-traditional' (i.e. non-White) source countries, due to 'the failure of an essentially unregulated auto-pass system' during 1994–95 (Bedford et al. 2005: 3). Seeing approvals shooting up, at the end of 1994, the government increased the number of points required for an 'automatic pass' – with no tangible impact on rising numbers, which substantially overshot the government's 'notional' annual target of 25,000 approvals (Bedford et al. 2005: 2–3). By October 1995, it was necessary to start 'monitoring and managing approvals on a weekly basis' to contain the blowout. Against this background, Peters had campaigned heavily on the imposition of a fixed target of 'ten thousand' resident visa grants – a demand that focused the debate, for the first time, on the idea of setting, monitoring, and meeting clear targets in line with broader government planning and policy (Bedford et al. 2005). Targets became a useful tool for channelling the emphasis on controlling immigration away from political debate towards a focus on target-setting that was followed through in the regulatory work of the immigration bureaucracy.

The National–New Zealand First Coalition Government initially marked a period of refinement rather than reworking of immigration policy, despite the anti-immigrant elements that joined the government. Bradford led incremental changes to immigration policy in the twenty-one months he was Minister of Immigration between December 1996 and the dissolution of the coalition in August 1998. The focus of this period, as we outline below, involved a sharpening emphasis on selection processes, what Bradford described in his interview as 'polishing the rules, ensuring that the right sort of people were made available to the New Zealand employment scene in terms of the skillsets that we had'. There was an increasing desire to manage immigration flows and outcomes in this period in a way that went beyond the less-regulated economic multiculturalism that had emerged since the early 1980s. One of the first steps in this direction involved conversations about the relationship of migration to population, which was specifically addressed in the 1997 Population Conference.

The 1997 Population Conference

As part of their coalition agreement with the National Party, New Zealand First had advanced the idea of a government-sponsored conference on immigration, although Max Bradford had managed to shift the conference focus towards the less incendiary concept of population change (Bedford & Ho 1998: 50–51). In many ways, the 1997 Population Conference at Te Papa Tongarewa (Museum of New Zealand) echoed the concerns of the Dominion Population Committee fifty years earlier, which Prime Minister Jim Bolger acknowledged in his opening address (Bolger 1997). The post-war Dominion Population Committee Report had attempted to retain the guiding principles of the imperial migration regime, but it had also gestured towards the emergence of a new approach in which migration would be driven by employer demand and the need for population growth as a macro-economic force. By the time the 1997 Population Conference took place, the new world prefigured by the Dominion Population Committee had become the new orthodoxy. The 1997 conference was an attempt to map what this new reality might mean for New Zealand's population futures.

Prime Minister Jim Bolger and his Deputy, Winston Peters, jointly announced the conference in late July 1997 and outlined its purpose and goals. Bolger acknowledged the profound changes to New Zealand society that had taken place since the mid-1980s and concluded that it was essential 'to become better acquainted with the changes that have occurred, the opportunities they bring, and to consider how our country will evolve demographically over the next decade and beyond' (Bolger & Peters 1997). Peters suggested that the conference offered 'an opportunity for New Zealand to explore the relationship between population change and immigration on economic activity and future demand for education, social services and business growth' (Bolger & Peters 1997). In his opening address, Bolger identified two key features of globalisation as central concerns for New Zealand society: economic integration, and cultural identity in an interconnected world. Fears about the loss of this cultural identity had become notable in New Zealand society by the mid-1990s, as evidenced by the prominence of immigration debates in the 1996 election campaign. While Bolger suggested it was important to retain such an identity, he also continued the National Party's emphasis on globalisation: 'we must be willing to embrace others who come to join us' (Bolger 1997).

The makeup of the conference delegates and speakers was varied, crossing governmental and non-governmental organisations, private and public sectors, and Māori and migrant interest groups (Bradford 1997). While there were concerns that the conference might be used as an occasion to announce new immigration policies, the emphasis was in fact much more on future migration policy and population concerns (Bedford & Ho 1998). In many ways, the conference discussion was about the difficulties of managing migration, not just the goals of the migration regime itself. Bedford and Ho (1998: 51) note, for instance, that the 'one session which dealt specifically with target-setting focused more on the problems of determining such targets, than the numbers per se'. While in Bradford's interview for this book he stated that the 'population conference never really led to anything in particular', many of the themes discussed made their way into migration policy over the coming decade. Future Minister of Immigration Tuariki Delamere, for example, put forward a proposal for New Zealand to follow the Australian three-stream model for migrants – skilled/business (60 per cent), family categories (30 per cent), and humanitarian (10 per cent) (Spoonley & Bedford 2012: 88) – which was subsequently implemented in 2001 by Lianne Dalziel.

Māori delegates also made notable contributions to the Population Conference, including Tipene O'Regan, Wira Gardiner, Whetu Wereta, Ranginui Walker, and Papaarangi Reid. O'Regan's talk placed a strong emphasis on the future and the importance of economic growth and development for Māori. He criticised arguments about restricting immigration – noting that even before the signing of Te Tiriti o Waitangi, Māori 'survived and thrived by reaching out to other cultures, for example trading with Australia in the early 19th century' (The Population Conference 1997). In a panel discussion that followed, O'Regan and the presenters (Gardiner, Wereta, Walker, and Reid) placed emphasis on inequities experienced by Māori and matters of economic development – not least in the context of recent Treaty of Waitangi settlements with Kāi Tahu (1995) and Waikato-Tainui (1996) – rather than the immediate matter of migration levels. Concerns about equity, tied up in the deficit language of 'closing the gaps' between Māori and non-Māori, were prominent at the time of the Population Conference, rather than migration. The urgency associated with this reflected anger and frustration towards the ongoing impacts of colonialism and persistent inequalities (Te Puni Kokiri 1998). The Māori unemployment rate had skyrocketed from 13.5 per cent in 1988 to 27.3 per cent in 1992 as Māori workers were disproportionately exposed to the neoliberal assault on the labour market (Poata-Smith 2013). Immigration's entanglement with agendas for national economic growth was not articulated as a central priority in these immediate and longer-term challenges.

Migration, however, was the key concern of the conference for Bradford and the National–New Zealand First Coalition Government. Bradford's closing remarks, which summarised the various keynotes and panels, raised questions about the extent to which governments could or should try to influence migration outcomes. In answering these questions, Bradford made the point that immigration policy had often orbited the seemingly more central economic and social policy arenas. He noted that 'for too long, immigration policy has been in a little cell on its own, without too much reference to other government policies or indeed to other things going on in the community, and we have to rectify that' (Bradford 1997). He pondered: 'it seems to me that one of the mistakes that we've made in policy in the past, is that we have fiddled with the target rate, the number of people who come under the controlled flow. We have fiddled with that in a way that has really been counter-productive' (Bradford 1997). Against this planned and active migration policy, he hypothesised a 'passive policy' in which the government set an annual number of migrants (Bradford 1997):

> Should we say one and a half per cent of the population is our immigration target each year, or should we try a rather more mishy-mashy approach, which is to make judgements about the people who we want in and leave either the bureaucracy or some appeal authority or the poor old Minister of Immigration to make those decisions. That's clearly an issue. We have to be alive to the fact of what it is we can control.

This proposed 'passive' system looked much like the auto-pass policy that operated in the immediate years after the introduction of the points system in 1991, where those who met the points threshold were automatically granted visas, irrespective of how their skills and qualifications related to labour needs or economic priorities. Bradford's perspective on immigration policy had substantial similarities to the impetus in the late 1980s and early 1990s; he described in his interview how he had been trained in economics with an emphasis on 'free-market development' that entailed 'letting the private sector run without the constraints that came out of war-time approach to running the economy'. Bradford had also worked in the Treasury in the 1970s before shifting to the International Monetary Fund and then representing the New Zealand Employers' Federation and becoming Chief Executive of the Bankers' Association in 1984. He was an avowed neoliberal politician, who had spent considerable parts of his career in the same institutional milieus as other revolutionary neoliberal change-makers of the 1980s. He not only saw little value in overt state planning and regulation but was committed politically to deregulation wherever possible.

In contrast to his neoliberal policy leanings and his musings at the conclusion of the Population Conference, Bradford's time in the role of Minister of Immigration was characterised by a continuation of the incremental introduction of changes to increase regulation to improve the selection and number of migrants. He acknowledged in his interview that the phenomenon of highly skilled migrants entering without job guarantees was a problem of the auto-pass system. He also continued the general emphasis of migration policy development of his predecessors – 'polishing the rules', as he put it, to make the right people available to New Zealand employers:

> But most of the time I spent was in polishing the rules around who could and could not come to New Zealand as immigrants. In that respect, I think I was probably pretty much the same as a lot of immigration ministers in the way in which the system needs to work. Polishing the rules, ensuring that the right sort of people were made available to the New Zealand employment scene in terms of the skillsets that we had.

This approach would seem to reflect the circumstances under which Bradford took on the role. In addition to the momentum generated by the changes Maxwell had implemented, and the latent concern about anti-immigration rhetoric following the election, shifts were also occurring internationally that were challenging the presumptions of the largely free-market approaches to migration policy that had emerged in New Zealand in the late 1980s and early 1990s and that Bradford seemingly preferred. The emphasis on 'migration management', first articulated as a principle by International Organization for Migration advisor Bimal Ghosh in 1995, asserted the desirability of a 'new international regime for orderly movements of people' (Ghosh 2000). Through its emphasis on 'regulated openness', the notion of migration management responded to the tensions that had emerged in neoliberal globalisation in the 1990s, which had embraced the liberalisation of trade and capital but had manifested in more ambivalent ways in relation to the freedom of people to move (Boucher 2008; Overbeek 2002). Migration that was deemed economically beneficial was framed as desirable, while family, humanitarian, and irregular migration became the focus of greater levels of scrutiny and control. As a result, 'migration policymaking at the global level [became] predominantly shaped by state preferences and characterized by utilitarian, macro-economic concerns' (Basok & Piper 2012: 41).

In New Zealand and Australia at the turn of the twenty-first century, the movement towards managerialism in migration was primarily evident in efforts to refine skilled migration programmes towards enhanced outcomes in settlement and economic benefit from immigration (Bedford 2004; Hugo 2004). A passive approach that relied on targets for entry could not achieve the goals that many governments were setting on attracting the right people, enhancing settlement and outcomes, regulating cross-border flows, or maximising the economic potential of immigration (Bedford et al. 2005). The Population Conference raised exactly these questions, and the policy responses that followed in subsequent years, under Tuariki Delamere and Lianne Dalziel, revealed an increasing interest in tracking and managing the volume, type, and benefit of immigration flows.

Distinct from both the calls to reduce immigration at the 1996 election and the economic multiculturalism of the previous decade, Bradford and the coalition government were now advancing a 'stable immigration' policy. Stability was to be achieved through a mix of annualised targets for new immigrants and longer-term targets for the contribution of net migration gain to population change. Bradford announced a new target of 38,000 residence approvals for 1998/1999 alongside a 'goal of a net gain of 10,000 people a year from permanent and long-term migration', which was to include movements of both New Zealand citizens and non-citizens (Bradford 1998). These approaches demanded more 'ad hoc' flexibility for employer requirements, and fine-tuned techniques for processing residence approvals to address positive economic growth in the late 1990s and growing demand for skilled labour while controlling immigration that was perceived to be non-beneficial:

> There was a fair bit of reacting to the squeaky wheel in the employment market, and the rules changed to reflect that pretty much on an ad hoc basis. There was also quite a lot of work done

on the family repatriation arrangement. In other words, what sort of people could be brought in with immigrants who had been granted permanent residency, what members of their family could come. . . . Some parts of the world, particularly India and the Asian regions, were inclined to bring large families in on the back of the permanent residency requirements and that required a lot of polishing of the rules so that the numbers weren't opened up too widely.

As Bradford described it in his interview, immigration policy was now 'very much an economic policy issue driven as much as anything by the Treasury and the other economic departments as by the immigration division'. Family immigration was a part of this approach, so far as it contributed to the attractiveness of New Zealand to the immigrants the government saw as desirable. Bradford's account and approaches at the time, then, speak to a desire to control for excess in areas of immigration that were deemed undesirable. Racial stereotypes played a significant role in these framings of desirability – larger families and perhaps especially large arrivals from Asia were deemed in need of management, particularly because they might generate political challenges to immigration that the government was seeking to avoid. While Treasury was driving the policy direction, the immigration division became significant in the operationalisation and modification of selection criteria – in fine-tuning overarching objectives into modifiable criteria to respond to needs and pressures. As Bradford explained:

For the most part a lot of the polishing, if we can use that term, was initiated by the department or by the immigration division of the Department of Labour. They would send to me proposals for change, we would review it, put it through our coalition committee with New Zealand First, discuss it at cabinet level and the change would either take place in a modified form or in the form that it came to us from officials.

This strict separation of strategy and operations in bureaucratic design is a fundamental component of a managerial approach to immigration that first emerged in this period (Geiger & Pécoud 2010). In accordance with management theories of 'good governance', the separation of strategic and operational roles creates both a division of labour and a separation of powers among immigration officials tasked with administering decisions, elite bureaucrats overseeing the design of operational approaches, and policymakers leading strategic framing of immigration policy and its objectives (Mountz 2010). This allows for the construction of immigration targets and selection criteria that abstract migrants as population groups and individuals to whom objective value can be ascribed in accordance with strict principles, without the empathy that could emerge through direct contact with the messy realities of human lives in motion (Wonders 2006). In the case of New Zealand immigration policymaking at the end of the twentieth century, the growing separation of roles in immigration management established a set of norms that were important for ongoing changes over subsequent decades, which we discuss in this and the following chapter.

Political Turmoil and Maverick Politics

The National–New Zealand First Coalition Government experienced significant turmoil from late 1997 until its dissolution in August 1998 (Boston et al. 2004). From mid-1997, Minister for State-Owned Enterprises Jenny Shipley (formerly Minister of Social Welfare, 1990–93, and Minister of Health, 1993–96) had started articulating concerns about the limited reforms being advanced by the government and the disproportionate influence exerted by New Zealand First. After a majority of National MPs expressed no confidence, Bolger resigned, and Shipley became Prime Minister in December 1997, remaining so for the rest of the parliamentary term. This change in leadership was accompanied by a deterioration in the relationship with New Zealand First, and, in August 1998, Shipley sacked Winston Peters from Cabinet. Following a subsequent New Zealand First meeting, seven MPs resigned from the party and Peters announced the dissolution of the coalition. To maintain the confidence of Parliament, Shipley relied on the support of the ACT party, independent MP Alamein Kopu, and eight former New Zealand First MPs whose support she was able to gain (Boston et al. 2004). Among these was Tuariki Delamere, who was announced as the new Minister of Immigration in Shipley's Cabinet starting from September 1998.

Delamere's time in the role of Minister of Immigration was characterised by the reversal of several existing restrictions, particularly key examples of discrimination, although as we note below, other restrictions were also introduced. Once appointed, Delamere described quickly signalling his new approach to senior civil servants:

> Shipley announced it at 10.30pm and about 10.31pm I had a message sent over to the general manager [of the New Zealand Immigration Service], to Chris [Hampton], and told Chris to be front and centre at midday. Came over and I say, 'How's Immigration, Chris?' 'It's

wonderful minister.' Going through all these wonderful things, how great they're doing. Oh yeah. Because I already had my ideas what I wanted to start off with.

Delamere described challenging Chris Hampton, the general manager of the New Zealand Immigration Service, on restrictions that needed to change. Firstly, in August 1998, there was a quota limit of 1000 on international students from China, while such limits did not apply to other nationalities. Naming the policy for what it was, 'a racist, discriminatory policy', Delamere insisted on its removal. By late 1998, the quota had been increased to 4000, and it was eventually removed completely in 1999.[12] Secondly, Delamere took aim at the $20,000 English Language Bond that had been required from business migrants from non-English-speaking backgrounds since 1995. This was replaced with pre-purchased $3,000 vouchers for English-language training; General Skills migrants still had to pass an English-language test. A third change that occurred soon after Delamere took office was the creation of equal rights for same-sex couples. Previously same-sex couples had to wait four years before being seen as in a legitimate relationship, in contrast to two years for heterosexual couples. Summing up his conversation with Chris Hampton, Delamere described his final word as follows:

> *I said, 'Look Chris, I ain't having no bullshit racist discriminatory anti-gender, anti-sexual whatever on my watch. They'll be equal.' And they became equal. That was all done by one o'clock.*

Delamere's tenure was characterised by a focus on business immigration and making New Zealand a more attractive destination for migrants. He highlighted the inability of highly qualified migrants to work in their field of expertise in New Zealand because their qualifications were not recognised, and the fact that they were subsequently unemployed or working in low-skilled jobs (Bedford et al. 2005: 8). A review into existing policies also showed that the information available to migrants about working and living conditions in New Zealand was lacking (Bedford et al. 2005: 8). Reflecting a growing focus on the importance of knowledge generation about migration, a migrant levy was introduced by the Immigration (Migrant Levy) Amendment Act 1998, which would be used to fund migrant settlement initiatives and research. In June 1999, Delamere

---

12   The quota had been shifted from 400 to 1000 during Max Bradford's time as Minister of Immigration – it had initially been in place because of perceptions of risk associated with overstaying (Evening Post 1998).

announced the development of the Longitudinal Immigration Survey New Zealand, an eight-year survey of the first three years of migrant experiences after gaining residency, which aimed to 'provide the basis for fine-tuning immigrant selection, as well as labour market, business investment and social service policies' (Delamere 1999). Entry for IT workers was given priority in November 1998 (Delamere 1998), following on from a pilot programme under Max Bradford that had targeted young migrants in the UK, Hong Kong, and Taiwan. Alongside these changes, new 'Entrepreneur' and 'Investor' categories were introduced, which streamlined the application process and included residence options for entrepreneurs. For Delamere, both in his time as minister and subsequently as an immigration consultant, business immigration was the priority for economic benefits:

> You want money, you want investors so it's all well and good having your skilled migrants. But skilled migrants by and large are not going to be catalysts for significant creation of jobs with companies and stuff. Rich people, most of them, they don't want to invest their money in a bank account, they want to do something. So, we worked on that philosophy. We had the entrepreneur policy, and the investor policy. . . . My legacy, if you like, when I left Parliament, if you look at the country's GDP, and in 2000 through to 2003/4 if you like, if you took out all the GDP impacts of international students, in particular those 40,000 Chinese and the impacts of the investor policies and stuff, New Zealand GDP would look pretty bloody sick.

Part of the process of promoting business immigration involved building international relationships and marketing New Zealand as an attractive destination. New Zealand joined the APEC Business Card Travel Scheme in September 1998, which allowed businesspeople to move between member nations for short periods without requiring a visa. Visa-waiver arrangements were announced for Argentina, Chile, Brazil, and Uruguay in October 1998. In April of the following year, they were announced for Saudi Arabia, the United Arab Emirates, Bahrain, Kuwait, Oman, and Qatar, 'in order to foster closer contacts with the Gulf States involved, particularly in trade and tourism' (Delamere & Smith 1999). New Zealand Immigration Service offices were also opened in Shanghai and Moscow in 1999, and planned for Pretoria in 2000. Reflecting migration's entrenchment as a part of economic policy, these changes aimed to smooth the pathway for investment and advance the potential for immigration to spill over into other forms of economic globalisation.

In contrast to other former ministers interviewed for this research, Delamere presented himself as something of a maverick in the role. He made no secret of his disdain for arrangements he saw as ineffective or unfair and was frequently in the public eye for immigration announcements or decisions. Delamere was not part of the National Party but was rather an independent MP whose support the government needed to continue. In that regard, his position was unusual given the centrality of the immigration portfolio to the exercise of state sovereignty and the impression of the competence of governments. He was also the first and (at the time of writing) only Māori Minister of Immigration; alongside Kris Faafoi (2020– 22), Delamere is one of only two former ministers who did not position themselves as solely Pākehā or New Zealand European. When asked about his position as a Māori Minister of Immigration, he characterised his approach to the role as one based on fairness that drew on Māori values: 'what's paramount is whakapapa' (genealogical/relational connections):

> *My guiding principle when I was minister was to do, within our policy, to make sure what was fair. What was appropriate for New Zealand and that it was fair and treated everyone where you could equally. I always tried to hold of that.*

Highlighting the importance of relationships and equality in the same instance could be seen as contradictory. In Delamere's case, it perhaps represents the rather distinct and individual approach he brought to the immigration portfolio, and his interactions with constituents and officials were unlike those of any other Minister of Immigration. He described signing off on a ministerial directive granting residence to fourteen monks while visiting a Buddhist temple in Auckland after realising their experience was not recognised in the same way as Christian priests. He received significant public criticism for not accepting the appeal of German citizens Gunter and Petra Schier against a removal order; the Schiers had overstayed their visas by many years, and Gunter Schier had an undeclared criminal record for narcotics trading. Facing down politicians and prominent media figures, Delamere highlighted the inconsistency and racism of public sympathy for the Schiers given that so little concern had been expressed for the much more numerous removals of people from Pacific countries, including those who had no criminal records. In the final weeks of the National-led Government, Delamere was sacked by Prime Minister Jenny Shipley for a controversy over the granting of residence to businesspeople from China. Delamere approved the grant of residence with a lower level of investment than regulations required, with the proviso that the businesspeople invested into Māori development schemes. The Prime Minister declared she would not 'tolerate one law for Māori and one law for the rest of New Zealand'. After leaving Parliament at the 1999 election, Delamere went on to set up Tuariki Delamere and Associates, which became a prominent and successful immigration consultancy. Delamere has remained a prominent public commentator on immigration in the years since leaving Parliament, and was also in the public eye following charges of fraud in 2005 related to his time as minister, for which he was found not guilty.

Managing Migration, Outsourcing Risk

The growing shift towards managerialism in migration policymaking was cemented and then extended with the election of the Labour-led Government in 1999 and the appointment of Lianne Dalziel as Minister of Immigration (1999–2004). The political tide had shifted significantly by 1999, and in the general election that year the Labour Party won forty-nine seats, well exceeding the National Party's thirty-nine seats. Among the small parties, the left-wing Alliance party secured ten seats, ACT nine, and the Green Party seven. New Zealand First slumped to five seats and United New Zealand gained one seat. Labour, led by Helen Clark, quickly formed a minority coalition with the Alliance party and was provided support on confidence and supply by the Green Party. Labour had campaigned on a platform of enabling 'New Zealand to develop as a knowledge-based, high skills, high income, and fully employed nation, *underpinned by an active government* committed to reducing inequalities and to building strong public services in health, education, and other areas' (New Zealand Labour Party 1999, emphasis added). Its policy platform emphasised pragmatic and achievable developments, in contrast to the blitzkriegs of ideologically driven policy change from 1984 until the mid-1990s (Rudd 2005). The party pledged to promote economic development, reduce profit, focus on health, introduce fairer funding of tertiary education, enhance superannuation and public housing, and increase the top income tax rate. These policies were accompanied by progressive commitments to reform the Employment Contracts Act 1991 and return state monopoly to workplace accident insurance alongside an emergent emphasis on promoting national identity (Skilling 2010b).

While there was a clear progressive dimension to these policies, and discursive resonances with traditional left-wing manifestos, none of these policies sought to unwind the systemic features of market-based rule that had been established since 1984. Rather, Labour's platform could be considered part of a wider 'Third Way' movement that brought a greater emphasis on state investment in social and economic development and a growing public sector alongside a continued commitment to free markets, competition, and efficiency (Larner et al. 2007; Tickell & Peck 2003). The so-called 'Third Way' approach advocated a middle path between the state-centric Keynesian approach of the 1970s and the radical free-market approach that had become synonymous with Margaret Thatcher in the UK, Ronald Regan in the US, and Roger Douglas in New Zealand. First formulated by British sociologist Anthony Giddens, who was Director of the London School of Economics from 1996 to 2003, the Third Way approach had propelled Tony Blair's UK NewLabour Party into government in 1997. Clark and some of her key Cabinet members, particularly Steve Maharey, stridently advocated the new approach, and Clark would eventually argue, in a speech to the London School of Economics, that New Zealand had moved beyond neoliberalism (Clark 2002). As Larner et al. (2007) point out, however, Labour retained a strong focus on participation in the globalising economy and continued to operate through political rationalities and governmental technologies crafted under neoliberalism. Their 'roll-out neoliberal' policy platform moderated and consolidated, rather than overturned, the 'roll-back neoliberalism' of the previous decade. It also articulated with an emerging knowledge economy discourse that emphasised the importance of embracing information and communication technologies, framing knowledge and innovation as the source of economic growth, and foregrounding the value of scientific and technical skills and a wider embrace of knowledge in society (Larner et al. 2007).

Labour's immigration policy in the 2000s was framed in relation to these imperatives, focused on developing strategies to compete for talent in a context of globalisation, while aiming for better outcomes that could mitigate the problems associated with looser selection criteria. Economic imperatives had to be managed alongside an emphasis on 'national unity' and development (Skilling 2010a). Dalziel had been opposition spokesperson for immigration and emphasised in her interview the extent to which Labour was prepared to govern in 1999, that 'ministers in waiting had done a lot of background research and work' and were prepared to implement refined policy shifts. This approach reflected the broader emphasis on 'evidence-based policy making' and the introduction of 'best practice' that was in ascendency in the Fifth Labour Government and other 'Third Way' administrations (Smith & Haux 2017). For Dalziel, policy was no longer ideological but rather programmatic, pragmatic, and outcomes driven:

The policy became my guiding light for what I did as minister. As I said it was 'reflecting our past, shaping our future'. It was about having a better-researched knowledge focusing on settlement outcomes and resettlement outcomes. That was very much a focus of it. Taking that emphasis off numbers, and also looking for the reasons that settlement outcomes are made more positive.

Where her predecessors had expressly taken an approach to immigration rules that was more 'ad hoc', in Bradford's words, Dalziel asserted that greater control could be achieved, castigating the previous government's management of the points system as 'blunt and ineffective' (Dalziel 2000). In her first month in office, Dalziel established a Ministerial Advisory Group on migration policy and immigrant settlement, which undertook a review of current policy. Dalziel issued regular press releases on migration numbers in the early days of her tenure, and there were numerous announcements on small tweaks to existing migration policy (Bedford et al. 2002b), indicating a much more hands-on engagement with migration than some of her predecessors:

We didn't separate operations from policy. I fundamentally believe that you cannot have a good operation unless it's fully informed by policy, and you cannot have good policy or keep it up to date if you're not well informed by the operational side of it.

The following five years ushered in what migration scholar Richard Bedford (2004) described as a 'quiet revolution' in migration policy – there was no new immigration Act or major amendment, but there were more than thirty-three policy changes, four major reviews, and the development of a more targeted approach to skills. As will become clear in the following chapters, Dalziel's quiet revolution also set the foundation for migration policy for the next two decades.

The flagship change was the establishment of the New Zealand Immigration Programme (NZIP) in October 2001, which integrated the different economic, family, and humanitarian streams into one overarching programme of work. Dalziel described the NZIP as an approach that 'actively manages the number of approvals for skilled and business migrants' (Dalziel 2001). The programme adopted the three-stream approach of the Australian system that, at the 1997 Population Conference, Delamere had suggested New Zealand should mirror. As in Australia, each stream would be allocated a proportion of an overall immigration planning target: 60 per cent skilled/business; 32 per cent family sponsored; 8 per cent humanitarian. With this streamed approach, the government proposed to better facilitate economic migration by placing a strict cap on social, family, and humanitarian migration, reflecting their 'desire to ensure that talent tops the list of residence approvals' (Dalziel 2001). The new programme increased the target for residence approvals from 38,000 to 45,000. By introducing measures that ensured economic migrants were granted most approvals, the government dulled 'anticipated criticism that the larger immigration target was simply adding to the numbers of new migrants who were not making an active contribution to the economy' (Bedford et al. 2005: 17). The NZIP, in this regard, reflected a more integrated approach to explicitly managing migration, focused not only on numbers but also on who would arrive and under what conditions.

The key problem that Dalziel had identified was that of settlement outcomes and the question of whether immigration was making the kinds of economic contributions that the government desired:

> *The big issue of the day, which had been resolved for some issues but not others, was what I call the 'doctors driving taxis' debate. It was a huge debate, which was that we were bringing in highly skilled migrants from a range of different countries who could not work in their professions. Again, this all came back to settlement and resettlement outcomes. . . . The previous government had changed the policy so you couldn't get your residence points or your immigration points for a qualification unless you had the registration to practise in New Zealand, which was a sensible change to make. The trouble is that not all professions require registration, but you have to have it [for residence]. . . . A classic example is a qualified nurse. We were bringing nurse aides in. They were fully qualified in the Philippines for example, but they would end up being nurse aides. Our rest-home sector would be completely devastated if they weren't allowed to come.*

These concerns for settlement outcomes, and the deskilling and under-employment of highly qualified migrants, was hardly a unique situation to New Zealand. In Australia (Miller & Neo 1997) and Canada (Galabuzzi 2005) too, issues around professional accreditation, alongside skills mismatches and labour-market discrimination, had contributed to ongoing incidences of unemployment, underemployment, and deskilling among migrants who had arrived under similar human capital–oriented migration regimes. The shift from focusing solely on the number and composition of migrants who entered New Zealand towards helping migrants adjust to life began in the

1990s (Bedford et al. 2005: 13), but it was Dalziel who focused her political rhetoric around successful outcomes (Bedford 2004: 60). In a speech to the 'New Settlers' academic seminar series in April 2002, Dalziel summed up the fundamental problem she saw: 'there were people in the country who had residence, but couldn't get work, and there were people in the country who had work, but couldn't get residence' (Dalziel 2003a). Pre- and post-settlement initiatives were central to solving this problem, Dalziel argued, to ensure that migrants had a 'realistic expectation of what they could expect to find in New Zealand, and a mechanism for hooking into the labour market and/or business communities after they arrived' (Dalziel 2003a). But the relationship between the rhetoric and realities of migrant settlement was not straightforward, with Bedford et al. (2005: 24) suggesting that while some support was provided to refugees and migrants for immediate settlement, there was limited ongoing financial support for societal integration. Instead, the government placed emphasis on selecting migrants who would find it easier to get work and settle in New Zealand.

Concerns about the ability of migrants to settle in New Zealand informed discussions at governmental level about population trends. In June 2003, the government released a report, with a foreword co-authored by Dalziel, titled *Population and Sustainable Development* (Anderton et al. 2003), which attempted to map future population trends in New Zealand. The report projected that New Zealand would have very limited population growth over the next century, suggesting that the 'population [was] unlikely to reach five million in the next forty years' and would peak in 2051 at 4.6 million before falling back to 4.2 million by 2101 (Anderton et al. 2003: 7). The projections, and the report's emphasis on population, had synergies with the 1997 Population Conference and gave priority to a focus on research, planning, and government-directed management of migration. Of course, with hindsight, these projections were far off the mark, with New Zealand's population hitting the five-million mark in 2020, not least because of high levels of migration in the 2010s – facilitated by policy approaches first initiated by Dalziel.

Key to Dalziel and the Labour Government's vision of effective outcomes from immigration was the proactive targeting and facilitation of 'talent'. The notion of talent loomed large in the government's strategic focus on 'economic transformation', through its overarching 'Growth and Innovation Framework' (Lewis 2011). The framework identified the steady decline of the New Zealand economy relative to OECD standards, articulating a growing fear that 'over time, we will become Fiji with snow' (David Skilling, interviewed in Macfie 2007). The framework attributed this long-term decline to New Zealand's dependence on primary exports to declining European markets, which involved 'sending heavy, low-value-added products very long distances', to paraphrase Treasury analyst David Skilling, who played a key role in the framework. Drawing heavily on the work of management consultants espousing 'New Growth Economics', which posited knowledge and innovation as fundamental sources of wealth creation (LEK Consulting 2001), Skilling and others argued that New Zealand required a more 'weightless economy', geared towards higher-value-added manufacturing and – most importantly – a stronger focus on the high-tech sector, where Silicon Valley had become the new benchmark. The Growth and Innovation Framework thus aimed, across a wide range of policy domains, 'at transforming New Zealand from an imperial hinterland that had lost its empire – an economy dependent on low value-added primary exports to distant and declining markets – into a globally integrated "knowledge economy"' (Gamlen 2010a). A key plank in this strategy was the need to attract and grow a talented workforce, which could enable the transformation of the economy along new growth lines.

Amid this purported global 'war for talent' (Beechler & Woodward 2009), Dalziel regularly highlighted the need to create the conditions to capture more 'talent' in the aid of developing the knowledge economy (Bedford et al. 2005).

> Interviewer: Was immigration part of the mix of trying to think about the knowledge economy, improve the population mix in terms of skills?

> Dalziel: That's where the talent visa came from and it was particularly driven out of that whole approach that government had on economic transformation. The talent visa was part of that. I was part of the group of ministers that looked at economic transformation, I was part of that group. The talent visa, again if you look at it, it stripped away everything from the government. So, what does the government need to retain for its risk management? Health and character. That's it. So, whether they're qualified, whether they've got work experience, if the employer is prepared to take that all on board, that's down to them. If they're going to stay in the country for two years, they've got a good job that's paying over a certain amount of money, what is the government's role in managing the risk?

The introduction of a new 'talent visa' was the most obvious representation of this drive for highly skilled applicants, although the outsourcing of responsibility for settlement was indicative of a wider shift in policy. The talent visa took two forms: one where accredited employers guaranteed a salary of at least $45,000 for two years, and another that involved sponsorship of outstanding artistic, cultural, and sporting talent. The visa enabled a pathway towards residency for migrants who had entered New Zealand on temporary work visas to fill labour shortages in high-skilled occupations. Many of these migrants did not qualify under current residency criteria, but as Dalziel noted, due to their perceived 'talent' and capacity to help drive growth and innovation, they remained critical to the New Zealand economy and its future.

Following the *Population and Sustainable Development* report, Dalziel introduced a new Skilled Migrant Category (SMC) in July 2003, which she described at the time as 'the most significant change in immigration policy in more than a decade' (Dalziel 2003b). The SMC focused on active recruitment of skilled migrants and was explicitly framed around the Growth and Innovation Framework objectives. The policy included a new approach to granting residence rights that required applicants who met the pass mark to submit an Expression of Interest (EOI). Bonus points were awarded to those whose skills and qualifications overlapped with New Zealand labour demands and economic objectives (Bedford & Spoonley 2014: 894). Applicants would then be pooled and those with the highest number of points would be invited to apply for residency. After application, two streams would emerge: one comprised those who could demonstrate that they could easily settle in New Zealand, especially those with previous study or work experience in New Zealand or with a skilled job offer; those in the other stream would be placed on a two-year work-to-residence visa in order to prove they could settle effectively (Bedford et al. 2005: 25–26). The new policy also broadened the 1991 points system by granting trade and postgraduate qualifications almost as many points as bachelor's-level qualifications, and subsequently, in 2004, provided points for having family in New Zealand (Bedford & Spoonley 2014).

The introduction of the SMC encapsulated the prioritisation of settlement outcomes and the focus on attracting talent that characterised the years of Dalziel's ministership. The earlier policy, where migrants were granted approval by meeting the points threshold, was replaced with a much more targeted policy, which granted the Immigration Service more control in selecting migrants with the specific skills required to fill labour shortages and to stimulate the knowledge economy. Dalziel's focus on migrant settlement was further cemented by the introduction of the Immigration Settlement Strategy in December 2003, which set out a series of goals for migrants and refugees, such as obtaining employment to align with their skills, accessing language skills support, and feeling safe to express their cultural identity within the wider community (New Zealand Immigration Service 2004).

The SMC, and the talent visa, also expressed a shift in immigration policy towards granting temporary status before permanent residence rights, in contrast to the 1990s policy that granted residence primarily to offshore applicants. In March 2000, a Job Search visa was introduced, which allowed applicants within five points of the pass mark for residence to gain temporary work permits to search for employment in New Zealand (Bedford 2004). A new Priority Occupation List was introduced in 2002, which operated in much the same way as its antecedent from the 1970s and provided successful applicants with qualifications and experience in the identified areas with a two-year work permit (Bedford et al. 2005: 21). Similarly, the talent visa provided for work rights without a guarantee of residence based on employers taking on the risk of international recruitment. And, as noted above, the second stream of the SMC provided for a 'work to residence' visa that allowed residence applicants time to prove they had the ability to settle in New Zealand, which was effectively measured in terms of what the government deemed appropriate employment. Even in relation to people who had become irregular migrants, Dalziel described in her interview a pro forma arrangement she had with the Immigration Service: for appeals she would ordinarily grant temporary visas of three or six months to 'give them adequate time to regularise their status'.

The shift towards temporary migration programmes also emerged in relation to two other realms that had a close connection to the diversifying export orientation of the New Zealand economy. Firstly, there was the announcement in 2000 that the annual number of working holiday visas allowed would be doubled to 20,000 – a scheme that linked temporary contributions to the labour market to growth in tourism and expanding bilateral arrangements (Tsai & Collins 2017). Over the course of the next two decades, the number of country-specific working holiday schemes would quintuple from nine in 2000 (Newlands 2006) to forty-five in 2020, and the number of working holiday visas approved annually would eventually grow from 9480 in 1999 to 73,338 in the twelve months to June 2017, before dipping slightly in the next three years and pausing completely during the Covid-19-related border closures (MBIE 2024).

More immediately consequential was the rapid growth in international student visas. Delamere had already started the process of loosening arrivals for international students from China, and by 1999, these restrictions had been removed. New Zealand education institutions of all kinds – primary, secondary, public tertiary, and private training establishments – rode a fast-rising wave of student numbers. Between 1999 and 2003, the number of international students increased from around 30,000 to over 120,000, 45 per cent of whom were from the People's Republic of China (Collins 2006). The growth in what became known as 'export education' reflected earlier changes to the Education Act in 1990, which had reduced state funding to education. The need to cover funding shortfalls led to aggressive overseas marketing by universities, schools, education agents, and eventually the state (Collins & Lewis 2016). While Dalziel described these changes as peripheral to her focus as immigration minister, they would over time become linked with broader approaches to temporary migration that we outline in greater depth in Chapter 6.

The full impact of these shifts towards temporary migration and away from a prioritisation of permanent settlement would not become fully apparent until well after Dalziel's time in office, and in her interview for this book she stated that she did not see these policy changes in this way. Nonetheless, notable growth in temporary visas did occur, with a doubling of work visas approved annually from 43,141 in 1998/99 to 97,118 in 2003/04 (Immigration New Zealand 2016). As noted above, the international education sector saw a quadrupling of student numbers between 1999 and 2003. Beyond these initial impacts, the growth in working holidays and international students started the process of pivoting towards temporary migration programmes. Alongside the introduction of staggered applications for residence, these changes also laid the ideological foundation for a migration regime that would focus increasingly on benefits and costs and the expectation that migrants were the ones responsible for the outcomes of migration. Dalziel explained:

> So, the question that I ended up asking myself is, what is the risk that the government actually has to hold, that it can't transfer? Can it transfer any other risks? Yeah, it can transfer a lot because if an employer is making the call and they're paying a decent salary and they don't get residence for two years, well that's pretty good to me. I would have liked to extend that even further.

Dalziel's account in her interview echoed comments she made at the time about migrants 'carry[ing] the risk of not achieving this outcome rather than the New Zealand welfare system' (Dalziel 2003c). This approach is indicative of the way neoliberal governmentality reworks relations of risk, community, and expertise, especially in the context of new forms of managerialism. Within such arrangements, 'relations of risk' are central to governing society – both 'the risks posed to the individual themselves if they cannot adequately manage their life within the community' and 'the risks the individual may pose to the community on account of their failure to govern themselves' (Miller & Rose 2008). Internationally, immigration has been a key terrain for addressing risks in welfare regimes that emerge out of the social rights accorded to immigrants through access to residence permits (Sainsbury 2012). Indeed, the critique of immigrants as a burden on welfare provision has been commonplace in major receiving countries, including in New Zealand (Johnston et al. 2010). Responses to this have included efforts to reduce access through changes to welfare provision itself and the kind of shift that Dalziel intimated towards, whereby migrants are excluded from welfare access for extended periods of time and thus are expected to be self-responsible. These moves by Dalziel signalled a desire to minimise risk for the government, by asking migrants to demonstrate that they are worthy of inclusion through the performance of appropriate economic and social behaviours during a trial period. Similarly, in diversifying modes of entry, in terms of time-limited work visas, working holiday visas, and international student visas, the immigration regime was starting to allocate different rights to different migrants, setting distinct conditions on migration, linking migration to outcomes, and creating the apparatus through which it would be possible to continuously refine, rework, and reconfigure the managerial dimensions of migration policy.

Borders, Citizenship, and Regional Relationships

Dalziel instigated shifts towards temporary migration as a pathway to distributing residence rights and long-term immigrant settlement – and these occurred alongside tensions in geopolitical relationships with Australia, as well as further reworking of the limited immigration pathways available to people from Pacific countries. Early in Dalziel's term, significant challenges emerged around citizenship, the political relationship with Australia, and trans-Tasman migration. Dalziel described in her interview how, prior to the 1999 election, the Australian Minister of Immigration Philip Ruddock met with Helen Clark and herself to indicate that the Australian Government was planning to limit New Zealand citizens' access to social security benefits in Australia. Over the late 1990s, New Zealand had been increasingly framed by Australian politicians as a 'back door' for immigration of people from Asian and Pacific countries, who would be able to gain citizenship quickly and then immigrate to Australia under the

Trans-Tasman Travel Arrangement (Hamer 2014). Reports in Australia had observed a growth in the proportion of New Zealand citizens born in third countries over the 1990s, leading to a characterisation of New Zealand as operating a 'revolving door migration policy' (Rapson 1998).

According to Hamer (2014), the situation was exacerbated in late 2000 because of two other developments: in September 2000, Dalziel announced the Transitional Immigration Policy, an effective amnesty for around 7000 people whose visas had expired (around half of whom were Samoan and Tongan), and then shortly thereafter announced the Pacific Access Category, which would replace existing work permit arrangements and introduce small quota categories for Pacific countries, akin to the existing Samoan Quota Scheme. Then-Australian Minister of Immigration Philip Ruddock described this as something that undermined aspirations for a shared border: 'Our preference is to have a common border. That means you apply the same criteria. . . . Every time you make decisions which are unique it degrades the quality of those border arrangements' (Wellwood 2000: 1). While the rhetoric around border controls and immigration regulations was general, it was clear, as it had been to Aussie Malcolm and Stan Rodger in the 1980s (see Chapter 2), that it was the specific risk of onward migration of Pacific people that mainly worried the Australian Government (Hamer 2014).

For a period, New Zealand media had reported that there was potential for the entire Trans-Tasman Travel Arrangement to be reworked by Australia (Barber 1999), and concern had been recorded among New Zealand government officials that only New Zealand-born citizens would maintain free-movement rights to Australia (Hamer 2014). Australia and New Zealand had also been in the process of reviewing bilateral social security arrangements in the final years of the National-led Government, which were a particular sticking point for the Australian Government because of the comparatively higher number of New Zealand citizens living in Australia. On 26 February 2001, Prime Minister Helen Clark and her Australian counterpart John Howard gave a joint press conference announcing a change in policy, which meant that New Zealand citizens who arrived in Australia after that date had to gain permanent residence through the Australian immigration programme before accessing certain social security payments, or sponsoring family members for residence or citizenship (Clark 2001). A resolution to the bilateral social security arrangement was also announced, which meant that each country would pay for their own citizens' superannuation and disability benefits when they lived in the other country. Compromise was key in this solution, as Clark made clear in her comments (Clark 2001):

If New Zealand were to demand that every New Zealander crossing the Tasman should get full social security entitlements, then Australia would be fully justified in asking for hundreds of millions of dollars more in reimbursement, given the disproportionate migration flows between our two countries.

Despite the strength of political rhetoric and feeling around the issue, Poot and Sanderson (2007) observe that there was not a clear influence on the volume of trans-Tasman migration in subsequent years; emigration from New Zealand did notably decline in 2002 and 2003 but research suggests this was associated with an economic improvement in New Zealand rather than a direct response to the altered rights of New Zealand citizens in Australia (Ho et al. 2003). Rather than necessarily dampening trans-Tasman migration, the shift added to earlier changes in Australia that positioned newly arrived New Zealand citizens in a peculiar and somewhat precarious position, holding visas that were technically temporary but with indefinite rights to remain while also providing only limited access to the social benefits associated with permanent residence and citizenship (McMillan 2017). The situation was hardly ideal for New Zealand political leaders, who were faced with the ignominy of New Zealand citizens in Australia experiencing uneven rights compared with Australian citizens in New Zealand. Australia had exercised asymmetrical power in the trans-Tasman relationship but, by accepting the unilateral action, Clark and the New Zealand Government had managed 'to protect the Trans-Tasman Travel Arrangement and the two countries' preferential relationship' (Leslie 2016: 317).[13]

Despite the Australian assertions, Pacific immigration to New Zealand was hardly prioritised, having been severely hampered by the human capital regime that had been established in the 1980s and 1990s. Nonetheless, the differences between the approaches of Australia and New Zealand to development in, and immigration from, Pacific countries had diverged over the latter part of the twentieth century as they withdrew from formal colonialism. In contrast to Australia's more exclusionary approach, New Zealand had articulated a 'special relationship' with the Pacific, and immigration policy had been shaped by the legacies of the Dawn Raids deportation campaign and the Treaty of Friendship with Western Samoa (Bedford et al. 2007). A consequence was that even as New Zealand shifted towards a human capital–centric immigration regime in the 1980s and

13   This asymmetrical arrangement persisted and, in some respects, worsened over the next two decades, regularly becoming an irritant in trans-Tasman relations, until it was finally addressed by the Albanese Labour Government in mid-2023 – after the period covered by this book.

1990s, there remained small carve-outs for specific Pacific nationalities to enter New Zealand, gain employment, and sometimes transition to residence. The Samoan quota was the most significant. Established under the Treaty of Friendship, this scheme allowed up to 1100 Samoan nationals to become permanent residents annually. There were also temporary work schemes for Fiji, Kiribati, Samoa, Tonga, and Tuvalu that dated back to the 1970s and allowed very limited numbers of workers from these countries for fixed periods. The very small island states of Kiribati and Tuvalu had also maintained visa-waiver arrangements, while all other Pacific waiver arrangements had been concluded in March 1987.

The Pacific Access Category (PAC) that Dalziel introduced in July 2002 effectively rationalised Pacific immigration schemes (Bedford 2008). This new class of residence visa provided 375 places to nationals of Tonga (250), Tuvalu (seventy-five) and Kiribati (fifty). Fiji (250) was added to the PAC in 2003, and the total number of places increased to 650 in 2003 and 777 in 2004 before returning to 650 in 2005. Fiji was suspended from the PAC between 2007 and 2015 as a New Zealand Government response to the establishment of military government in the country. The existing Pacific temporary work schemes were terminated alongside the introduction of the PAC, and in late 2003, the visa waivers with Kiribati and Tuvalu were also terminated so that 'the adverse impacts of immigration are properly managed' (Dalziel 2003b).

While these schemes are sometimes described as 'preferential' to Pacific countries, not least by the Australian Government, which saw them as a 'back door' to trans-Tasman migration (Hamer 2014), they reflect the way in which New Zealand policy shifts towards human capital measures have led to limited migration for Pacific nationals. Between 1997 and 2005, fewer than 10,000 people from Pacific countries gained residence visas within the skills or business categories. Almost all were from Fiji (8144), with a much smaller number from Tonga (1106) (MBIE 2017a). This pattern reflects how educational credentials in Pacific countries do not match the skilled migration criteria or business/investor capital requirements of New Zealand's immigration policy. The notable exception is Fiji, where Fiji Indians have had the economic and cultural capital needed to gain access through the primary business/skilled residence pathways (Friesen 2008; Khan 2011). For most other Pacific peoples, quotas allow for small, sustained entry, but that occurs in a situation whereby the dominant skills-based selection criteria do not recognise education or employment in the Pacific as making people worthy of inclusion.

The interchange with Australia over social rights in the Trans-Tasman Travel Arrangement also articulated with subsequent shifts in citizenship arrangements in New Zealand. Dalziel recalled how she had responded to the Australian pressure on New Zealand by advocating for a change to New Zealand citizenship policy:

> I got the impression that [the Australian concerns were] largely off the back of how quickly people could get citizenship, so actually that was one of the rules that I did promote to the Minister of Internal Affairs was to extend the period of residence to five years. I was definitely supportive of that. I thought that might assist but Australia made the changes to the rules anyway.

At the time, people who entered New Zealand legally and gained a residence visa could apply to become New Zealand citizens after three years (two years for spouses of New Zealand citizens). Citizenship could be acquired by birth in New Zealand regardless of whether parents were residents or citizens. The three-year residence requirement mirrored the situation in Canada and was already longer than the two years required in Australia (subsequently increased to four years). The change that Dalziel advocated was eventually implemented in the Citizenship Amendment Act 2005, which changed eligibility requirements substantially so that applicants had to first gain residence and then reside for five years in New Zealand. Through the same legislation, birthright citizenship was removed, as were provisions for special treatment of New Zealand citizens' spouses.

Internationally, there was increased political and media attention on citizenship in the early 2000s (Nyers 2009), notably in the US (Spiro 2008), Ireland (Tormey 2007), and Canada (Macklin & Crépeau 2010) in relation to birthright citizenship and non-residents holding dual citizenship. Claims of strategic forms of citizenship acquisition, particularly what has been called 'birth tourism' (Balta & Altan-Olcay 2016; Wang 2017), were particularly controversial. In New Zealand, the opposition National Party raised similar concerns, describing New Zealand as 'a birthplace of convenience' (Gregory 2004). The Minister of Internal Affairs, George Hawkins, introduced the Identity (Citizenship and Travel Documents) Bill to Parliament in 2004 by highlighting this issue (Hawkins 2014):

> Some people may come to New Zealand on temporary permits solely to give birth, so that their New Zealand-born children are citizens. Under current law those children are entitled to access publicly funded services such as health care and education. Restricting citizenship by birth will ensure that citizenship and its benefits are limited to people who have a genuine and ongoing link to New Zealand.

The opposition National Party and New Zealand First supported the changes, while the Green Party raised concerns and questioned the extent to which there was actually a pattern of birth tourism. Green MP Keith Locke highlighted in the media a specific connection to pressure from Australia (Dominion Post 2004a):

> When the Government talks about coming into line with other countries, they mean Australia. We shouldn't tail Australia in citizenship matters, particularly when the Howard government is so driven by anti-immigrant, anti-refugee paranoia. We must challenge their charges that New Zealand is a soft-on-migrants back door to Australia.

Australia had abolished birthright citizenship through an amendment to the Australian Citizenship Act in 1986 (Prince 2003), a move that had been catalysed by a 1985 case of a Tongan citizen who had given birth to a child in Australia after their student visa had expired. Dalziel's comments and Locke's critique suggest that aligning arrangements with Australia was a significant motivation for the citizenship changes in 2005. These shifts were also indicative of trends observed internationally as part of nation-state responses to the effects of globalisation in other key policy domains (Joppke 2010), including perceptions of risk associated with border security that are discussed in the next section and chapter. Dauvergne (2007: 489) framed this trend as a pattern of 'citizenship with a vengeance' wherein 'immigration and citizenship law are transformed into a last bastion of sovereignty', increasing regulation over migrant mobilities and reinforcing state authority through the control of national borders.

The Emerging Threat of (Irregular) Migration

Risk was not only a matter of potential economic and social downside outcomes. It also took shape around the perceived threat of irregular migration, and led to an emphasis on border and internal security that followed the arc of international migration politics (Ceyhan & Tsoukala 2002). From the mid-1990s, immigration and border officials, and eventually immigration ministers, were facing a larger number of claims for asylum and 'irregular' arrival. In 1994, only eighty-eight persons arrived at New Zealand airports wishing to apply for refugee status, but this number increased each of the following four years to a peak of 342 in 1998/99 and remained over 200 annually until 2003/04 (Refugee

Statistics 2010). Similarly, in terms of expulsion, the number of people who were refused entry to New Zealand upon arrival grew from 379 in 1994 to what was then a record of 1239 in 1999/2000. Expulsion of irregular arrivals would reduce to 357 by 2000/01 but quickly increased again to a new record of 1455 in 2005/06 and remained around 1000 annually into the earlier 2010s (Refugee Statistics 2010). While these numbers are small in comparative terms, and notably so in relation to Australia (Dickson 2015), they indicate what was seen as a growing trend in irregular migration. Speaking at the closing of the 1997 Population Conference, Max Bradford signalled exactly these concerns around migration control and border security (Bradford 1997):

> It is an emerging problem for many countries as organised crime attempts to move in to have people cross other country's borders against policy or against the wishes of that nation. It's an issue which is extraordinarily sensitive because of its relationship with refugee policy, but frankly it is one that we have to come to grips with.

This balance between determining and addressing irregular migration on the one hand and maintaining refugee policy on the other became a significant theme from the late 1990s onwards. In their interviews for this book and elsewhere, immigration ministers often adopted a rather self-congratulatory tone when discussing New Zealand's refugee policies. In the same speech, Max Bradford described New Zealand's refugee policy as 'one of the most generous policies in the world', even though, with a quota of only 750 per year until 2020, the country's per capita intake of refugees through the United Nations High Commissioner for Refugees (UNHCR) system has been modest (de Lapaillone 2012) and very few asylum seekers have been accepted (Kennedy 2016). Lianne Dalziel was similarly proud of her work in the refugee space, in particular the introduction of programmes to improve resettlement procedures and social and economic outcomes. In 2001, during Dalziel's tenure, Prime Minister Helen Clark negotiated a high-profile agreement with Australia to take 131 asylum seekers on board the Norwegian MV *Tampa*. The *Tampa* had been denied entry into Australian waters and precipitated the 'Pacific Solution', where people seeking asylum in Australia were detained extraterritorially on Nauru, Christmas Island, and Manus Island (Mountz 2011). It served as a useful political distinction that represented New Zealand as a humanitarian state in contrast to Australia's increasing focus on extraterritorial border control and pre-emptive intervention. As Dalziel explained:

Then there was the boat people and the Tampa incident, which is probably actually still the thing I'm most proud of and that was the ability of New Zealand to be a circuit breaker in what was a standoff situation. I still know people today who came on the Tampa as kids. One of the young guys is over in DC at the moment doing a Fulbright scholarship. They're just fantastic migrants. But I think the Australian government knew that at the time, they were just playing a hard-line role.

Contemporaneously, New Zealand had tacitly supported the Australian measures, with Dalziel stating in 2000 that 'although Australia has borne the brunt of seaborne illegal arrivals, I believe it is important that we work with Australia to address what is an international problem' (Dalziel 2000). Political scientist Kate McMillan (2008) framed this view as the 'hydraulic logic' of irregular migration: 'suppress it in one place and it will pop up in another. New Zealand does not want to be the place it "pops up" when other countries are successful in deflecting it. It is possible, for example, that Australia's recent success in deterring irregular migration onto its shores will encourage potential migrants to look to New Zealand as an alternative destination.' These sentiments, and those expressed by Bradford and Dalziel, demonstrate an increasingly established political claim that irregular migration presented national and human security risks to New Zealand and needed to be responded to through enhanced security measures and international cooperation.

By the turn of the millennium, New Zealand had already started to introduce legislation designed to deter or manage perceived migration threats. Two further amendments to the Immigration Act were passed in 1999. In April, measures were introduced to enable faster removal of overstayers, reducing the amount of time between a removal order and an appeal claim to three months and allowing the immediate removal of any person unlawfully in New Zealand who had not appealed within forty-two days of their visa expiry (Delamere 1998). The amendment also introduced a 'Limited Purpose Visa', which targeted applicants who the Immigration Service believed might stay beyond the expiry of their visa. The Limited Purpose Visa granted entry, but the holder was not allowed to apply for an extension or any other kind of visa and was not able to lodge an appeal against any removal order (Delamere 1998). In June, what was euphemistically called the 'Boat People' Bill was passed in Parliament. This was effectively a pre-emptive response to the unconfirmed news that a ship had left the Solomon Islands on 12 June, carrying over one hundred Chinese migrants, with the intention of landing in New Zealand (Delamere 1999). The new Bill allowed for asylum seekers to be detained for longer periods and made it easier to return migrants to the departure country.[14]

New immigration legislation also intersected with security measures introduced in the wake of the 11 September 2001 terrorist attacks in the US. Following the attacks, the UN Security Council passed Resolution 1373 on 28 September 2001, which called on states to 'prevent and suppress terrorist acts' through policing, surveillance, security, and financing controls. It also urged them to introduce measures to 'prevent the movement of terrorists or terrorist groups by effective border controls'. In response to this call, New Zealand's Terrorism Suppression Act was passed in 2002; it provided wider powers and new resources to police and intelligence agencies to undertake surveillance and respond to perceived terrorist threats, despite their relatively low risk in New Zealand (Small 2008). This legislative move towards securitisation created a much more restrictive and hostile environment for some migrants, especially those from the Middle East and North Africa (Bedford et al. 2005: 23), and later provided for the domestic deployment of anti-terrorism resources against Māori and other activist groups (Keenan 2008).

A particularly notable case was Ahmed Zaoui, an elected MP of Algeria exiled by the military, who arrived in New Zealand in 2002 and was determined as meeting the threshold for refugee status. The Security Intelligence Services (SIS), however, issued Zaoui with a security risk certificate, determining that he posed an unacceptable risk to New Zealand. Zaoui had been a long-term activist in Algeria's Islamic Salvation Front, a militantly anti-government Islamist group, and had been convicted of involvement in terrorist and/or criminal activity first by Algeria – whose government actively pursued him around the world – and later by several states where he sought shelter, including Belgium, Switzerland, and France. However, the contents and intelligence source of the New Zealand security risk certificate were not revealed to Zaoui or his lawyer, and he spent ten months in near-solitary confinement in

14   Other moves were also indicative of divergence between economic value and perceived security risk in migration. While visa waivers were being introduced for countries the government wished to connect with, Indonesia's waiver was rescinded in late 1998 after the government received more than 300 refugee applications from Indonesian citizens, many fleeing the economic and political turmoil that erupted following the collapse of President Suharto's authoritarian regime. Delamere also advanced a proposal to test all immigrants for Human Immunodeficiency Virus (HIV), a move that was criticised publicly and by a range of officials – while it was not implemented, a modified version with a quota was introduced by Delamere's successor Lianne Dalziel in 2004. In stark contrast to the facilitation of business immigration, and the efforts to manage labour migration in more orderly ways, such moves substantially hardened the New Zealand border for refugees and asylum seekers and strengthened the state's authority over determining the place of different migrants in New Zealand.

a maximum-security prison and further time in a remand facility until receiving bail in a Supreme Court ruling in December 2004, which allowed him to reside in a Dominican priory in Auckland. It was not until September 2007 that the security risk certificate was withdrawn by the SIS, at which point it was declared that additional information, Zaoui's cooperation, and the length of time he had been in New Zealand were justifying reasons. Zaoui's case demonstrated how racialised anti-terrorism measures, the hard edge of securitisation (Ibrahim 2005; Simmons 2007), were becoming integral to immigration regulation and creating conditions for increasingly differentiated control of mobile people (Dauvergne 2007).

The legislative and policing focus on terrorism also played out domestically in dramatic fashion in the mid-2000s. On 15 October 2007, the New Zealand Police undertook house raids across New Zealand and arrested seventeen Māori and environmental activists under suspicion of being involved in organised criminal activity, firearms offences, and running a terrorist training camp in Te Urewera mountains (Keenan 2008). The township of Rūātoki in Ngāi Tūhoe territory was locked down with media publishing images of armed police corralling residents. Among those arrested was Tame Iti, prominent Ngāi Tūhoe activist and former member of Ngā Tamatoa, which had led protests for Indigenous rights and against land confiscation by the Crown in the 1970s. While the Solicitor-General declined police requests to charge suspects under the Terrorism Suppression Act 2002, four people, including Tame Iti, were brought to trial and eventually convicted on firearms charges in 2012 (Devadas 2008). While nominally distinct from migration matters, the drawing of anti-terrorism activities into domestic spaces provides a sense of the wider implications of the 'war on terror' and this growing emphasis on border security. Identifying and responding to external and internal threats – including 'homegrown terrorism' among Indigenous people – are key parts of the consolidation of sovereign power in the twenty-first century (Hokowhitu & Devadas 2013).

Security, especially around asylum and refugee processing, became an increasing dimension of political activity and campaigning in the early 2000s. A key focus of Dalziel's first three years as Minister of Immigration was a reduction in the backlog of refugee cases, from more than 3000 when she took office to less than 600 by the 2002 General Election. Most of these cases were determined as 'unfounded' and thus declined. In public addresses at the time and during her interview, Dalziel (2002) characterised these applications as a 'scam' and said: 'New Zealand has been the victim of thousands of manifestly unfounded claims which have effectively clogged up our system of determination and appeal.' Following September 2001, the government introduced a much harder-line detention policy for refugee claimants, which effectively meant that almost all claimants were detained (in the past as few as 5 per cent had been) and, as Zaoui's case shows, some were detained in maximum-security prisons. The new detention policy was successfully challenged in the High Court by the Human Rights Foundation and the Refugee Council, but a full ruling of the Appeal Court overturned this earlier decision, and thus the detention policy was declared legal (New Zealand Herald 2003).

In the 2002 General Election, the opposition National Party, New Zealand First, and ACT all targeted the government around security risks emerging from asylum seeker processing, and around various challenges to the integrity of the immigration system. Nonetheless, Labour was returned to power in a coalition with the Progressive Party, which had splintered out of the Alliance. Labour's immigration policy also took a harder line on irregular migration, upholding a rhetoric of working with the UNHCR on quota refugees, while also highlighting responses to security matters, including introducing an Advance Passenger Processing System and mandatory fingerprinting of onshore asylum seekers (already in practice at that time for border claimants) (New Zealand Labour Party 2002). While migration and security threats proved productive electioneering tactics, almost all political representatives supported moves towards greater security and threat management in migration and border control.

Conclusion

The period 1996 to 2004 marked a fundamental development in the history of migration policy in New Zealand. The introduction of the points system in 1991 had cemented the neoliberalisation of migration policy, but the political atmosphere of the mid-1990s forced the National Government to make changes to the points system to curb migration from Asia and respond to anti-Asian anti-immigrationism led by Winston Peters. The Population Conference in 1997, which was more focused on migration than on any other issue, symbolised the increasingly important role migration would play in shaping New Zealand's future into the twenty-first century. The conference also signalled the direction of policy development from approaches focused on setting targets and accepting migrants based simply on qualifications towards more interventionist policy aimed at controlling the types of migrants entering the country and more closely aligning migration trends with labour and economic objectives.

When Lianne Dalziel became Minister of Immigration, it was immediately clear that a more active policy programme would emerge in the early twenty-first century. The introduction of the Skilled Migrant Category (SMC) with the Expression of Interest (EOI) component in 2003 was the culmination of Dalziel's focus on 'talent' and better migrant settlement outcomes that characterised her years as minister. The dilemma she identified when she took office – that 'there were people in the country who had residence, but couldn't get work, and there were people in the country who had work, but couldn't get residence' – had been partially solved by the SMC, a booming international student market, and new temporary migration programmes that provided more pathways to residency. By the time Dalziel left office in 2004, migration management had been streamlined and optimised for the new knowledge economy. But the tightening of humanitarian migration, and growing fears over global terrorism, pointed towards a new focus on securitisation in migration governance, which would come to dominate policy in subsequent years. It is this next step in security, integrity, and modernisation that we address in the following chapter.

CHAPTER 5

Security, Integrity, and Modernisation, 2005–2011

B y the first decade of the new millennium, New Zealand migration policies mirrored a global trend towards favouring the economic characteristics of migrants over social and cultural ones. This had been precipitated by the overhaul of the migration system in the 1980s, especially the Immigration Act 1987, but had really taken shape as part of a more concerted programme of socially progressive, neoliberal, and managerial transformations by National-led and Labour-led governments in the 1990s and early 2000s. As discussed in the previous chapter, Lianne Dalziel's tenure from 1999 to 2004 was especially notable. That period was characterised by a shift in migrant selection away from a deregulated human capital approach – which granted visas to those who met points thresholds, irrespective of labour-market needs – towards a more targeted selection process that aligned skilled migrants with labour shortages and economic objectives. These shifts represented the first substantive moves towards a New Zealand variant of what has internationally been described as migration management (Collins & Bayliss 2020; Friesen 2017), which focuses on targeting and managing the potential value of economic migration through regulatory innovation and increased monitoring of outcomes (Kalm 2010). Under Dalziel, migration management took shape through the establishment of temporary migration, for labour and education purposes, as a central element of the migration regime. These policy developments led New Zealand towards a higher rate of immigration over the first decade of the twenty-first century than countries such as Australia, Canada, and the US (Akbari & MacDonald 2014: 804).[15]

The economic imperatives in migration policy were also accompanied by a greater concern with security and risk internationally (Geiger & Pécoud 2017), which would come to resonate in New Zealand in important ways over the first decade of the twenty-first century. In Western Europe especially (Ceyhan & Tsoukala 2002), but also in the Americas (Ackleson 2005) and Australia (Ruddock 2000), security emerged as a key dimension

---

15   However, New Zealand's population growth was slower than that of these countries because of a high rate of emigration in the same period.

of thinking about migration in the context of the fall of the Berlin Wall and the end of the Cold War. The collapse of the Soviet Union had led to claims that neoliberalism and democracy would extend their reach into formerly socialist and authoritarian states (Poku et al. 2000). The post-Cold War world promised globalisation, characterised by the freer flows of goods and ideas, but it was also deemed risky for the threat of uncontrolled migrations, not least refugees and labour migrants who emerged out of state implosions, interethnic conflicts, and civil wars (Walters 2015).

As we have seen in the closing of the previous chapter, security discourses were also amplified in response to terrorist attacks in major Western cities in the early 2000s. In this chapter we focus on how governmental concern about security and risk took on a more urgent character in the years after the global 'war on terror' was declared (Ibrahim 2005). The terrorist attacks that occurred in September 2001 in New York and Washington DC, as well as those in Bali (2002), Madrid (2004), London (2005), and Mumbai (2005), among other places, led to significant changes to New Zealand's immigration and border policies. New Zealand was deeply entangled in the geopolitical response to these events through its position within the US-centred Anglosphere, and specifically within the Five Eyes security alliance, which first became prominent in this period. Intensified security at airports, the introduction of biometric technologies, and an extension of border practices beyond the territorial limits of nation-states have since all become normalised and taken-for-granted elements of international mobility (Jones & Johnson 2016).

Within this new context, accompanied by the growing dominance of neoliberal thought and market economics, migration came to occupy a bifurcated position in the establishment and maintenance of national and global liberal order (Rudolph 2003). On the one hand, migrants who were deemed to be skilled or entrepreneurial, or otherwise desirable, were the target of the kinds of migration policies developed in New Zealand in the 1990s. On the other hand, the figure of the 'irregular' migrant – especially racialised visions of refugees, trafficked persons, criminals, and terrorists – appeared 'as the anchoring point of securitarian policies and fierce public debates that gained momentum in the 1990s' (Ceyhan & Tsoukala 2002). Security discourses and the purported threat of migration cut across these diverse forms of migration and the ways that governments responded to them. On the one hand, security appeared most stringent in relation to the framing of irregular migration as a threat – one that was linked to terrorism and the wholehearted embrace of new border technologies for surveillance, control, and removal (Ibrahim 2005). On the other hand, regular migration, especially that associated with lower-skilled labour, became viewed in terms of the risks of migrants not returning to their countries of origin, and considerable effort was invested in new programmes for managing migration (Kalm 2010). In New Zealand, this emerged most notably in the 'circular mobility' schemes aiming to promote Pacific seasonal worker migration. Security assessments, status determination, and border enforcement have consequently become key tasks for immigration authorities.

In this chapter we explore the response to security and risk as key concerns within migration policymaking in New Zealand. We also address the relationship of discourses of security and risk to a focus on modernisation and the integrity of the immigration system. Our primary focus is on the Ministers of Immigration in office between 2004 and 2011: Paul Swain (who chose not to be interviewed for this book), David Cunliffe, Clayton Cosgrove, and Jonathan Coleman. Extending our account of early expressions of security and risk in Chapter 4, this chapter explores the substantive responses developed during this period: a focus on integrity and modernisation of the migration regime and its bureaucratic functions; the development of new innovations in the space of circular labour mobility; and a new drive to link securitised migration to a global economic-development agenda. We conclude the chapter by returning to the question of the skills, outlooks, and aptitudes desired in the role of Minister of Immigration. By the early 2010s, the role of Minister of Immigration had become much more complex because of shifts in the economic and security dimensions of this portfolio, demanding not only political nous but also the capacity to engage in sophisticated technocratic managerialism.

Security and Integrity

Liannne Dalziel was forced to resign from the immigration portfolio in February 2004 over a scandal involving the leaking of legal notes regarding the deportation of a Sri Lankan teenager (Espiner 2004). Despite this resignation, the final four years of Helen Clark's Labour Government largely saw the continuation of policies initiated under Dalziel, especially those that related to linking migration with economic development, settlement outcomes, temporary migration programmes, and a growing emphasis on security and risk management. She had laid the template for how migration policy would evolve over the final years of the Labour Government and beyond, with the Skilled Migrant Category (SMC) and Expression of Interest (EOI) set up to target specific skillsets and temporary migration increasingly filling in a range of labour shortages. Alongside these, the onshore transition from temporary work and study visas to the permanent residence scheme was also well established. And, by this stage, enhanced security measures in border processing and the management of irregular migration were becoming seen as normal features of the migration regime. Rather than these broad policy directions, the challenge for Dalziel's immediate successors related much more closely to the operation of Immigration New Zealand, especially regarding integrity and risk management.

Dalziel was replaced by Paul Swain, who held the role of Minister of Immigration from February 2004 until the general election in October 2005. Swain was one of two former ministers (alongside Nathan Guy, 2011–13) who chose not to be interviewed for this research. While in the immigration portfolio, Swain was concurrently Minister of Corrections (2003–5), and he also inherited the commerce portfolio from Dalziel; this was an unusual combination that reflects the unexpected departure of Dalziel from these roles. Swain was particularly public in advancing new measures to amplify immigration and security linkages domestically, and in raising questions about the integrity of Immigration New Zealand.

By the time Swain became Minister of Immigration, a Border Security Bill was being debated in select committee that was designed to 'strengthen border control security measures against terrorism and other suspicious activities relating to cross-border crime organisations' (Parliamentary Counsel Office 2003). The Bill led to amendments to the Customs and Excise Act and the Immigration Act, intended to reduce identity fraud, such as requiring airlines and other carriers to undertake sophisticated pre-boarding checks on anyone intending to travel to New Zealand. In the early months of his tenure, Swain publicly articulated the possibility that police officers would undertake roadside checks for immigration status (Dominion Post 2004b), although this was later rolled back to a Memorandum of Understanding. The MoU between the New Zealand Police and Immigration New Zealand noted that 'Police came across illegal immigrants in the course of their day-to-day duties and inquiries', and made it possible for police 'to access an Immigration Service 24-hour helpline where significant doubt existed around an individual's immigration status' (Swain & Hawkins 2004).

The transition between Dalziel and Swain, and the period leading up to the end of the second term of the Fifth Labour Government, also coincided with a series of accusations of fraud that threatened to undermine confidence in the integrity of the government's management of migration. Within a month of becoming minister, Swain was given the Ombudsman's report (Office of the Ombudsman 2004) into the 'lying in unison' scandal, which involved accusations that Immigration New Zealand officials had misled the Ombudsman in relation to official information requests regarding the Ahmed Zaoui case discussed in Chapter 4. While the report did not assert that coordinated lying had occurred, it identified several shortcomings in departmental processes, which became the subject of significant media and parliamentary debate. A KPMG report commissioned during Dalziel's tenure was also released in 2004, which identified seventy-eight allegations of fraudulent practices between 2001 and 2003, involving forty-nine staff in Immigration New Zealand. The report provided political traction for opposition parties both publicly and in Parliament. Notably, New Zealand First leader Winston Peters (2004: 14525) asserted in Parliament that Immigration New Zealand 'has been riddled with fraud and corruption over many years', and amplified this critique of shortcomings around security in the media: 'The security of New Zealand is at stake. We must stamp out the fraud and corruption within the Immigration Service, both here and overseas, and try to find out who has slipped through border surveillance into New Zealand' (New Zealand First 2004).

The report led to several resignations as well as a series of internal changes at Immigration New Zealand, including 'a new integrity policy, improved investigation processes, increased investigation capability, and code of conduct training for all staff' (Swain 2004: 14525). These specific accusations echoed an upward trend in complaints about processes at Immigration New Zealand. In its 2005/06 annual report, the Office of the Ombudsman (2006) highlighted a 35 per cent year-on-year increase in complaints received against Immigration New Zealand (309 in the twelve months to June 2006), which raised questions about the effectiveness of decision-making and processes. In its subsequent 2006/07 annual report, the Office of the Ombudsman (2007) received a similar number of complaints (290), and noted delays in providing reasons for decisions and investigating complaints, as well as inaccuracies in documentation and factual errors in relation to ministerial direction. In conclusion, the Ombudsman asserted that because Immigration New Zealand 'stated that it did not intend to mislead the investigation, the only other conclusion that could be reached was that there had been a serious oversight, or a lack of knowledge, of relevant statutory obligations on the part of the officers who had handled the request and dealt with the investigation' (Office of the Ombudsman 2007: 16).

The public attacks on Immigration New Zealand's migration-management integrity were sustained. Media reports indicated that the agency 'appears to be struggling against fraud and corruption' as the number of immigration applications increased in the reworked immigration system (Waikato Times 2004). Security checks on applications were seen as inconsistent. On the one hand, applications that were deemed risky were kept quiet with no ability for applicants to gain information about the status of processing or the information being drawn on (Dominion Post 2005). On the other hand, media had reported high-profile cases where seemingly problematic applicants were easily granted visas, such as a former minister in Saddam Hussein's Iraqi Government who was granted residency despite his known record of human rights violations (Martin 2005). Immigration New Zealand was similarly reported to be dealing with scams associated with refugee applicants, including what were determined to be unfounded claims of asylum upon arrival in New Zealand, and asylum seekers switching passports after arrival, in order to access public support (Kiong 2005). Other challenges to the systems of Immigration New Zealand had been raised regarding the number of people unlawfully in the country, estimated at over 20,000 in 2005. This was partly blamed on issues with Pacific migration schemes, and the processing of international student visa applications following completion of study (Hutchinson 2005).

Many of these issues came to a head in the 2005 General Election campaign. The administrative failings described here led to the National Party's proposal to merge Immigration New Zealand with the Citizenship Office of the Department of Internal Affairs, creating a new 'Department of Immigration and Citizenship'. Then National Party leader Don Brash argued that 'the Immigration Service is currently a shambles, characterised by administrative delays, secrecy, bureaucratic blunders and ineffective audit and fraud investigation. The integrity of our borders and homeland security are at risk from this failing agency' (Brash 2005). Integrity and security in relation to immigration had political traction, partly because Brash and his party were able to invoke American notions of 'homeland security' and the need to protect core national values. A rejuvenated New Zealand First party similarly advocated for widespread change in the portfolio, including establishing an 'Immigration Inspectorate' to independently monitor Immigration New Zealand. Hyping anxiety about fraud, they also proposed a 'flying squad' of officers to rapidly investigate crime and fraud in immigration management (Berry 2005). While these approaches provided fodder for political attacks on the government, there was in fact no substantive distinction between the major parties in these matters, as a result of a basic international security environment that they had limited autonomy to change: New Zealand's government security apparatus was by now fully entangled in the US-led Anglosphere (Vucetic 2020).

Although the election was closely contested, the Helen Clark-led Labour Party secured a third term after gaining fifty seats (compared with National's forty-eight). To shore up its slim majority, Labour also secured support on confidence and supply from both New Zealand First (seven seats) and United Future (three seats). Although the confidence-and-supply agreement was not a full coalition, it echoed the 1996 coalition agreement with the National Party, in which New Zealand First neither sought nor secured specific commitments to change immigration policy. The only substantive commitment was that the Labour Government would carry out a 'a full review of immigration legislation and administrative practices within the immigration service, to ensure the system meets the needs of New Zealand in the twenty-first century and has appropriate mechanisms for ensuring the system is not susceptible to fraud or other abuse' (New Zealand Labour Party 2005).' Swain's successor, David Cunliffe, would take up this significant task with gusto.

Modernisation and the Culture of Immigration New Zealand

Following the 2005 election, David Cunliffe was appointed Minister of Immigration, a position he would hold for two years before the role was taken over by Clayton Cosgrove (his Associate Minister) for the final twelve months of the Fifth Labour Government. Cunliffe and Cosgrove pursued a significant programme of change in the structure and systems of Immigration New Zealand. Having taken up the role, one that he described as not being previously familiar with, Cunliffe found Immigration New Zealand to be in disarray:

> It was a department of very uneven management practice and its IT backbone was broken. Its processing systems were very mixed, and it screamed risk. It was a very substantial management challenge. . . . It was a) a busted processing system; with b) a poor customer focus; c) a relatively undifferentiated approach to who got taken; and d) made very little difference to the broader economic output.

Prior to entering politics, Cunliffe had worked for a number of years as a management consultant with global firm Boston Consulting Group, and his education included a Master of Public Administration from Harvard University. Cunliffe explicitly brought this managerial perspective and thinking to the role:

> My very first take on this as a management consultant out of Boston Consulting was, crikey, this doesn't work. This boat is leaking, we have to plug the leaks before we – I don't mean that in a security

sense but in an operational sense – before we sail it anywhere. . . .
I had to start, I felt, with the basics which are de-risk the system,
build the system so it can deliver the capabilities to deliver the
policy. Then work with colleagues to edge the policy towards a more
value-based rather than volume-based set of outcomes.

The technocratic management impulses expressed here were evident in Cunliffe's approach. Initially, the focus was on addressing policy criteria that were creating backlogs and other problems. Cunliffe immediately instigated a review of the SMC selection process, because the low points threshold of one hundred was creating an excess of selected EOIs, with around 9500 unselected applicants in the pool in December 2005 (Bedford & Spoonley 2014: 899). This had downstream effects on processing and complaints about Immigration New Zealand decision-making. The government added another 3000 places to the SMC over the next three years, taking the potential total up to nearly 30,000. It also introduced a two-tier system to the SMC, which pooled applicants meeting the one-hundred-points minimum for up to six months, with selections made on a fortnightly basis. Those with 140 points or above were automatically selected, while those below 140 were ranked on their points and whether they had a job offer. Those without job offers could be selected in each draw, but only if places had not been taken up by those with a job offer (Bedford et al. 2010: 12; Bedford & Spoonley 2014: 899). Under previous work-to-residence schemes, work visa recipients had two years to find permanent skilled positions in New Zealand, but this was reduced to six months to encourage a swifter transition to residency (Bedford et al. 2010: 12). Changes to the investor category in 2005 also introduced an EOI procedure like that in use for skilled work. In early 2007, a review of family policies recommended that family sponsorship applications should be assessed with an additional objective of contributing to 'New Zealand's economic transformation and social development' (Cunliffe 2007b: 6). This marked an important change, which would be taken up in further regulatory shifts by Cunliffe's successors, Jonathan Coleman (2008–13) and Michael Woodhouse (2014–17). This trajectory culminated in a two-tiered system in 2012 and the closure of the parent category in 2016 (Bedford & Didham 2018; Bedford & Liu 2013). Cumulatively, these shifts further sharpened the focus of Dalziel's reforms on targeting the selection of migrants with settlement potential and skills that were deemed beneficial to the economy.

Technical changes to immigration processing, criteria, and quotas paved the way for a wider comprehensive review of the migration policy framework in the final term of the Fifth Labour Government. In his early months as minister, Cunliffe had instigated a review of the 1987 Immigration Act that would eventually lead to the Immigration Act 2009 (passed by Jonathan Coleman in the successor National Government). The 2009 Act both fulfilled Labour's commitment to New Zealand First and advanced an agenda that had been underway since Labour took office in 1999. In July 2006, Cunliffe announced the Immigration Change Programme, which entailed the 'most radical review of our immigration policy in 20 years' (Cunliffe 2006b). In a speech outlining the programme, Cunliffe painted current immigration policy as 'outdated', and outlined four main drivers for change: circulation; competition for skills, talent, and labour; diversity; and heightened risk and pressure on the border.

An important feature of the Immigration Change Programme was addressing what was seen as significant shortcomings in the technology used by Immigration New Zealand. For Cunliffe, the key issue was that 'as a business system it was broken'. The language of business is notable here, echoing not only Cunliffe's own background but a broader trend of integrating management practices from the private sector into public-sector operations in New Zealand (Chapman & Duncan 2007; Yui & Gregory 2018). This was a question of modernisation to address the core challenge of risk management, as Cunliffe explained:

> Much of its information store about migrants was retained on Excel databases. That will cause a smile because you can imagine how many visas it processed. There was no global wide, secure wide area network that would allow every office and every embassy to be able to check an application in real time against the collective store of knowledge. It was unacceptably risky from a security perspective, and it also made it very difficult for New Zealand to achieve its economic and cultural aims just because there was such a random process.

The New Zealand Immigration Programme was renamed the New Zealand Residence Programme in 2006 (Cunliffe 2006b). Cunliffe also announced that a new IT system would be put in place to improve the experience for users of the service as well as 'manage risk assessment, and facilitate centralised key decision-making' (Cunliffe 2006a). This was an example of the increasing technologically integrated management of migration that is now a taken-for-granted feature of the migration system. A substantial element of this was the introduction of CusMod, which merged systems in Immigration with those in Customs. For Cunliffe, this was about establishing a 'modern border interface' that could achieve 'security, global reach, ubiquity, [and] real time processing' (Cunliffe interview).

Other initiatives included the standardisation of electronic transactions (which also aimed to eliminate potential fraud within the system), and the establishment of a new centralised student visa processing centre in Palmerston North. Cunliffe saw these changes in system architecture and operational procedure as urgent priorities, and left internal processes and culture change to the senior management of Immigration New Zealand and his successor Clayton Cosgrove.

Cosgrove took over the role of Minister of Immigration in November 2007 when Cunliffe was made Minister of Health and promoted to the Labour Party's front bench. Having served as Associate Minister of Immigration under Cunliffe, Cosgrove also already had significant concerns about the operational dimensions of Immigration New Zealand. He recalled an encounter in 2005 with Mary-Anne Thompson (then Deputy Secretary of the Department of Labour, in charge of Immigration New Zealand):

> I remember being briefed when I became Associate Minister, there was David Cunliffe and myself, we met with Mary-Anne Thompson. I remember this vividly. I just listened to the initial brief and I said to her at one point, 'So, tell me, when we go down to the Chamber to answer parliamentary questions, what is the level of accuracy that we should expect coming out of the department in terms of information?' She looked rather nonchalantly at both of us – I don't think David picked it up until I talked to him afterwards – and said, 'Something like 80%.' I said to David afterwards, 'Do you realise 20% of the time we are going to be boxing blind?'

While Cosgrove continued with the more technical aspects of the Immigration Change Programme initiated by Cunliffe, he also faced challenges associated with the integrity of Immigration New Zealand and articulated a view that the culture of the agency needed to change. As Associate Minister, he described being responsible for hundreds of direct-intervention requests, many of which were being brought for ministerial determination 'where the bureaucracy deemed it too tough and too hot to make a decision themselves'. Moving into the role of full Minister of Immigration, Cosgrove pursued a focus on accountability in the work of the bureaucracy:

> I said to the officials, 'Listen, we're going to make decisions and we're going to do it appropriately. If it is the case that we've made decisions and we've done it appropriately with proper process, considered all the information and it gains media traction because

it's controversial, then I will stand up and defend it. I will defend you and I will defend the department because we've acted appropriately, if it is the right decision and we've observed the proper process. If we've stuffed it up, I will go and take the hit as the minister, because that's what you do. Then the 'bullet' that hit me when I get back to the office will start ricocheting off my skull looking for targets because there will be accountability for decision-making. We are actually going to stand on our own feet as a department. We're not going to be susceptible to media or other pressure. We're going to do our job properly. Okay, we may get it wrong, and that's always correctable. It doesn't mean we're going to be inflexible but we're actually going to do it properly. We're going to be humanitarians but we're going to do it properly.'

In his interview, Cosgrove described Immigration New Zealand as being 'under siege' when he took over, and there was growing public concern about its efficacy and the security of the border. Early in Cosgrove's tenure as minister, an independent investigation was launched into the irregular issuing of visas to applicants from Kiribati, who it became clear were relatives of Immigration New Zealand head Mary-Anne Thompson (Young 2008). The investigation found that the applications were received outside the normal timeframe and approved despite the quota for Kiribati being full. A subsequent inquiry uncovered that Thompson had lied about having a PhD on several occasions in her public service career, including in gaining her role as Deputy Secretary for Immigration (Young 2008). At the same time, it was claimed that up to a third of Immigration New Zealand's Pacific Division were committing serious offences (Trevett 2008), while questions were raised about the deportation of Iranian Christians despite well-founded claims about their likely persecution (Donnell 2008). These ongoing concerns about integrity and decision-making at Immigration New Zealand raised questions for Cosgrove about accountability and public confidence. He articulated a view that to be 'humanitarian' in relation to immigration, the wider public needed confidence in the systems and practices of officials:

My philosophy in immigration, because at the time the department was under siege, was – to be blunt with you, and I said this publicly – the public want to know we're secure at the border. The truth is if we're keeping bad guys out and booting the bad guys out and people know that, then the generosity of the Kiwi spirit is that when we need to do the humanitarian stuff or let folks in because there's a good reason, most people will say 'yep, that's okay'. They want to know the border is secure, the bad guys are kept out, the bad guys are being booted out. My objective was to raise the public confidence level that would allow me then to do the right thing on the other side. To say to people, come on, you know this family does need to be allowed into New Zealand, it might hit the headlines, they may be refugees, if they stay in their own country they may be killed. What Helen Clark did with the Tampa kids was high risk, high political risk and it showed a ton of guts. It was the right decision to make. It's a sense of fairness. If Kiwis believe you're doing the right thing, they'll give you plenty of rope.

In May 2008, Cosgrove and Prime Minister Helen Clark officially requested that the Office of the Auditor-General undertake an inquiry into Immigration New Zealand to address the wide-ranging issues that had emerged in the public sphere. The inquiry, which was not released until May 2009 when a new government and minister were in office, 'did not find widespread integrity and probity issues' but did identify systems, processes, and organisational issues that were in need of remedy: Immigration New Zealand was overly focused on quantity over quality in visa decision-making; the workplace culture was unsafe for raising concerns about departmental processes; a silo culture existed between units and branches that was compounded by poor management practices; and there were specific concerns about resourcing, capability, and subsequent problems in the Pacific Division (Auditor-General 2009). Specific focus was also given to the position and practices of Mary-Anne Thompson, and questions were raised as to whether ministers or the State Services Commission (SSC) had fulfilled their duty. The Auditor-General agreed with an earlier SSC finding about Thompson's actions and clarified that the SSC and ministers across this period (Swain, Cunliffe, and Cosgrove) had all acted appropriately.

In the final year of their term, Cunliffe and then Cosgrove were putting a Bill in place to establish a new Immigration Act, based on the findings of the review initiated in 2006 and the changes introduced with the Immigration Change Programme. The Bill was introduced to Parliament in August 2007, marking two decades since the Fourth Labour Government had passed the Immigration Act 1987. In its first reading, Cunliffe (2007b: 11231) was clear that this new legislation was about formalising a transformation of immigration policy towards a greater emphasis on managing the dual challenges of economic value and security:

Over the last 20 years the world has changed. There are greater flows of people around the world. There is greater global competition for skills, talent, and labour, and, of course, there are heightened risks and pressures on the border. Those changes are real. They are significant. New Zealand needs to recognise the realities of the global labour market and the risks in the modern security environment. It is not a matter of either/or. We need to be better at managing both. That is why we need to adapt the immigration system to ensure the best outcomes for the country.

The new Bill centred on three pillars that reaffirmed the by-then-dominant framing of migration as a tool for economic development, emphasising competition between countries for talented migrants, including students, and the need to provide a service that attracts such migrants while also underscoring border security to respond to irregular migration and international terrorism. The Bill included a focus on immigration's contribution to 'the goals of economic transformation, families, and building national identity' as well as a focus on the systems that sought nothing less than 'to transform the business of immigration from end to end' (Cunliffe 2007b: 11231). The Bill introduced new technological requirements (such as the use of biometrics, and requirements for fingerprints and iris scans for non-citizens), as well as delegation of discretionary decision-making to bureaucrats, alterations to refugee status and asylum claims, and the ability to use classified information (Bedford et al. 2010: 46).

While the Bill was pitched as a comprehensive overhaul that reflected the outcomes of the Immigration Change Programme, in many respects it represented an effort to legislatively formalise trends that had been in development since at least Dalziel's time in office. The shift reflected the fact that immigration had become a much more complex and vexed portfolio than it had been even just a decade earlier, let alone in the halcyon days of the liberalising 1987 Immigration Act and the economic multiculturalism of the late 1980s and early 1990s. The shift towards migration management, advanced significantly by Lianne Dalziel, had led to a much greater variety of immigration pathways and associated procedures and regulations. In turn, the amplified emphasis on security and risk in migration placed a media, political, and public spotlight on the operation of immigration and, as a result, the performance of the Minister of Immigration. Technocratic managerialism and a sustained focus on accountability constitute indicative responses to such complexity. They also aligned with the kinds of public managerialism that had become a key feature of the governing of New Zealand in the first decade of the twenty-first century (Chapman & Duncan 2007; Yui & Gregory 2018).

Migration, Development, and Circular Mobility in the Pacific

A landmark development during the third term of the Fifth Labour Government was the introduction of the Recognised Seasonal Employer scheme, which facilitated the 'circular' labour mobility of people from Pacific countries to work in New Zealand horticulture and viticulture. Since the era of the Dawn Raids and the 1982 foreclosure of Western Samoan citizenship rights (discussed in Chapters 1 and 2), Pacific migration had held a marginal position in New Zealand's immigration system. The Samoan Quota Scheme and, since 2002, the Pacific Access Category, provided the primary pathways to Pacific immigration. New Zealand's orientation towards the Pacific had been shaped by 'broad objectives in the region of encouraging economic development, regional integration and stability' (Ramasamy et al. 2008: 171), which had taken shape through foreign aid initiatives, diplomacy, and sometimes security interventions alongside Australia (Bryant-Tokalau & Frazer 2006). By the mid-2000s, this Pacific development agenda came to intersect with ideas that had emerged internationally around the relationship between migration and development. Since the mid-1990s, a new 'optimistic school of thought' on migration was in ascendency in international dialogue and scholarship, asserting that migration can bring shared benefits for all parties involved if the settings are appropriately configured (Gamlen 2010a). What has been known as the 'triple-win' or 'win-win-win' formulation – 'bringing benefits to destination countries, origin countries and migrant workers themselves' – captured the imagination of international organisations in a way that became a 'mantra' (Kapur 2003; Wickramasekara 2011). New Zealand participated in these developments, particularly via the High-Level Dialogue on Migration and Development in the UN General Assembly. Then-UN Secretary-General Kofi Annan had been advocating for the inclusion of migration on the UN agenda, seeing it as a blind spot for international affairs (Annan 2006). Aiming for a bottom-up global governance regime, Annan worked the dialogue through the UN Development Agenda, an area that had high consensus and few conflicts – in contrast to international security, for example (Gamlen 2019).

One of the most prominent responses to the question of migration and development was the proposition for 'circular migration', wherein labour migrants from developing countries shuttled back and forth between origin and destination countries according to shifts in labour-market demand (Vertovec 2006). It was claimed that this would benefit the migrants themselves by increasing their incomes massively. But it would also benefit destination countries by providing a flexible labour source for spikes in seasonal demand, while minimising long-term settlement and its purported problems of integration into the local labour market and community: workers would be present when employers and governments desired and then disposed of when they were not. Crucially, this approach was claimed to benefit origin countries as well, by relieving unemployment and providing remittances and potential for investment (Basok 2003). Critics called this the 'resurrection of guestworker schemes', which had been famously problematic in post-war Europe and North America (Castles 2006). But these concerns were dismissed in a new surge of optimism about migration for development, with circular migration as the leading case study (Gamlen 2010a; 2014d).

While New Zealand did not have experience with institutionalised guestworker programmes, these had been a key feature of European and North American immigration policy in the post-World War II period (Castles 1986; Wong 1984). A primary governmental concern within earlier programmes had been the issue of return, wherein people granted temporary rights to live and work had eventually either overstayed the length of their visa or had applied for long-term residence rights, often leading to subsequent family migration. The Bracero Programme in the US (Massey & Liang 1989) and the German guestworker programmes (Chin 2007) were indicative cases where large permanent migrant populations had developed after temporary labour entry. Because of the unplanned nature of this settlement, these populations had become excluded, leading to complex social problems such as poverty, racism, housing, and crime concentrated in 'ethnic enclaves' within major cities. While not formalised in the same way, the New Zealand Government's enticement of Pacific people to migrate for work in the 1950s–70s had generated similar unintended consequences. From a migration management perspective, then, the challenge for 'circular migration' programmes was to preclude any kind of inclusion and long-term settlement through robust 'recruitment policies and procedures, enforcement of employment and housing-related minimum standards, and the size of the programme' (Basok 2000: 215). Participants in circular migration programmes then needed to be constructed as good workers, who were dependent on employers, committed to returning (Binford 2009), and content with 'social quarantining' (Horgan & Liinamaa 2017) to limit their interaction with wider society.

Domestically, circular migration offered a response to the increasing labour demands New Zealand was facing in the horticulture and viticulture industries by the mid-2000s because of a prolonged period of economic growth (Ramasamy et al. 2008: 173). While many of these roles were taken up by people on student visas or working holiday schemes, the latter could not cover all demand. Another perceived problem was that employers had limited control over workers. Reports suggested that a consequence of such shortages was an estimated 20,000 people on visitor visas being illegally employed in these industries (Bedford & Spoonley 2014). Moreover, employers complained of the high staff turnover, which made it difficult to train workers effectively and led to varying quality in work undertaken (Ramasamy et al. 2008: 174). As a response, the government introduced the Seasonal Work Permit pilot in 2006, which eventually became the Recognised Seasonal Employer (RSE) scheme from 2007. The scheme allowed approved employers in the horticulture and viticulture industries to recruit overseas workers, primarily from the Pacific, on short-term visas to fill vacancies that could not be filled by New Zealand workers. Cunliffe, who was immigration minister at the time that the RSE was introduced, described the scheme in exactly the optimistic lexicon that was internationally in ascendency at the time:

> There are several areas where it is traditionally very difficult for New Zealand to recruit enough domestic labour to fill the labour demand requirements. One is the fishing industry, another is seasonal horticulture and viticulture. A third is the aged care sector and the health sector. It is reasonable to try, in my view, to find win/wins in those situations. In respect of the RSE scheme, possibly coloured by the fact that I'd run an aid programme while I was working at Foreign Affairs and have a deep and abiding affection for the South Pacific, it wasn't lost on me that the RSE scheme became the second single largest source of foreign exchange for Vanuatu, for example. Much bigger than New Zealand's aid programme, so it was genuine win/win.

As a policy development, the RSE was unique in the migration sphere as it involved the collaboration of three key governmental agencies: the Department of Labour, the Ministry of Social Development, and the overseas aid programme, NZAID, overseen by the Ministry of Foreign Affairs and Trade (Ramasamy et al. 2008: 177). The collaboration of these agencies was deemed essential to ensure that employers were accredited and monitored, recipients were adequately prepared and aware of the working conditions prior to departure, and the development outcomes of the scheme for Pacific nations were assessed (Ramasamy et al. 2008: 177–78). For Cunliffe, the scheme hinged on good management and accountability:

I do recall working from first principles with the RSE scheme to think about how to get the best balance between the needs of some industries in New Zealand for seasonal labour peaks and the need for it to be humane, sustainable, and good for the workers and their communities. That led us to the emphasis on number one, protect the New Zealand labour force first; number two, have high standards of pastoral care; number three, have long-standing relationships between employers and source villages, and manage quality in that way through accountability.

The introduction of the RSE scheme also speaks to other channels for the development of migration policy (Gamlen 2014d). The value of migrant remittances was being rethought internationally as part of the new optimism around migration and development, and New Zealand economist David McKenzie was involved in World Bank work in this area while also undertaking research with John Gibson at the University of Waikato on migration and remittances in the Pacific region (McKenzie et al. 2006; Gibson 2006). The empirical evidence they generated would support the triple-win theory, and frame countries like Tonga as exemplary of the potential benefits of circular migration. Geographer Richard Bedford, whom we have quoted extensively in this book, was also crucial to the establishment of the RSE scheme. He had been a contributor to dialogue on these issues in Europe, at the World Bank, and at the UN migration and development discussions, and he made a strong argument for New Zealand to ride the wave of enthusiasm he had encountered in these forums, by setting up a seasonal scheme. Bedford was strongly networked and influential with government officials in the region, with a deep commitment to the benefits of New Zealand and Australia's increased openness to Pacific migration, a lifelong research interest of his (Peace 2015). Bedford's perspectives on Pacific migration and population were captured in an influential 2012 report with Australian geographer Graeme Hugo, highlighting the region's primary population growth in Melanesia, which lacked emigration channels, leading to potential risks from rising unemployment and unrest (Bedford & Hugo 2012). They similarly noted the increasing threats from environmental change and its interaction with rapid unregulated development, suggesting that Pacific countries would also need increasing emigration options in the coming decades. Although his views on the subsequent development of the scheme are more mixed, Bedford at that time saw the Recognised Seasonal Employer scheme as a partial solution to all these problems.

It was partly through the advocacy of this community of influential New Zealand migration researchers that the RSE scheme became seen as a global 'model' for circular migration (Lewis 2014). Supporters of the scheme described it as a way to 'square the policy circle around inter-national migration' (McKenzie et al. 2008: 205), because of its potential to simultaneously 'relieve labour shortages in developed countries and aid development in sending countries' (Gibson et al. 2008: 187). In the case of New Zealand, the RSE scheme initially allowed for up to 5000 workers per season but increased year on year, and by 2019, the number stood at 14,400. It was initially aimed primarily at Pacific Island Forum member nations (Lee 2009: 10), with the aim of at least 50 per cent of places for forum nations in the first five years (Ramasamy et al. 2008: 180). Temporary migration from the Pacific would thus help fill shortages in unskilled labour but would also, as one economist at the World Bank argued, expand 'employment opportunities by allowing access to labour-starved regional labour markets', which was 'considered one of the surest ways to build economic resilience and stability in the Pacific' (Luthria 2008: 166).

As a circular migration scheme, the RSE scheme sought to achieve its claimed triple wins without the risk that migrants would remain after their seasonal contract concluded. Workers therefore had to be highly managed by employers and intermediaries, and the terms of the RSE scheme needed to preclude workers applying for any other visa under any circumstances. To avoid the perceived problem of unintended family reunification that had plagued post-war European guestworker schemes, the RSE scheme also denied entry for any accompanying family members (Bailey 2009). The RSE thus became New Zealand's harshest labour migration regime: it was set up to provide very limited rights, and to sit in stark contrast to the open rights accorded to working holiday visa holders, primarily from Europe and North America, many of whom worked in the same horticultural and viticultural roles. Other criticisms of the scheme have highlighted a 'lack of engagement with unions, the community sector and Pacific diaspora communities', as well as raising concerns about substandard social and pastoral care of workers, especially in terms of housing (Maclellan 2008: 2–4). Furthermore, the scheme created the potential for exploitation of temporary workers because of its restrictions on workers' rights, its articulation of social networks and intermediaries that governed worker activities, and its effect of isolating workers in employer-provided accommodation in rural areas (Collins 2017; Collins & Stringer 2019; Stringer 2016; Stringer & Michailova 2019a).

The RSE was indicative of the zeitgeist of the late 2000s: that migration could be managed in relation to controlling the arrival and con-ditions of temporary migrants; that such controls minimised the risks of irregular migration; and that effective management demanded constant oversight and assessment of processes and outcomes. Alongside Dalziel's earlier pivot to temporary migration, and Cunliffe and Cosgrove's instigation of modernisation in the immigration system, the RSE was – and at the time of writing remains – one of the most significant legacies of immigration policy from the Fifth Labour Government. Over the coming two decades, the RSE scheme would spawn numerous copycat initiatives elsewhere in the world, and would itself survive and indeed flourish through the global economic-development agenda of the new John Key-led National Government.

'New Zealand IS Open for Business'

We must create an environment that sends the message loud and clear: New Zealand IS open for business.

— Maiden speech to the New Zealand Parliament, 29 August 2002
John Key, Prime Minister, 2008–16

The National Party swept to power in the 2008 General Election with a campaign centred on economic transformation in the aftermath of the Global Financial Crisis (GFC). The popularity of the three-term Helen Clark-led Labour Government had been in decline well before the election, especially following the rise of future Prime Minister John Key to the National Party leadership in 2006 (Chen n.d.). Labour and Clark had also faced increasing conservative electoral backlashes in relation to a range of progressive social policies, and Clark herself had become a sustained target of sexism and ageism (Ross & Comrie 2012). The domestic political challenges facing the Labour Government had also been compounded by the GFC, which had led to a recession in New Zealand and an increasing number of job losses before the 2008 election campaign began.

The election results saw the National Party secure 44.93 per cent of votes (fifty-eight seats) to the Labour Party's 33.99 per cent (forty-three seats), from which they were easily able to govern through confidence-and-supply agreements with the Māori Party (five seats), the ACT party (five seats), and the United Future party (one seat). New Zealand First and Winston Peters gained 4.07 per cent of the vote but did not return to Parliament, having neither reached the 5 per cent threshold nor won any electoral seats. This failure was at least partly related to controversy surrounding a donation by expatriate billionaire Owen G. Glenn to New Zealand First, and to John Key's assertion early in the campaign that Peters would not be a minister in a National-led government.

During the election campaign, there were serious concerns about operational matters at Immigration New Zealand that were headline news, but the focus of immigration policy debate didn't reveal substantive differences between the major parties. National's immigration policy emphasised *emigration* in highlighting the departure of more than 80,000 people in the year to June 2008, and proposed again the integration of immigration and citizenship functions to facilitate the return of New Zealand expatriates. An evocative image was published of John Key, a returned expat himself, standing in an empty Westpac Stadium in Wellington bemoaning that 'the equivalent of this entire stadium and more leaves every year' (Miller 2015). This campaign tactic echoed similar efforts early in Helen Clark's term, when opponents of the Labour Government had stirred up a moral panic about 'the brain drain', including by taking out a full-page national newspaper advertisement listing the names of people who had supposedly emigrated because of the Labour Government's policies (Gamlen 2005; 2013a). During the 2008 election campaign, National's immigration spokesperson Lockwood Smith described a policy agenda – including tax, regulatory, and infrastructure reforms – intended to make 'returning home an attractive prospect for highly skilled expat Kiwis' (Eaton 2008). National also proposed new visa categories, a 'silver fern visa' to fast-track the entry of qualified applicants to look for work, and a retirement visa for wealthy people to live in New Zealand. Cosgrove countered by describing these policies as 'chequebook immigration' and accusing National of preparing too little detail to deal with the complex issues in the portfolio. In reality, there was little substantive difference between the two parties on immigration in 2008, and National's proposals were very much a continuation of the direction established under Labour governments since 1999 (Bedford et al. 2010). Indeed, it was not long before future Labour leader David Shearer himself was replicating Key's stunt of being photographed in an empty stadium (Gamlen 2014b).

A key feature of the 2008 election was the growing success of the Māori Party (now Te Pāti Māori), which secured 2.4 per cent but won five of the Māori electorate seats, thereby displacing Labour from one of its key constituencies. The Māori Party had been formed in 2004 when Tariana Turia resigned from the Labour Party in protest against the Foreshore and Seabed Act 2004, which had overturned a Court of Appeal ruling indicating the potential for Treaty claims in relation to ownership of New Zealand's foreshore and seabed (Bargh 2006). The Māori Party had gained four seats in 2005, with Turia joined by prominent academic and kapa haka (performing arts) exponent Pita Sharples, as well as Hone Harawira and Te Ururoa Flavell. In the lead-up to the 2008 election, Turia articulated several important positions on immigration policy: firstly, that Te Tiriti o Waitangi needed to be centred in immigration policy discussions (Turia 2007). She highlighted how Māori assertions about immigration had been consistently ignored (Turia 2007), and proposed amendments to the Immigration Act that would require cultural education programmes, including in relation to Te Tiriti o Waitangi, along with basic training in tikanga (Māori protocol) and te reo (Māori language), for all immigration advisors (Turia 2008). After the election in 2008, the Māori Party entered into a confidence-and-supply agreement that would help the National Party to govern without depending on the far-right ACT party. The agreement included a commitment to review the Foreshore and Seabed Act, which was repealed in 2011, but the rest of the agreement was heavily geared towards establishing a relationship between the two parties and negotiating differences. The Māori Party would provide support for National-led governments right through to 2017.

Some comments on John Key and his symbolism for the National-led governments of 2008–17 are worth including at this juncture. Key was a former currency trader for investment firm Merrill Lynch and came to politics in 2002 with an unapologetic focus on economic development and the promotion of business, captured evocatively in his maiden speech claim that the task of government was to make sure that 'New Zealand IS open for business'. National's campaign was partially inspired by the success that same year of Barack Obama, whose lofty and non-specific slogans promised 'hope' and 'change'. Similarly, National's campaign in 2008 was framed around a nondescript invitation to 'Choose a Better Future', and emphasised the need for a refresh in government and the development of an aspirational direction. Light on policy detail, National's campaign in 2008 (and 2011 and 2014) promoted Key's rags-to-riches story, his claims to global economic knowledge, and his ability to network, socialise, and have influence with global luminaries – from CEOs of the largest corporations to the President of the US, Barack Obama. 'Brand Key' indexed a new embrace of neoliberal triumphalism, which for Devadas and Nicholls (2012; see also Jones 2016; Tie 2016) centred the organisation of social relations in a way that 'regularises the hegemony of neoliberal capitalism' and places an unquestionable emphasis on property rights, free markets, and free trade. As we shall see in the remainder of this chapter, but especially in the next chapter, this coalescence of achieving globalising economic aspirations through the reworking of social relations and international networks would be enormously consequential for New Zealand's approach to immigration policy in the second decade of the twenty-first century.

Jonathan Coleman was appointed Minister of Immigration in the first term of the John Key-led National Government.[16] He described being 'really desperate to get into Cabinet full stop' because, somewhat similarly to John Key, he did not see himself as a career politician but rather was focused on having impact in the short term. A trained medical doctor, Coleman had also undertaken a Master of Business Administration at the London Business School. He had spent time working in Australia, the UK, and the US and had been a consultant on health issues for the multinational professional services consultancy PriceWaterhouseCoopers. Like Cunliffe and Cosgrove before him, then, Coleman brought an orientation towards business practice and administration to the immigration portfolio. And in many respects, he continued their legacy of modernising Immigration New Zealand, amplifying the emphasis on economic transformation through immigration, and addressing risk and security through technocentric managerialism.

By the time the National Party was in power and Coleman was overseeing the immigration portfolio, the new immigration Bill had already been through its first reading and select committee. In May 2009, before the third reading of the Bill, the aforementioned Auditor-General's review was released, which identified significant issues in Immigration New Zealand. Coleman took the report as a sign that the previous government had left a mess in immigration that needed a 'total overhaul of processes and a change in culture' (Coleman 2009). While criticising the previous government's stewardship, Coleman echoed sentiments that were surprisingly like those of Cunliffe and Cosgrove:

> Looking back, it felt very dysfunctional and if you recall, Immigration was within the Department of Labour. . . . [The officials] really struggled to present a clear picture up front of the key elements of the system and how it worked and what was going on. It was like you were trying to view this huge system, but you were constantly looking down the narrow shaft of a telescope. It took probably nine months to really understand how this ecosystem all fitted together.

Carrying on the themes introduced by Cunliffe and Cosgrove, Coleman described in his interview a focus on 'getting your own patch sorted out'

16   While former Associate Minister of Immigration Lockwood Smith had been the National Party's immigration spokesperson while in opposition, his position had become untenable after making racist remarks: that 'some of the Asian workers have been more productive . . . because their hands are smaller' and that employers are 'having to teach [Pacific workers] things like how to use a toilet or shower' (*Otago Daily Times*, 22 October 2008).

before 'driving down policy detail': 'it starts with closer to home, with actually trying to work out who you've got there working for you, how good they are and whether they're going to be the right people for the future'. Coleman described working with Nigel Bickle, a seasoned public service administrator who had held public management and executive positions since the late 1990s, to advance a more streamlined and rigorous approach to the department:

> He really put some rigour into it. He made things a lot simpler and we really started to get some traction there. But it did feel a bit of a shambles initially. A really disjointed network. Things happened very slowly, very paper based.

Having continued the process of modernising Immigration New Zealand, Coleman prioritised linking immigration more clearly into the government's economic-development agenda. In the early days of his tenure, Coleman confirmed that he would keep in place the SMC selection process that had been established under Labour and would maintain the average number of accepted EOIs over the following six months (Bedford et al. 2010: 16). But in July 2009, several occupations were removed from the skills shortage list, which led to a reduction in applications through the SMC. However, the same target of residence approvals was maintained at between 45,000 and 50,000, and there was a much higher proportion (78 per cent) of residence approvals for applicants with job offers, which meant that these migrants were much more likely to take up residence (Bedford et al. 2010: 17–18). In a speech in 2009, Coleman argued that attracting skilled migrants was essential so that New Zealand would 'remain competitive in the international market'. This emphasis, and several other policy changes discussed below, reflected a strategic focus on using immigration to 'drive the economy':

> It was all about recovering from the GFC and starting to grow the New Zealand economy again, making sure that government resources were focused productively in areas that would produce outcomes for New Zealand. Now, I'm talking about that across all portfolios. . . . For Immigration, it became about how can we actually use immigration to help drive the economy, to make sure we've got this flow of skills that we need. How can we actually help to bring capital into the country and also beyond are we making sure that people that did come to New Zealand are able to make a contribution to the economy.

This integration of immigration policy with other areas of government had some resonance with the approach taken under the preceding Labour Government, but it also clearly reflected a sharper focus on linking immigration explicitly into economic development. The attractiveness of New Zealand in immigration terms was articulated as part of a renewed emphasis on 'New Zealand Incorporated' (NZ Inc) in the Key-led National Government (Coleman 2009). NZ Inc is a term that signals an integrated approach to promoting New Zealand overseas and linking government and industry in a way that supports business growth and internationalisation (Hamilton-Hart 2021).[17] It had emerged in policy talk in the late 1980s and early 1990s and was also taken up by governments in the 1990s and 2000s. NZ Inc gained new life under the Key-led National Government in a concerted focus on export growth, especially in primary industries that scaled up trade and export-oriented activity substantially in the 2010s.

In immigration policy, this approach was apparent in the introduction of new visas such as the 'Silver Fern Visa', introduced in April 2010, which granted visas to those between the ages of twenty and thirty-five with high-ranking qualifications and skills, and provided a fast track to residence rights for those who gained permanent employment. Coleman further refined the changes to the family stream that Cunliffe had initiated in 2007, shifting the parent policy away from settlement outcomes and towards a focus on family sponsorship as one of the ways to attract and retain skilled migrants. New instructions for Immigration New Zealand were that parent applications should be streamlined for 'high-contributing sponsors' (Bedford & Liu 2013: 31). A new marketing initiative was announced for the SMC, which specifically targeted online environments through a 'combination of search engine optimisation techniques and online advertising to target skilled migrants in the United States and the UK' (Coleman 2009). These changes also intersected with an intensifying focus on tourism under the new government. This new tourism focus linked short-term arrivals with New Zealand's image and its relationship with key economic partners, especially in Asia. In his role as Associate Minister of Tourism, Coleman emphasised the economic potential of tourism, noting in 2011 that the Chinese tourist market alone was adding $365 million to the economy annually (Coleman 2011). Several Visa Acceptance Centres were established in the first term of the new government, which enabled the administration of visas to take place offshore for tourists,

---

17   NZ Inc was shaped around a desire to emulate the cooperative, global-facing approaches of Japan, Singapore, and South Korea and to stitch together a shared front for New Zealand in the aftermath of the stripped-back post-Rogernomics economy (Hamilton-Hart 2021).

international students, workers, and other migrants. Offices were set up in Beijing, Shanghai, Hong Kong, Mumbai, Ho Chi Minh City, and Pretoria. This reorientation reflected a broader pivot being undertaken across trade, foreign affairs, and immigration that prioritised engaging with Asia, especially China, India, and the ASEAN (Association of Southeast Asian Nations) region. Coleman explained:

> We also made sure that we made the network more efficient around the world, so there was a big drive to digitalise the Immigration New Zealand operation but also to align the footprint with New Zealand's broader strategic and economic issues. Rather than having Immigration officers align with traditional embassies that we've had say in Europe, we started saying well actually, we're going to need people from China and India, that's where the skills are going to come from, that's where a lot of the capital will also come from. So, while [the Ministry of Foreign Affairs and Trade] was realigning its footprint, we were mapping the Immigration New Zealand footprint to that same matrix to make sure that we had alignment across all New Zealand's external-facing agencies.

In line with these changes in footprint, new Investor and Entrepreneur visas were introduced that eased criteria for potential investors and allowed for fast-tracking of applications. The old Investor policy had higher investment requirements – $20 million for the Global Investor category and $10 million for the Professional Investor category – and required four years of business experience to apply. The new Investor and Investor Plus categories reduced the minimum investment to $1.5 million (Investor) and $10 million (Investor Plus). While three years of business experience was required for the Investor category, no business experience was required for the Investor Plus category. The new Entrepreneur Plus category offered 'a faster path to residence for applicants who create at least 3 fulltime jobs and invest $500,000 in their business' (Brownlee & Coleman 2009). In 2010, an Immigration Retirement Package was also introduced, which targeted 'high-income' retirees, with two categories: Temporary Retirement and Parent Retirement. Under the temporary scheme, retirees were expected to invest $75,000 over two years of the visa, which could be renewed if these conditions were met. The parent category enabled retirees who were parents of New Zealand citizens or permanent residents to apply for permanent residence if they had an annual income of $60,000, invested at least $1 million in the first four years, and had another $500,000 to live on after this period.

Again, it was the links with the large economies in Asia that were at the forefront of Coleman's focus, reflecting the broader government view that immigration-based connections had potential to generate wider value for New Zealand as a whole:

> It's a matter of how can we harness immigration to the wider benefit of the country, because as a small trading nation becoming more and more insular and isolated is going to affect our interest at a whole lot of levels, whether it's foreign policy or trade. The networks that migrants have brought in terms of small business, exchange between here and India, here and China, it's been invaluable. There's a whole lot of benefits which are in the end you can quantify them, but you may not be able to quantify them immediately but they're definitely there. There's linkages that just wouldn't happen with China without the benefit of having New Zealand Chinese here.

Throughout his tenure, Coleman reiterated the importance of business migration to economic development, especially the regeneration of economic growth in the wake of the GFC. In a speech to the New Zealand and Australia Business Investment Forum in March 2010, Coleman echoed John Key's maiden speech claim that 'New Zealand is open for business' and that attracting investors was 'an important component of ensuring we continue to compete on the world stage'. He also emphasised preferential treatment for investors, as the new immigration policies had to 'ensure that business migrants are treated as the premium clients they are' (Coleman 2010).

While many of the major legislative changes brought in under the new government were grounded in the review and change programme introduced by the previous Labour Government, the changes to the SMC and business migration categories had already signalled, if not a radical overhaul, at least a shift in the focus of immigration policy towards more actively influencing economic development. The Immigration Act passed its third reading in Parliament in November 2009 and came into effect the following year, further indication of the bipartisan foundation of immigration policy change. The new Act included several system-based changes that built on reviews undertaken under Cunliffe and Cosgrove. A universal visa system was introduced with the new Act, which got rid of entry documents titled 'permit' or 'exemption'. An integrated appeal tribunal was also established, which replaced the existing four separate appeal tribunals. And, of particular importance to temporary migrants, a new 'interim' visa enabled those awaiting a decision on a visa application to remain in New Zealand while their application was being processed.

The political rhetoric around the new Immigration Act focused primarily on the issue of border security, which continued to be a prevalent theme during National's term in government. The Act confirmed the increasing use of biometrics and classified information in the immigration system, including the ability to share this information with international partners, as well as the ability of the Minister of Immigration to use classified information in cases related to security or criminal conduct. The new Act enabled Immigration New Zealand to collect photographs, fingerprints, and iris scans from any foreign national to verify their identity. By this point, biometrics had become central to international border-security procedures. As critics pointed out at the time, the 'biometric border' reshaped the very idea of a geographical border as fixed to a nation-state (Amoore 2006). Instead, the sharing of biometric information not only entrenched profiling at the heart of international border policy but also enabled various nation-state borders, especially across the Anglosphere, to become increasingly internationally connected and enforced through the sharing of information. Coleman observed:

> In the post-9/11, there's just been much more interest in migration of people, security, understanding who is coming into your country, what their background is, what their possible links and sympathies may be. It's something that's created momentum over a long period of time, and then as these various events, whether it's Afghanistan boat people phenomenon as well as opportunities through international collaboration, data tracking, whether it's come together, it's all come together to sort of support a more collective view on border security. ... There was opportunity enabled by technology but I think also in the post-Afghanistan era where all those nations were cooperating around international security issues and the effort in Afghanistan, and then this fear that illegal migration would not only produce a wave of migration that wasn't economically driven but in fact could also be a security threat, I think there was that aspect to it as well.

As we outlined at the beginning of this chapter, and as Coleman narrates above, the emphasis on border security arose initially in the context of the 'war on terror' in the immediate period after high-profile terrorist attacks in the US. By the time of the first term of the National Government, this emphasis was taking a new, more integrated turn that involved new alignments across immigration, intelligence, border security, and foreign affairs.

International dialogue about border alignment had been in process for some time before Coleman was in office. In the late 1990s, for example, the New Zealand and Australian governments explored the possibility of creating a common border for immigration and customs, but such a border contravened visa-waiver provisos in several treaties New Zealand was involved in (Bedford et al. 2000: 15). New Zealand's then–more lenient citizenship policy had, as we noted in the previous chapter, also been a concern for Australia. Lianne Dalziel indicated in her interview for this book that she had pushed changes to citizenship and passport legislation in order to try and maintain greater access for New Zealand citizens to social security in Australia. Beyond growing trans-Tasman alignment in border security, the early-to-mid-2000s saw New Zealand engaging more actively in international organisations around migration and border security, including being elected to the UNHCR Executive Committee for the first time in October 2002,[18] and joining the International Organization for Migration in 2003.[19] For Dalziel, joining these organisations was about cooperating more widely on migration: 'whether in a global sense we should be thinking a little bit more broadly about whether we collectively could trust each other's determination systems to undertake what is a massive effort worldwide' (Dalziel interview).

By the early 2010s, New Zealand was explicitly drawing immigration into international engagement with key security and intelligence partners in the Anglosphere. While a common trans-Tasman border never eventuated, in December 2009, the Smartgate system was introduced in New Zealand airports, making it possible for Australian and New Zealand citizens with e-passports to cross the border without a customs officer identity check, and facilitating much greater information-sharing (McMillan 2015). Perhaps most notably, in June 2009, New Zealand joined the Five Country Conference, now frequently known as the Migration Five, which mirrors the Five Eyes intelligence alliance of the US, the UK, Canada, Australia, and New Zealand, as discussed in the Introduction. The Migration Five received little press at the time but has become much more prominent in the decade since (Bonnett 2024; Radio New Zealand 2020a). Coleman explained the Migration Five in the context of security and immigration:

18   New Zealand was elected to the UNHCR Executive Committee (ExComm) for the first time in October 2002 (having acceded to the UNHCR Convention in 1960). The ExComm advises the High Commissioner for Refugees, reviews funds and programmes administered internationally, and approves annual budgets for the UNHCR.

19   In 2003, New Zealand joined the International Organization for Migration (IOM), at that stage an institution that represented and carried out migration management operations (including resettlement, detention, and deportation of irregular migrants) for member nation-states but was neither part of the UN system nor an NGO (the IOM became a 'Related Organization' to the UN in 2016). As Ashutosh and Mountz (2011) put it, the IOM then represented 'a novel form of neoliberal governance and is indicative of the transformations of sovereignty that extend beyond capital flows to include the management of migrant bodies'.

It springs more from the security side of things. Probably tied in with Five Eyes which, when I became a minister, no one even mentioned Five Eyes. It was the policy that no one discussed in the media at the time. It was all to do I think with illegal migration, boat people and movements from Afghanistan/Sri Lanka down through Indonesia's archipelago to this part of the world. Whether those people ended up in Canada, Australia or here . . . there was a bit of diplomatic toing and froing, but Australia's argument on these things being 'if you guys don't participate these boats would end up coming to New Zealand'. It was all sort of a bit of a political construct which had some practical outcomes in terms of sharing intelligence around the movements of illegal migrants. But also, being as a mutual security pact around movement of illegal migrants as well. But it wasn't something that a huge amount of time was spent on between immigration ministers, because immigration ministers never all met together. But it would have been something I think foreign ministers had as a diplomatic tool and something that they would have discussed more together.

Coleman's comments speak to the emergent characteristic of these arrangements at the end of the first decade of the twenty-first century. They would, as he implies, however, become much more substantial over the years that followed, as would a wider range of international dialogues and collaborations, which drove technological changes to further integrate migration into the space of border security and intelligence (Amoore 2024; Collins 2023). Coleman also gives us some insight into the position of the Minister of Immigration in these developments. Rather than the Minister of Immigration, it is the Minister of Foreign Affairs (Murray McCully during Coleman's tenure as minister) who takes the lead where relations with key intelligence partners are involved. This division of labour indicates the mid-ranking status of the Minister of Immigration. Coleman's comments also illustrate how immigration itself was becoming a much more central concern for government as a whole, whether that be in terms of economic agenda, export and trade, or foreign affairs and border security. This is a theme we take up in greater detail in the next chapter.

Conclusion

In terms of the broad direction of immigration policy, the focus on economic development, and more-targeted selection criteria, the period from 2004 to 2011 consisted of an evolution rather than a revolution.

Certainly, the change in government in 2008 brought with it a shift in rhetoric – an avowed emphasis on global aspirations and immigration as a driver rather than contributor to economic development – but the orthodoxy of migration management that had been previously established remained the political rationality and toolkit for achieving these ends. The main tenets of the Immigration Change Programme instigated by Cunliffe and Cosgrove were to all intents and purposes adopted into policy under the National Government. Likewise, the modernisation of the immigration system in this period, especially the shift from paper-based to electronic applications, represented a shared interest across the major parties in developing a modern immigration system capable of extracting economic value and managing security risks. Perhaps most notably, as in the 1980s, the introduction of the new Immigration Act 2009 was instigated by one party (Labour) and then passed into law by the other (National), although the order had now reversed from the introduction of the Immigration Act 1987. Despite attempts to score political points off each other, especially at election time, the approaches to immigration policy adopted by both National and Labour governments tended to continue the direction of change initiated by the prior government.

If anything, geopolitical developments – especially the war on terror and the Global Financial Crisis – were the main drivers of changes in migration policy in this period. The war on terror had cemented the rationality of border security at the heart of migration policy in North America, Europe, and Australia. By 2011, this had come to influence New Zealand's own border practices, immigration policy, and international engagement. The normalisation of security at the heart of border and immigration policy is highlighted by the increased use of biometrics to identify and surveil foreign nationals, and the willingness to link immigration to intelligence and international data-sharing. As a result of the sharing of biometrics with other governments, mainly through the Five Eyes alliance, the New Zealand border became implicated in, and often mirrored, border-security programmes across the Anglosphere. The 2008 Global Financial Crisis sharpened the symbiosis between immigration and economic growth in the eyes of the new National Government, but this symbiotic relationship outlasted their entry into government. The introduction of new business and entrepreneur visas and changes to the SMC, RSE, and international student visas certainly aligned with the core principles of the National Government under Key, and had been shaped in response to the global recession. These developments were, however, largely updates to policies that already existed. In short, there were many more continuities than differences between the Labour and National governments on migration policy in this period.

Amid these bipartisan orientations and policy continuities, the discussion in this chapter has revealed how the role of the Minister of Immigration took on a new character in this period. As we have outlined in previous chapters, many former Ministers of Immigration saw their core task as either doing the political work to achieve change in legislation (Malcolm, Burke, Maxwell) or working with the bureaucracy to conceive and initiate new regulatory approaches (Douglas, Birch, Dalziel), all while fending off political attacks surrounding migration (Rodger, Bradford, Delamere). Cunliffe, Cosgrove, and Coleman were faced with a different challenge – with immigration both massively expanded as a system and involving enormous complexity in operations, their shared objectives all centred on achieving technocratic management. As former business consultants with extensive international experience and either an MPA or MBA, each was very well suited to this task and epitomised the introduction of managerialism into the role of Minister of Immigration. The questions they raised were not about the why of immigration, or even necessarily what core selection criteria ought to be, but rather about *how the immigration regime operates* in a modern and efficient way capable of managing the risks that were now seen as inherent in the mobility of people.

CHAPTER 6

A New Migration Boom and the Politics of Immigration Policymaking, 2012–2020

I n the earlier chapters of this book, we traced the emergence of a new migration regime in New Zealand in the 1980s and early 1990s. This new regime was framed as a conclusion of the imperial regime dominant in the nineteenth and twentieth centuries and as advancing a new liberalised vision of immigration as multicultural nation-building. Immigration policy operated in the mould of *laissez-faire* multiculturalism by the early 1990s (Spoonley & Meares 2011), providing pathways to residence and citizenship for people with desired qualifications or financial resources to invest. Country of origin was nominally less relevant (cf. Bedford et al. 1987; Simon-Kumar 2015). Immigration in the early 1990s was also positioned rhetorically within a globalisation agenda that had extended a geopolitical pivot from the UK and Europe towards Asia and the Pacific since the 1970s. Long-term non-citizen immigration increased substantially in the 1990s alongside a diversification of immigrant origins, especially in relation to the Asian region.

By the turn of the twenty-first century, the economic and human capital bases of immigration policy were advanced by governments led by both major political parties. Even as migration was contested in the public domain, policymaking across different governments and ministers was characterised by evolutionary change rather than sharp policy shifts or reversals. Most of this tinkering took the form of regulatory changes driven by small differences of approach among ministers and – more often – expert civil servants, with occasional minor fine-tuning of the underlying legislation. The migration problematic turned in the early 2000s towards governmental questions of how to manage enlarged and diversified migration flows, especially in relation to enhancing purported economic benefits. Immigration ministers became tasked with a greater focus on overseeing the technical operation of immigration policy and regulation, the introduction and tweaking of categories, and the assessment of what were deemed to be appropriate numbers for settlement, humanitarian, family, economic, labour, and educational migrants. Amid this growing complexity, Immigration New Zealand came under scrutiny in the mid-2000s, with questions raised about its capacity to manage increased volumes and types of applications, the state of its technological apparatus, and its integrity in relation to decision-making and fraud. Added to this, immigration became entangled in security matters related to controlling border crossings, restricting irregular arrivals, and identifying potential threats and risks. Cumulatively, migration became a much higher-stakes matter for government, a long way from the reflection of ministers in the 1980s, who had asserted that it was peripheral to political agendas. To use James Hollifield's (2004) phrase, in this period migration rose from an issue of secondary importance into the realm of 'high politics', involving matters of security, diplomacy, and reasons of state.

This chapter examines the culmination of these diverse forces and transformations in the decade leading up to the Covid-19 global pandemic and its associated border closures and suspension of immigration. In the three decades since the Immigration Act 1987, the government of immigration in New Zealand has become laden with enormous complexity and interdependence on other areas of state practice. The tenures of the final three ministers covered by this book (Nathan Guy, Michael Woodhouse, and Iain Lees-Galloway) speak to this complexity and its implications for the role of Minister of Immigration.[20] As we detail in this chapter, Woodhouse and Lees-Galloway came into the role of immigration with this portfolio now centrally positioned in government agendas, especially in relation to economic development and population growth. They were also faced with the highest levels of net migration since World War II (Department of Labour 2012), along with new challenges such as migrant exploitation, a higher-pressure policy environment, and a renewed questioning of the relationship between Te Tiriti o Waitangi and immigration policy.

Prelude to the New Migration Boom

Despite aspirations towards globalisation and economic openness, the first five years (2008–12) of the John Key-led National Government coincided with substantial declines in net migration (see Figure 6.1). The emigration of New Zealand citizens continued, cumulatively reaching a net migration loss of -125,718 between July 2008 and June 2012. The net migration gain of non-citizens had also declined. When National entered government in 2008, the net migration gain of non-citizens had been 50,590, but by 2012 this figure had fallen to 28,894 – the lowest figure since the turn of the twenty-first century. The cumulative result was an overall net migration loss

---

20   Nathan Guy chose not to be interviewed for this book.

Figure 6.1. *Estimated Net Migration by Country of Citizenship, 12/16-Month Rule (Annual–June)*
(Source: Statistics New Zealand; analysis by Collins)

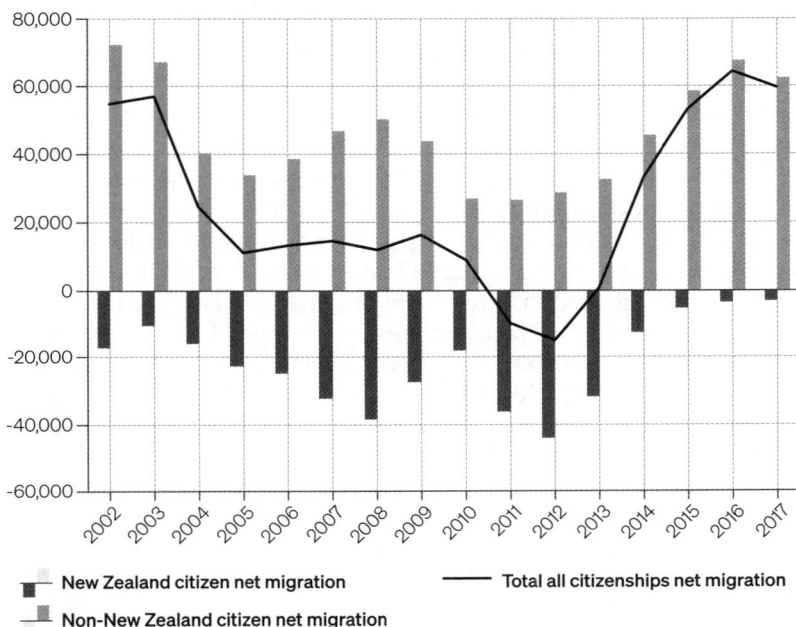

Legend:
- New Zealand citizen net migration
- Non-New Zealand citizen net migration
- Total all citizenships net migration

of -9,404 in 2011 and -14,983 in 2012. These were the largest net migration losses New Zealand had experienced since 1989, and were interrupted only by a modest net migration gain of 809 in 2013.

These substantial shifts in emigration and immigration were largely driven by broader political-economic conditions, especially the Global Financial Crisis (GFC) of 2007–8, rather than changes in immigration policy. Unemployment had increased considerably in New Zealand, from 3.8 per cent in 2008 to 6.4 per cent in 2012 (Razzak 2016). The GFC was also having a broader dampening effect on international migration (Koser 2010). New Zealand citizen emigration was disproportionately directed towards Australia and often involved people moving to undertake work in the mining boom in Western Australia and Queensland (Hamer 2012; Scott 2018). A smaller contributor to emigration was the devastating Christchurch earthquake in 2011, which led to a significant and disproportionate increase in international emigration from Christchurch, especially between February and December 2012 (Fabling et al. 2022). Emigration was more common among foreign-born residents of Christchurch and overall contributed to a loss of 21,000 people (5.6 per cent of the population) between 2010 and 2012. This set the scene for rapid migration-led demographic change in the city later that decade (Collins & Friesen 2022).

Despite these political-economic challenges, the National Party and John Key continued to ride a wave of popularity. In most opinion polls between 2008 and 2011, the party garnered more than 50 per cent support, while Labour remained below 30 per cent, with their new leader, Phil Goff, struggling to gain public traction. In some ways, the GFC and the Christchurch earthquakes bolstered National's claimed position as a stable government, especially in contrast to Labour, which appeared disorganised and characterised by internal feuds (Johansson & Levine 2012). In the 2011 election, National cruised to victory, receiving 47.31 per cent of the vote for a total of fifty-nine seats in the 121-member Parliament. Labour secured 27.48 per cent, the Green Party 11.06 per cent, New Zealand First 6.59 per cent, the Māori Party 1.43 per cent (gaining three electorate seats), ACT 1.07 per cent (gaining one electorate seat), and United Future 0.6 per cent (also gaining one electorate seat). National quickly made governing arrangements with the Māori Party, ACT, and United Future, providing several possible ways to pass legislation.

Immigration policy gained relatively little attention in the 2011 election campaign. Labour advocated for the introduction of an independent ombudsman to take the politics out of immigration, and highlighted the importance of skills attraction in a way that was barely distinct from National. Even Winston Peters hardly mentioned immigration in his successful campaign to return to Parliament (Skilling 2012). The Māori Party, who had positioned themselves as a Māori political partner for the ascendant National Party from 2008 to 2011, linked National's economic-development agenda to Te Tiriti o Waitangi, arguing that 'to compete globally it is important that new citizens share our understanding of history', which could be achieved through a 'course in the history of Te Tiriti o Waitangi as part of receiving citizenship' (Māori Party 2011). Also, in the lead-up to the election, academic Margaret Mutu advocated for the reduction of migration from White majority countries like South Africa, the UK, and the US because of their influence in sustaining the White supremacist dimensions of settler colonialism in New Zealand. Mutu's comments were quickly criticised by politicians, commentators, and officials, such as Human Rights Commissioner Joris de Bres, who described them as 'racial prejudice and racial discrimination' (Hill 2011). Kukutai and Rata (2017: 27) argue that this is part of a 'widespread vilification [of Māori perspectives on migration] by mainstream media and politicians' that has 'effectively (and, we argue, deliberately) erased Māori from national conversations on immigration'. We discuss this argument further below.

After the election, Jonathan Coleman was appointed Minister of Defence and Minister of State Services, while Nathan Guy took over the immigration portfolio. Guy was a farmer and electorate MP for the lower North Island constituency of Ōtaki; alongside the immigration role, he served as Minister for Racing and was subsequently Minister for Primary Industries. Guy continued the direction of policy under Coleman, especially the emphasis on distinguishing different streams of immigration, introducing tougher border controls, and reworking refugee resettlement.

National's 2011 manifesto focused on improving 'immigration's contribution to entrepreneurship and innovation' alongside implementing an 'Attraction and Retention Strategy' for skilled migration. More significant changes occurred to family policies: the sibling category was removed and a new parent category was introduced in July 2012, modelled on the Expression of Interest (EOI) system for the Skilled Migrant Category (SMC). Applicants were placed in one of two tiers based on their income, ability to bring settlement funds ($500,000), and whether they had sponsoring children with sufficient income to support them. Tier 1 applications had an eighteen-month wait-time by 2013, and those in Tier 2 were estimated to be in a seven-year queue (Bedford & Liu 2013). The intent to favour wealthier migrants was clear, and the change had significant impacts for New Zealand citizens and residents with Pacific connections, who were less able to sponsor family under these criteria.

The government responded to the Christchurch earthquakes through the expansion of temporary migration schemes to initiate the rebuild process. The Canterbury Employment & Skills Board (CESB) was set up to identify labour-market shortages and assess the skilled migrants that were required. In August 2011, the CESB estimated that at least 30,000 additional workers would be needed over five to ten years, and marketing campaigns were launched to attract migrants to Christchurch (Wood 2011). Guy reassured the region that Immigration New Zealand would streamline the process for bringing skilled migrants to Canterbury, especially through the new Canterbury Skills Shortage List (Guy 2012a). Construction work visa approvals increased as the rebuild got underway, from 375 in the year to June 2012 to 1338 in 2013, 2484 in 2014, and 2677 in 2015, before starting to decline. Beyond occupations in the construction sector, a further 77,160 work visas were approved for the Canterbury region between 2011 and 2019, including 19,089 to people from the Philippines, 8997 from the UK, and 8118 from India. Rebuild-related migration led to rapid growth in the overseas-born and Asian-ethnicity population of Christchurch, which respectively increased from 21 per cent to 27 per cent and 9 per cent to 15 per cent between the 2013 and 2018 censuses (Collins & Friesen 2022).

In relation to the securitised focus on irregular migration, the government introduced legislation in 2012 that mirrored elements of Australia's deterrence-focused border regime. The two countries' policies have developed in tandem since the early days of colonisation, and the increased focus on deterrence at this time may have represented New Zealand following a multilateral script, in which New Zealand's legitimacy with respect to its larger international allies depends on a commitment to deepening security cooperation and taking their security issues seriously – rather than an actual concern about trends in irregular arrivals, smuggling, or trafficking. Eventually passed as the Immigration Amendment Act 2013, this legislation was framed around renewed claims that New Zealand was becoming a target for illegal migrants and people smugglers (an echo of claims during Tuariki Delamere's tenure, 1998–99). The Act sought to 'enhance New Zealand's ability to deter people-smuggling to New Zealand by making it as unattractive as possible to people-smugglers and the people to whom they sell their services' (Immigration Amendment Bill 2012 (16-1), explanatory note). Under this new policy, a mass arrival was deemed to be more than thirty people, who could then be detained for up to six months, with the detention period able to be increased by twenty-eight days at a time thereafter. Minister of Foreign Affairs Murray McCully also advocated the use of Australian extraterritorial detention centres to process asylum seekers (Radio New Zealand 2013).

New Zealand authorities had already been carrying out military-style exercises to demonstrate their readiness for such an arrival. In June 2012, Immigration New Zealand, the Ministry of Health, and the Customs Service carried out 'Exercise Barrier', involving one hundred role players 'acting as potentially illegal immigrants being processed through health, customs and immigration checks following their simulated arrival by boat' (Williamson & Guy 2012). The exercise was something of a 'border spectacle' (De Genova 2015) aimed at manifesting a message of fealty to global regimes of border control and the suppression of irregular migration. It was also premised on building inter-agency relationships and included observers from Canada and Australia who provided feedback and advice after the event. As Guy stated in a press release, 'all of this sends a strong message that New Zealand is well prepared and will not tolerate illegal people smuggling operations' (Williamson & Guy 2012).

Guy oversaw the development of the Refugee Resettlement Strategy, which was released in 2013, early in the tenure of his successor, Michael Woodhouse. The strategy had an overarching vision of a future where 'refugees are participating fully and integrated socially and economically as soon as possible so that they are living independently, undertaking the same responsibilities and exercising the same rights as other New Zealanders and have a strong sense of belonging to their own community and to New Zealand' (Immigration New Zealand 2013). To achieve this aim, five goals were established for refugee resettlement: (1) Self-sufficiency; (2) Participation; (3) Health and Wellbeing; (4) Education; (5) Housing. The strategy strengthened existing commitments to good settlement outcomes for refugees, including the provision of access to language assistance, housing, healthcare, and education.[21] Undoubtedly, the new strategy established a more structured and transparent resettlement programme, but its introduction was also driven by ideological and political motives. In 2012, for instance, Guy suggested that the proposed resettlement strategy would 'support refugees to become self-sufficient and reduce dependency on state support' (Guy 2012b). Connecting refugees to employment opportunities can help refugees settle more quickly in the community, but it also alleviates state responsibility to support them. 'Responsibilisation' has been core to the achievement of neoliberal agendas (Brown 2015; Vallelly 2021) and was a central plank in the agenda of the National Government in the early 2010s, with Key advocating for 'a society fostering personal responsibility' (Campbell 2016). In this respect, the refugee strategy entailed assimilation into a New Zealand 'way of life' that was now reworked in neoliberal terms to prioritise personal responsibility and self-sufficiency.

A final important development during Guy's tenure as Minister of Immigration was the reconfiguration of the administrative functions of immigration governance. Early in 2012, Steven Joyce, the Minister for Economic Development and a key policy architect in Key's National Government, announced the formation of the Ministry of Business, Innovation and Employment. Established in July 2012, the new supra-agency integrated the functions of the Department of Labour (which since 1932 had been responsible for immigration policy), the Ministry of Economic Development, the Ministry of Science and Innovation, and the Department of Building and Housing. It was claimed that MBIE, as it became known, would generate efficiencies across these agencies, lead a business growth agenda, and 'have clear, co-ordinated and focused government policy leadership' to achieve the government's agenda of building 'a more competitive and

21   Seen as central to this strategy was the Māngere Refugee Resettlement Centre, where on arrival, refugees would enter a six-week programme to assist in adaptation to New Zealand society (Mitchell & Kamenarac 2021). A particular emphasis was placed on connecting refugees to employment opportunities.

internationally-focused economy' (Joyce 2012). The rhetoric referenced similar initiatives in the UK, Australia, and Canada that placed emphasis on centring and integrating diverse economic advice to government. Over the decade since, MBIE has become a behemoth of policymaking, advice, and regulation – growing to over 5000 staff and extending its operations into forty-six New Zealand-based and fourteen international offices. In relation to immigration, MBIE has built significant capacity in data and policy analytics and amplified the already-existing emphasis on economic growth and border control at the heart of immigration policymaking.

Economic Development and the New Migration Boom

Michael Woodhouse took over as Minister of Immigration in February 2013 when Nathan Guy was appointed Minister of Primary Industries. Woodhouse didn't 'think there was a great deal of thought put into the portfolios that I got, to be fair. [But] John [Key] had probably said something like, "we know Woody's a pretty safe pair of hands, Immigration's a bit risky but we think he'll be all right with it"' (Woodhouse interview). Like many other ministers, Woodhouse suggested that his existing knowledge of immigration was limited to addressing constituency issues,[22] but the portfolio would become a significant passion:

> I quickly came to realise how ubiquitous but important immigration was. It affects every other corner of New Zealand public policy and New Zealand life. Whether it's economic development, foreign policy, housing policy, social policy, education, health, you name it, decisions that I and my department were making, and Cabinet was making, were going to impact on just about every other corner of government. That put me in a really, really interesting position.

Woodhouse was outside of Cabinet for the first year and was promoted to Cabinet in a January 2014 reshuffle in advance of the election that year. National won the general election in September 2014 with ease, securing 47 per cent of the party vote and sixty out of 121 seats in Parliament. Meanwhile Labour, now led by David Cunliffe, secured a mere 25 per cent and thirty-two seats. The Green Party won fourteen seats, New Zealand First

22   Woodhouse was elected from the National Party list but was based in Dunedin. Although he never won the Dunedin seat, he actively participated in electorate activities and campaigns to build party support.

eleven seats, and the Māori Party two seats, while United Future and ACT took one seat each. Immigration again remained a relatively minor part of the election campaign, with fewer than 2 per cent of voters rating it as a major concern (Vowles et al. 2017). National quickly re-established governing arrangements with the Māori, ACT, and United Future parties. Following the election, Woodhouse was reappointed Minister of Immigration and remained in the role until National's unexpected electoral defeat in 2017.

Woodhouse's time as Minister of Immigration was characterised by an amplified political focus on the relationship between economic development and migration and a substantial increase in net migration (Spoonley 2020). In his interview for this book, Woodhouse consistently emphasised that migration should be 'demand driven': i.e. that it should fluctuate in response to job growth, lower unemployment, skills shortages, and employer demand. In policy terms, many of the initiatives developed during his tenure built on the framework established by Lianne Dalziel and her successors but also incorporated a more explicit emphasis on extracting economic value from migration, more varied regulatory mechanisms, and an increased stratification of migrant rights. According to Woodhouse, immigration held an important but understated place in National's political agenda. The portfolio was subject to influence from senior ministers, and Woodhouse noted that, because he was junior and initially outside Cabinet, he 'wasn't in some of those more detailed conversations right at the get-go'. He also described how the diversity of viewpoints demanded complex negotiation and meant that the government was often not publicly forthright about its position:

> My experience in the cabinet room particularly, if not in the wider caucus, was that there were as many views around the cabinet table around liberal versus conservative immigration policy as there was in the country at large. . . . To try and find an agreed position on this was actually quite difficult and I suspect, although it was a bit above my pay grade, that that was one of the reasons why we weren't out there really, really banging the drum for a particular position on immigration.

Previous ministers, including Cunliffe, Coleman, and even Dalziel, had given a sense of how some elements of immigration policy, especially those associated with borders and security, were handled by more senior members of government. What Woodhouse indicated reflected a different situation, where the actual contours of immigration policy and levels of immigration had become recognised as an important part of the broader political agenda to such an extent that there were elements that were 'above [his] pay grade'.

Despite a relatively muted public position on immigration, National's approach during this period situated immigration within its wider economic development and globalisation agenda. John Key articulated this agenda in a 2016 contribution to the *New Zealand International Review*:

> *No-one should fear people who want to come here and contribute, no matter where in the world they are from. There is no worldwide conspiracy to take jobs from New Zealanders or suppress wages or buy all of our houses. Immigrants make an incredible contribution, bringing capital, skills, knowledge, and experience. They support existing businesses or start their own. And they bring contacts, expertise and differing views and ideas that contribute to the richness of our communities. They join the tens of thousands of Kiwis moving home because they want to live, work and raise their families in New Zealand. We should embrace that.*

The discursive groundwork for this approach was laid in July 2014 with the launching of the *Migration and Integration Strategy*, an update on the 2006 *New Zealand Settlement Strategy*. While the 2006 and 2014 strategies have overt similarities, their differences indicate a subtle further shift in discourse and thinking around migration, especially from cultural towards economic benefits (Simon-Kumar 2020). The 2014 strategy placed emphasis on gaining 'the best economic and social benefits from migrants when they settle here', prioritisation of employment and education outcomes in settlement, and the removal of reference to diversity or the cultural value of migration that had been prominent in the 2006 strategy. The 2014 strategy also established 'priority groups', defined as those 'who make the largest potential economic contribution' and would be granted settlement and other government support denied to other migrants.

Woodhouse's tenure also saw the practical apotheosis of John Key's and National's neoliberal vision that New Zealand should be open to the world. Unlike Coleman and Guy, who were faced with the GFC and its aftermath, Woodhouse oversaw and had to grapple with the consequences of substantial growth and diversification of migration. He viewed his role as one of improving the perceived skills mix of migrants coming to New Zealand and managing migrant expectations through delinking temporary migration from residence:

> *What were the things that I was most concerned about? There were two principal ones. The first was, are we a net importer or exporter of skills? We say we've got the skilled migration policy but*

*are we exporting our doctors and accountants and surveyors, and
importing burger flippers and baristas? Because at that time we
weren't filling the planning range for our skilled migrant quota, which
was 50,000 or something. We were down around 37,000, 38,000,
and Nigel Bickle [Deputy Chief Executive, Immigration New Zealand]
came to me and he said, we've got a choice. Effectively what he was
saying was, "do we lower the bar?", and I went "absolutely not!" We
have a standard for skilled migrants. The price of entry should be
high and I'm not going to drop it just because we're in a recession.
The second thing, and the thing that dominated my thinking right
through my years, was the mismatch between temporary and
permanent migration. The fact that, try as we might, we could not fit
all of the temporary migrants who were already in country into our
residency programme.*

Concerns about low immigration were particularly pronounced following
the GFC and the net migration losses between 2008 and 2012. By the time
Woodhouse was minister, some indicators were shifting, however: the
unemployment rate, which had peaked at 6.7 per cent in December 2012,
was starting a long period of decline to the 4 per cent figure reached in
June 2020. GDP growth, which had dipped again after the Christchurch
earthquakes, rose from 2.5 per cent in December 2012 to 3.8 per cent in
December 2014 and remained above 3 per cent until December 2019. And
the period from 2013 to 2017 constituted a new migration boom and a
period of unprecedented population growth.

Net migration grew to 33,462 in the year to June 2014, then further
to record levels of 53,427 in 2015, 64,613 in 2016, and 59,533 in 2017, raw
figures that for the first time exceeded the great settler migration in the
nineteenth century.[23] The net migration loss of New Zealand citizens
declined continuously from -12,224 in 2014 to -2915 in 2017,[24] and non-
citizen net migration grew every year from 2013 through to 67,776 in 2016

23   It is noteworthy that the formula for calculating net migration was revised in 2017 from a calculation
of migration intentions based on airport arrival cards (i.e. arrivals would indicate if they intended to remain
in New Zealand for twelve months or more) to one based on more sophisticated and modelled estimates of
border cross data (i.e. tracking administrative records for individual arrivals and departures). The latter model
estimated whether people were in New Zealand for twelve out of a given sixteen-month period. The change
actually reduced the net migration numbers, which had been reported as being as high as 72,300 in the twelve
months to June 2017 (and was higher than the 12/16-month rule calculation in each of the previous four years).
In this chapter we draw on the new system, which is further explained by Statistics New Zealand: https://www.
stats.govt.nz/methods/defining-migrants-using-travel-histories-and-the-1216-month-rule
24   Rather than a change in patterns of returns of expatriates (for which Key and National had so
vociferously campaigned), the change reflected a reduced departure of citizens, declining from a peak of
71,963 in 2012 to between 40,000 and 44,000 in the years 2015–19.

and 62,448 in 2017 (see Figure 6.1).[25] Combined, these migration patterns substantially impacted population growth: in the five years between the 2013 and 2018 censuses, the New Zealand population grew from 4,242,048 to 4,699,755. Net migration over those five years combined was 250,167, meaning it constituted nearly 55 per cent of all population growth – 'the most significant in New Zealand's migration history, both in size and as a proportion of the population' (Spoonley 2020: 62).

Managing Temporary Migration

In contrast to previous periods of growth in net migration, increases in the mid-2010s were driven primarily by people arriving through temporary migration programmes rather than the residence programme. At the time of the 2013 census there was a population of 105,891 people on work visas resident in New Zealand and 57,234 on student visas (total 163,125), making up 3.8 per cent of the census-night population. By 2018, the work visa–holding population had grown to 180,273 and that of the student visa to 84,627, a total of 264,900, which would constitute 5.6 per cent of the New Zealand population (see Figure 6.2). Put another way, increases in the number of people on temporary work and study visas constituted 22.2 per cent of all population growth between 2013 and 2018. Of course, residency was still important to this new temporary migration trend, and part of the reason for the rise in temporary migration were the work- and study-to-residence visas that had been introduced and refined under both Labour and National governments. Residence visa approvals had, however, remained relatively static at 40,000 to 50,000 per year throughout the early 2010s, while around 80 per cent of residence approvals (and over 90 per cent of principal applicant approvals) were for people already in New Zealand on a temporary visa (MBIE 2016).

The shift towards temporary migration programmes followed the arc of similar developments in Australia (Howe et al. 2020) and Canada (Vosko 2022). Within these reconfigured migration regimes, settlement and access to long-term residence rights were subject to increased scrutiny and an expectation that migrants had to work for several years to demonstrate their worthiness for societal inclusion (Robertson 2015). Work and study visas were claimed to give temporary migrants the opportunity to move from

25   This reflected an inverse shift from changes in citizen migration. The number of non-citizen arrivals grew from 71,951 in the year to June 2013, reached 105,175 in 2016, and would remain above 100,000 per year through to 2020. Non-citizen departures were more stable, reducing from 39,198 in 2013 to 37,399 in 2016, before growing to over 48,000 by 2019–20.

Figure 6.2. *The Rise of Temporary Migration to New Zealand: Permanent and Temporary Visa Approvals, 1997/98–2019/20*
(Source: Ministry of Business, Innovation and Employment; analysis by Gamlen)

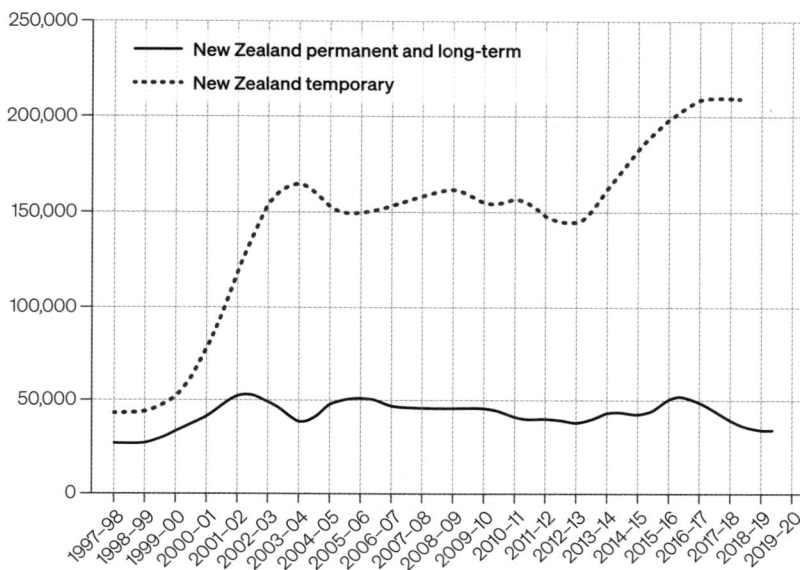

temporary to resident visas while in New Zealand; there was a widespread expectation among people arriving on temporary visas that there were viable pathways to residence rights (Collins 2018). The reality, however, which Woodhouse alluded to above, was that there were not residence pathways for most temporary migrants, which generated uncertainty in migrant populations about their prospects and dependency on employers to support work visa renewals or progression to residency that would contribute to growing migrant exploitation (Collins & Stringer 2019).

There were many policy strands to the increase in the number of people holding temporary work visas. By the time Woodhouse was in office, the Recognised Seasonal Employer (RSE) scheme was well established and being held up globally as a 'model' of how other countries could foster 'circular migration' (Gibson & McKenzie 2014). The annual RSE cap had been set at 5000 in 2007 but had been increased in every year subsequently – under Woodhouse, from 8000 in the 2013/14 year to 11,100 in 2017/18. The RSE represented the primary pathway for migrants from the Pacific during this time, making up around 60 per cent of all temporary

Figure 6.3. *Visa Approvals for Major Temporary Migration Programmes, 1997/98–2019/20*
(Source: Ministry of Business, Innovation and Employment; analysis by Collins)

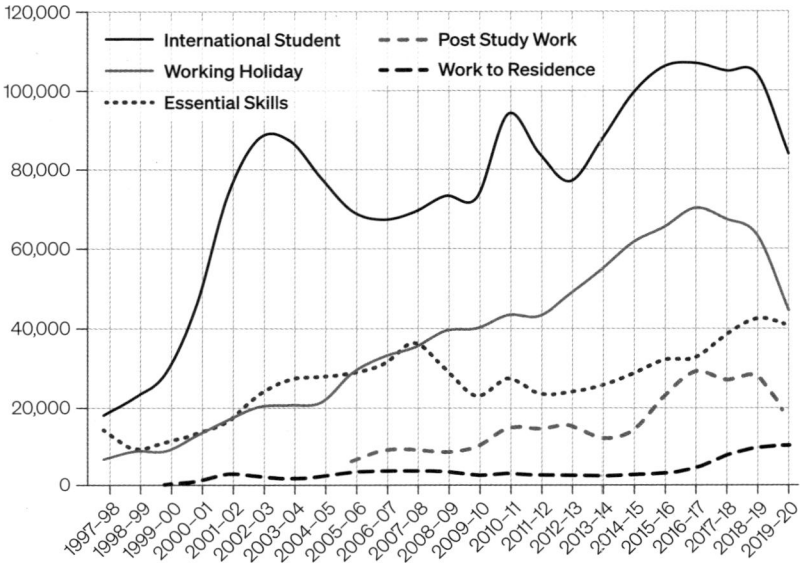

work visas for people from the region. The scheme was also now deeply embedded in the labour-supply models of the horticulture and viticulture industries, especially in regions like Marlborough and Hawke's Bay. While Woodhouse highlighted disagreements with employers in his early years, he viewed the RSE as an ideal way to manage temporary labour needs, describing it as 'the best guestworker scheme in the world' (interview).

Under Minister of Foreign Affairs Murray McCully, another twenty-two working holiday agreements were signed between 2008 and 2017, bringing the total to forty-eight, including several with Eastern European and South American countries. Working holiday visas reflected international trade and diplomatic relationships, were linked to a boom in tourism and youth mobility, provided short-term labour supply to hospitality, and supplemented the RSE in horticulture and viticulture (Opara 2018; Tsai & Collins 2017). Working holiday visa approvals grew from 48,699 in the year to June 2013 to 70,002 in 2017 (MBIE 2017a), although the short-term character of working holidays means actual population numbers peaked at 47,007 in February 2017. Notwithstanding nationality diversification

Figure 6.4. *Population of Temporary Visa Holders, 30 June 2011–2020*
(Source: Ministry of Business, Innovation and Employment; analysis by Collins)

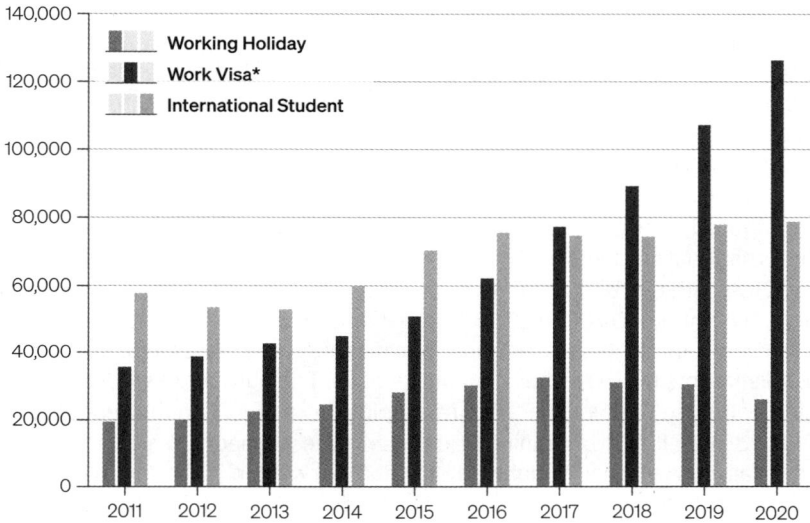

* Work Visa includes Essential Skills, Work to Residence, Post Study Work, Recognised Seasonal Employer

during the 2010s, at the time of writing the working holiday scheme remains dominated by young people from Western Europe and North America, who have the most streamlined entry requirements and advantageous conditions, and made up 75 per cent of this population in 2017.

What Woodhouse referred to as 'demand driven' work visas included the Essential Skills and Work to Residence visas. These work visas were either for jobs on Immigration New Zealand's skills shortage lists or were 'labour market tested', meaning that employers had to demonstrate the unavailability of local workers. Essential Skills and Work to Residence visa holders were restricted by the terms of their visa to specific occupations, with specific employers and in specific regions, with any variations requiring prior approval from Immigration New Zealand. These visas were thus subject to considerable government oversight and monitoring and also subject to changes in regulation, such as assessed skills shortages, qualification criteria, terms of employment, family and social rights, and much more. Visas were issued for between one and three years, dependent on occupation and income, with those on longer visas typically granted more settlement support, family reunification, and access to public healthcare. Essential Skills visa approvals grew from 24,792 in the year to June 2013 to 37,713 in 2017. Meanwhile, Work to Residence visa approvals were much lower at 2307 in 2013 and 4794 in 2017 (see Figure 6.4 for changes in the resident populations of these temporary migrant categories). Notably, many Essential Skills and Work to Residence visa holders could be accompanied by partners, who were also granted work visas, with 'partner of a worker' visa approvals growing from 12,150 in the year to June 2013 to 19,779 in 2017.

International student mobility also became more prominent and was reconfigured in relation to the attainment of residence rights. The numbers of international students in New Zealand had not increased much during the 2010s, with the 2017 student visa approval total of 106,710 still lower than the high point of 120,000 in 2003. International students were, however, increasingly enrolling in sub-degree qualifications at private training establishments (PTEs) rather than universities. The number of students being approved to study in PTEs grew rapidly from 20,826 in the year to June 2013 to 36,807 in 2016, meaning that these students made up around 35 per cent of all international students (up from 27 per cent in 2013). Much of this growth emerged because of changes by the New Zealand Qualifications Authority in 2013, overseen by Stephen Joyce as Minister of Tertiary Education, which allowed PTEs to undertake their own English-language testing rather than having to use external tests like IELTS.[26] In 2014, changes were also introduced that permitted all international students enrolled in a full-time course (fourteen weeks or more) to work part-time, with those enrolled for a full academic year or longer allowed to work full-time in holiday periods. Postgraduate students were given unlimited working rights (Fry & Wilson 2018). While this market-driven shift increased the number of students and the tax revenue the sector was generating, it created substantial challenges for Woodhouse's approach to managing migration.

Many international students became eligible for post-study work visas on completion of their courses and aspired to settle in New Zealand, adding even larger numbers of temporary migrants at the same time as the government was insisting on limiting onward pathways to residence. Post-study work visa approvals doubled from 14,190 in the year to June 2015 to 29,190 in 2017. In 2016, however, media investigations (Laxon 2016a; 2016b) and academic research (Collins 2016; Stringer 2016) began to emerge that outlined the entanglement of international education in debt-financing, migration and education agent fraud, unsubstantiated

---

26   IELTS is the International English Language Testing System.

promises of pathways to residence, and labour-market exploitation. Union leader Dennis Maga described the arrangement as 'education trafficking' (Weekes 2016), wherein syndicates of agents, who recruited students for educational institutions, employers, and, in effect, the New Zealand Government, operated by 'luring students to New Zealand by deception for the fees or commission they bring' (Laxon 2016a). In one particularly striking case, 400 international students from India had their visas cancelled after Immigration New Zealand found that education agents had submitted fraudulent documents about students' financial status to gain visas. While many of these students never came to New Zealand, nine appealed to Woodhouse to remain and continue their study but were issued deportation notices. The students sought sanctuary in a central Auckland church, where they remained for two weeks before voluntarily leaving New Zealand, many with debts exceeding $30,000 and none of the educational qualifications or post-study work opportunities they had migrated for. Subsequent investigations in 2019 showed that the students had been unaware of the fraud, and they were granted work visas to return to New Zealand (Kumar 2019).

Political Management and 'Quality' Control

For Woodhouse, these different temporary migration programmes constituted distinct policy challenges. On the one hand, RSE workers were subject to strict regulation that assured their departure annually, even if many returned in subsequent years. Similarly, working holiday visa holders were deemed to be associated with the tourism industry and unlikely to remain long term. They were framed as young people undertaking work-travel experiences, although research suggested that certain sectors had become dependent on working holiday visa holders (Opara 2018) and workplace exploitation was also apparent (Collins & Stringer 2019). In contrast, people taking up Essential Skills work visas, international students, and post-study work visa holders all occupied an intermediate position, wherein they were potentially in New Zealand for many years and could often be accompanied by partners and children. Moreover, many aspired for long-term settlement, but the limited opportunities for residence made this unlikely. Michael Woodhouse explained:

> The pathway for them to residency was not only a long narrow one, it was completely blocked. I thought we were selling – well rather, the government was very careful, and I encouraged Immigration

New Zealand to be very careful, particularly in [the] essential skills work visa area not to portray the labour market tested work visa as – a pathway to residency. But what was happening was it was being drowned out by immigration agents and education agents overseas and other people with an interest, like lobby groups, like I'll name them, Federated Farmers, hospitality industry, Tourism New Zealand as a way of getting here and getting residence.

In his interview, Woodhouse described how he sought to increase the regulation of temporary migration but noted that the political management needed to deliver such changes was challenging.

The overall emphasis of the Key Government in relation to immigration was an embrace of economic value that prioritised globalisation. Woodhouse, however, described his political philosophy as one that hinged on the free movement of goods and capital but was circumspect about the free movement of people: 'residency and citizenship does have a price, and it should be a high price, and . . . we need to control our growth'. Cabinet included quite different views on immigration, ranging from liberal to conservative perspectives on the openness of borders.

The issue of international education, and the volume and purported quality of international students, and its entanglement with exploitative business activity, illustrated these debates. On the one hand, there was Steven Joyce, who advocated an economic growth agenda through international education, and on the other, there was Woodhouse, whose focus was on maintaining quality and managing migration. Joyce regularly defended the 'robustly monitored' approach to international education (Weekes 2016) and highlighted the industry's multi-billion-dollar value (Laxon 2016a; 2016b), saying, 'We're bringing in graduates who are adding significantly to the New Zealand workforce, there's no doubt they're doing that' (Otago Daily Times 2017). In contrast, Woodhouse became embroiled in managing the outcomes of fraud and the growing evidence of exploitation (author emphasis added):

Steven [Joyce], of course, was the Tertiary Education minister for several years, so he was particularly keen to ensure that this very large service export earner, our second largest service export earner behind tourism, was able to thrive. I had concerns about the quality of some of the education offerings, particularly among PTEs. . . . We had some quite robust discussions about the degree to which a) there was a quality product being offered, b) whether there was incorrect messaging that we knew education agents globally were selling at least level 5 and 6 qualifications [sub-degree diplomas] as a pathway to residence when, frankly, there was both from a numbers perspective and a policy perspective it just couldn't be the case. We tightened things up, actually. At least around the margins. I would have gone further.

Woodhouse also noted in his interview that international education was an 'area where I think we wanted to really increase the numbers' but that 'I thought we had a quality issue that needed to be watched'. Woodhouse introduced measures that sought to bring more regulatory control to this area, and Joyce oversaw the reintroduction of independent English-language testing for students from India in 2016. He also launched a revamp of the 'Code of Pastoral Care of International Students' that same year. The new code specifically addressed concerns around education agents, requiring educational providers to assure that agents 'provide international students with reliable information and advice about studying, working, and living in New Zealand' and 'act with integrity and professionalism'. These measures addressed some of Woodhouse's concerns, but he was clear that he 'would have gone further'. This was a regular theme in his interview, and he described the challenge of negotiating around the cabinet table as a matter of compromise over conviction:

Trying to find the sweet spot is a bit like the search for truth and wisdom; it's just going to mean different things to different people. That's the wonderful challenge actually that I thoroughly enjoyed. Trying to firstly listen really carefully and then form a view that was acceptable to the majority. I would much rather be a conviction politician but actually immigration policy involves compromise.

Media discourse on the rise of temporary migration represented a second political management challenge. By 2016, the claim that migration was out of control and leading to unsustainable population growth was becoming common. Commentary would emerge monthly, each time record net migration numbers were reported, and significant attention was paid to the purported effects of migration on housing, employment, and workplace exploitation. Auckland had seen record property price increases over the 2010s, with the average property price increasing from under $496,274 in 2010 to $913,938 in early 2017 (Barfoot and Thompson 2017). The opposition Labour Party and Winston Peters were frequently amplifying public anxiety and directing it towards migration. In one particularly infamous incident in 2015, Labour MP Phil Twyford released research that calculated the percentage of 'Chinese-sounding surnames' in a home buyer survey to argue that migrants were driving house prices up. The approach was lambasted as xenophobic and racist, with critics noting that Chinese were among New Zealand's long-standing settler groups, and therefore many of those with 'Chinese-sounding names' were New Zealand-born or New Zealand citizens (Ng 2017). As subsequent research would show, claims about the impact of migration on housing were significantly overstated (Hyslop et al. 2019).[27] More broadly, media discourse presented net migration figures as if they were indicative of long-term immigration and as such did not account for the government's approach to managing migration through temporary programmes. Woodhouse explains:

> I did an interview with Damian Christie on One News once to talk about Auckland house prices and the impact of foreign buyers. It might have been around the time of the Chinese-sounding surnames saga. I made the flippant, well it wasn't a flippant comment, but he thought it was, I said look, net migration is being driven by students and working holiday makers and frankly, a backpacker going to Wānaka is hardly driving up the Auckland housing market. And he looked at me just with incredulity as if I didn't know what I was talking about, that surely all these migrants were driving up the Auckland housing market. I'm going, 'No mate, you've got to look behind the numbers.'

The third political management issue emerged from representatives of labour unions and migrant advocates, as well as industry representatives, many of whom had come to rely on consistently growing temporary migration to meet labour needs. For Woodhouse, this was a question of listening and then developing policy that from his perspective was considered holistic and supportive of economic development without creating additional risks:

> The employer industry groups were very prominent . . . Hospitality, Business New Zealand, the EMA [Employers and Manufacturers Association], various chambers of commerce. There were also the

27 ˙ Labour's research was dismissed as a political stunt: an effort to win back working-class voters who had been gradually defecting to the right wing for several decades, in protest at Labour's perceived support for increasing immigration. Indeed, the exact same tactic was simultaneously being attempted – with equally unsuccessful results – by the UK Labour Party under Ed Miliband, the son of a prominent Marxist refugee, who was widely criticised for inauthenticity when his party attempted to court anti-immigrant voters by aping UKIP and the UK Conservatives by rebranding the party as 'One Nation Labour' – echoing a slogan embraced by the far right around the world (Gamlen 2013b).

migrant workers unions and the trade unions more generally who were opposed very strongly to certain immigration trends. . . . The immigration industry obviously. Migrant groups, so the likes of the Indian Community Association, basically every country with a large enough diaspora would be lobbying me quite a bit. Refugee community, obviously. And you listen extremely carefully to all of them but ultimately, you have to walk a fine line down the middle of some of the more extreme desires that these groups would have.

Walking the fine line between different interests, Woodhouse undertook what he described as 'nip and tuck policies' to try to manage immigration demand and conditions. These included 'special instructions' introduced in 2015 to address the Christchurch earthquake rebuild and evident exploitation in construction work in the city – temporarily creating additional labour-market rights for construction workers to change employers and remain longer in New Zealand. There was constant modification of skills shortage lists regulating approvals for different sectors. From April 2016, a new rule required employers to engage Work and Income (New Zealand's social welfare agency) prior to undertaking a labour-market test. Also in 2016, the points required for Skilled Migrant Category residence applications increased for the first time in fourteen years, from 140 points to 160 points, a shift specifically designed to prioritise 'the highest value migrants'. And, in February 2017, changes were introduced to forbid employers who breached immigration or employment law from recruiting people on temporary work visas.

Family migration also came under scrutiny in the context of high net migration and the government's stated desire to enhance migration management and outcomes. In his interview, Woodhouse emphasised the problem with open categories that did not have a clear focus on outcomes:

The reason they were relevant was because they were uncapped, so if you wanted to reduce the number of people coming and staying permanently, the only place that they could really come from was skilled migrant category. You had your Pacific and Samoan quotas, you had your refugee quota and you had uncapped partnership. There was a cap on the parent category as well but at that time it was 5500 a year, it was quite a big number. I distinctly remember getting a briefing about parent category showing the costs on the health system, the costs of emergency benefits and anecdotes, very strong – actually, not just anecdotes, information about how it was going, that I was concerned enough

*about to announce a review. . . . Suffice to say, I reduced the
number, I think it was in the two-year planning range from 11,000
down to 4000 and then suspended the parent category.*

The focus on regulating family categories that were not explicitly
economically oriented was not new. David Cunliffe and Jonathan Coleman
had already introduced an emphasis on economic value into family policy
and, as noted above, a two-tiered parent category had been introduced
under Nathan Guy that effectively precluded applications from migrants
without high incomes or significant capital (Bedford & Didham 2018;
Bedford & Liu 2013). Woodhouse took this further, introducing a strict
cap of 2000 for the parent, sibling, and adult child category and then
'temporarily' terminating selection of parents to 'reduce the total number
of migrants being granted residence' (Woodhouse 2016). The temporary
closure wouldn't be reversed until the next government was in office,
and in his interview, Woodhouse indicated that the similarly uncapped
partnership category had been unfinished business in his effort to achieve
more-effective management of residence approvals. Set alongside the
changes introduced in the previous decade, these restrictions were
indicative of how family migration had shifted increasingly to the periphery
of an immigration policy regime that was focused on human capital
priorities and managing temporary labour migration.

Each of these initiatives focused on managing migration for
'quality' and incrementally stratified the rights of migrants who were
deemed lower skilled from those deemed higher skilled. Despite the
changes, an increasing number of work visas were still being approved
for occupations that were classified in the Australia and New Zealand
Standard Classification of Occupations (ANZSCO)[28] framework as 'lower
skilled', with the proportion of skill level 4 and 5 visas approved growing
from less than 30 per cent in the year to June 2013 to nearly 40 per cent in
2017. In April 2017, however, Woodhouse announced a wide-ranging reform
of the temporary migrant work regime and associated changes to the SMC.
From August 2017, the conditions of Essential Skills work visas would be
determined by a combination of occupational classification in ANZSCO and
remuneration bands pegged to the median wage. Those classified as 'lower
skilled' would be restricted to twelve-month visas, which they could renew
only twice before a twelve-month 'standdown' outside of New Zealand,

---

28   ANZSCO, the Australian and New Zealand Standard Classification of Occupations, is used in both
Australia and New Zealand to classify different occupational types in order to organise data about individuals
or jobs. It has also been used in immigration assessments in both countries, although New Zealand has
increasingly moved towards remuneration bands as a means to evaluate the skill level of migrants.

and became ineligible to support partners or children. Those deemed 'mid-skilled' or 'higher skilled' would gain three-year and five-year visas respectively with unlimited renewals, which meant they could also access public healthcare, and retained eligibility to support partners and children. SMC changes for residence applications included related shifts to allocate more points to applicants with higher incomes, while close family support was removed as a factor in selection.

The reforms bore some resemblance to approaches in countries like Singapore, where highly regulated temporary programmes had long been the central plank of governing migration (Yeoh 2006). They also epitomised Woodhouse's approach to immigration, centred on his political philosophy of free mobility of capital and goods and restricted labour, and the capacity of regulatory settings to direct migration outcomes. Press releases for the reforms made clear that their aim was to increase stratification in migrant rights and inclusion by 'prioritis[ing] higher-paid and higher-skilled migrants' and 'ensuring that migrants with no pathway to residence do not become well-settled in New Zealand' (MBIE 2017b). In his interview, Woodhouse also consistently stated that there ought to be distinctions between lower-skilled migrants, who could be permitted where demand genuinely existed, and higher-skilled migrants who could meet the 'price' of residence and citizenship. Migrants deemed to be lower skilled were given a stark message – 'the conditions of those visas now reinforce that temporary means temporary' (MBIE 2017b) – implying a shift towards guestworker programmes that Woodhouse had long favoured (Collins 2017). Indeed, Woodhouse finished his interview by arguing that the 'RSE is the solution to problems right across our economy', not least because it reduces 'our stated permanent and long-term migration data because they only stay for up to seven months'. Notwithstanding his desire to extend such arrangements across the migration regime, the August 2017 reforms became Woodhouse's last contribution to the immigration portfolio, as National's seemingly impregnable hold on government came to an unexpectedly early conclusion in September 2017.

Electoral Change and 'Population Shock'

Nearing the end of 2016, the National Party was performing so well in opinion polls (at times reaching 50 per cent support) that they seemed likely to gain a fourth term in office, a feat not achieved by any government since the 1960s. This situation shifted when John Key unexpectedly announced his resignation as Prime Minister in December, effectively handing the leadership to Deputy Prime Minister Bill English. Initially, National's polling held up, despite the issues that the government was facing, which included criticisms linking high net migration to inequality as well as shortages of housing and infrastructure (Spoonley 2020). Labour leader Andrew Little picked up on these issues with policy announcements committing to reduce net migration to between 20,000 to 30,000 annually, a figure that Winston Peters bested by aiming for 10,000 per year. More broadly, commentators had become convinced that immigration settings were the cause of a wide range of societal issues, from housing to roads, schools, water, and other infrastructure (Dominion Post 2017).[29] These emergent anti-immigration approaches in Labour reflected trends observed elsewhere, notably in the UK and US, of political parties seeking to connect with voters who expressed disillusionment with the effects of globalisation (Portice & Reicher 2018).

While immigration, inequality, and housing were clearly of popular concern (Hall 2017c), it was a series of dramatic political events that led to the unexpected demise of National at the general election in 2017. Andrew Little had taken over leadership of Labour after the disastrous 2014 election but had struggled to gain much popular support for the party. His leadership came under question in 2017 with Labour still languishing below 30 per cent support. Labour support dropped further to less than 25 per cent following a spike in Green Party support, after co-leader Metiria Turei spoke publicly about her struggles as a beneficiary in the 1990s.[30] In response to Labour's dire polling numbers, Andrew Little resigned on 31 July, less than two months before the election. On the same day, deputy leader Jacinda Ardern was elected as his replacement. Ardern's leadership transformed the public representation of Labour, and the party's support increased to consistently exceed 35 per cent, largely at the expense of the Green Party and New Zealand First. At least part of Ardern's success was her ability to put to rest the Labour Party's anti-immigration experiment under Little (Gamlen & Sherrell 2022).

When the election was held on 23 September 2017, National secured the highest party vote (44.4 per cent), followed by Labour (36.9 per cent), New Zealand First (7.2 per cent), and the Green Party (6.3 per cent). ACT gained one electoral seat, but United Future and the Māori

29   One *Dominion Post* editorial exemplifies this kind of commentary: 'Net immigration is at unprecedented levels and is causing serious economic trouble. It is helping stoke the fires of house prices. It is helping clog the already-clogged roads of Auckland. It is putting a strain on schools, transport services, even on the decaying water pipes. Nobody disputes that these problems are real or that they will cost a fortune to fix.'
30   These events also subsequently led to Turei's resignation after being hounded by media for the minor fraud involved in her past engagements with social welfare agencies.

Party did not return to Parliament. The result positioned New Zealand First (nine seats) as able to decide government, since neither National and ACT (fifty-six seats and one seat respectively) nor Labour and the Green Party (forty-six and eight seats respectively) could command a majority in the 120-seat Parliament. After four weeks of post-election negotiation, New Zealand First opted to form a coalition with the Labour Party. Meanwhile, the Green Party remained outside of Cabinet with a confidence-and-supply arrangement and some ministerial portfolios. Jacinda Ardern became Prime Minister and Winston Peters became Deputy Prime Minister and Minister of Foreign Affairs.

In the new Coalition Government, Iain Lees-Galloway was appointed Minister of Immigration, as well as holding the Workplace Relations and Accident Compensation Corporation portfolios. Prior to being elected in 2008, Lees-Galloway had served as an organiser and advisor for the New Zealand Nurses Organisation (the national trade union for nurses). Lees-Galloway recounted growing up in a politically conservative family before making connections with the Labour Party and its social democratic values during his studies at Massey University. When he was elected, Lees-Galloway had not envisaged himself as working in the immigration portfolio because, as he described it in the interview, 'it always looked like a terrible poisoned chalice'. Over time, however, the portfolio seemed like an 'intellectual challenge', and he had advocated in 2014 to shadow Woodhouse as opposition spokesperson for immigration and workplace relations.

Lees-Galloway had to grapple with very similar issues to Woodhouse. Net migration had been running at very high levels for several years and was clearly speeding up population growth. There were numerous issues with the temporary migration system, especially in terms of workplace exploitation. While most of the public commentary blamed the preceding National Government, migration had become a significant issue that Lees-Galloway and the Coalition Government were expected to deal with. Exemplary of the wider discourse was prominent economic commentator Bernard Hickey, who from 2018 onwards consistently described the situation as a 'population shock' and 'crisis' (Hickey 2018):

> News in recent weeks of raw sewage running down the walls of leaky buildings at Middlemore hospital and exhausted midwives quitting in droves across Auckland is just one of the signs. There are many others in Auckland and elsewhere to indicate our largest city has just suffered a population shock that is now generating an infrastructure crisis. . . . New Zealand's population grew by over 430,000 to 4.9 million in the last five years, mostly from net migration, but also from

*relatively high birth rates in Auckland and the upper North Island.
... Auckland's population shock on top of decades of infrastructure
under-spending and a budgetary squeeze from Wellington has
created a man-made crisis.*

The release of data from the 2018 census fuelled this discourse by
highlighting that New Zealand would soon reach a population of five
million, which eventually occurred in March 2020. Data from the census
revealed that the country had grown at its fastest rate ever: 2.1 per cent
annually between 2013 and 2018 (compared with 0.7 per cent annually
between 2006 and 2013). The coming milestone of five million would
also be the fastest million in New Zealand's history, taking only seventeen
years.[31] As we have documented in this book, the transformation in
immigration policy since the early 2000s laid the groundwork for this rapid
and diversified population growth, which was then supercharged by the
economic-development agenda of the Fifth National Government. In the
two and a half years leading up to the Covid-19 pandemic, it was Lees-
Galloway who was tasked with managing the consequences.

Managing Conflict

The notion of a 'population shock' fed into the broader claims of the first
Labour–New Zealand First Coalition Government. Despite their differences,
the two parties had both been critical of National's unrelenting economic-
development agenda, and they thus asserted a focus on becoming 'a
transformational government, committed to resolving the greatest long-term
challenges for the country' (New Zealand Labour Party & New Zealand First
2017). However, the coalition agreement included only two commitments
related to immigration: 'Ensure work visas issued reflect genuine skills
shortages and cut down on low quality international education courses';
and 'Take serious action on migrant exploitation, particularly of international
students'. Neither of these commitments matched pre-election rhetoric
about reducing net migration. Both the brevity and the substance of these
priorities reflected the fine line Labour needed to walk to govern, balancing
the pro-diversity message that helped Ardern resuscitate the party's
polling, with the imperative to keep New Zealand First's anti-immigration
constituency on side. To achieve this, Gamlen & Sherrell (2022) argue, the

31   New Zealand's population had reached 4 million in 2003 (3 million in 1973) and, as we noted in
Chapter 4, mid-range projections in 2003 suggested the population would peak at 4.6 million in 2051.

Labour–New Zealand First Government assembled a particular version of an 'illiberal paradox' in its approach to migration policy (Natter 2018), positioning themselves as focused on regulating for migrants' own wellbeing while continuing the development of policy that reduced residence opportunities and stratified migrant rights (Collins 2020; Simon-Kumar 2020).

In her speech at the opening of Parliament in November 2017, the new Prime Minister, Jacinda Ardern, argued that curbing immigration numbers would be essential to ease 'pressures on our housing, infrastructure and public services' (Ardern 2017). Both Labour and New Zealand First had campaigned on reducing net migration, but their policy preferences differed considerably. New Zealand First aimed to substantially reduce net migration to 10,000 annually, but this was now hard for any government to engineer given the diversity of migration programmes – residence, work, study, humanitarian, working holiday, business, and so on – each of which had its own internal configurations. It was the residence programme that became the target, likely because it was an area where numerical results could be achieved relatively easily and quickly. During the preceding National Government, the two-year planning range for residence had been slightly reduced (from 90,000–100,000 down to 85,000–95,000 in 2016). Under Labour–New Zealand First, the planning range was modified more substantially to 50,000–60,000 over eighteen months (1 July 2018 – 31 December 2019), the equivalent of a 66,000–80,000 two-year range. Actual residence approvals declined rapidly from 47,685 in the year to June 2017 to 37,947 in 2018 and 34,515 in 2019.

Despite reductions in residence planning and approvals, net migration continued to be very high at 48,995 in 2018 and 52,101 in 2019, primarily because of ongoing growth in temporary migration. While attempting to curb residence approval numbers, the Labour–New Zealand First Government also introduced measures to increase visas options in specific industries facing labour shortages. A new KiwiBuild Skills Shortage List was established for construction companies, and the cap on RSE workers was raised to 12,850 for 2018/2019, then to 14,400 the following year (Lees-Galloway 2019). A new marketing campaign was introduced in October 2018 that targeted overseas teachers to fill expected shortages in the education sector (Hipkins 2018). And the parent category for skilled migrants, closed under the previous government, was reopened in October 2019, with the hope that allowing skilled migrants to bring parents would increase the quality of work and residence applicants. Overall, the number of people on temporary work and study visas living in New Zealand continued to grow, from 248,094 when the Labour–New Zealand First Government entered office in October 2017 to a peak of 305,469 at the end of February 2020. The growing discrepancy between residence reductions and ongoing temporary migration increases seemed to extend the stratification of migrant rights that had been introduced by Woodhouse, and rhetorically aligned with Labour and New Zealand First's election campaign. Lees-Galloway, however, made it clear that coalition arrangements with New Zealand First had determined this approach:

> It is one of the things that I was very disappointed to leave the role not having to be able to attend to, was really to do something for the group of people who had been stuck waiting for the opportunity to get a residency visa. Especially those who met the criteria but because we have essentially an arbitrary cap on how many residency visas we issue, that again people are stuck on that waiting list. It was something the media picked up on and we got quite hammered over but I don't mind saying now that coalition arrangements made that particular policy a little tricky.

Lees-Galloway had entered the role of Minister of Immigration with a sustained focus on migrant exploitation, which was by then seen as at least partly a result of the migration regime itself. Migrant exploitation had been a serious issue for years, with people on temporary work and study visas being subject to a wide range of criminal and non-compliant employment practices, often connected to their visa status. Common forms of exploitation included being paid below minimum or contracted wages, being forced to return money to employers, paying premiums for jobs or visas, having passports confiscated, and being denied leave and other basic work rights (see Collins & Stringer 2019). Addressing exploitation articulated with Lees-Galloway's background in unions and the Labour Party focus on workers' rights:

> We saw, especially with the growing number of people on temporary visas, that there was quite a bit of evidence that the exploitation of migrants was growing in New Zealand. We saw that as a risk to our international profile, but obviously exploitation of migrants largely happens in the workplace, so you not only had those migrant workers' rights being undermined but that meant that you created the opportunity for everybody's working rights to be undermined.

Several initiatives were undertaken to address exploitation. In May 2018, a $30.4 million injection was made to Immigration New Zealand to better detect workplace exploitation. Changes were made to post-study work visas, which from November 2018 were no longer linked to a specific employer. And, in 2019, MBIE commissioned a series of studies, which reported on the extent and implications of workplace exploitation (Collins & Stringer 2019) and surveyed international findings and policy responses (Stringer & Michailova 2019a; 2019b). This research led to changes to 'prevent' exploitation through reworking employment restrictions in relation to work visa holders; to 'protect' migrants through a dedicated phone helpline and a bridging visa for victims; and to 'enforce' labour protections through new powers granted to the Labour Inspectorate branch of MBIE.

An immediate immigration crisis emerged in the aftermath of the 15 March 2019 terrorist attacks on two mosques in Christchurch. Brenton Tarrant, a twenty-eight-year-old Australian White supremacist who had been living in Dunedin, violently attacked the Linwood Mosque and Masjid Al Noor with assault weapons, murdering fifty-one people and injuring forty more in a horrific live-streamed atrocity. The attack has been described as 'New Zealand's Darkest Day' (Radio New Zealand 2019) and led to sustained global attention on New Zealand, the victims and their families, and the lack of attention to White supremacist terrorism by security agencies. Lees-Galloway worked with Jacinda Ardern to develop a package of visas and residence pathways for the families of victims and those affected, many of whom were on temporary visas. These included people who had lost partners and/or parents who were principal work visa holders, thus making their partner/dependent visas invalid. Lees-Galloway asserted in his interview that, given these people had suffered immeasurable trauma, 'we owe it to them to provide them with some security and stability, and the opportunity to have a range of options available to them and to be able to decide what was in the best interests of their family'. In the background to these well-made points of principle, the regularisation of temporary workers was also consistent with the government's broader strategy of greater labour-market regulation, under the banner of cracking down on 'exploitation'.

The terrorist attack also supported some arguments for changes in regulation by raising significant issues around border security. A subsequent Royal Commission of Inquiry found that there had been 'an inappropriate concentration of counter-terrorism resources on the threat of Islamist extremist terrorism' (Royal Commission of Inquiry 2019), which had come at the expense of relatively little attention being paid to the risks posed by extreme right-wing and White supremacist groups. New Zealand governments had continued to invest in and build security capability in relation to immigration and increase the use of automated and 'smart' processes at the border. Woodhouse, for example, during his tenure, had worked to develop online visa processing and extend e-border technology use, increased the powers of immigration authorities to work with police to take biometric information forcibly, and participated in Migration Five meetings, describing the 2017 meeting as 'an opportunity to share intelligence and ideas with our Five Country colleagues, particularly in relation to border security issues and the general movement of people' (Woodhouse & Finlayson 2017). Lees-Galloway had carried on the process of technological development and securitisation, through proposals to develop an Electronic Travel Authorisation (like Australia and the US) for visa-waiver countries. Eventually legislated in June 2019, three months after the terrorist attack, the NZeTA was designed specifically to increase information available to border agencies, speed up approved crossings, and 'bring New Zealand's border in line with international best practice' (Davis et al. 2019). Despite these latter developments, it is unlikely that border security would have picked up Tarrant's movements because of his Australian citizenship and the free-movement privileges accorded across the Tasman. Moreover, it is notable that the Royal Commission found that because he was Australian, he was granted a firearms licence and was able to purchase assault rifles with limited and questionable checks on his character, which would have been much harder for people of other nationalities (Royal Commission of Inquiry 2019).

To address some of the broader structural issues that were being observed in immigration, Lees-Galloway began a major revision of how demand-driven work visas were issued in late 2018. He focused on simplifying a 'system [that] is overly complex, includes a number of different visa options and isn't adequately responsive to sectoral or regional differences in the labour market' (Lees-Galloway 2018). Proposals in December 2018 included: replacing the nationwide Skills in Demand Lists with Regional Skills Shortage Lists tailored to different parts of the country; accreditation of employers and the creation of a new framework for assessing visa applications that was employer-led rather than migrant-led; and the introduction of 'sector agreements' to smoothen recruitment of migrants 'in return for commitments by the sector to employ and train more New Zealanders' (Lees-Galloway 2018). The system re-envisaged the management of temporary migration through a series of 'gates' that assessed elements of an application including the 'employer check', the 'job check', and the 'migrant check'. Following six months of consultation, the Accredited Employer Work Visa (AEWV) scheme was formally announced in September 2019. While the AEWV was a new technocentric approach to managing migrant selection and tenure, it also retained key control features of the previous system, such as the employer link on work visas and the distinction between skill levels, remuneration, and migrant rights. The new scheme was due to be introduced incrementally from 2020 and finalised by 2021. However, the Covid-19 pandemic restrictions from March 2020 meant that many features of the AEWV transformation were suspended and then revised for introduction in late 2022.

Like Woodhouse, Lees-Galloway was caught between multiple intersecting interests and pressures. Having been in opposition for nine years, he described entering government with 'a pretty strong understanding of what it was that we wanted to achieve', not least in relation to matters such as migrant exploitation. What he found, however, was a complex landscape of policy information, advice, and countervailing viewpoints that demanded constant negotiation:

> *What you realise is in opposition you don't have a lot of resources to really be developing good robust-costed thought-through policy. Then you bring your manifesto and then suddenly you've got an army of officials who are there, a) to help you implement your manifesto, but b) to scrutinise it. That's one of the greatest challenges of government, is getting your manifesto through the layers of bureaucracy and all the absolutely appropriate levels of reporting and transparency and feedback that you get from the officials. But sometimes as the elected part of the government you do feel like you're perhaps doing battle with the permanently employed part of the government.*

This statement is indicative of a wider theme of this book, which is the extent to which New Zealand immigration policy is institutionalised and subject to various forms of 'nondecision-making' (Bachrach & Baratz 1963). While the engagement between government politicians and officials is likely to be challenging across a range of portfolios, one of the characteristics of the managerial shift in migration policy that we have traced in this book has been the increasingly technocratic dimensions of policymaking and thus its reliance on a sizeable bureaucratic apparatus and its growing focus on data generation and analysis. The formation of MBIE in 2012 had led to expanded policy, research, and operational expertise in relation to migration and labour. The agency undertook administrative analysis of visa processing and approvals, monthly migrant population counts, and regional and national labour-market contributions and outcomes, among other things. For a Minister of Immigration like Lees-Galloway, articulating a rights-based approach to rethinking immigration policy, grappling with the bureaucracy raised challenges, especially in relation to the claimed implications of any changes:

Sometimes the things that look sensible to do in the immigration system actually have arguably a negative impact on them because you're actually saying we're going to make it harder for you to get a visa, or it's not going to be so easy for employers to turn to the immigration system. That's really challenging because you want to do the right thing, you want to improve standards, but you know that in this system there are tens of thousands of real human beings with real human lives who are just looking for an opportunity to get ahead. Often, it's that desire to get that opportunity that makes them vulnerable, that makes them exploitable. In order to make them less exploitable, you often end up reducing the number of opportunities there are available to them.

Like Woodhouse, Lees-Galloway also had to deal with lobbyists and industry groups on a regular basis in relation to these policy developments, suggesting in his interview that 'immigration probably attracted the most requests for face time with the minister out of all of my portfolios'. Lees-Galloway listed a range of interests, from Business New Zealand, Recognised Seasonal Employer groups, trade unions, migrant worker groups, and local chambers of commerce, among others, and highlighted the development of 'bespoke' 'policy responses to the various lobby groups that were out there'. As he put it in the interview, 'sometimes those things just crashed into each other head on and there was no avoiding the fact that you would have people who would have legitimate grievances around what you were trying to do'.

Then there were the cabinet negotiations, which as we have already noted were tense, given the diversity of viewpoints and the power struggle between Labour and New Zealand First, as well as the Green Party's less direct influence on migration policymaking. The Labour–New Zealand First Coalition had inherited the National Government's commitment to increasing the refugee quota from 750 to 1000 in 2018, but the Labour Party had further committed to the campaign in 2016–17 to double the quota to 1500. The Green Party confidence-and-supply agreement included a commitment to 'review, and adequately fund and support, the family re-unification scheme for refugees'. New Zealand First had other views, with Winston Peters declaring publicly in early September 2018 that 'we never made a commitment to double the refugee quota'. Two weeks later, following cabinet negotiations that likely involved other compromises, Peters had reversed that position and New Zealand First agreed with the proposed change.[32] Lees-Galloway also

---

32   The refugee quota was due to increase to 1500 in July 2020, but like the AEWV this did not occur until 2022 due to the impacts of the Covid-19 pandemic response.

described grappling with New Zealand First in relation to the removal of what had become known as the 'family link policy', a racist restriction requiring refugee applications from Africa and the Middle East to already have family in New Zealand. This had been instituted in the securitisation push by Jonathan Coleman in 2010 and effectively limited refugee resettlement from those regions. For Lees-Galloway, getting agreement between coalition partners on this matter was a significant achievement:

> The big one for me was removing the arbitrary restriction on people from Africa and the Middle East. That was an important one to me personally. Again, you don't have to read too far between the lines to figure out why it took so long to get that one over the line. . . . Part of that was just the time that it took, part of it was that we were not able to get consensus across the three parties of government around some stuff.

A proposal to remove the family link requirement had been put to Cabinet in May 2018, which then became public a year later in May 2019 when a campaign gathered pace. Peters challenged the proposed policy change in a major television interview in June 2019, claiming that the family link policy 'can hardly be racist. How could it possibly be racist when all the [refugees] coming in are brown or black? How could that possibly be racist?' (One News 2019). It was not until October 2019, eighteen months after initial proposals had been put forward, that this relatively simple policy change was confirmed. Such moves were indicative of the broader 'handbrake' that New Zealand First and Winston Peters had claimed to represent in the coalition arrangement, limiting the most progressive initiatives of the Labour Party and, from the perspective of Green Party leader James Shaw, acting as 'an agent of chaos' in government (Trevett 2020). Reports after the Coalition Government ended in 2020 confirmed difficulties in the immigration portfolio. Lees-Galloway was described as 'at the front line of the differences between Labour and NZ First'; 'NZ First had expected Labour to go further on its own policy to reduce net migration', and consequently 'every single immigration issue was absolute torture' (Trevett 2020).

Iain Lees-Galloway's term as Minister of Immigration came to an end in July 2020 when he was sacked by Prime Minister Jacinda Ardern for having a consensual but 'inappropriate' relationship with a former electorate staff member. His final six months in office were dominated by the impact of the Covid-19 pandemic and the government's rapid border closure and immigration suspension, which we cover in the conclusion of this book. Lees-Galloway's tenure as Minister of Immigration and the Labour–New Zealand First Coalition Government's three-year term was shaped around clear plans to manage immigration numbers in light of the rapid growth in net migration overseen by Michael Woodhouse. Residence approval numbers were reduced, but this did not equate to reductions in net migration, which increased further between 2018 and 2020. At the same time, policy shifts created sharper distinctions between temporary migrants in states of extended temporariness and smaller proportions of these temporary migrants were able to gain residence rights. Migrant exploitation represented a constant challenge and, despite new investment and regulation, continued to be regularly and prominently reported. The 15 March 2019 terrorist attack represented a more immediate crisis and one that revealed the unevenness of border securitisation and immigration control over the preceding two decades.

As we shall describe in the conclusion that follows, the Covid-19 global pandemic emerged in early 2020, postponing several of the new policy initiatives that Lees-Galloway had been leading and demanding a completely different approach to the border and migration. Overall, Lees-Galloway's tenure highlighted how complex the migration regime had become, how much it was in the crosshairs of multiple political, bureaucratic, business, and public interests, and perhaps how the control supposedly enabled by migration management was at least somewhat illusory. However, first we discuss a major topic that has emerged in recent years regarding the proper role of Māori in the immigration policymaking process.

Te Tiriti o Waitangi and Immigration

In their chapter in the 2017 book *Fair Borders? Migration Policy in the Twenty-First Century* (Hall 2017b), published in the lead-up to the 2017 election, Tahu Kukutai and Arama Rata (2017: 27) identify what they refer to as 'a yawning hole in policy making and research relating to immigration; that is, the exclusion of indigenous peoples and perspectives'. Māori are 'erased . . . from national conversations on immigration'. This 'yawning hole' has manifested itself in different ways across the four decades covered by this book, and as we mentioned in the Introduction, we do not agree as authors on the width or depth of this hole. These questions can also be raised in the era covered by this chapter. For Woodhouse, questions relating to Te Tiriti o Waitangi were other politicians' responsibility: 'our Treaty obligations are, I think, pretty broadly understood and I wasn't part of any conversation philosophically about where immigration policy fits into that'. In slight contrast, Lees-Galloway did acknowledge the fact that 'the Treaty [of Waitangi] was set up around migration. Something that's overlooked. . . . I think we do have obligations to talk about that', but framed such matters in the limited terms of consultation. He gave an example of an instance where mana whenua had not been consulted by MBIE on the development of refugee resettlement in a new region, stating that 'in this day and age it's just a given you would consult with iwi on that'.

Rather than substantive engagements with the relationship of Te Tiriti o Waitangi to immigration policy, or questions of Māori sovereignty as outlined in Te Tiriti, both Woodhouse and Lees-Galloway were more comfortable talking about Māori as stakeholders. Woodhouse reported some interactions with the Māori Party, who were in governing arrangements with National between 2008 and 2017, about concerns over a proposed increase in RSE numbers (which went ahead regardless) and its implications for Māori workers who might be competing for similar opportunities in horticulture and viticulture. Similarly, Lees-Galloway also reported being questioned by 'Māori workers' about migrants taking their jobs or impacting the conditions of available work. Such accounts arguably position Māori as one of many labour-force stakeholders and in doing so reconstitute in economic terms the 1980s and 1990s framing of Māori as simply another ethnic group, thus minimising Indigenous status (Walker 1994). In Lees-Galloway's contemporary articulation of this perspective, Māori and Treaty concerns are just one of many 'lenses':

> It's true, there's a whole range of lenses. You do need to think about things like social cohesion. You do need to think about the Treaty obligations. You do need to think about the migrant communities themselves and what you're doing to support them and enable them to flourish and so there are multiple lenses through which immigration needs to be looked at. I suspect that probably most governments recently have, I think rightly emphasised the labour-force lens of migration, perhaps have overlooked the others and maybe have thought that's for the Office of Ethnic Affairs or for some other part of government to worry about.

Both Woodhouse and Lees-Galloway also articulated a view that Māori businesses had a stake in immigration; that, as Woodhouse put it, 'iwi up and down the country own a substantial swag of land and business and were, you could say, beneficiaries of immigration policy that enabled overseas workers to work in their industries'. Such claims assert a promissory view of the Māori economy as leading to social, political, and economic improvement for Māori without addressing structural alterations to governing arrangements and power sharing. Such a view was expressed by John Key in 2009 when he made it clear that he wanted to resolve Treaty settlements and discussions because he was 'impatient to see all Māori standing strong, economically independent and fulfilling their potential' (Key 2009). As Maria Bargh put it in relation to this 'post-settlement world', Treaty breaches and addressing The Treaty are framed as *historical* rather than contemporary influences on the constitution of New Zealand: 'The Crown's position does not question the fundamentals upon which its political power is based and instead continues behaviour already proven to be contrary to Te Tiriti' (Bargh 2012: 146).

And yet, in relation to immigration policy, there have been alternative articulations between 2011 and 2020 that reflect more substantive engagements with Te Tiriti o Waitangi and governing arrangements, although these were largely unrecognised publicly or in our interviews. As we have already noted, the Māori Party had highlighted alternative, Te Tiriti-based policies in 2011 and 2014, and Margaret Mutu had publicly raised questions about the socio-cultural impacts of immigration policies for Māori in 2011. Immigration featured in *The Report of Matike Mai Aotearoa – The Independent Working Group on Constitutional Transformation* (2016), convened by Moana Jackson and chaired by Margaret Mutu. *Matike Mai* seeks '[t]o develop and implement a model for an inclusive Constitution for Aotearoa based on tikanga and kawa, He Whakaputanga o te Rangatiratanga o Niu Tireni of 1835, Te Tiriti o Waitangi of 1840, and other indigenous human rights instruments'. The report highlighted how questions of immigration were central to the maintenance of mana (authority) and rangatiratanga (sovereignty), that '[a]s with any concept of power, mana or rangatiratanga always included the right to determine who could live or pass through one's jurisdiction. It implied an authority to control the flow and conduct of immigrants . . .'). The various constitutional arrangements proposed in *Matike Mai* separate out a rangatiratanga sphere (iwi/hapū assembly) from a kāwanatanga sphere (the Crown in Parliament) and a relational sphere, bringing these together, offering potential to rethink immigration policy authority and forms of decision-making.

Kukutai and Rata (2017) have also outlined an approach to immigration that is based in Te Tiriti o Waitangi, that recognises and asserts rangatiratanga and prioritises manaakitanga. They describe manaakitanga as relating to 'mutual care and respect for people, honouring one another or power sharing, and the protection of our environments' (Kukutai & Rata 2017: 40–41). As Kukutai and Rata (2017) outline, drawing on manaakitanga would not simply erase economic dimensions of migration but rather recognise that there is a need for mutual benefits between migrants and the nation. They also argue for a different way of thinking about how migration is organised: that care is needed in accommodating and including new arrivals and their families without the burdens of over-bureaucratisation, that whakapapa (ancestral, genealogical) relationships with countries in the Pacific need to be prioritised in encouraging migration, and that the minimalist approach to refugee resettlement needs to be redressed. It is notable that such assertions were absent from and differ both discursively and practically from much of the 2011–20 push towards temporary migration overseen by Guy, Woodhouse, and Lees-Galloway that we have discussed in this chapter.

Conclusion

The nine years from 2011 to the Covid-19 border closure in 2020 represented the culmination of significant transformational developments in New Zealand migration policy since the 1980s. As we have traced earlier in this book, the Immigration Act 1987 and the Immigration Amendment Act 1991 opened the possibility of large-scale immigration but only tentatively provided the tools for Ministers of Immigration to manage the type and number of migrants. In the following two decades there was consistent, cumulative policy development focused on selecting economically valuable migrants, enhancing security, and paying greater attention to managing temporary residents. By 2011, these foundations of twenty-first-century migration policy had been laid. The Ministers of Immigration covered in this chapter (Nathan Guy, Michael Woodhouse, and Iain Lees-Galloway) were tasked with managing the outcomes of those settings. As we have seen, this decade was a period of intense development and modification of technologies for managing migration – new visas, pathways, regulations, monitoring, and border control. Migration became more complex, more interconnected with other social, economic, and political domains, and more salient as a political issue, especially as net migration rates reached highs that exceeded even those in the nineteenth century.

It is notable, especially in comparison to the 1980s, that migration policymaking has shifted from the peripheries of political agendas to holding a central place in government decision-making, perhaps to an extent not seen since the nineteenth century when immigration policy was a central plank in the project of settler colonialism. Unlike in the nineteenth century, however, the immigration portfolio itself remained a middling political role that brought as much career risk as it did opportunity for advancement.

Migration policymaking sometimes became a protracted matter of cabinet debate, in a manner that was less apparent in the preceding three decades covered by this book. Woodhouse spoke of positioning migration policy in National's economic-development agenda while negotiating the sometimes competing interests of senior ministers in other portfolios. For Lees-Galloway, the challenge was the 'torturous' negotiations with Winston Peters and New Zealand First in a complex three-way governing arrangement with the Green Party. Record high net migration also meant that these debates took place in a public sphere characterised by an avalanche of data on migration and population growth and considerable anxiety about their impact on housing, infrastructure, and employment.

The migration regime that had been developed by the 2010s also raised questions of ethics, rights, and inclusion. The temporary migration regime first initiated in the early 2000s was by the mid-2010s doing much more than just serving as a tool to facilitate the growth of international education or resolve short-term labour shortages and address skill gaps. Rather, temporary migration had become an established part of educational and labour markets, and while both National and Labour governments increasingly framed temporary migration as distinct from permanent migration, migrants, employers, educational providers, and migration industry actors all promoted and sought to achieve pathways to residence and long-term settlement and inclusion. Defining the line between permanent and temporary migration – between those who can become part of society and those who will be used and then discarded – raises fundamental ethical questions about the government of migration. Indeed, reports of migrant exploitation and fraud became increasingly common during this decade, leading to new efforts to manage the consequences that the migration regime itself was central in producing. To manage these distinctions and consequences, Woodhouse and then Lees-Galloway oversaw an increasing stratification of rights accorded to migrants who were deemed to be lower skill, lower quality, and only short-term residents. Woodhouse viewed such regulations as appropriate mechanisms to 'keep the price of residence and citizenship high', while Lees-Galloway empathised with temporary migrants but maintained an incapacity to operate any other kind of migration regime. Regardless of their framing, ministers in this period were entangled in constructing new ethical positions on migration and overseeing a complex bureaucratic apparatus needed to establish and regulate the distinction between temporary and permanent migrants.

CODA

The Covid-19 Interregnum

From 11:59pm tonight we will close our border to any non-residents and citizens attempting to travel here. This will stop tourists or temporary visa holders, including students or temporary workers, from coming to and entering into New Zealand.

— Prime Minister Jacinda Ardern, 19 March 2020
  (Radio New Zealand 2020b)

On 19 March 2020, Prime Minister Jacinda Ardern announced the full closure of the New Zealand border to anyone who was not a New Zealand citizen or permanent resident. The border closure in response to the effects of the global Covid-19 pandemic was an unprecedented form of border enforcement. Indeed, as Ardern noted in her announcement, 'at no time in New Zealand's history has a power like this been used'. Ardern was unrelenting in the intention to maintain border closure, asserting that she was 'not willing to tolerate risk at our border, that is where predominantly most of our cases are coming from' (Radio New Zealand). The New Zealand border would remain closed for much of the next two years, with only brief openings to Australia and exempt travellers, before fully reopening on 31 July 2022. Iain Lees-Galloway, who stood in the background while the Prime Minister made her speech and answered questions from reporters about the details and consequences of the move, was Minister of Immigration at the time of the border closure, but by July 2020 he had resigned.

The New Zealand Government's border closure in response to the Covid-19 pandemic initially appeared to mark an end to the four decades of significant transformation in migration policymaking since the 1980s – and to top the growing significance of migration to population, culture, economy, and politics in New Zealand. The year to June 2020 recorded New Zealand's highest net migration rate to date, but this was largely due to the sudden return of New Zealand citizens and permanent residents and the inability of many visitors, tourists, and temporary visa holders to depart during lockdowns. By June 2021, net migration had plummeted to -6585, and in June 2022 New Zealand recorded a -17,270 net migration loss (Statistics New Zealand 2022). These very low migration numbers, especially in contrast to the previous five years of record net migration gains, did include a substantial net gain of 13,642 New Zealand citizens in the year to June 2021. This gain would turn out to be temporary. Emigration took off again in the year following, with a net loss of -11,789 citizens by June 2022. By May 2023, the loss had grown to -30,800. Among temporary migrants, most working holiday visa holders departed within 2020, and international students followed suit, often as they completed their studies. Work visa holders and their families remained, however: excluding working holiday visa holders, the population of people on work visas in New Zealand only reduced from 187,191 in April 2020 to 171,246 in December 2021 (MBIE 2024).

While it seemed to signal a closure to the world at the time, the border closure during the Covid-19 pandemic turned out to be an interregnum rather than a collapse. During this time, it was possible for government, academics, commentators, and the public to muse over migration, its significance for population and society, and the potential ways forward for migration policymaking. For its part, the government undertook reviews of different elements of the migration regime. In 2021, the New Zealand Productivity Commission (2022) was tasked by Minister of Finance Grant Robertson to undertake a review of 'Immigration Settings for New Zealand's Long-Term Prosperity and Wellbeing'. The Commission reported back in 2022 and, among other things, recommended that the government address Te Tiriti o Waitangi in migration policymaking; be more transparent about migration policy; address the relationship between migration, population growth, and infrastructure development; and reduce restrictions on work visa holders that were underpinning workplace exploitation.

In the meantime, new Minister of Immigration Kris Faafoi launched an 'Immigration Reset' in May 2021. Initially, the reset was framed as a sharp departure from previous approaches to migration policy, 'a once-in-a-generation opportunity to take a different path for immigration' (Nash & Faafoi 2021). Two months later, a cabinet paper rebranded the process as a 'rebalance' with the more modest goal of addressing 'the volume and skill mix of immigration' (Faafoi 2021a). Once finalised, the rebalance included the relaunch of the Accredited Employer Work Visa scheme, which had been developed under Lees-Galloway, although this was now twinned with a 'Green List' of very high-skilled occupations that would be fast-tracked to residency (something akin to the auto-pass policy of the 1990s). In a short space of time, migration policy looked like it would go in a different direction before returning to the trajectory of policy development underway in Woodhouse and Lees-Galloway's tenures.

The New Zealand Government was also faced with significant issues related to the very large population of people on temporary visas in New Zealand. When borders closed in March 2020, there were more than 300,000 people on temporary work and study visas in New Zealand, constituting more than 6 per cent of the resident population. Many did not have access to basic rights or welfare during the pandemic, leading to particularly challenging situations in places like Queenstown that had especially high numbers of unemployed temporary migrants

(Collins 2021). While most working holiday visa holders and international students departed over the course of 2020, most work visa holders and their families remained. Many of these people had been affected by the 2017 reforms to work visas that Woodhouse had overseen, which would have seen them depart New Zealand by August 2021 (having hit the three-year limit for lower-skilled work visas). The potential impacts on the labour market were significant, as was the risk of a large undocumented population. In September 2021, Faafoi (2021b) announced the 2021 Resident Visa, a 'one-off pathway' for people who had been on temporary work visas for three years or more to gain a residence class visa following police and health checks. Effectively an amnesty for temporary visa holders, this initiative led to 211,401 residence visas being issued to workers and their families between December 2021 and October 2024 (MBIE 2024). Thus, when the Accredited Employer Work Visa scheme kicked off in late 2022, it was to some extent a blank slate. By December 2023, when this book was being finalised, the population on AEWV had grown already to 75,501. The RSE scheme, which had been paused in 2020 and 2021 while thousands of workers were stranded in New Zealand, was kickstarted in late 2022 with a new increase in the total cap to 19,000 for the year to June 2023 (Immigration New Zealand 2022) and 19,500 for the year to June 2024 (Immigration New Zealand 2023). International student numbers have been slower to recover, but by October 2023 they had reached 57,828 (before the seasonal decline in students over school and university summer holidays). All signs pointed to a return to reliance on high-volume temporary migration as a crucial feature of labour and educational markets (MBIE 2024).

The 2023 General Election took place shortly before this book was finalised. In early 2023, Jacinda Ardern resigned as Prime Minister, with the leadership of the Labour Party and prime ministership quickly transitioning to Chris Hipkins, a senior cabinet minister who had overseen the education and health portfolios and was prominent as the Minister for Covid-19 Response. Following Kris Faafoi's resignation from Parliament in June 2022, Michael Wood had taken over as Minister of Immigration, but he succumbed to a scandal around non-declaration of investments in June 2023, and the role was passed to Andrew Little for the four months leading up to the general election. While Labour initially maintained reasonable polling following the change in leadership, by the middle of 2023 it became clear that they were unlikely to win a third term. The election campaign was dominated by populist politics from the ACT party and New Zealand First, especially in relation to the growing significance of Te Tiriti o Waitangi and Māori involvement in governance. Meanwhile, the National Party lambasted

Labour for government debt and inflation. Immigration played little role in the campaign, even though New Zealand was experiencing higher net migration figures than it had before the Covid-19 pandemic – 128,900 in the twelve months to October 2023 (Statistics New Zealand 2023) – and serious issues were emerging over the operation of the Accredited Employer Work Visa scheme (Burns 2023).

On election night, National won 38.06 per cent of the vote (forty-eight seats), in comparison to the Labour Party's 26.91 per cent (thirty-four seats), the Green Party's 11.6 per cent (fifteen seats), the ACT party's 8.64 per cent (eleven seats), and New Zealand First's 6.08 per cent (eight seats). Te Pāti Māori won six of the seven Māori electorate seats. National formed a three-way coalition with the ACT party and New Zealand First and promptly issued a 100-day plan that was dominated by commitments to repeal legislation introduced by the preceding Labour and Labour–New Zealand First governments, especially those surrounding issues of co-governance with Māori. Immigration did not feature in the 100-day plan but it was a focus of each of the coalition agreements. These included commitments to: increase the RSE cap and enhance its flexibility, introduce a five-year parent visa with no social security rights, remove wage requirements for the Skilled Migrant Category, and liberalise rules for family members of visa holders (New Zealand National Party 2023). The plan also promised to: improve the AEWV, ensure Immigration New Zealand is addressing risk and verification of applicants properly, investigate the establishment of an 'essential worker' planning mechanism, commit to enforcement of migrant exploitation issues, and address lack of focus in immigration policy (New Zealand National Party 2023). Erica Stanford of the National Party was appointed as the new Minister of Immigration, only the third woman to hold the role after Annette King and Lianne Dalziel.

The Covid-19 border closure, and its consequences for immigration flows and the then-ruling Labour Government, marked a dramatic end to the period of migration policymaking that we have focused on in this book. The research for this book had been developed in 2017 and the first set of interviews completed in 2019, at a time when a complete closure of the New Zealand border seemed impossible. In many respects, the border closure and suspension of many immigration operations between 2020 and 2022 provide closure for the stories and histories that we have explored in this book, while also reinforcing some of the key themes that we have addressed. For a time, it seemed like a complete reset and redirection was possible, but it was clear by the end of 2023 that immigration policy was continuing to build on the direction of travel established over the course of the period we have discussed in this book. The objectives of immigration policy were focused on economic benefits; the shift from permanent settlement to the management of high-volume temporary migration programmes was entrenched; and risk and security were upheld as key priorities in the management of migration and border control. As we discuss in the Conclusion, the continuity of migration policy that we observe here and over this period speaks to the ways in which immigration has been institutionalised as a common-sense feature of the operation of government in New Zealand.

Conclusion

T his book has provided an account of New Zealand migration policymaking over the past half-century through the insights of the most senior government official within this country's migration system: the Minister of Immigration. Our primary source material has been interviews with all but three of the eighteen Ministers of Immigration in office between 1981 and 2020, whom we interviewed in person and by Zoom video-conferencing between December 2019 and February 2021. In addition to these interviews, our narrative has drawn extensively on secondary material such as academic histories and social scientific articles in peer-reviewed journals, and to a limited extent on other primary sources such as contemporary and historical media articles and government records. Our analysis of this material has aimed to produce a historically situated account of a particularly rapid period of change in New Zealand's migration regime, with sufficient historical analysis of earlier periods to frame the context out of which these more recent changes have emerged.

Our aim in this conclusion is to draw together and synthesise some key dimensions of governing migration in New Zealand that have emerged across the last half-century. We begin by outlining key elements of transformations in immigration policy, including: the introduction of new ideas about liberal multiculturalism into immigration policymaking; the increasing adoption of neoliberal market logic in migration management; the expansion of temporary migration through a diverse range of socio-legal channels; the rise of a technocratic-managerial approach to the increasingly complex migration system; the shifting political and ethical framing of immigration and migrant rights; and the consequences these shifts have for the role of the Minister of Immigration. We also highlight some key themes shaping New Zealand migration governance across the period of interest, including: the ongoing influence of empire and New Zealand's particular version of colonialism; the significance of emigration to Australia; and the mobility and diffusion of migration policy 'models' and 'best practices'. In this conclusion, we argue that there has been an institutional entrenchment of a New Zealand migration regime based on liberal and neoliberal ideas about multiculturalism and market-led economic growth – ideas which were thought strange and new in the early 1980s, but which have now become taken for granted as such basic common sense that it appears unthinkable to question them (see Gamlen & Sherrell 2022).

The Transformation of New Zealand's Migration Regime

In our analysis, we have identified several major shifts in migration policy across the period from 1981 to 2020. Firstly, New Zealand's migration system has transformed over the past four decades from a racially exclusive system underpinned by ideas of empire and colonisation into an economically exclusive one underpinned by ideas of liberal multiculturalism, neoliberal economics, and geopolitical reorientation towards the Asia-Pacific. We have traced the growing perception, since the 1970s and 1980s, that New Zealand's pre-1986 immigration policy favouring 'traditional source countries' was a legacy of an imperial racism, and that – as an independent country in the Asia-Pacific region – New Zealand ought to welcome immigrants of any nationality. The ethno-demographic implications of this shift have been clear in the significant immigration-led diversification of New Zealand society from the 1990s onwards. While the multicultural underpinnings of immigration policy nominally assert non-discrimination in immigration selection, our analysis has shown how different forms of discrimination and differential inclusion of migrants into society have emerged over these four decades as central characteristics of New Zealand's approach to migration.

The increasingly multicultural and economic discourse under-pinning immigration policy has not been without challenges, however. Not least among these has been significant friction with the increasing focus on bicultural policy in New Zealand, which focuses on addressing the ills of settler colonialism and affirming Māori sovereignty, and which resists the idea that Indigenous Māori are simply one of multiple cultural groups of equal status (Spoonley 2015b; Spoonley et al. 2003). At the same time, a politics of anti-immigration has emerged periodically. It has particularly targeted Asian peoples. In New Zealand, the label 'Asian' is an ethnic meta-category that denotes a diverse range of peoples who identify and/or connect with various regions of East and Southeast Asia (in contrast with British usage, where 'Asian' typically denotes people from South Asia). More broadly, anti-immigrationism has resisted diverse immigration flows as a clash with the dominant White and/or bicultural identity and culture of New Zealand. Specific policies have occasionally been aimed at Asian, Pacific, Middle Eastern, and African immigration, but there have not been any successful major political challenges to the discourse of liberal multiculturalism and neoliberal economics that now underpins New Zealand's migration regime. These ideas dictate that immigration should advance the broader neoliberal globalisation of New Zealand's economy and society.

The increasingly multicultural orientation of New Zealand's immigration policy has not, however, led to equal treatment of all migration flows. The liberalisation of immigration policy initiated by the 1987 Immigration Act has, over three decades, been configured through the neoliberal economic orthodoxies that have reshaped state and society in New Zealand since the 1980s. We have shown how the reforms of the Act grew out of the progressive, anti-racist, and pro-equal-opportunity stance of the Third Labour Government, and were drafted under the Muldoon-led National Government in the late 1970s and early 1980s, initially focusing on overturning race-based immigration controls. The Act itself was eventually passed by the Fourth Labour Government, however, where it eventually became incorporated into a much wider transformation of New Zealand society and state based on the discourses and principles of neoliberal economics. And yet, the 1987 legislation was not initially part of the economic agenda of neoliberalism. Rather, it was only after initial liberalisation that the opportunity emerged for key reformers such as Roger Douglas and Bill Birch to work with bureaucrats to reconfigure immigration policy in a way that would prioritise economic benefits, target skills and investment, and respond to gaps in the labour market. They saw an opportunity to harness socially liberal ideas associated with multiculturalism in service of their economically liberal priorities. Throughout the 1990s and into the twenty-first century, this neoliberal transformation of immigration policy took shape through an increasing emphasis on the perceived need for New Zealand's economy and society to become more 'global' in outlook, leading to ever-more monitoring and refinement of immigration targets and outcomes, to experimentation with new market-oriented immigration regulations and technologies, and to the development of different and unequal socio-legal statuses for different categories and nationalities of migrants. While diverse and mutable, all of these developments have been framed around the basic claims that immigration should economically benefit New Zealand, that the state should regulate immigration to maximise these economic benefits, that immigration policy should be outwardly neutral in relation to nationality, and that immigrants should instead be selected based on abstract assessments of economic value in terms of wealth, age, and skills.

Perhaps the most striking element of this neoliberal shift in immigration policy has been a declining focus on permanent settlement and a growing emphasis on temporary migration, through a wide range of socio-legal channels. Until the mid-1990s, even after the first wave of neoliberal reforms, immigrants were still viewed as permanent settlers and future New Zealand citizens. Permanent residence rights were usually granted before immigrants even arrived. In contrast, since the late 1990s, we have seen the widespread emergence of staggered and stepwise immigration pathways into long-term settlement and residence. For most immigrants, the first step to permanent settlement is now not an offshore application, but entry on one of an increasingly complex range of temporary visas for work and study. While discursively framed as giving immigrants an opportunity to experience living in New Zealand and demonstrate their desirability as potential settlers, the effect of this transformation has been to generate an unprecedentedly large temporary migrant population, with different groups holding widely different socio-legal statuses, and some groups effectively becoming 'permanently temporary'. It is striking that at the time the New Zealand border closed in response to the Covid-19 pandemic in March 2020, more than 6 per cent of people living in New Zealand were on a temporary work or study visa. The rights of migrants are stratified by notional skill levels and perceived economic potential in ways that are now difficult even for professional immigration experts to comprehend, and temporary migrants are increasingly vulnerable to exploitation and fraud.

The growing complexity of New Zealand's migration system, alongside increasing dependence on temporary migration, has created significant challenges for successive New Zealand governments. Over the course of our study period, we have observed a growing ethos of technocratic managerialism in the development of immigration policy and the work of the Minister of Immigration, which has become increasingly prominent over the past two decades. Government operations have become ever-more reliant on a complex range of computer systems and other technologies designed to categorise, assess, process, and monitor immigrants and their interactions with broader society, in line with a growing spectrum of key performance indicators, designed to suit a range of stakeholders in government and in private-sector companies.

The basic points system, first introduced in the 1991 Immigration Amendment Act, remains central to the New Zealand Residence Programme. By 2020, however, it was surrounded by an array of other technologies: metrics for establishing skills of migrants; techniques for assessing the legitimacy of qualifications, job offers, health, language ability, relationships, wealth, and other characteristics; and border-surveillance measures that offer data on passenger movements, to enable new forms of control and monitoring. These technologies make migration governable in a way that articulates with the wider neoliberal economic logic driving other areas of policy. Governing migration has become an exercise in optimising the migration market and regulating against 'market failures' such as irregular migration. Moreover, the points system now relates to a permanent immigration programme that accounts for a small fraction of actual immigration. Most people now immigrate through a variety of temporary migration programmes that have made it possible for policymakers to shape, monitor, and enforce selection criteria with far greater power and far less scrutiny than is possible through the points system.

The transformations we outline have not only involved a change in the technical, econometric methods of managing migration; they have also entailed the emergence of a new kind of ethics surrounding what were once called 'rights' and are now more often described in terms of 'social inclusion'. The imperial migration regime was deeply exclusionary, but its harshest exclusions occurred at the border: immigrants, especially 'White' ones, were formally accepted as residents with near-automatic pathways to naturalisation and citizenship. Discrimination against non-Whites, non-English-speaking Whites, and 'less-White' groups was rife. But it did not involve the creation of formally separate legal statuses. This commitment to equality before the law for all residents is now largely gone. Elements of it remained during the initial liberalisation of immigration policy in the 1980s and 1990s, but the last two decades have seen the deliberate creation of multiple socio-legal statuses for different groups within New Zealand society. People holding temporary work and study visas now have different bundles of rights, stratified by the length of time they can live in the country, the work that they can undertake, whether they can live with family, and whether they can access public healthcare, education, and other basic social services. The shift from permanent to temporary migration has profoundly changed what it means to be 'a New Zealander'. Prior to the period of our study, this label was deeply racialised but did imply a formal status of equality under law and an attached bundle of standard rights and obligations. By the end of the period, it was a much more contested category, claimed by an increasingly diverse range of groups with different ethnic identities, demographic characteristics, mobility patterns, legal statuses, and levels of inclusion within New Zealand society.

A key feature of the transformation of immigration policy and its implications for New Zealand society has been the increasingly peripheral position of family immigration. Under the imperial migration regime, family was a central concern because immigration was oriented towards population-building. The increasing focus on economic returns from immigration has positioned family in a quite different way. Especially since the 2010s, migrants who gain residence rights have been able to bring their partners and dependent children if they have them, but they are effectively unable to bring parents or children over the age of eighteen unless those people can gain entry themselves. For temporary migrants, the restrictions are even greater, with people on many work and study visas precluded from family sponsorship. Thus, even those migrants who gain residence must often spread their lives transnationally if they want to maintain a meaningful family life, through regular interactions with their wider families, siblings, parents, and grandparents. As Ran and Liu (2021: 148) have recently put it, this situation constitutes 'the emergence of forced multi-location and multi-generational immigrant families whereby family members have limited choice but to live across different national, geographic, cultural, and linguistic localities'.

The transformation of immigration policy has thus also generated a different ethics of migration, one where migrants have increasingly been valued and granted socio-legal statuses according to how much human capital and economic capital they are deemed to possess. While inclusion is still offered up for the small minority who qualify for residence rights, immigration policy has become increasingly transactional and extractive towards most arrivals. They are now framed as temporary contributors to labour and educational markets, without the prospect of full, long-term inclusion. In a word, many of them have effectively become guestworkers. In the final years covered in this book, former ministers such as Michael Woodhouse and Iain Lees-Galloway have framed migrants in these stratified, commodifying – and to some extent dehumanising – terms, emphasising the 'price of citizenship' and the 'quality' of migrants as factors determining whether they deserve to remain long term in New Zealand. Thus, while immigration policy has been increasingly influenced by socially liberal ideas of multiculturalism over the last four decades, at an even more fundamental level it has been shaped in conformity with the neoliberal economic ideas that have taken hold across New Zealand society.

Fragments of Empire and Colonialism

These transformations in New Zealand immigration policy have taken place on the edges of a changing but persistent global empire. From the signing of Te Tiriti o Waitangi and through most of the twentieth century, immigration policy in New Zealand evolved as part of Great Britain's imperial and colonial expansion. The incorporation of New Zealand into this imperial migration regime involved rapid White settler immigration and population growth in the nineteenth century, supported by the usurpation of Māori sovereignty, the acquisition of Māori land, and the exclusion of almost all non-White immigrants. Like its settler colonial kin-nations, Australia and Canada, New Zealand relied on encouraging and subsidising inflows of largely British immigrants, and over time establishing and refining legal and administrative systems for processing them. New Zealand maintained a colonial-era preference for immigrants from 'traditional source countries' long after its post-colonial peers, Australia and Canada, had dropped their White immigration policies.

While immigration is no longer framed in the terms of the British Empire, New Zealand remains part of the empire-like Anglosphere alliance that has succeeded Great Britain. Like the three other primary British settler colonies – Canada, Australia, and the US – New Zealand has opened its doors to an increasingly diverse range of ethnicities during the period covered by this book. In New Zealand, the initial shift reflected chronic and growing concern about the viability of immigration flows from Britain to sustain population growth and labour-market needs. The gradual opening of immigration opportunities to nationals of other European countries represented a first tentative step beyond British-centric immigration policy. More notable was the encouragement of temporary labour migration from Pacific countries from the 1950s, which represented New Zealand's version of the temporary immigration programmes that America, Britain, and Northern European countries implemented to fuel post-World War II reconstruction and economic expansion. Just as the US took braceros from Mexico, European countries took guestworkers from its southern and eastern peripheries, and Britain opened to immigrants from former colonies, New Zealand encouraged Pacific migration and was relaxed about visa overstaying as long as the economy boomed and employer demand for migrant labour remained high. The result of this, New Zealand's first experiment with guestworker programmes, was a relatively small uptick in ethnic diversification – but one that set the stage for the wholesale liberalisation of immigration policy in the 1980s and the subsequent shift towards more highly regulated temporary migration programmes in the twenty-first century.

Alongside these developments has been a geopolitical and geoeconomic pivot towards Asia and the tentative crafting of a new identity for New Zealand as an independent nation in the Asia-Pacific region. Of all Britain's colonies, New Zealand was one of the most reluctant to leave the imperial nest, because of its deep economic and cultural dependence on Britain for its lifelines of trade, investment, and migration. This reluctance extended, perhaps surprisingly, to generations of Māori leaders who perceived that alliance with the Empire was a way to ensure, as Apirana Ngata famously put it, that 'the future of our race as a component and respected part of the New Zealand people will be less precarious' (Ngata 1943). In 1973, when Britain withdrew from its preferential colonial agreements and joined the European Economic Community instead, New Zealand leaders felt betrayed, and recognised the imperative to find new geopolitical and geoeconomic allies. This recognition formed the immediate historical background to the liberalisation of immigration policy in the 1980s and 1990s, which became an integral part of New Zealand's reorientation towards Asia and the Pacific. In 1981, only 14.8 per cent of the population was born overseas (mostly in Britain), but by 2018 this had risen to 27.4 per cent. In 1981, 85.8 per cent of New Zealand residents identified as European and 8.9 per cent as Māori; in 2018, major ethnic identifications were 70.2 per cent European, 16.5 per cent Māori, 15.1 per cent Asian, 8.1 per cent Pacific, and 1.5 per cent across Middle Eastern, Latin American, and African.

The immigration ministers we interviewed have highlighted how shifts in immigration policy emerged through shifting political rationalities about the diversity of people entering New Zealand. In the initial period of significant legislative change in the 1980s, ending race-based criteria was understood by Anthony 'Aussie' Malcolm, Kerry Burke, Stan Rodger, and others as a matter of 'fairness' and righting the wrongs of the prior regime. Their view reflected a version of liberal multiculturalism and openness to the discourse of globalisation that was then gaining ascendency. Over time, the diversification of immigration has increasingly been framed in terms of a need for economic rather than cultural openness. Immigration, alongside international trade and investment, has come to represent just another cross-border flow of capitalism – a means to improve the skill level of the New Zealand population, labour-market flexibility, and international connections, towards the aim of market-led economic growth.

While the specific policy positions of governments and ministers have varied, in principle the idea still stands that immigration should be open to all nationalities. In practice, however, the race-based exclusiveness of New Zealand's colonial migration regime has been replaced by class-based exclusivity that is expressed in different socio-legal pathways open to different nationalities. Previously immigrants could come from any class if they were White. Now they can come from any race if they are rich. Others who are deemed lower skilled, and are typically from outside Europe and North America, are contingently welcome, within restrictive temporary migration programmes that preclude societal inclusion. And in contrast to the colonial period – during which arrivals were fewer and came more slowly, and New Zealand's border was a rudimentary paper-based (and indeed mostly paperless) affair – the hundreds of thousands of people who arrive annually in New Zealand today are filtered and stratified with bureaucratic precision by an extremely broad array of biometric and other border technologies.

Our analysis also reveals how New Zealand's migration regime has been developed on the foundational legacies of the prior imperial migration regime. While the British Empire has lapsed, to this day New Zealand retains the British monarch as head of state. Te Tiriti o Waitangi remains an agreement between 'The British Crown' and 'Māori', and New Zealand remains a member of the Commonwealth of Nations, 'a voluntary association of 56 independent and equal countries' whose 'roots go back to the British Empire' (The Commonwealth 2025). In many respects, the modern Commonwealth echoes central features of the migration regime of the former British Empire, wherein movement between the White settler colonies and Britain is relatively frictionless while migration from the non-White former subject colonies is more difficult. Today those restrictions are discursively framed in terms of economic criteria rather than racial ones, but the effects are often similar in terms of which source countries are excluded – which raises the question of whether the underlying motivations and policy logics are similar too. In New Zealand, a range of migration policy settings reveals strong traces of intra-imperial mobility, including the Trans-Tasman Travel Arrangement – a fragment of the former British imperial migration space that now constitutes one of the most open borders in the world – as well as its range of visa-waiver programmes, working holiday schemes, bilateral social security and taxation arrangements, and advantageous opportunities for achieving permanent residence and citizenship.

The period of immigration policy change that we have traced in this book has occurred at a time of other transformations in the character of New Zealand society, most notably a growing emphasis on redressing colonial wrongs driven forward by Māori political movements, and a new wave of questioning of the colonially imposed nation-state model and its governance arrangements. Te Tiriti o Waitangi has become an increasingly central element of national life and is now expected to be a touchstone for all government agencies; the 2020 Public Service Act now requires 'the Public Service to engage with Māori and to understand Māori perspectives' (though by early 2024, the new National-led Coalition Government was promising to abolish such requirements and hold a referendum on the constitutional status of The Treaty). For the Ministers of Immigration interviewed for this book, Te Tiriti o Waitangi was not considered central to the making of immigration policy, as we discussed in detail in Chapter 2, where we outlined the fact that as authors we do not all agree on precisely how and why Te Tiriti was absent from such policymaking.

The government emphasis on Treaty-partnership and expectations for substantive engagement with Māori are relatively new. As Ganesh Nana (New Zealand Productivity Commission 2022: 3), Chair of the New Zealand Productivity Commission, put it after overseeing the Commission's extensive inquiry into immigration history and policy settings, 'tāngata whenua have not had an opportunity to present their views on immigration policy since 1840'. An alternative perspective may be that Māori are prominently represented, both formally and informally, across all branches of the New Zealand Government and so have an indirect impact on the direction of policy, including migration policy, more broadly. The process of rethinking the involvement of Māori and the place of Te Tiriti o Waitangi in relation to immigration policy is beyond the scope of this book. But given the fierce political debates on issues of 'co-governance' at the time of writing, it is a challenge that future governments may have to address. Overall, while governments and Ministers of Immigration since the 1980s have advanced a programme of change that departs from imperial approaches and methods, their changes have also sometimes reinforced other aspects of the old ways of doing things.

The transformations of immigration policy that have occurred since the 1980s are also striking for how they have reinforced colonial relationships between New Zealand and Pacific countries. The initial period of Pacific labour migration to New Zealand in the 1950s–70s is well documented, as are the racist Dawn Raids campaigns that disproportionately targeted Pacific people for deportation. In the period covered by this book, we have observed how governments have sought to limit and control migration from the Pacific. Limitations came in the bipartisan agreement to legislatively block access for Samoans to New Zealand citizenship in 1982, the introduction of the points system in 1991 that defined 'high skill' to be inaccessible to people in Pacific countries, the effects of family immigration policies that prioritise the income and wealth of applicants, and the very limited increases in quotas for arrivals from the Pacific.

As our interviews highlight, these limits on Pacific migration have recently been reconfigured. The 2007 introduction of the Recognised Seasonal Employer (RSE) scheme now echoes the guestworker programmes of the post-war period, albeit in the guise of a 'new' form of 'circular labour mobility' – a type of international movement that is proudly 'flexible' from the perspective of employers who want cheap temporary labour, but highly restrictive for migrants and their countries of origin. By ministers interviewed for this book, and in sources dating from the time of its inception, the RSE has been publicly presented as a type of development aid project, in which circular migration is supposedly a triple win for migrants as well as their countries of destination and origin. However, critics continue to maintain that these programmes largely benefit New Zealand employers and are detrimental for migrants (who are vulnerable to exploitation) and their origin countries, which suffer depletion of labour and human capital and become dependent on emigration to relieve unemployment and generate cash remittances.

These programmes can also be conceived as a form of economic and social paternalism, in which Pacific countries are framed as needing New Zealand's support and direction. Such criticisms are often countered by the claim that governments and inhabitants of Pacific countries have often been the most enthusiastic supporters of the RSE, and that one of their most common requests is that such programmes should take more temporary workers. And yet, in 2023 when we were finishing this book, Samoan Prime Minister Fiamē Naomi Mata'afa (Neilson 2023) highlighted the above issues in the RSE (and Australia's Seasonal Worker Programme) and called for an EU-style free-mobility regime in the Pacific, a demand that has been echoed by other Pacific leaders since (Fotheringham 2023). Relatedly, in 2022 the New Zealand Human Rights Commission's (2022) review of the RSE highlighted how it reduces Pacific people's freedom in a way that sustains human rights abuses and, according to Equal Employment Opportunities Commissioner Saunoamaali'i Karanina Sumeo (Radio New Zealand 2022) leads to 'what can be seen as modern day slavery'. At the time of writing, the RSE cap had increased to 20,000 annually, cementing its role as a solution to labour-market shortages for New Zealand's horticultural and viticultural industries, while precluding any pathway to residence rights or social inclusion. In this sense, while the RSE has been seen as a beneficent act on the part of New Zealand, it also conforms to a long-standing and familiar pattern in which richer coloniser countries at the core of the global economy exploit the raw materials and human resources of poorer colonised countries on the peripheries, whose emigrants are reduced to the status of a disposable labour force.

The stories and histories presented in this book also highlight how New Zealand immigration policy is still made in a context of international security alliances that descend directly from the British Empire. New Zealand's immigration policy is still set in compliance with the strategies and policies of a wider five-country alliance with the UK, the US, Canada and Australia. For this group, migration policy is closely associated with the powerful and secretive UK–US agreement on signals intelligence – colloquially known as the 'Five Eyes alliance' – which was formed immediately after World War II to formalise key elements of the UK–US 'special relationship' and of intra-imperial cooperation among Britain's White Dominions, which had already been taking place for centuries by that time. Senior ministers of these countries have always met regularly to ensure their migration policies and operations are in alignment; they have evolved and modernised their migration systems in cooperation with each other over the decades, and they have rarely made any major changes to immigration policy without consulting each other.

The role of this post-imperial alliance in shaping New Zealand's migration policy has grown stronger, not weaker, in the past two decades. Security was a seldom-mentioned word in discussions of immigration policy in New Zealand in the 1980s and 1990s. But after high-profile terrorist attacks in the early 2000s (especially the 11 September 2001 attacks in New York and Washington DC, and the 7 July 2005 bombings in London), persistent murmurings about the need to link migration and security suddenly grew into a sustained roar. In the other countries of the alliance, immigration has been brought under the umbrella of stern new 'homeland security' agencies, which aim to address the problem of large transit regions such as the colossal US–Mexico and US–Canada land borders, Australia's vast coastline, and the UK's integration with an effectively borderless European Union. The result has been that New Zealand – despite being far removed from any similar type of border action – has also increasingly bundled up migration policy with multilateral responses to terrorism and 'securing the border'.

The migration focus of Five Eyes ministerial meetings has deepened significantly since the late 2000s, particularly under the auspices of the so-called 'Anglosphere Five Country Conference on Migration' (the so-called 'Migration Five'), but also through their co-sponsorship of other international forums (such as the Bali Process on People Smuggling, Trafficking in Persons and Related Transnational Crime). In keeping with this growing securitisation of migration, the ministers we interviewed often described key aspects of their role in terms of securing the border and managing security risks associated with immigration. They explained to us how the discourses, technologies, and practices that emerged from the aftermath of the terrorist attacks of the early 2000s and the Migration Five meetings had become central to the government of immigration. Thus, while the leadership of this centuries-long alliance of five rich, predominantly White, English-speaking former British colonies has gradually shifted from the UK to the US, the alliance remains profoundly influential over many aspects of New Zealand's migration regime. In New Zealand, migration control is still often conducted as part of formal international collaborations that represent only the most recent manifestations of a continuous alliance between the core states of Britain's former empire.

Trans-Tasman Connections

One particular legacy from the imperial past looms especially large in New Zealand's migration system: the open border with Australia, which has been proactively maintained since the earliest days of both colonies. The efforts to manage migration since the 1980s that have been discussed in this book have been set against the backdrop of New Zealand's formative geopolitical, economic, social, and cultural connections with Australia. In the early days of settler colonisation, New Zealand often experienced net migration gains from trans-Tasman population movement, alongside its substantial net inflows from Britain and elsewhere. But since the 1970s, New Zealand's consistent net migration gains, which had underpinned its colonial model of development for more than a century, have given way to more-complex patterns of immigration *and* emigration (Gamlen & Sherrell 2022). These have included substantial periodic net migration losses, particularly to Australia. Consistent emigration over the last half-century has led to claims that up to one million New Zealand citizens live in other countries (Gamlen 2011), which would constitute the equivalent of 20 per cent of the resident population. By far the largest proportion is in Australia, where an estimated 670,000 New Zealand citizens now live – equivalent to nearly 15 per cent of New Zealand's population (DFAT n.d.). This dynamic profoundly affects the overall demographic and macro-economic sources of demand for immigration to New Zealand. The trans-Tasman dimension of New Zealand migration governance is therefore an important strand in this book.

In the period 1981–2018, there was a cumulative net loss of -648,448 New Zealand citizens to Australia among a total net loss of -743,861 citizens to all countries (Poot 2010; Statistics New Zealand 2024, for 2011–18). While former ministers interviewed in this book did not dwell on these flows of New Zealand citizens to any great extent, it is clear that these emigration patterns have been a major factor in the formulation of immigration policies. According to conventional New Zealand wisdom, the basic purpose of immigration is to 'replace' New Zealand's population in the context of population ageing and, more importantly, consistent emigration. The link between reliable emigration of New Zealand citizens to Australia, alongside reliable immigration gains, reflects a deep structural entanglement with the Australian economy and labour markets, and the problems that emerge are then resolved through immigration policy.

The trans-Tasman migration connection indirectly affects an extremely broad range of New Zealand policy areas, and sometimes explodes into the foreground of public debate. It did so in the case of the 'Brain Drain Debate' of the 1980s (Reserve Bank of New Zealand 1986), which resurfaced in the early 2000s in relation to efforts to engage with the New Zealand diaspora as part of new knowledge economy shifts (Gamlen 2005). Emigration was also a key narrative in the 2008–17 National Government's emphasis on opening New Zealand to the world: the John Key-led administration sought to turn around net migration losses of citizens by crafting an image of an aspirational New Zealand that would be desirable to both New Zealand citizens abroad and to new migrant arrivals. As New Zealand experienced massive net migration gains in the late 2010s, Michael Woodhouse would highlight these citizen flows as evidence that the government was exercising sufficient controls on immigration policy. Keeping tally of trans-Tasman migration flows has become a common theme in New Zealand politics: when in government, the political parties are always careful to frame emigration as caused by global forces beyond their control. Then when in opposition, they chase headlines by blaming the government of the day for causing a brain drain. As they take turns in this cat-and-mouse game, the parties recycle each other's stunts – such as being photographed in an empty sports stadium symbolising the number of people who have emigrated (Gamlen 2014b). Though made to look like pitched political battle, the national debate over emigration has become more of a ritualised blood sport.

The trans-Tasman connection has also had other indirect influences on immigration policy in New Zealand. Our interviews drew attention to instances where Australian disquiet about the migration of Pacific New Zealanders to Australia surfaced in political interactions. Both Aussie Malcom and Stan Rodger, for instance, described being questioned about this by their Australian counterparts. As Rodger put it, 'they used to take me aside and chew my ear'. New Zealand was framed as a 'back door' for migration to Australia for Pacific people, and Australian disquiet about this phenomenon underpinned restrictions that were placed on New Zealanders between 2001 and 2023 (Hamer 2014). The Australian view of New Zealand as a back door was also noted by Lianne Dalziel, and contributed to legislative changes to citizenship requirements in New Zealand, even though this did not have the desired effect of changing

Australia's position on New Zealand citizen rights. More recently, other changes to Australian immigration legislation and practice have included deportation of New Zealand citizens with criminal convictions, regardless of how long they have lived abroad (Hamer 2023), a move that, until the rapprochement of 2023 under the Albanese Government, had disrupted the typically smooth diplomatic relations between the two countries.

Policy Mobility and Diffusion

The trans-Tasman migration connection is constituted not only in flows of migrants between New Zealand and Australia, but also in the mobility of migration policy models and best practices between the two countries. Put differently, because they share one of the most open borders in the world, their migration governance arrangements are typically either shared or duplicated on both sides of the Tasman. This aspect of New Zealand migration policy is particularly surprising because migration is routinely seen as one of the last areas of international policy where governments claim absolute sovereign control and refuse international oversight as interference. And yet, New Zealand is an example of how the world of international migration policymaking is characterised not by separate sovereign countries each doing their own thing, but by the adoption of almost identical international migration policies in very different countries (Gamlen 2019).

As this book has demonstrated, immigration policy mobility and diffusion is happening both between Australia and New Zealand, and between these states and a range of others. On the one hand, New Zealand functions as one of the laboratories where 'new' migration policies are developed before they are shipped off to other governments, which adopt and adapt them into local policies as examples of 'international best practice'. The well-known policy approach of multiculturalism, which New Zealand policymakers helped refine during the 1970s–80s, can now be found in a range of countries, including those without significant recent histories of immigration. The points-based model of immigration management, refined by Commonwealth settler societies in the 1980s and 1990s, has been touted in quite different contexts, such as China and Kazakhstan (Bedford & Spoonley 2014; Gamlen 2014a). Meanwhile, programmes like New Zealand's Recognised Seasonal Employer scheme have been emulated so often around the world that they have significantly contributed to the emergence of a new generation of guestworker programmes (Castles 2006; Gibson & McKenzie 2014).

On the other hand, New Zealand does not develop migration policies unilaterally, but does so in cooperation with its closest peer states – notably Australia and Canada, both kin-settler colonial nations and members of the five-country alliance to which New Zealand has belonged ever since British colonisation. All of the above-mentioned examples of international migration policy best practice – the end of colonial race controls, the emergence of multiculturalism, the development of the points approach, and the resurgence of temporary labour migration programmes – have been evolved as part of international collaborations between New Zealand and these major peer states.

Ministers of Immigration interviewed for this book frequently drew attention to examples of policy emulation, learning, and adaptation. Kerry Burke and Stan Rodger, for example, both highlighted the significance of Australian and Canadian policy articulations of multiculturalism as an influence in the undertaking of the Immigration Review in 1986 and the formulation of the Immigration Act 1987. Roger Douglas described drawing up the initial approach to the points system (later introduced under Bill Birch in 1991) through interactions that he and senior bureaucrats had with Australian officials. Tuariki Delamere explicitly referenced the Australian residence programme when he proposed a new approach at the 1997 Population Conference that was introduced in a modified form by Lianne Dalziel in the New Zealand Residence Programme in 2002.

Some of these dynamics of policy diffusion have been driven by peer-to-peer engagements among nominally equal allies – but as we intimated above, others have been imposed on New Zealand by its more powerful allies. New security requirements in immigration and border policy reflected US-centred international responses to terrorism in the early-to-mid-2000s, which would then continue to develop and be circulated through the Migration Five network. And the Recognised Seasonal Employer scheme reflected the international establishment of circular labour mobility as a new orthodoxy in migration and development, articulated in high-level international forums and institutions surrounding the United Nations, and developed in parallel with Australia's Seasonal Worker Programme.

These instances of policy mobility and diffusion are indicative of the way that New Zealand has evolved its major migration management frameworks as part of international 'benchmarking loops' (Gamlen 2019). In this form of policy mobility, 'Rather than being imposed coercively, the models and best practices of [migration policy] being traded, adapted, and adopted . . . are derived and distilled from specific national experiences, held up as exemplars' (Gamlen 2019: 229). Our research suggests that New

Zealand frequently adopts and adapts new migration policy innovations that are purportedly derived from Australian or Canadian models. However, it is likely that these same policies were previously adopted and adapted in Australia and Canada, where they were framed as 'New Zealand models'. In this way, migration policymakers in New Zealand, Australia, and Canada are constantly monitoring, measuring, and refining their regulatory practices in order to compete and collaborate with each other to be the 'best in the international class' in the area of migration management.

The circuit-like forms of policy exchange and development between Australia, Canada, and New Zealand come in a range of configurations and are often recursive, involving mutual and overlapping emulation and adaptation between these countries, and also involving other nations at times, as well as international institutions such as the World Bank and the International Organization for Migration (Gamlen 2019). Benchmarking loops and recursive modelling processes have increased the ability of many policy actors to promulgate certain types of migration policies under the auspices of 'transferring international recognition as best practice'. Among the most important policies to achieve such institutionalisation around the world, partly through the benchmarking loops New Zealand is involved in, are multiculturalism, the points system, temporary labour migration programmes, and border-security imperatives. In addition to the observed convergence in immigration policies, the analysis here and elsewhere also suggests that benchmarking loops of this kind provide legitimacy for policy innovation by ministers and officials – because a particular policy or idea has a supposedly successful precedent elsewhere, there is a licence to experiment in a new context (Gamlen 2019).

The Institutionalisation of Immigration

The accounts of Ministers of Immigration interviewed for this book make it clear that migration is deeply institutionalised in the context of late twentieth-century and early twenty-first-century New Zealand. Migration has been fundamental to populating the islands now known as New Zealand ever since the establishment of colonial rule following the signing of Te Tiriti o Waitangi. The imperial migration regime that was developed and maintained over the subsequent thirteen decades was characterised by key shared assumptions, most notably that migrants ought to be White and preferably British, and that immigration was a means of growing the settled population. In the period covered by this book, these assumptions underpinning immigration policy have been reconfigured. They now revolve around a nominally non-discriminatory 'multicultural' intake. They take a neoliberal approach to the market value of immigration, while emphasising the need to regulate against market failures such as security threats, and restrict the unintentional long-term settlement of temporary migrants. In this sense, the period covered by this book has been one of profound disruption and transformation of New Zealand's migration regime.

The period that our book has considered, however, has been generally one of consolidation rather than ruptures or radical departures. While the four decades from 1981 to 2020 have been characterised by significant changes, the development of immigration policy both within and across governments has been cumulative and incremental. It has been neither partisan nor abrupt. New Ministers of Immigration have built on the approach of their predecessors rather than reversing or reworking policy platforms, and some key pieces of legislation and regulation have been developed across transitions in government. These include the 1987 Immigration Act; the points system embedded in the 1991 Immigration Amendment Act; the security provisions of the 2009 Immigration Act; the Recognised Seasonal Employer scheme; and the realisation of the National Government's 'temporary-means-temporary' vision for labour migration in the Accredited Employer Work Visa scheme, which was finally enacted by the Labour Government as the Covid-19 border closure ended. A key factor behind this continuity and stability in immigration policymaking has been the establishment of durable institutions within and around the civil service, universities, and media for reliably understanding and managing New Zealand's migration system (Gamlen & Sherrell 2019). More so than in many places, migration policy in New Zealand is made by immigration experts in governmental, academic, and non-governmental organisations that are dedicated to issues of immigration, rather than by the elected officials who transit through the office of the Minister of Immigration as they build their political careers (Gamlen & Sherrell 2022).

Such consensus and institutional embeddedness cannot be found in the migration politics of many other countries. Fellow Five Eyes countries such as Australia and Canada display similar patterns of institutionalisation to varying extents. But further afield, immigration policy often remains fiercely political, to the extent that it can topple governments. At the time of writing, in mid-2023, the Dutch Government had just collapsed after failing to reach an agreement on immigration policy. Earlier, during the planning for this book, Donald Trump's successful campaign to become President of the United States of America was initiated around a focus on Mexican and other immigrants, and his presidency was characterised by extreme border and migration policies, including bans on migrants from several predominantly Muslim countries, and the practice of separating families of undocumented migrants. Hard-line anti-immigrant political parties have also been successful at driving harsh border-control policies in many European countries. Moreover, in contrast to the South Pacific, where New Zealand migration policy usually moves in lockstep with neighbouring Australia, immigration elsewhere is often such an international flashpoint that it can lead to fundamental changes to the external relations of states. The UK voted to exit the neighbouring European Union in 2016 largely because of concerns that immigration was out of control, with at least one famous British economist opining that immigration levels had breached a threshold beyond which they could be sustained (Collier 2013). At that time, immigrants accounted for merely 12–14 per cent of the total UK population. The proportion of immigrants in New Zealand's total population has never been below this level since the mid-nineteenth century, and for the vast majority of the past 183 years, it has been far higher.

And yet, by international standards, the politicisation of migration in New Zealand has been mild and has not disturbed a dominant consensus on immigration policy. Winston Peters and his fellow New Zealand First party members are the most obvious exponents of anti-immigration politics in New Zealand. However, as we noted in Chapters 4–6, whenever New Zealand First has actually entered government, they have only moderately affected the policies and regulatory settings around migration. For example, while the party sought to reduce immigration in the 2017–20 coalition with Labour, their focus was only on the level of residence approvals, and they seemed satisfied to leave untouched the rapidly growing student and work visa numbers at that time. Labour similarly dabbled in anti-immigration electioneering in 2016 and 2017 under the brief leadership of Andrew Little, and even offered its own version of commitments to reduce net migration to set numbers, which was already a tried-though-untrue tactic in the UK (Gamlen 2014c). However, once in office, Labour simply carried on the policy development direction of the previous National-led government. Undoubtedly, these periodic small-scale political mobilisations around immigration are significant, especially for peoples who become racialised in the process and must endure bouts of racist abuse and discrimination (McCarthy 2022). In governmental terms, however, while immigration is standard fodder for opposition politics, to date there seems to have been limited potential to transform this into the lightning-rod issue it has become in other parts of the world.

Our analysis suggests that there are several forces at play in constituting and maintaining the institutionalisation of immigration in twenty-first-century New Zealand. The immigration policymaking that we have traced in this book has tended to be characterised by what political scientists sometimes call 'nondecision-making'. Nondecision-making occurs 'when the dominant values, the accepted rules of the game, the existing power relations among groups, and the instruments of force, singly or in combination, effectively prevent certain grievances from developing into full-fledged issues which call for decisions' (Bachrach & Baratz 1963: 641). Nondecisions occur when policy ideas – even though they began their lives once upon a time as the exciting new innovations of passionate policy entrepreneurs and advocates – have been copied, emulated, or imposed so often that they have proliferated and become normal (DiMaggio & Powell 1983; Finnemore & Sikkink 1998; Haas 1992). Nondecisions operate through a 'logic of appropriateness' as opposed to a logic of consequences (March & Olsen 2011): under nondecisions, behaviour is not calculated strategically to achieve some specific objective, but adopted because it symbolises adherence to the norms that constitute the status quo in a specific cultural context (Meyer 2017). In the realm of migration policy, the status quo is characterised by particular ideas, expectations, informal codes of behaviour, and enforceable rules that have become embedded within the formal institutions overseeing and influencing immigration policy and practice.

One of the key contributions of this book has been to trace the assembly and entrenchment of a new 'status quo' for immigration policy over the course of the four decades from 1980 to 2020. In the period we have covered, New Zealand has been transformed by the introduction of neoliberal thought, policy, and practice, with its emphasis on market rule and individualism as common sense. The migration regime has, like all other areas of state and society, also been transformed by this new wave of orthodoxy. Sometimes this has reflected a need to find quick solutions to urgent problems, such as when the New Zealand Treasury briefed the incoming Fourth Labour Government in 1984 that the urgency of the country's crises demanded an immediate neoliberal revolution. Other times, the adoption of specific neoliberal ways of doing things has happened because of pressure to align with powerful partners (such as when New Zealand's powerful Migration Five partners push new alliance-wide initiatives). And often the adoption of neoliberal policies reflects genuine beliefs that New Zealand should emulate overseas policy models – such as in the early 1980s when ministers believed that introducing a multicultural intake was simply the right thing to do, as long as that intake was based on market-led economic principles.

Networks of scientific experts and policy advocates have been key to shaping and promoting the new immigration policy status quo, particularly those who have circulated through key centres of neoliberal thinking such as the New Zealand Treasury (which was at the forefront of the 1980s neoliberal reforms), and other ideological hothouses such as the World Bank (which has played a key role in the development of New Zealand's new Pacific guestworker programme). Indeed, some of the ministers we interviewed were themselves products of these neoliberal networks: Max Bradford worked at both the Treasury and the IMF; David Cunliffe, Clayton Cosgrove, and Jonathan Coleman all carried their experiences as management consultants into their roles, during a period when technocratic managerialism came to dominate immigration policy. By tracing four decades of immigration policy evolution through a range of primary and secondary source materials, we have shown how certain ideas have become internalised as 'common sense' to the extent that they cease to be consciously noticed as expectations or rules. Instead, these status quo ideas and norms operate at an ideological level, where it would be unthinkable for immigration policymakers not to at least pay lip-service to them.

While the most obvious instances of the institutionalisation of immigration policy orthodoxy are the codification of norms in written rules that are enforced and implemented by dedicated bureaucracies, informal norms can also become deeply entrenched. Such norms can be hard for politicians to shift: on the one hand, they lie outside the scope of formal laws that governments can hope to change through their dominance of the legislative branch. On the other hand, such norms fall within the scope of the bureaucrat's 'technical expertise', which is somewhat insulated from the dictates of the executive branch. There are examples of the influence of technical expertise in the persistent emphasis on the economic valuation of immigration as well as the twenty-first-century emphasis on using temporary migration programmes, skills assessments, and monitoring technologies to simultaneously address labour-market gaps, while holding temporary migrants in socio-legal statuses that limit rights and societal inclusion. One example, reported by Bill Birch, was the way that bureaucrats insisted on staying the course in immigration policy development during his negotiations with them. Iain Lees-Galloway's stories of an 'army of officials', 'layers of bureaucracy', and 'doing battle with the permanently employed part of the government' provided further examples. Added to this has been a growing sense of 'regulatory capture', which is 'the process through which special interests affect state intervention in any of its forms' (Dal Bó 2006: 203). In the past decade or so, this regulatory capture has become increasingly evident in the influence exercised by business lobbies in crafting immigration policies to address labour shortages in New Zealand.

Our main point is that many key ideas, norms, and practices concerning immigration and its place in New Zealand society are so deeply internalised that they now form part of unquestionable common sense. New Zealand's regulatory systems for maintaining and managing internationally high immigration rates are embedded deeply not just within formal government agencies but within social organisations more broadly – including in media, research communities, the health and education system, social security provisioning, community group charters, codes of conduct, and so forth – such that many aspects of immigration policy remain essentially off limits to tinkering by elected officials representing formal political positions. Put differently, many aspects of migration management in New Zealand have become effectively pre-political or depoliticised in the sense that they are not only agreed upon by the major political parties, but it would be almost inconceivable for any political party to hold a dissenting view or to implement an alternative model once in power. Many of the issues that animate other countries less used to large-scale immigration are, in the New Zealand case, non-issues. Either they are simply considered unimportant, or they are subject to nondecision-making and the force of the status quo that impedes any challenge to what is conceived to be common sense.

Acknowledgements

Francis: I am very grateful for the opportunity to collaborate with both Alan Gamlen and Neil Vallelly and I thank them for their significant contributions to the conceptualisation and writing of this book. The conversations we have had while bringing this book to press have expanded my perspectives on migration research and the politics of knowledge production that it entails. Neil, your patience appears to be without measure.

This project was conceived partway through a Rutherford Discovery Fellowship (2015–20) entitled 'Nation and Migration: Population Mobilities, Desires and State Practices in 21st Century New Zealand', which was generously funded by Te Apārangi Royal Society of New Zealand. The development of the research first emerged in a discussion with Nicolas Lewis in 2016, and was significantly influenced by conversations with Alan, as well as other collaborators on the Fellowship, Richard Bedford and Wardlow Friesen. Most of the research was undertaken when I was based at Te Ngira: Institute for Population Research (formerly NIDEA) at the University of Waikato, and my thinking towards this project benefited enormously from discussions with Tahu Kukutai, Polly Atatoa Carr, Moana Rarere, Arama Rata, and Yara Jarallah, among others. Renae Dixon, project manager at Te Ngira, provided invaluable assistance in background research and support in planning for the interviews.

Without doubt, the opportunity to speak to former Ministers of Immigration represents a particular privilege. The ministers who participated in the interviews approached the interviews with candour, providing immensely valuable insights into their time in politics, the challenges of migration policymaking, and their current positionalities and outlooks. I would also like to thank Len Cook, Robert Didham, and Richard Bedford, who went out of their way to help me find crucial materials on the 1997 Population Conference and provided their insight into that event and its outcomes. Sam Elworthy has been a significant support through the process of writing, helping to gather what were really valuable commentaries from two anonymous reviewers of the book and a specialist Treaty historian, and to navigate a complicated revision process.

Like all intellectual projects, this one has a personal side too – my daughter, Molly, has been with me throughout, and my partner, Katie, has provided the support I needed to get this done. My mother, Jenny, as always the holder of family wisdom, provided valuable feedback on historical writing, and both her and my father, John, often provided the space I needed to write many of the chapters that now make up the book. Thank you, and I hope you can all see your contributions in the book that has emerged.

Alan: I am deeply grateful to Francis for initiating this project and sustaining it over the years. Since he approached me about the Rutherford Discovery Fellowship collaboration in 2014, Francis has been an invaluable partner, engaging in countless discussions and debates that shaped this work. I also extend my heartfelt thanks to Neil, whose exceptional intellectual and research skills propelled this book to completion, transforming his initial role into that of a co-author. Special thanks to Sam Elworthy for his stewardship of the manuscript, to the anonymous reviewers for their helpful feedback, and to mentors such as Paul Spoonley who helped things along. To the interviewees, your generosity and insights were fundamental – and more broadly, thank you for your service as Ministers of Immigration. Lastly, my deepest appreciation goes to my family for their patience and support throughout this journey.

Neil: I am very fortunate to have had the opportunity to collaborate on this book with scholars with the standing of both Francis and Alan. I came on board the project in 2021 as a research fellow, and I was honoured to be asked to become a co-author of the manuscript in early 2022. I am deeply grateful for their guidance and encouragement in the early stages of drafting the manuscript, and I learned so much from our discussions. I have deep respect for their academic rigour and intelligence, and while developing a single authorial voice for a co-authored manuscript is never easy, I am proud of the book we have produced.

I worked on this project while holding a Rutherford Postdoctoral Fellowship (2022–24) entitled 'The Borders of Capital: Neoliberalism and Regimes of Migrant Detention in Aotearoa New Zealand', which was funded by Te Apārangi Royal Society of New Zealand. I would like to extend a heartfelt thanks to Sam Elworthy for his work on getting the manuscript to publication, organising helpful peer-reviews, and his patience during the final revisions of the manuscript. My colleagues and friends Miranda Johnson and Simon Barber at Ōtākou Whakaihu Waka, University of Otago, have both added valuable insights into the material, and I would like to thank my colleagues in the Sociology, Gender Studies and Criminology programme at Otago for helping me settle into my new role as a permanent lecturer since 2023. My thanks are also extended to Andrew Campbell for his meticulous editing of the manuscript, and to Lauren Donald at AUP for project managing this book.

Finally, I would like to thank my family in Ireland, especially my sister, Lisa, for all their support. And most importantly, my enduring love goes to my partner, Lynley, who has been patient and encouraging throughout, and my son, Molloy, who will hopefully one day understand why his mum and dad write books.

References

Abu-Laban, Y., & Stasiulis, D. (1992). Ethnic pluralism under siege: Popular and partisan opposition to multiculturalism. *Canadian Public Policy/ Analyse de Politiques*, 18(4), 365–86.

Ackleson, J. (2005). Constructing security on the US–Mexico border. *Political Geography*, 24(2), 165–84.

Akbari, S., & MacDonald, M. (2014). Immigration policy in Australia, Canada, New Zealand, and the United States: An overview of recent trends. *International Migration Review*, 8(3), 801–22.

Alchin, T. (1990). The role of the CER – Closer Economic Relations Agreement – in improving Australian/New Zealand relations. *Australian Quarterly*, 62(1), 21–35.

Amoore, L. (2006). Biometric borders: Governing mobilities in the war on terror. *Political Geography*, 25(3), 336–51.

Amoore, L. (2024). The deep border. *Political Geography*, 109, 102547.

Anae, M. (1997). Towards a NZ-born Samoan identity: Some reflections on 'labels'. *Pacific Health Dialog*, 4(2), 128–37.

Anae, M. (2020). *The platform: The radical legacy of the Polynesian Panthers*. Bridget Williams Books.

Anae, M., Tamu, L., & Iuli, L. (2015). *Polynesian Panthers: Pacific protest and affirmative action in Aotearoa New Zealand 1971–1981*. Huia Publishers.

Anderson, A. (2016). The making of the Māori middle ages. *Journal of New Zealand Studies*, 23, 2–18.

Anderson, A., Binney, J., & Harris, A. (2015). *Tangata whenua: A history*. Bridget Williams Books.

Anderton, J., Maharey, S., Wilson, M., Dalziel, L., & Hobbs, M. (2003). *Population and sustainable development*. New Zealand Government.

Andrews, K. (2021). *The new age of empire: How racism and colonialism still rule the world*. Penguin.

Ang, I., & Stratton, J. (1998). Multiculturalism in crisis: The new politics of race and national identity in Australia. *TOPIA: Canadian Journal of Cultural Studies*, 2, 22–41.

Annan, K. (2006). Address of Mr. Kofi Annan, Secretary-General, to the High-Level Dialogue of the United Nations General Assembly on International Migration and Development, New York, 14 September. *International Migration Review*, 40(4), 963–65.

Anonymous. (2014). Peopling New Zealand. *New Zealand History*, https://nzhistory.govt.nz/culture/assisted-immigration/administration

Appadurai, A. (1996). *Modernity at large: Cultural dimensions of globalization*. University of Minnesota Press.

Archives New Zealand. (2022). *He Whakaputanga o te Rangatiratanga o Nu Tireni: The Declaration of the Independence of New Zealand*, https://www.archives.govt.nz/discover-our-stories/the-declaration-of-independence-of-new-zealand

Ardern, J. (2017). *Speech from the throne*. 8 November, https://www.beehive.govt.nz/speech/speech-throne-2017

Ashton, J. (2015). *At the margin of empire: John Webster and Hokianga, 1841–1900*. Auckland University Press.

Ashutosh, I., & Mountz, A. (2011). Migration management for the benefit of whom? Interrogating the work of the International Organization for Migration. *Citizenship Studies*, 15(1), 21–38.

Attwood, B. (2020). *Empire and the making of native title: Sovereignty, property and indigenous people*. Cambridge University Press.

Auditor-General. (2009). *Inquiry into immigration matters*. Controller and Auditor-General.

Bachrach, P., & Baratz, M. S. (1963). Decisions and nondecisions: An analytical framework. *American Political Science Review*, 57(3), 632–42.

Bade, J. N. (1993). *The German connection: New Zealand and German-speaking Europe in the nineteenth century*. Oxford University Press.

Badkar, J., Callister, P., Krishnan, V., Didham, R., & Bedford, R. (2007). Gender, mobility and migration into New Zealand: A case study of Asian migration. *Social Policy Journal of New Zealand*, 32, 126.

Bailey, R. L. (2009). *Unfree labour? Ni-Vanuatu workers in New Zealand's Recognised Seasonal Employer scheme*. University of Canterbury.

Balch, A. (2013). *Managing labour migration in Europe: Ideas, knowledge and policy change*. Manchester University Press.

Ballantyne, T. (2012). *Webs of empire: Locating New Zealand's colonial past*. Bridget Williams Books.

Ballantyne, T. (2014). The theory and practice of empire-building: Edward Gibbon Wakefield and 'systematic colonisation'. McKenzie, K., & Aldrich, R. (Eds.), *The Routledge history of western empires*, pp. 89–101. Routledge.

Ballantyne, T. (2015). *Entanglements of empire: Missionaries, Māori, and the question of the body*. Auckland University Press.

Ballara, A. (1998). *Iwi: The dynamics of Māori social organisation from c.1769 to c.1945.* Victoria University Press.

Ballara, A. (2003) *Taua: Musket wars, land wars or tikanga? Warfare in Māori society in the early 19th century.* Penguin.

Balta, E., & Altan-Olcay, Ö. (2016). Strategic citizens of America: Transnational inequalities and transformation of citizenship. *Ethnic and Racial Studies, 39*(6), 939–57.

Banivanua Mar, T. (2009). Frontier space and the reification of the rule of law: Colonial negotiations in the Western Pacific, 1870–74. *Australian Feminist Law Journal, 30*(1), 23–39.

Barber, D. (1994). The dawning of a significant sun. *National Business Review,* 9 September, 41.

Barber, D. (1999). Canberra threatens curbs on Kiwis crossing Tasman. *National Business Review,* 23 July.

Barber, S. (2020). In Wakefield's laboratory: Tangata whenua into property/labour in Te Waipounamu. *Journal of Sociology, 56*(2), 229–46.

Barber, S., & Davidson, M. (Eds.). (2021). *Through that which separates us.* Te Reo Kē/The Physics Room.

Barfoot and Thompson. (2017). *January 2017 housing market update,* https://www.barfoot.co.nz/market-reports/2017/january/market-update

Bargh, M. (2006). Changing the game plan: The Foreshore and Seabed Act and constitutional change. *Kōtuitui: New Zealand Journal of Social Sciences Online, 1*(1), 13–24.

Bargh, M. (2012). Post settlement world (so far): Impacts for Māori. In Wheen, N., & Hayward, J. (Eds.), *Treaty of Waitangi Settlements,* pp. 166–81. Bridget Williams Books.

Barlow, C. (1991). *Tikanga whakaaro: Key concepts in Māori culture.* Oxford University Press.

Basok, T. (2000). He came, he saw, he stayed: Guest worker programmes and the issue of non-return. *International Migration, 38*(2), 215–38.

Basok, T. (2003). Mexican seasonal migration to Canada and development: A community-based comparison. *International Migration, 41*(2), 3–26.

Basok, T., & Belanger, D. (2016). Migration management, disciplinary power, and performances of subjectivity: Agricultural migrant workers in Ontario. *Canadian Journal of Sociology, 41*(2), 139–64.

Basok, T., & Piper, N. (2012). Management versus rights: Women's migration and global governance in Latin America and the Caribbean. *Feminist Economics, 18*(2), 35–61.

Bassett, M. (2000). Kirk, Norman Eric. *Te Ara – the Encyclopedia of New Zealand*, https://teara.govt.nz/en/biographies/5k12/kirk-norman-eric

Bayly, C. A., & Harper, T. N. (2008). *Forgotten wars: The end of Britain's Asian empire*. Penguin.

Beaglehole, A. (n.d.). Refugees. *Te Ara – the Encyclopedia of New Zealand*, https://teara.govt.nz/en/refugees

Beaglehole, A. (2009). Looking back and glancing sideways: Refugee policy and multicultural nation-building in New Zealand. In Neumann, K., & Tavan, G. (Eds.), *Does history matter? Making and debating citizenship, immigration and refugee policy in Australia and New Zealand*, pp. 105–23. ANU Press.

Beaglehole, A. (2013). *Refuge New Zealand: A nation's response to refugees and asylum seekers*. Otago University Press.

Becker, G. (1964). *Human capital: A theoretical and empirical analysis with special reference to education*. University of Chicago Press.

Bedford, R. (1984). The Polynesian connection: Migration and social change in New Zealand and the South Pacific. In Bedford, R. (Ed.), *Essays on urbanisation in South East Asia and the Pacific*, pp. 131–41. University of Canterbury.

Bedford, R. (1994). Pacific Islanders in New Zealand. *Espace Populations Sociétés*, 12(2), 187–200.

Bedford, R. (2004). The quiet revolution: Transformations in migration policies, flows and outcomes, 1999–2004. *New Zealand Geographer*, 60(2), 58–62.

Bedford, R. (2005a). International migration and globalization: The transformation of New Zealand's migration system since the mid-1980s. In Patman, R., & Rudd, C. (Eds.), *Sovereignty under siege: Globalization and New Zealand*, pp. 129–56. Ashgate.

Bedford, R. (2005b). Meta-societies, remittance economies and internet addresses: Dimensions of contemporary human security in Polynesia. In Graham, D., & Poku, N. (Eds.), *Migration, globalisation and human security*, pp. 109–36. Routledge.

Bedford, R. (2008). Pasifika mobility: Pathways, circuits and challenges in the 21st century. In Bisley, A. (Ed.), *Pacific interactions: Pasifika in New Zealand, New Zealand in Pacifika*, pp. 85–134. Institute of Policy Studies.

Bedford, R. (2019). Australasia and the Pacific Islands. In Inglis, C., Li, W., & Khadria, B. (Eds.), *The SAGE handbook of international migration*, pp. 311–25. SAGE.

Bedford, R. D., Bedford, C., Ho, E. S., & Lidgard, J. M. (2002a). The globalisation of international migration in New Zealand: Contribution to a debate. *New Zealand Population Review*, 28(1), 69–97.

Bedford, R., & Didham, R. (2018). Immigration: An election issue that has yet to be addressed? *Kōtuitui: New Zealand Journal of Social Sciences Online*, 13(2), 177–94.

Bedford, R. D., Farmer, R. S., & Trlin, A. D. (1987). The immigration policy review, 1986: A review. *New Zealand Population Review*, 13(2), 49–65.

Bedford, R., & Ho, E. (1998). The Population Conference: 'Talkfest' or turning point? *New Zealand Geographer*, 54(1), 50–54.

Bedford, R., Ho, E., & Bedford, C. (2010). Pathways to residence in New Zealand, 2003–2010. *New Zealand and International Migration: A Digest and Bibliography*, (5), 1–49.

Bedford, R., Ho, E., Krishnan, V., and Hong, B. (2007). The neighbourhood effect: The Pacific in Aotearoa and Australia. *Asian and Pacific Migration Journal*, 16(2): 251–69.

Bedford, R., Ho, E., & Lidgard, J. (2000). International migration in New Zealand: Context, components and policy issues. Population Studies Centre, Discussion Paper 37, University of Waikato.

Bedford, R., Ho, E., & Lidgard, J. (2002b). International migration in New Zealand: Context, components and policy issues. *Journal of Population Research*, Special Ed., 39–65.

Bedford, R., Ho, E. S., & Lidgard, J. (2005). From targets to outcomes: Immigration policy in New Zealand, 1996–2003. *New Zealand and International Migration: A Digest and Bibliography*, (4), 1–43.

Bedford, R., & Hugo, G. (2012). *Population movement in the Pacific: A perspective on future prospects*. Department of Labour.

Bedford, R. D., & Larner, W. (1992). Pacific Islanders in New Zealand in the 1980s. *New Zealand and International Migration: A Digest and Bibliography*, (2), 65–81.

Bedford, R., & Lidgard, J. (1997). Visa-waiver and the transformation of migration flows between New Zealand and countries in the Asia-Pacific Region, 1980–1996. In Lee, B-T., & Bahrin, T. S. (Eds.), *Vanishing borders: The new international order of the twenty-first century*, pp. 91–110. Ashgate.

Bedford, R., Lidgard, J., & Ho, E. (2003). International migration during election years: The evidence for 1996, 1999 and 2002. *New Zealand Journal of Geography*, 115(1), 26–43.

Bedford, R., & Liu, L. (2013). Parents in New Zealand's family sponsorship policy: A preliminary assessment of the impact of the 2012 policy changes. *New Zealand Population Review*, 39, 25–49.

Bedford, R., & Spoonley, P. (2014). Competing for talent: Diffusion of an innovation in New Zealand's immigration policy. *International Migration Review*, 48(3), 891–911.

Beechler, S., & Woodward, I. C. (2009). The global 'war for talent'. *Journal of International Management*, 15(3), 273–85.

Belgrave, M., Kawharu, M., & Williams, D. V. (Eds.). (2005). *Waitangi revisited: Perspectives on the Treaty of Waitangi*. Oxford University Press.

Belich, J. (1986). *The New Zealand Wars and the Victorian interpretation of racial conflict: The Maori, the British, and the New Zealand Wars*. McGill-Queen's University Press.

Belich, J. (2002a). Imperial myth and colonial actuality: Findings from a New Zealand laboratory. *Melbourne Historical Journal*, 20, 7–13.

Belich, J. (2002b). *Making peoples: A history of the New Zealanders from Polynesian settlement to the end of the nineteenth century*. University of Hawaii Press.

Belich, J. (2002c). *Paradise reforged: A history of the New Zealanders from the 1880s to the Year 2000*. Allen Lane Penguin Press.

Bell, A. (2014). *Relating indigenous and settler identities: Beyond domination*. Springer.

Bellamy, P. (2018). Immigration chronology: Selected event, 1840–2008. New Zealand Parliamentary Library Research Paper 2008/01.

Bellamy, R. (2008). *Citizenship: A very short introduction*. Oxford University Press.

Berry, M. (2013). Developments in New Zealand competition law and policy. *Antitrust Chronicle*, 2.

Berry, R. (2005). Peters wants migrant flying squad. *New Zealand Herald*, 27 May.

Binford, L. (2009). From fields of power to fields of sweat: The dual process of constructing temporary migrant labour in Mexico and Canada. *Third World Quarterly*, 30(3), 503–17.

Birch, W. F. (1989). National Party guidelines for 1990. In Arbuckle, R. (Ed.), *A positive immigration policy for New Zealand*. Proceedings of the Top Tier Immigration Seminar, Wellington, pp. 12–14.

Birch, W. F. (1990a). Migrant labour. *New Zealand Parliamentary Debates*, 506, 1063.

Birch, W. F. (1990b). Occupational Priority List. *New Zealand Parliamentary Debates*, 511, 272.

Birch, W. F. (1991). *Immigration policy*. Press statement, 3 July. New Zealand Government.

Bolger, Hon. J. (1997). *Knowing who we are*. Speech to the Population Conference, 9 May 1997, https://www.beehive.govt.nz/speech/knowing-who-we-are

Bolger, J., and Peters, W. (1997). *The Population Conference: People, communities and growth*, New Zealand Government Press Release, 31 July, https://www.beehive.govt.nz/release/population-conference-people-communities-and-growth-0

Boltanski, L., & Chiapello, E. (2005). The new spirit of capitalism. *International Journal of Politics, Culture, and Society*, 18, 161–88.

Bonnett, G. (2024). The truth about the shadowy 'Migration 5'. *Radio New Zealand*, 17 June, https://www.rnz.co.nz/programmes/in-depth-special-projects/story/2018942836/the-truth-about-the-shadowy-migration-5

Boshier, J. (2023). Six unique years: Why did Think Big happen? *Policy Quarterly*, 19(1), 19–26.

Boston, J., Church, S., & Pearse, H. (2004). Explaining the demise of the National–New Zealand First coalition. *Australian Journal of Political Science*, 39(3), 585–603.

Boston, J., Levine, S., McLeay, E., & Roberts, N. S. (1997). The 1996 General Election in New Zealand: Proportional representation and political change. *The Australian Quarterly*, 69(1), 1–14.

Boswell, C. (2003). The 'external dimension' of EU immigration and asylum policy. *International Affairs*, 79(3), 619–38.

Boswell, C. (2008). *European migration policies in flux: Changing patterns of inclusion and exclusion*. Blackwell Publishing Ltd.

Boucher, G. (2008). A critique of global policy discourses on managing international migration. *Third World Quarterly*, 29(7), 1461–71.

Boyer, T. (1996). Problems in paradise: Taiwanese immigrants to Auckland, New Zealand. *Asia Pacific Viewpoint*, 37(1), 59–79.

Bradford, M. (1997). *Transcript of closing speech: New Zealand Population Conference*, https://www.beehive.govt.nz/speech/transcript-closing-speech

Bradford, M. (1998). *Government seeks skilled migrants*, New Zealand Government Press Release, 3 June, https://www.beehive.govt.nz/release/government-seeks-skilled-migrants

Brady, A. (2002). *Friend of China: The myth of Rewi Alley*. Routledge.

Brash, D. (2005). *National's immigration plan: A responsible middle course*. Campaign speech, 9 August, https://www.donbrash.com/national-party/nationals-immigration-plan-a-responsible-middle-course/

Brown, W. (2015). *Undoing the demos: Neoliberalism's stealth revolution*. Zone Books.

Brownlee, G., & Coleman, J. (2009). *Business migration scheme revamped.* New Zealand Government Press Release, 29 July, https://www. beehive.govt.nz/release/business-migrant-scheme-revamped

Bryant-Tokalau, J., & Frazer, I. (Eds.). (2006). *Redefining the Pacific? Regionalism past, present and future.* Ashgate.

Burke, K. (1979). Imprest Supply Bill. *New Zealand Parliamentary Debates,* 422, 46.

Burke, K. (1986). Review of Immigration Policy, August 1986. *Appendices to the Journals of the House of Representatives,* G.42. Government Printer.

Burns, A. (2023). NZ govt warns migrant workers of employment scams amid immigration review. *Radio New Zealand,* 20 September, https:// www.rnz.co.nz/news/business/498410/nz-govt-warns-migrant-workers-of-employment-scams-amid-immigration-review

Cahill, D. (2018). Polanyi, Hayek and embedded neoliberalism. *Globalizations,* 15(7), 977–94.

Campbell, C. Y. (1986). Ambition without substance: Waikato Immigration Scheme. *Archifacts: Bulletin of the Archives and Records Association of New Zealand,* (June), 54–60.

Campbell, J. (2016). Brand John: The Key to National's success. *Radio New Zealand,* 15 December, https://www.rnz.co.nz/news/on-the-inside/320458/brand-john-the-key-to-national's-success

Carmichael, G. A. (Ed.). (1993). *Trans-Tasman migration: Trends, causes and consequences.* Bureau of Immigration Research and New Zealand Immigration Service. Australian Government Publishing Service.

Castles, S. (1986). The guest-worker in Western Europe – An obituary. *International Migration Review,* 20(4), 761–78.

Castles, S. (2004). Why migration policies fail. *Ethnic and Racial Studies,* 27(2), 205–27.

Castles, S. (2006). Guestworkers in Europe: A resurrection? *International Migration Review,* 40(4), 741–66.

Ceyhan, A., & Tsoukala, A. (2002). The securitization of migration in western societies: Ambivalent discourses and policies. *Alternatives,* 27(1), 21–39.

Chandramohan, B. (2012). India and New Zealand: Strengthening ties. *New Zealand International Review,* 37(1), 20–23.

Chapman, J., & Duncan, G. (2007). Is there now a new 'New Zealand model'? *Public Management Review,* 9(1), 1–25.

Chen, A. (n.d.). New Zealand political opinion polls, https://www. andrewchen.nz/polls

Chin, R. (2007). *The guest worker question in postwar Germany.* Cambridge University Press.

Chishti, M., & Yale-Loehr, S. (2016). *The Immigration Act of 1990: Unfinished business a quarter-century later*. Migration Policy Institute.

Clark, C., & Clark, E. A. (2016). *Challenging neoliberalism: Globalization and the economic miracles in Chile and Taiwan*. Edward Elgar.

Clark, H. (2001). *New Social Security Agreement with Australia*. New Zealand Government Press Release, 26 February, https://www.beehive.govt.nz/release/new-social-security-agreement-australia

Clark, H. (2002). *Implementing a progressive agenda after fifteen years of neoliberalism: The New Zealand experience*. Address to London School of Economics, 21 February.

Coalition Agreement. (1996). *Agreement between NZ First Political Party and the New Zealand National Party*. Thomson Wilson.

Cobarrubias, S. (2019). Mapping illegality: The i-Map and the cartopolitics of 'migration management' at a distance. *Antipode*, 51(3), 770–94.

Coleman, J. (2009). *The economic impact of immigration*. New Zealand Government Press Release, 3 November, https://www.beehive.govt.nz/speech/economic-impact-immigration

Coleman, J. (2010). *New Zealand/Australian Business Investment Forum*. New Zealand Government Press Release, 11 March, https://www.beehive.govt.nz/speech/new-zealandaustralian-business-investment-forum

Coleman, J. (2011). Lexis Nexis Immigration Law Conference – Speech notes, 12 August, https://www.beehive.govt.nz/speech/lexis-nexis-immigration-law-conference-speech-notes

Collier, P. (2013). *Exodus: Immigration and multiculturalism in the 21st century*. Penguin.

Collins, F. L. (2006). Making Asian students, making students Asian: The racialisation of export education in Auckland, New Zealand. *Asia Pacific Viewpoint*, 47(2), 217–34.

Collins, F. L. (2016). *Temporary migration and urban incorporation in Auckland*. University of Auckland.

Collins, F. L. (2017). We are creating a guest-worker programme. *New Zealand Herald*, 21 April, https://www.nzherald.co.nz/nz/francis-collins-we-are-creating-a-guest-worker-programme/QONKABTLY76M64LLLA4DWUBYMA/

Collins, F. L. (2018). Keeping bodies moving: Hope, disruption and the possibilities of youth migration. *Journal of Intercultural Studies*, 39(6), 626–41.

Collins, F. L. (2020). Legislated inequality: Provisional migration and the stratification of migrant lives. In Simon-Kumar, R., Collins, F. L., and Friesen, W. (Eds.), *Intersections of inequality, migration and diversification*, pp. 65–86. Palgrave Pivot.

Collins, F. L. (2021). Temporary migration and regional development amidst Covid-19: Invercargill and Queenstown. *New Zealand Geographer*, 77(3), 191–205.

Collins, F. L. (2023). Geographies of migration III: The digital migrant. *Progress in Human Geography*, 47(5), 738–49.

Collins, F. L., & Bayliss, T. (2020). The good migrant: Everyday nationalism and temporary migration management on New Zealand dairy farms. *Political Geography*, 80, 102193.

Collins, F. L., & Friesen, W. (2022). Excess aspirations: Migration and urban futures in post-earthquake Christchurch. *Urban Studies*, 59(16), 3253–70.

Collins, F. L., & Lewis, N. (2016). New Zealand universities: The prospects and pitfalls of globalizing higher education. In *The Palgrave handbook of Asia Pacific higher education*, pp. 597–613. Palgrave.

Collins, F. L., & Park, G. S. (2016). Ranking and the multiplication of reputation: Reflections from the frontier of globalizing higher education. *Higher Education*, 72(1), 115–29.

Collins, F. L., & Stringer, C. (2019). *Temporary migrant worker exploitation in New Zealand*. Ministry of Business, Innovation and Employment.

Collins, J. (2008). Globalisation, immigration and the second long post-war boom in Australia. *The Journal of Australian Political Economy*, 61, 244–66.

Collins, J. (2012). Perspectives from the periphery? Colombo Plan scholars in New Zealand universities, 1951–1975. *History of Education Review*, 41(2), 129–46.

Commission on Immigration Reform. (1997). *Becoming an American: Immigration and immigrant policy*. US Commission on Immigration Reform.

Constantine, S. (2002). The British government, child welfare, and child migration to Australia after 1945. *The Journal of Imperial and Commonwealth History*, 30(1), 99–132.

Constantine, S. (2003). British emigration to the Empire-Commonwealth since 1880: From overseas settlement to diaspora? *Journal of Imperial and Commonwealth History*, 31(2), 16–35.

Consterdine, E. (2017). *Labour's immigration policy: The making of the migration state*. Palgrave.

Cooke, H. (2018). A brief history of Winston Raymond Peters. *Stuff*, 18 June, https://www.stuff.co.nz/national/politics/97547465/a-brief-history-of-winston-raymond-peters

Cooper, L. (2017). Europe's problem with nationalism. In Hudson, K. (Ed.), *Free movement and beyond: Agenda setting for Brexit Britain*, pp. 64–70. Public Reading Rooms.

Crosby, R. D. (2001). *The musket wars: A history of inter-iwi conflict 1806–1845*. Reed Publishing Limited.

Cunliffe, D. (2006a). *Future proofing immigration: The Immigration Change Programme*. New Zealand Government Press Release, 15 July, https://www.beehive.govt.nz/speech/future-proofing-immigration-immigration-change-programme

Cunliffe, D. (2006b). *Immigration Change Programme: A framework for the future*. Address to Auckland District Law Society, 31 October.

Cunliffe, D. (2007a). *Review of family sponsorship policies*. Paper for the Cabinet Policy Committee attached to POL (07) 160, 21 May.

Cunliffe, D. (2007b). Immigration Bill – First Reading. *New Zealand Parliamentary Debates*, 641, 11231.

Curtin, J., Kerby, M., & Dowding, K. (2023). Sex, gender, and promotion in executive office: Cabinet careers in the world of Westminster. *Governance*, 36(1), 233–54.

Dal Bó, E. (2006). Regulatory capture: A review. *Oxford Review of Economic Policy*, 22(2), 203–25.

Dalziel, L. (2000). *Changes on the way to attract more skilled migrants*. New Zealand Government Press Release, 20 October, https://www.beehive.govt.nz/release/changes-way-attract-more-skilled-migrants

Dalziel, L. (2001). *NZ Immigration Programme to attract talent*. New Zealand Government Press Release, 17 September, https://www.beehive.govt.nz/feature/nz-immigration-programme-attract-talent-24

Dalziel, L. (2002). *NZ keen to ensure protection of genuine refugees*, 2 October, https://www.scoop.co.nz/stories/PA0210/S00033/nz-keen-to-ensure-protection-of-genuine-refugees.htm

Dalziel, L. (2003a). *Immigration and New Zealand society*. Seminar presentation, 6 March, https://www.beehive.govt.nz/speech/immigration-and-new-zealand-society

Dalziel, L. (2003b). *Tuvalu, Kiribati and Nauru no longer visa free*. New Zealand Government Press Release, 5 December, https://www.beehive.govt.nz/release/tuvalu-kiribati-and-nauru-no-longer-visa-free

Dalziel, L. (2003c). *Skilled immigration policy announcements – Notes*. New Zealand Government Press Release, 1 July, https://www.scoop.co.nz/stories/PA0307/S00036/skilled-immigration-policy-announcements-notes.htm

Dalziel, R. (2013). *Julius Vogel: Business politician*. Auckland University Press.

Dalziel, P., & Lattimore, R. (2001). *The New Zealand macroeconomy*. Oxford University Press.

Dann, L. (2017). The crash. *New Zealand Herald*, https://www.nzherald.co.nz/indepth/business/1987-stock-market-crash/

Dardot, P., & Laval, C. (2014). *The new way of the world: On neoliberal society*, trans. Gregory Elliot. Verso.

Darwin, J. (2009). *The empire project: The rise and fall of the British world-system, 1830–1970*. Cambridge University Press.

Dauvergne, C. (2005). *Humanitarianism, identity and nation: Migration laws of Australia and Canada*. UBC Press.

Dauvergne, C. (2007). Security and migration law in the less brave new world. *Social & Legal Studies*, 16(4), 533–49.

Dauvergne, C. (2016). *The new politics of immigration and the end of settler societies*. Cambridge University Press.

Davis, K., Lees-Galloway, I., and Sage, E. (2019). *Legislation passed for visitor levy and smart border systems*. New Zealand Government Press Release, 1 June, https://www.beehive.govt.nz/release/legislation-passed-visitor-levy-and-smart-border-systems

Day, R. J. (2000). *Multiculturalism and the history of Canadian diversity*. University of Toronto Press.

Dean, J. (2009). *Democracy and other neoliberal fantasies: Communicative capitalism and left politics*. Duke University Press.

Delamere, T. (1998). *Entry for IT workers given high priority*. New Zealand Government Press Release, 12 November, https://www.beehive.govt.nz/release/entry-it-workers-given-high-priority-0

Delamere, T. (1999). *Government approves ambitious immigration survey*. New Zealand Government Press Release, 1 June, https://www.beehive.govt.nz/release/government-approves-ambitious-immigration-survey

Delamere, T., & Smith, L. (1999). *Visa waiver for six Gulf states*. New Zealand Government Press Release, 21 April, https://www.beehive.govt.nz/release/visa-waiver-six-gulf-states-0

De Genova, N. (2015). The border spectacle of migrant 'victimisation'. *OpenDemocracy*, 20 May, https://www.opendemocracy.net/en/beyond-trafficking-and-slavery/border-spectacle-of-migrant-victimisation/

de Lapaillone, M. C. (2012). *New Zealand's approach to refugees: Legal obligations and current practices*. The United Nations Association of New Zealand.

Denord, F. (2009). French neoliberalism and its divisions: From the Colloque Walter Lippmann to the Fifth Republic. In Mirowski, P., & Plehwe, D. (Eds.), *The road from Mont Pèlerin: The making of the neoliberal thought collective*, pp. 45–67. Harvard University Press.

Department of Labour. (2009). *New faces, new future: Immigration policy changes between 2001–2008*. Department of Labour.

Department of Labour. (2012). *Permanent and long-term migration: The big picture*. Department of Labour.

Devadas, V. (2008). 15 October 2007, Aotearoa: Race, terror and sovereignty. *Sites: A Journal of Social Anthropology and Cultural Studies*, 5(1), 124–51.

Devadas, V., & Nicholls, B. (2012). The meaning of John Key. *New Zealand Journal of Media Studies*, 13(2), 18–31.

DFAT. (n.d.). *New Zealand country brief*. Australian Department of Foreign Affairs and Trade, https://www.dfat.gov.au/geo/new-zealand/new-zealand-country-brief

Dickson, A. (2015). Distancing asylum seekers from the state: Australia's evolving political geography of immigration and border control. *Australian Geographer*, 46(4), 437–54.

DiMaggio, P. J., & Powell, W. W. (1983). The iron cage revisited: Institutional isomorphism and collective rationality in organizational fields. *American Sociological Review*, 147–60.

Dominion Post. (2004a). Citizenship law change 'bowing to Australia'. *Dominion Post*, 1 September, 6.

Dominion Post. (2004b). No soft touch – and no police state. *Dominion Post*, 17 June, Edition 2, 6.

Dominion Post. (2005). Immigration in secret. *Dominion Post*, 15 August.

Dominion Post. (2017). Editorial: Immigration cuts are not xenophobic, but economically necessary. *Dominion Post*, 13 June, https://www.stuff.co.nz/dominion-post/comment/editorials/93639140/editorial-immigration-cuts-are-not-xenophobic-but-economically-necessary

Donnell, H. (2008). Christian refugee sent back to Iran. *North Shore Times*, 3 April.

Drummond, J. (2013). *The life and work of Richard John Seddon (Premier of New Zealand, 1893–1906): With a history of the Liberal Party of New Zealand*. Cambridge University Press.

Duncan, N. T. (2012). *Immigration policymaking in the global era: In pursuit of global talent*. Palgrave Macmillan.

Durand, C. (2017). *Fictitious capital: How finance is appropriating our future*. Verso.

Eaton, D. (2008). Policy release. *The Press*, 5 September, 5.

Eldred-Grigg, S. (2014). *Diggers, hatters & whores: The story of the New Zealand gold rushes*. Random House.

Ellermann, A. (2021). *The comparative politics of immigration: Policy choices in Germany, Canada, Switzerland, and the United States*. Cambridge University Press.

Encel, S. (1988). The FitzGerald report on Australia's immigration policies. *Patterns of Prejudice, 22*, 48–49.

Espiner, C. (2004). Dalziel's downfall. *The Press*, 21 February, 2.

Evening Post. (1998). More Chinese students. *Evening Post*, 19 June, 15.

Faafoi, K. (2021a). *Long-term direction for the immigration portfolio: A rebalance*. Cabinet Social Wellbeing Committee.

Faafoi, K. (2021b). *One-off residence pathway provides certainty to migrants and business*. New Zealand Government Press Release, 30 September, https://www.beehive.govt.nz/release/one-residence-pathway-provides-certainty-migrants-and-business

Fabling, R., Grimes, A., & Timar, L. (2022). Emigration and employment impacts of a disastrous earthquake: Country of birth matters. *Regional Studies, 57*(12), 2491–2502.

Farmer, R. S. J. (1985). International migration. In Pool, D. I. (Ed.), *The population of New Zealand*, Country Monograph Series Number 12. United Nations Economic and Social Commission for Asia and the Pacific.

Farmer, R. S. J. (1996a). Economic deregulation and changes in New Zealand's immigration policy: 1986 to 1991. *People and Place, 4*(3), 55–63.

Farmer, R. S. J. (1996b). New Zealand's 'targeted' immigration policy, 1991 to 1996. *People and Place, 5*(1), 1–15.

Finnemore, M., & Sikkink, K. (1998). International norm dynamics and political change. *International Organization, 52*(4), 887–917.

Foks, F. (2022). Emigration state: Race, citizenship and settler imperialism in modern British history, c. 1850–1972. *Journal of Historical Sociology, 35*(2), 170–99.

Fotheringham, C. (2023). RSE schemes in question. *Radio New Zealand*, 30 November, https://www.rnz.co.nz/international/programmes/datelinepacific/audio/2018917426/rse-schemes-in-question

Franks, P., & McAloon, J. (2016). *The New Zealand Labour Party, 1916–2016*. Victoria University Press.

Fraser, L. (2019). Both sides of the Tasman: History, politics and migration between New Zealand and Australia. In Henrich, E., & Simpson, J. (Eds.), *History, historians and the immigration debate*, pp. 55–70. Palgrave Macmillan.

Friesen, W. (2008). The evolution of 'Indian' identity and transnationalism in New Zealand. *Australian Geographer*, 39(1), 45–61.

Friesen, W. (2017). Migration management and mobility pathways for Filipino migrants to New Zealand. *Asia Pacific Viewpoint*, 58(3), 273–88.

Friesen, W. (2018). Beyond the RSE: Systems of Pacific labour migration to New Zealand. *New Zealand Population Review*, 44, 111–29.

Fry, J., & Glass, H. (2016). *Going places: Migration, economics and the future of New Zealand*. Bridget Williams Books.

Fry, J., & Wilson, P. (2018). *Better lives: Migration, wellbeing and New Zealand*. Bridget Williams Books.

Fukuyama, F. (1989). The end of history? *The National Interest*, (16), 3–18.

Galabuzzi, G. E. (2005). Factors affecting the social economic status of Canadian immigrants in the new millennium. *Canadian Issues*, Spring, 53–57.

Gamlen, A. (2005). 'The brain drain is dead; long live the New Zealand diaspora', WP-05-10, Centre on Migration, Policy and Society, University of Oxford.

Gamlen, A. (2010a). The new migration and development optimism: A review of the 2009 Human Development Report. *Global Governance*, 16(3), 415–22.

Gamlen, A. (2010b). *The emigration state system: New Zealand and its diaspora in comparative context*. Doctoral Dissertation in Geography, University of Oxford.

Gamlen, A. (2011). Engaging Asia: The role of the diaspora. *Outlook*, 15, Asia New Zealand Foundation.

Gamlen, A. (2013a). Creating and destroying diaspora strategies: New Zealand's emigration policies re-examined. *Transactions – Institute of British Geographers*, 38(2), 238–53.

Gamlen, A. (2013b). Tory immigration policy is not doomed to fail – it is designed to do so. *The Guardian*, 14 January, http://www.theguardian.com/commentisfree/2013/jan/14/immigration-policy-designed-to-fail

Gamlen, A. (2014a). Editorial: Celebrating excellence in migration studies. *Migration Studies*, 2(3), 295–99.

Gamlen, A. (2014b). Inequality drives many to quit New Zealand. *New Zealand Herald*, 9 April, https://www.nzherald.co.nz/nz/alan-gamlen-inequality-drives-many-to-quit-nz/RTX5DZY2SJCCLTTSTTBE6SK4PE/

Gamlen, A. (2014c). Why do politicians break their promises on migration? *OUPBlog*, Oxford University Press, 18 December.

Gamlen, A. (2014d). The new migration-and-development pessimism. *Progress in Human Geography*, 38(4), 581–97.

Gamlen, A. (2019). *Human geopolitics: States, emigrants, and the rise of diaspora institutions*. Oxford University Press.

Gamlen, A., & Sherrell, H. (2019). Australian immigration policy: The role and scope of points-tested visas. *Compas*, 22 November, https://www.compas.ox.ac.uk/article/australian-immigration-policy-the-role-and-scope-of-points-tested-visas

Gamlen, A., & Sherrell, H. (2022). Australia and New Zealand: Classical migration states? In Hollifield, J., Martin, P., Orrenius, P., & Héran, F. (Eds.), *Controlling immigration: A comparative perspective*, 4th Edition, pp. 175–210. Stanford University Press.

Garson, J.-P. (2004). *Migration in Europe: Trends and perspectives*. OECD.

Garten, J. E. (2021). *Three days at Camp David: How a secret meeting in 1971 transformed the global economy*. HarperCollins.

Geiger, M., & Pécoud, A. (Eds.). (2010). *The politics of international migration management*. Palgrave Macmillan UK.

Gentry, K. (2015). *History, heritage, and colonialism: Historical consciousness, Britishness, and cultural identity in New Zealand, 1870–1940*. Manchester University Press.

Georgi, F. (2010). For the benefit of some: The International Organization for Migration and its global migration management. In Geiger, M., and Pécoud, A. (Eds.), *The politics of international migration management*, pp. 45–72. Palgrave Macmillan UK.

Ghosh, B. (2000). Towards a new international regime for orderly movements of people. In Ghosh, B. (Ed.), *Managing migration: Time for a new international regime*, pp. 6–26. Oxford University Press.

Ghosh, B. (2007). Managing migration: Towards the missing regime? In Pécoud, A. (Ed.), *Migration without borders: Essays on the free movement of people*, pp. 97–118. Berghahn.

Gibson, J. (2006). *Efficient financial services for development in the Pacific*. Institute of Policy Studies.

Gibson, J., & McKenzie, D. (2014). The development impact of a best practice seasonal worker policy. *Review of Economics and Statistics*, 96(2), 229–43.

Gibson, J., McKenzie, D., & Rohorua, H. (2008). How pro-poor is the selection of season migrant works from Tonga under New Zealand's Recognised Seasonal Employer (RSE) Program?, Working Papers in Economics 8/08. Department of Economics, University of Waikato.

Gilbertson, A., & Meares, C. (2013). Ethnicity and migration in Auckland. Auckland Council Technical Report, TR2013/012.

Glick Schiller, N., & Salazar, N. B. (2013). Regimes of mobility across the globe. *Journal of ethnic and migration studies*, 39(2), 183–200.

Goldberg, D. T. (2009). *The threat of race: Reflections on racial neoliberalism*. John Wiley & Sons.

Gordon, C. (1991). Governmental rationality: An introduction. In Burchell, G., Gordon, C., & Miller, P. (Eds.), *The Foucault effect: Studies in governmentality*, pp. 1–51. Harvester Wheatsheaf.

Grace, P., Ramsden, I., & Dennis, J. (Eds.). (2001). *The silent majority: Ngati Poneke Young Maori Club, 1937–1948*. Huia Publishers.

Gregory, A. (2004). Automatic citizenship for review. *New Zealand Herald*, 15 June, https://www.nzherald.co.nz/nz/automatic-citizenship-for-re view/7GPWG44XMFHVUUUGI33GKH3SJU

Greif, S. W. (1995). *Immigration and national identity in New Zealand: One people, two peoples, many peoples?* Dunmore.

Grey, G. (1890). Immigration of Chinese into the colony. *New Zealand Mail*, 2 August, 20.

Guy, N. (2012a). Speech to the 2012 New Zealand Association for Migration and Investment, 31 August, https://www.beehive.govt.nz/speech/ speech-2012-new-zealand-association-migration-and-investment

Guy, N. (2012b). Speech to the Massey University conference 'Pathways to metropolis in the 21st century: Immigration issues and futures', 24 October, https://www.beehive.govt.nz/speech/speech-massey-university-conference-pathways-metropolis-21st-century-immigration-issues-and

Haas, P. M. (1992). Introduction: Epistemic communities and international policy coordination. *International Organization*, 46(1), 1–35.

Hage, G. (2000). *White nation: Fantasies of white supremacy in a multicultural society*. Routledge.

Hage, G. (2010). Intercultural relations at the limits of multicultural governmentality. In Ivison, D. (Ed.), *Ashgate research companion to multiculturalism*, pp. 235–54. Ashgate.

Hall, D. (2017a). *Emerging from an entrenched colonial economy: New Zealand primary production, Britain and the EEC, 1945–1975*. Springer.

Hall, D. (Ed.). (2017b). *Fair borders?: Migration policy in the twenty-first century*. Bridget Williams Books.

Hall, D. (2017c). With the election looming, a new poll reveals New Zealanders' views on immigration. *The Spinoff*, 12 June, https:// thespinoff.co.nz/society/12-06-2017/as-we-gear-up-for-an-election-a-new-poll-reveals-nzers-views-on-immigration

Hamer, D. A. (1990). *New towns in the New World: Images and perceptions of the nineteenth-century urban frontier*. Columbia University Press.

Hamer, P. (2008). One in six? The rapid growth of the Māori population in Australia. *New Zealand Population Review*, 33(34), 153–76.

Hamer, P. (2012). Māori in Australia: An update from the 2011 Australian Census and the 2011 New Zealand general election. Available at SSRN 2167613.

Hamer, P. (2014). 'Unsophisticated and unsuited': Australian barriers to Pacific Islander immigration from New Zealand. *Political Science*, 66(2), 93–118.

Hamer, P. (2023). Australia's NZ migration reforms: Pacific implications. *DevPolicy Blog*, Australian National University, 13 June, https:// devpolicy.org/australias-nz-migration-reforms-pacific-implications-20230613/

Hamilton-Hart, N. (2021). *NZ Inc: Supporting international business growth*. University of Auckland, New Zealand Asia Institute.

Hansen, R. (1999). The politics of citizenship in 1940s Britain: The British Nationality Act. *20th Century British History*, 10(1), 67–95.

Hansen, R. (2000). *Citizenship and immigration in postwar Britain*. Oxford University Press.

Harris, A. (2004). *Hīkoi: Forty years of Māori protest*. Huia Publishers.

Hartog, J., & Winkelmann, R. (2004). Comparing migrants to non-migrants: The case of Dutch migration to New Zealand. In Zimmermann, K. F., & Constant, A. (Eds.), *How Labor Migrants Fare*, pp. 97–119. Springer.

Harvey, D. (2005). *A brief history of neoliberalism*. Oxford University Press.

Hastings Standard. (1906). His first speech. *Hastings Standard*, 14 June, 3.

Hawkins, F. (1988). *Canada and immigration*. McGill-Queen's University Press.

Hawkins, G. (2014). Identity (Citizenship and Travel Documents) Bill. *New Zealand Parliamentary Debates*, 618, 14496.

Hayek, F. A. (2001). *The road to serfdom with the intellectuals and socialism*. Institute of Economic Affairs.

Hayward, J., & Shaw, R. (2016). *Historical dictionary of New Zealand*, 3rd ed. Rowman & Littlefield.

Henry, M. (2008). Border geostrategies: Imagining and administering New Zealand's post-World War One borders. *New Zealand Geographer*, 64(3), 194–204.

Hickey, B. (2016). The year in really big numbers. *New Zealand Herald*, 18 December, https://www.nzherald.co.nz/nz/bernard-hickey-the-year-in-really-big-numbers/M7K6KTJJJHX77CPEIDQHG5FE4M/

Hickey, B. (2018). The case to borrow and invest. *Newsroom*, 10 April, https://www.newsroom.co.nz/the-case-to-borrow-and-invest

Hill, M. (2011). Curb white immigrants: Academic. *Stuff*, 4 September, https://www.stuff.co.nz/auckland/5561230/Curb-white-immigrants-academic

Hipkins, C. (2018). *New plan to address teacher shortage*. New Zealand Government Press Release, 14 October, https://www.beehive.govt.nz/release/new-plan-address-teacher-shortage

Hjerm, M. (2000). Multiculturalism reassessed. *Citizenship Studies*, 4(3), 357–81.

Ho, E. (2002). Multi-local residence, transnational networks: Chinese 'astronaut' families in New Zealand. *Asian and Pacific Migration Journal*, 11(1), 145–64.

Ho, E. (2003). Reluctant exiles or roaming transnationals? The Hong Kong Chinese in New Zealand. In Ip, M. (Ed.), *Unfolding history, evolving identity: The Chinese in New Zealand*, pp. 165–84. Auckland University Press.

Ho, E., Bedford, R., & Goodwin, J. (1997). 'Astronaut' families: A contemporary migration phenomenon. In *East Asian New Zealanders: Research on new migrants*. Aotearoa New Zealand Migration Research Network Research Paper. Albany: Department of Sociology, Massey University, 20–41.

Ho E., & Farmer R. (1994). The Hong Kong Chinese in Auckland. In Skeldon R. (Ed.), *Reluctant exiles? Migration from Hong Kong and the new overseas Chinese*, pp. 215–33. M. E. Sharpe.

Ho, E., Hugo, G., & Bedford, R. (2003). Trans-Tasman migration in context: Recent flows of New Zealanders revisited. *People and Place*, 11(4), 53–62.

Ho, E., Ip, M., & Bedford, R. (2001). Transnational Hong Kong Chinese families in the 1990s. *New Zealand Journal of Geography*, 111, 24–30.

Hokowhitu, B., & Devadas, V. (Eds.). (2013). *The fourth eye: Māori media in Aotearoa New Zealand*. University of Minnesota Press.

Hollifield, J. F. (2004). The emerging migration state. *International Migration Review*, 38(3), 885–912.

hooks, b. (1992). Representing whiteness in the Black imagination. In Grossberg, L., Nelson, C., & Treichler, P. A. (Eds.), *Cultural studies*, pp. 338–46. Routledge.

Horgan, M., & Liinamaa, S. (2016). The social quarantining of migrant labour: Everyday effects of temporary foreign worker regulation in Canada. *Journal of Ethnic and Migration Studies, 43*(5), 713–30.

Horn, G. (2014). Ulster Protestants in New Zealand: A bibliographic essay. *Immigrants & Minorities*, 32(3), 315–42.

Houkamau, C. A. (2019). Māori identity and economic wellbeing. In Fleming, C., & Manning, M. (Eds.), *Routledge handbook of indigenous wellbeing*, pp. 209–20. Routledge.

Howe, J., Charlesworth, S., & Brennan, D. (2019). Migration pathways for frontline care workers in Australia and New Zealand: Front doors, side doors, back doors and trapdoors. *University of New South Wales Law Journal*, 42(1), 211–41.

Howe, J., Reilly, A., Clibborn, S., van den Broek, D., & Wright, C. F. (2020). Slicing and dicing work in the Australian horticulture industry: Labour market segmentation within the temporary migrant workforce. *Federal Law Review*, 48(2), 247–71.

Hugo, G. (2004). *A new paradigm of international migration: Implications for migration policy and planning for Australia.* Australian Government, Information and Research Services, Parliamentary Library.

Human Rights Commission. (2022). *The RSE Scheme in Aotearoa New Zealand: A human rights review.* Human Rights Commission.

Humphrys, E. (2018). *How Labour built neoliberalism.* Brill.

Hutching, M. (1999). *Long journey for sevenpence: An oral history of assisted immigration to New Zealand from the United Kingdom, 1947–1975.* Victoria University Press.

Hutchinson, D. (2005). Over 1000 overstayers deported but 20,000 still here. *The Press*, 8 July, 3.

Hyslop, D., Le, T., Maré, D. C., & Stillman, S. (2019). Housing markets and migration–Evidence from New Zealand. Available at SSRN 3477071.

Ibrahim, M. (2005). The securitization of migration: A racial discourse. *International Migration*, 43(5), 163–87.

Immigration New Zealand. (2013). *New Zealand Resettlement Strategy.* Ministry of Business, Innovation and Employment.

Immigration New Zealand. (2016). *W1 Work Applications Decided Database.* Ministry of Business, Innovation and Employment.

Immigration New Zealand. (2022). Recognised Seasonal Employer scheme cap increased to 19,000. https://www.immigration.govt.nz/about-us/media-centre/news-notifications/recognised-seasonal-employer-scheme-cap-increased-to-19-000

Immigration New Zealand. (2023). Recognised Seasonal Employer scheme. https://www.immigration.govt.nz/about-us/media-centre/common-topics/recognised-seasonal-employer-rse-scheme

Ip, M. (2000). Beyond the 'settler' and 'astronaut' paradigms: A new approach to the study of Chinese immigrants in New Zealand. In Ip, M., et al. (Eds.), *Migration and travel patterns between Asia and New Zealand*. Aotearoa/New Zealand Migration Research Network, Department of Sociology, Massey University, 3–17.

Ip, M. (2003a). Chinese immigrants and transnationals in New Zealand: A fortress opened. In Ma, L., & Cartier, C. (Eds.), *The Chinese diaspora: Space, place, mobility, and identity*, pp. 339–58. Rowman and Littlefield.

Ip, M. (2003b). Seeking the last Utopia: The Taiwanese in New Zealand. In Ip, M. (Ed.), *Unfolding history, evolving identity: The Chinese in New Zealand*, pp. 185–210. Auckland University Press.

Ip, M. (Ed.). (2003c). *Unfolding history, evolving identity: The Chinese in New Zealand*. Auckland University Press.

Ip, M. (2013). Chinese immigration to Australia and New Zealand: Government policies and race relations. In Tan, C.-B. (Ed.), *Routledge handbook of the Chinese diaspora*, pp. 156–75. Routledge.

Ip, M., & Friesen, W. (2001). The new Chinese community in New Zealand: Local outcomes of transnationalism. *Asian and Pacific Migration Journal*, 10(2), 213–40.

Ip, M., & Liu, L. (2008). Gendered factors of Chinese multi-locality migration: The New Zealand case. *Sites: A Journal of Social Anthropology and Cultural Studies*, 5(2), 31–56.

Jacobs, J. M. (2002). *Edge of empire: Postcolonialism and the city*. Routledge.

Johansson, J. (2006). What if Ruth Richardson had never delivered the 'Mother of All Budgets'? In Devine, S. (Ed.), *New Zealand: As it might have been*, pp. 213–22. Victoria University Press.

Johansson, J., & Levine, S. I. (Eds.). (2012). *Kicking the tyres: The New Zealand general election and electoral referendum of 2011*. Victoria University Press.

Johnson, M. (2016). *The land is our history: Indigeneity, law, and the settler state*. Oxford University Press.

Johnston, R., Gendall, P., Trlin, A., & Spoonley, P. (2010). Immigration, multiculturalism and geography: Inter-group contact and attitudes to immigrants and cultural diversity in New Zealand. *Asian and Pacific Migration Journal*, 19(3), 343–69.

Jones, C. (2016). John Key the biofinancial entrepreneur. *Kōtuitui: New Zealand Journal of Social Sciences Online*, 11(2), 89–103.

Jones, C., & Linkhorn, C. (2017). 'All the rights and privileges of British subjects': Māori and citizenship in Aotearoa New Zealand. In Mann, J. (Ed.), *Citizenship in transnational perspective: Australia, Canada, and New Zealand*, pp. 139–55. Springer.

Jones, D. S. (2013). *Masters of the universe: Hayek, Friedman, and the birth of neoliberal politics*. Princeton University Press.

Jones, M. J. (2012). Dalmatian settlement and identity in New Zealand: The Devcich farm, Kauaeranga valley, near Thames. *Journal of the Australasian Society for Historical Archaeology, 30*, 24–33.

Jones, R. (2016). *Violent borders: Refugees and the right to move*. Verso.

Jones, R., & Johnson, C. (2016). *Placing the border in everyday life*. Routledge.

Joppke, C. (2003). Citizenship between de- and re-ethnicization. *Archives Européennes de Sociologie, 44*(3), 429–58.

Joppke, C. (2010). *Citizenship and immigration*. Polity.

Jourdain, W. R. (1925). *Land legislation and settlement in New Zealand*. W. A. G. Skinner, Government Printer.

Joyce, S. (2012). *MBIE to drive Govt's Business Growth Agenda*. New Zealand Government Press Release, 30 June, https://www.beehive.govt.nz/release/mbie-drive-govt%E2%80%99s-business-growth-agenda

Kalm, S. (2010). Liberalizing movements? The political rationality of global migration management. In Geiger, M., & Pécoud, A. (Eds.), *The politics of international migration management*, pp. 21–44. Palgrave Macmillan UK.

Kapur, D. (2003). *Remittances: The new development mantra?* Paper prepared for the G-24 Technical Group Meeting, 15–16 September. United Nations.

Kasper, W. (1990). *Populate or languish? Rethinking New Zealand's immigration policy*. New Zealand Business Roundtable.

Kawharu, M., Williams, D. V., & Belgrave, M. (Eds.). (2005). *Waitangi revisited: Perspectives on the Treaty of Waitangi*. Oxford University Press.

Keeley B. (2007). *Human capital: How what you know shapes your life*. OECD Publishing.

Keenan, D. (Ed.). (2008). *Terror in our midst? Searching for terrorism in Aotearoa New Zealand*. Huia Publishers.

Kelsey, J. (1995). *The New Zealand experiment: A world model for structural adjustment?* Auckland University Press.

Kennedy, M. (2016). Putting our refuge hand up. *New Zealand International Review, 41*(5), 13–17.

Key, J. (2009). Towards 2014: Speech at Te Kōkiri Ngātahi National Hui to progress Treaty settlements. 22 April, https://www.beehive.govt.nz/speech/towards-2014-speech-te-k%C5%8Dkiri-ng%C4%81tahi-national-hui-progress-treaty-settlements

Key, J. (2016). Punching above our weight. *New Zealand International Review*, 41(4), 13–15.

Khan, R. L. (2011). A study of Fiji Indian migrants in New Zealand: Their migration and settlement management and experiences. Unpublished PhD Thesis, Massey University, Palmerston North.

Kingfisher, C. (2013). *A policy travelogue: Tracing welfare reform in Aotearoa/New Zealand and Canada*. Berghahn Books.

Kiong, E. (2005). Immigration, police seek passport scam fugitives. *New Zealand Herald*, 30 May, https://www.nzherald.co.nz/nz/immigration-andnbsppolice-seek-passport-scam-fugitives/3P7AA6GNQIZOJBP54WZINL54UU/

Klikauer, T. (2015). What is managerialism? *Critical Sociology*, 41(7–8), 1103–19.

Knafo, S. (2020). Neoliberalism and the origins of public management. *Review of International Political Economy*, 27(4), 780–801.

Koram, K. (2022). *Uncommon wealth: Britain and the aftermath of empire*. John Murray.

Koser, K. (2010). The impact of the global financial crisis on international migration. *Whitehead Journal of Diplomacy and International Relations*, 11(1), 13–20.

Koslowski, R. (2014). Selective migration policy models and changing realities of implementation. *International Migration*, 52(3), 26–39.

Kukutai, T., & Broman, P. (2016). From colonial categories to local culture: Evolving state practices of ethnic enumeration in Oceania, 1965–2014. *Ethnicities*, 16(5), 689–711.

Kukutai, T., & Rata, A. (2017). From mainstream to manaaki: Indigenising our approach to immigration. In Hall, D. (Ed.), *Fair borders? Migration policy in the twenty-first century*, pp. 26–44. Bridget Williams Books.

Kumar, A. (2019). Deported Indian students granted work visas to return after fraud allegations cleared. *Stuff*, 24 April, https://www.stuff.co.nz/tarana/112211634/deported-indian-students-granted-work-visas-to-return-after-fraud-allegations-cleared

Kundnani, A. (2021). The racial constitution of neoliberalism. *Race & Class*, 63(1), 51–69.

Kymlicka, W. (2013). Neoliberal multiculturalism. In Hall, P., & Lamont, M. (Eds.), *Social resilience in the neoliberal era*, pp. 99–125. Cambridge University Press.

Laffey, M. (1999). Adding an Asian strand: Neoliberalism and the politics of culture in New Zealand, 1984–97. In Weldes, J. (Ed.), *Cultures of insecurity: States, communities, and the production of danger*, pp. 233–60. University of Minnesota Press.

Larner, W. (1998). Hitching a ride on the tiger's back: Globalisation and spatial imaginaries in New Zealand. *Environment and Planning D: Society and Space*, 16(5), 599–614.

Larner, W. J., Le Heron, R., & Lewis, N. (2007). Co-constituting 'after neoliberalism': Political projects and globalizing governmentalities in Aotearoa/New Zealand. In England, K., and Ward, K. (Eds.), *Neoliberalization: States, networks, peoples*, pp. 223–47. Blackwell.

Laxon, A. (2016a). Student visa fraud: 'It's not about education'. *New Zealand Herald*, 5 December, 14.

Laxon, A. (2016b). Students' NZ dream turns to nightmare. *New Zealand Herald*, 6 December, 12.

Le Heron, R., & Pawson, E. (Eds.). (1996). *Changing places: New Zealand in the nineties*. Longman Paul.

Leay, B. (1999). Commentary on Sir Robert Muldoon's 1984 Sir Robert Menzies Lecture by Barrie Leay. In Gregory, A. (Ed.), *The Menzies Lectures 1978–1998*, pp. 122–25. Sir Robert Menzies Lecture Trust.

Leckie, J. (2021). *Invisible: New Zealand's history of excluding Kiwi-Indians*. Massey University Press.

Leckie, J. (2022). 'Go back to your country!' Excluding Indians in contemporary Aotearoa New Zealand. In McCarthy, A. (Ed.), *Narratives of migrant and refugee discrimination in New Zealand*, pp. 28–49. Routledge.

Lee, H. (2009). Pacific migration and transnationalism: Historical perspectives. In Lee, H., & Francis, S. T. (Eds.), *Migration and transnationalism: Pacific perspectives*, pp. 7–42. ANU Press.

Lees-Galloway, I. (2018). *Regions and industries will benefit from temporary work visa proposals*. New Zealand Government Press Release, 18 December, https://www.beehive.govt.nz/release/regions-and-industries-will-benefit-temporary-work-visa-proposals

Lees-Galloway, I. (2019). *Helping our regions get seasonal support*. New Zealand Government Press Release, 26 September, https://www.beehive.govt.nz/release/helping-our-regions-get-seasonal-support

LEK Consulting. (2001). *New Zealand talent initiative: Strategies for building a talented nation*. LEK Consulting.

Leslie, J. (2016). Sequencing, people movements and mass politicization in European and trans-Tasman single markets. *Government and Opposition*, 51(2), 294–326.

Levick, W. (1988). *Contract labour migration between Fiji and New Zealand: A case study of a South Pacific work scheme*. Master's Thesis, University of Canterbury.

Levick, W., & Bedford, R. (1988). Fiji labour migration to New Zealand in the 1980s. *New Zealand Geographer*, 44(1), 14–21.

Levine, S., & Roberts, N. S. (1994). The New Zealand electoral referendum and general election of 1993. *Electoral Studies*, 13(3), 240–53.

Lewis, N. (2011). Political projects and micro-practices of globalising education: Building an international education industry in New Zealand. *Globalisation, Societies and Education*, 9(2), 225–46.

Lewis, N. (2014). Comparative perspective: Insights from New Zealand's Recognised Seasonal Employer scheme. In Gertel, J., & Sippel, S. (Eds.), *Seasonal workers in Mediterranean agriculture*, pp. 257–63. Routledge.

Ley, D. (2003). Seeking homo economicus: The Canadian state and the strange story of the business immigration program. *Annals of the Association of American Geographers*, 93(2), 426–41.

Ley, D. (2011). *Millionaire migrants: Trans-Pacific life lines*. John Wiley & Sons.

Li, P. H. (2014). New Chinese immigrants to New Zealand: A PRC dimension. In Zhang, J., & Duncan, H. (Eds.), *Migration in China and Asia*, pp. 229–44. Springer.

Liu, J. H., & Mills, D. (2006), Modern racism and neo-liberal globalization: The discourses of plausible deniability and their multiple functions. *Journal of Community & Applied Social Psychology*, 16, 83–99.

Liu, L. S. (2017). New Chinese immigration to New Zealand: Policies, immigration patterns, mobility and perception. In Zhou, M. (Ed.), *Contemporary Chinese diasporas*, pp. 233–59. Palgrave Macmillan.

Liu, L. S. (2018). *Chinese transnational migration in the age of global modernity: The case of Oceania*. Routledge.

Lloyd, D., & Wolfe, P. (2016). Settler colonial logics and the neoliberal regime. *Settler Colonial Studies*, 6(2), 109–18.

Luthria, M. (2008). Migration and development: A framework to identify the links, policies and institutions that matter. *Labour, Employment and Work in New Zealand*, 39–47.

Macfie, R. (2007). New gold dreams. *New Zealand Listener*, 210 (3511).

Macklin, A., & Crépeau, F. (2010). *Multiple citizenship, identity and entitlement in Canada*. Institute for Research on Public Policy.

Maclellan, N. (2008). *Workers for all seasons? Issues from New Zealand's Recognised Seasonal Employer (RSE) Scheme*. Institute for Social Research, Swinburne University of Technology.

Magretta, J. (2012). *What management is: How it works and why it's everyone's business*. Profile.

Mallon, S., Māhina-Tuai, K. U., & Salesa, D. I. (Eds.). (2012). *Tangata o le Moana: New Zealand and the people of the Pacific*. Te Papa Press.

Manuka, H. (1994). Human labour as a commodity: A Maori ethical response. In Morrison, P. (Ed.), *Labour, employment and work in New Zealand*. Conference proceedings, Victoria University, Wellington.

Māori Party. (2011). *Our whānau; our future*. https://img.scoop.co.nz/media/pdfs/1110/FINAL_policy_document_4_0__20111027.pdf

March, J. G., & Olsen, J. P. (2011). The logic of appropriateness. In Goodin, R. (Ed.), *The Oxford handbook of political science*, pp. 478–97. Oxford University Press.

Marlowe, J., & Elliott, S. (2014). Global trends and refugee settlement in New Zealand. *Kōtuitui: New Zealand Journal of Social Sciences Online*, 9(2), 43–49.

Martin, K. (2005). Saddam minister files claim for refugee status. *Dominion Post*, 10 May, 3.

Martin, L. L. (2021). Carceral economies of migration control. *Progress in Human Geography*, 45(4), 740–57.

Mason-Bish, H. (2019). The elite delusion: Reflexivity, identity and positionality in qualitative research. *Qualitative Research*, 19(3), 263–76.

Massey, D. (1991). A global sense of place. In Robertson, S. (Ed.), *Defining travel: Diverse visions*, pp. 167–77. University Press of Mississippi.

Massey, D. S., & Liang, Z. (1989). The long-term consequences of a temporary worker program: The US Bracero experience. *Population Research and Policy Review*, 8, 199–226.

Matike Mai Aotearoa. (2016). *The report of Matike Mai Aotearoa – The Independent Working Group on Constitutional Transformation*. https://nwo.org.nz/resources/report-of-matike-mai-aotearoa-the-independent-working-group-on-constitutional-transformation/

May, A. (2001). 'Commonwealth or Europe?': Macmillan's dilemma, 1961–63. In May, A. (Ed.), *Britain, the Commonwealth and Europe*, pp. 82–110. Palgrave Macmillan.

Mayell, P. (2004). Beyond the 'outer crescent': The Mackinder century in New Zealand geopolitics. *Geographical Journal*, 170(4), 368–76.

MBIE. (2016). *Migration trends 2015/2016*. Ministry of Business, Innovation and Employment.

MBIE. (2017a). *Migration trends 2016/2017*. Ministry of Business, Innovation and Employment.

MBIE. (2017b). *Essential Skills Visa Policy: Report following consultation on proposed changes*. Cabinet Economic Growth and Infrastructure Committee.

MBIE. (2024). *Migration data explorer*. https://mbienz.shinyapps.io/migration_data_explorer/

McAloon, J. (2013). The state and economic policy in twentieth century Australia and New Zealand: Escaping the staples trap? In Lloyd, C., Metzer, J., & Sutch, R. (Eds.), *Settler economies in world history*, pp. 521–43. Brill.

McCarthy, A. (2015). *Migration, ethnicity, and madness: New Zealand, 1860–1910*. Otago University Press.

McCarthy, A. (Ed.). (2022). *Narratives of migrant and refugee discrimination in New Zealand*. Routledge.

McCluskey, N. (2008). *A policy of honesty: Election manifesto pledge fulfilment in New Zealand 1972–2005*. PhD Thesis, University of Canterbury.

McCully, M. (1989). Immigration (Miscellaneous) Bill. *New Zealand Parliamentary Debates*, 503, 13707–8.

McDougall, H. (2021). Buttering up: Britain, New Zealand and negotiations for European Community enlargement, 1970–71. *International History Review*, 43(2), 333–47.

McKenzie, D., Gibson, J., & Stillman, S. (2006). How important is selection? Experimental versus non-experimental measures of the income gain from migration. Motu Working Paper, https://www.motu.nz/our-research/population-and-labour/migration/how-important-is-selection-experimental-vs-non-experimental-measures-of-the-income-gains-from-migration/

McKenzie, D., Martinez, P. G., & Winters, L. A. (2008). Who is coming to New Zealand under the new Recognised Seasonal Employer (RSE) Program? CReAM Discussion Paper 806, Centre for Research and Analysis of Migration, Rockwool Foundation Berlin.

McKinnon, M. (1996). *Immigrants and citizens: New Zealanders and Asian immigration in historical context*. Institute of Policy Studies.

McMillan, K. (2008). Irregular migration: New Zealand's experience and response. *New Zealand International Review*, 33(4), 2–6.

McMillan, K. (2015). Moving freely, but taking a different route: Comparing trans-Tasman and European Union norms of human mobility. In Björkdahl, A., Chaban, N., Leslie, J., & Masselot, A. (Eds.), *Importing EU norms: Conceptual framework and empirical findings*, pp. 97–113. Springer.

McMillan, K. (2017). 'Affective integration' and access to the rights of permanent residency: New Zealanders resident in Australia post-2001. *Ethnicities*, 17(1), 103–27.

McMillan, K. (2020). The intersecting electoral politics of immigration and inequality in Aotearoa/New Zealand. In Simon-Kumar, R., Collins, F. L., & Friesen, W. (Eds.), *Intersections of inequality, migration and diversification: The politics of mobility in Aotearoa/New Zealand*, pp. 87–108. Palgrave.

Meares, C. (2007). From the Rainbow Nation to the Land of the Long White Cloud: Migration, gender and biography. PhD Thesis, Massey University, Albany.

Meares, C., Bell, A., & Peace, R. (2010). Migration, gender and economic integration: International scholarship (2006–09) and an Aotearoa New Zealand research agenda. *Kōtuitui: New Zealand Journal of Social Sciences Online*, 5(2), 61–80.

Meyer, J. W. (2017). Reflections on institutional theories of organizations. In Greenwood, R., Lawrence, T., Meyer, R., & Oliver, C. (Eds.), *The Sage handbook of organizational institutionalism*, pp. 831–52. SAGE.

Mikecz, R. (2012). Interviewing elites: Addressing methodological issues. *Qualitative Inquiry*, 18(6), 482–93.

Miller, P. W., & Neo, L. M. (1997). Immigrant unemployment: The Australian experience. *International Migration*, 35(2), 155–85.

Miller, P., & Rose, N. (2008). *Governing the present: Administering economic, social and personal life*. Polity.

Miller, R. (2015). *Democracy in New Zealand*. Auckland University Press.

Mincer, J. (1958). Investment in human capital and personal income distribution. *The Journal of Political Economy*, 66(4), 281–302.

Mirowski, P., & Plehwe, D. (Eds.). (2009). *The road from Mont Pèlerin: The making of the neoliberal thought collective*. Harvard University Press.

Mitchell, K. (2004). *Crossing the neoliberal line: Pacific Rim migration and the metropolis*. Temple University Press.

Mitchell, L., & Kamenarac, O. (2021). Refugee children and families' positioning within resettlement and early childhood education policies in Aotearoa New Zealand. *Kōtuitui: New Zealand Journal of Social Sciences Online*, 17(2), 224–41.

Mosley, L. (2013). *Interview research in political science*. Cornell University Press.

Mountz, A. (2010). *Seeking asylum: Human smuggling and bureaucracy at the border*. University of Minnesota Press.

Mountz, A. (2011). The enforcement archipelago: Detention, haunting, and asylum on islands. *Political Geography*, 30(3), 118–28.

Muldoon, R. D. (1984). The international economic debate: The 1984 Sir Robert Menzies Lecture. In Gregory, A. (Ed.), 1999, *The Menzies Lectures 1978–1998*, pp. 122–25. Sir Robert Menzies Lecture Trust.

Munshi, D. (1998). Media, politics, and the Asianisation of a polarised immigration debate in New Zealand. *Australian Journal of Communication*, 25(1), 97–110.

Murphy, N. (2003). Joe Lum v. Attorney-General: The politics of exclusion. In Ip, M. (Ed.), *Unfolding history, evolving identity: The Chinese in New Zealand*, pp. 48–68. Auckland University Press.

Mutu, M. (2022). Mana Māori Motuhake: Māori concepts and practices of sovereignty. In Andersen, C., Larkin, S., Tuhiwai-Smith, L., Moreton-Robinson, A., & Hokowhitu, B. (Eds.), *Routledge handbook of critical indigenous studies*, pp. 269–82. Routledge.

Nash, S., & Faafoi, K. (2021). *Immigration reset: Setting the scene.* New Zealand Government Press Release, 17 May, https://www.beehive.govt.nz/speech/immigration-reset-setting-scene

Natter, K. (2018). Rethinking immigration policy theory beyond 'Western liberal democracies'. *Comparative Migration Studies*, 6(1), 2–21.

Neilson, M. (2023). Samoa PM calls out NZ and Australia over 'Pacific family', urges EU-style free movement of labour and travel. *New Zealand Herald*, 22 March, https://www.nzherald.co.nz/nz/politics/samoa-pm-calls-out-nz-and-australia-over-pacific-family-urges-eu-style-free-movement-of-labour-and-travel/E2JBKV5OU5CEXJBCIRJL3GFPSM/

Nelson, G. (2012). *'In quietness and in confidence shall be your strength': Vicesimus Lush and his journals, 1850–1882.* Master's Thesis, Victoria University of Wellington.

New Zealand Census (1945). *Census of Population and Housing, New Zealand, 1945.* Department of Census and Statistics.

New Zealand Census. (1971). *New Zealand Census of Population Dwellings.* Department of Statistics.

New Zealand First. (2004). Official papers reveal serious corruption in NZIS. *Scoop*, 13 April, https://www.scoop.co.nz/stories/PA0404/S00193/official-papers-reveal-serious-corruption-in-nzis.htm

New Zealand Herald. (1879). Chinese immigration. *New Zealand Herald*, 1 August, 5.

New Zealand Herald. (1920). Asiatic influx. *New Zealand Herald*, 15 September, 8.

New Zealand Herald. (1989). Immigration criteria set for overhaul. *New Zealand Herald*, 9 November, 9.

New Zealand Herald. (1990). Immigrant selection uses point system to bring in skilled. *New Zealand Herald*, 21 March, 4.

New Zealand Herald. (2003). Top court clears refugee detention. *New Zealand Herald*, 17 April, https://www.nzherald.co.nz/nz/top-court-clears-refugee-detention/ZDAZC57K4RMXA6TF4I3K5SUICM/

New Zealand Herald. (2007). Ex-immigration minister cleared of fraud. *New Zealand Herald*, 2 March, https://www.nzherald.co.nz/nz/ex-immigration-minister-cleared-of-fraud/OPUF5UT6Z7RLY43GHZTN4KCO3Y/

New Zealand Immigration Service. (2004). *National Immigration Settlement Strategy*. Department of Labour, Wellington.

New Zealand Labour Party. (1984). *The 1984 Policy Document of the New Zealand Labour Party*. New Zealand Labour Party.

New Zealand Labour Party. (1999). *Key policies 1999: The future is with Labour*. New Zealand Labour Party.

New Zealand Labour Party. (2002). *Labour's immigration policy*. https://www.scoop.co.nz/stories/PA0207/S00372.htm

New Zealand Labour Party (2005). Confidence and Supply Agreement with New Zealand First, 17 October. https://www.mcguinnessinstitute.org/wp-content/uploads/2020/08/Confidence-and-Supply-Agreement-with-New-Zealand-First.pdf

New Zealand Labour Party & New Zealand First. (2017). Coalition Agreement: New Zealand Labour Party & New Zealand First. https://www.parliament.nzmedia/4486/362429780labourandnewzealandfirstcoalitionagreement.pdf

New Zealand National Party. (1975), *The National Party 1975 General Election Policy*. New Zealand National Party.

New Zealand National Party. (1990). *National Party policies for the 1990s: Creating a decent society*. National Party of New Zealand.

New Zealand National Party. (2023). *National, ACT and New Zealand First to deliver for all New Zealanders*. https://www.national.org.nz/national_act_and_new_zealand_first_to_deliver_for_all_new_zealanders

New Zealand Productivity Commission. (2021). *International migration to New Zealand: Historical themes and trends*. Working Paper 2021/04, https://www.productivity.govt.nz/publications/immigration-history/

New Zealand Productivity Commission. (2022). *Immigration – Fit for the future: Final report*. https://www.productivity.govt.nz/inquiries/immigration-settings

Newlands, K. J. (2006). *The modern nomad in New Zealand: A study of the effects of the Working Holiday Schemes on free independent travellers and their host communities*. Unpublished Master's Thesis, Auckland University of Technology, https://core.ac.uk/reader/56361040

Ng, K. E. (2017). *Old Asian, new Asian*. Bridget Williams Books.

Ngata, A. T. (1943). *The Price of Citizenship*. Wellington: Whitcombe & Tombs.

Noakes, S., & Burton, C. (2019). Economic statecraft and the making of bilateral relationships: Canada–China and New Zealand–China interactions compared. *Journal of Chinese Political Science, 24*, 411–31.

Nugent, D. (1997). *Modernity at the edge of empire: State, individual, and nation in the northern Peruvian Andes, 1885–1935*. Stanford University Press.

Nyers, P. (Ed.). (2009). *Securitizations of citizenship*. Routledge.

Oakman, D. (2010). *Facing Asia: A history of the Colombo Plan*. ANU Press.

Office of the Ombudsman. (2004). *Report on 'Lie in unison' memo*. Office of the Ombudsman.

Office of the Ombudsman. (2006). *Report of the Ombudsman for the year ended 30 June 2006*. Office of the Ombudsman.

Office of the Ombudsman. (2007). *Report of the Ombudsman for the year ended 30 June 2007*. Office of the Ombudsman.

O'Malley, V. (2015). *Haerenga: Early Māori journeys across the globe*. Bridget Williams Books.

O'Malley, V. (2016). *The Great War for New Zealand: Waikato 1800–2000*. Bridget Williams Books.

O'Malley, V. (2017). *He Whakaputanga: The Declaration of Independence, 1835*. Bridget Williams Books.

O'Malley, V. (2019). *The New Zealand wars / Ngā pakanga o Aotearoa*. Bridget Williams Books.

O'Malley, V., Stirling, B., & Penetito, W. (2011). *The Treaty of Waitangi companion: Māori and Pakeha from Tasman to today*. Auckland University Press.

One News. (2019). Winston Peters argues NZ's Africa and Middle East refugee policy 'can hardly be racist'. *One News*, 25 June, https://www.1news.co.nz/2019/06/24/winston-peters-argues-nzs-africa-and-middle-east-refugee-policy-can-hardly-be-racist/

Ong, A. (2006). *Neoliberalism as exception: Mutations in citizenship and sovereignty*. Duke University Press.

Ongley, P., & Pearson, D. (1995). Post-1945 international migration: New Zealand, Australia and Canada compared. *International Migration Review, 29*(3), 765–93.

Opara, O. (2018). From settler society to working holiday heaven? Patterns and issues of temporary labour migration to New Zealand. *New Zealand Sociology, 33*(1), 29–52.

Orange, C. (2015). *The Treaty of Waitangi*. Bridget Williams Books.

Otago Daily Times. (2017). Too many international students: Officials. *Otago Daily Times*, 3 March, https://www.odt.co.nz/news/national/too-many-international-students-officials

Overbeek, H. (2002). *Globalisation and governance: Contradictions of neo-liberal migration management.* HWWA Discussion Paper.

Palmer, G. (2013). *Reform: A memoir.* Victoria University Press.

Papps, T. (1985). Growth and distribution of population. In Pool, D. I. (Ed.), *The population of New Zealand.* Country Monograph Series Number 12. United Nations Economic and Social Commission for Asia and the Pacific.

Parekh, B. (2000). *Rethinking multiculturalism: Cultural diversity and political theory.* Harvard University Press.

Parker, B. J. (2002). At the edge of empire: Conceptualizing Assyria's Anatolian frontier ca. 700 BC. *Journal of Anthropological Archaeology, 21*(3), 371–95.

Parliamentary Counsel Office. (2003). *2003 Annual report.* New Zealand Parliament.

Parr, A. R. (2000). Immigration and New Zealand: From localism to globalism? *New Zealand Sociology, 15*(2), 304–34.

Paul, D. B., Stenhouse, J., & Spencer, H. G. (Eds.). (2017). *Eugenics at the edges of empire: New Zealand, Australia, Canada and South Africa.* Springer.

Peace, R. (2015). Islands, islanders and a man and his manuscripts: Richard D. Bedford writing Pacific geographies, 1968–2015. *New Zealand Population Review, 41,* 3.

Peck, J. (2010). *Constructions of neoliberal reason.* Oxford University Press.

Peck, J., & Theodore, N. (2015). *Fast policy: Experimental statecraft at the thresholds of neoliberalism.* University of Minnesota Press.

Peck, J., & Tickell, A. (2002). Neoliberalizing space. *Antipode, 34*(3), 380–404.

Pécoud, A. (2021). Narrating an ideal migration world? An analysis of the Global Compact for Safe, Orderly and Regular Migration. *Third World Quarterly, 42*(1), 16–33.

Perry, A. (2001). *On the edge of empire: Gender, race, and the making of British Columbia, 1849–1871.* University of Toronto Press.

Peters, W. (2004). Questions for Oral Answer – Questions to Ministers. *New Zealand Parliamentary Debates, 619,* 14525.

Phillips, J. (n.d.). History of immigration. *Te Ara – the Encyclopedia of New Zealand,* https://teara.govt.nz/en/history-of-immigration

Phillips, J., & Hearn, T. (2008). *Settlers: New Zealand immigrants from England, Ireland and Scotland 1800–1945.* Auckland University Press.

Pickles, K. (2001). Empire settlement and single British women as New Zealand domestic servants during the 1920s. *New Zealand Journal of History, 35*(1), 22–44.

Pickles, K. (2016). *Christchurch ruptures.* Bridget Williams Books.

Pihama, L. (1993). No, will not be a post… *Te Pua*, 2(1/2), 35–37.

Piper, N. (2013). *New perspectives on gender and migration: Livelihood, rights and entitlements.* Routledge.

Plehwe, D., & Mirowski, P. (2009). *The road from Mont Pèlerin: The making of the neoliberal thought collective.* Harvard University Press.

Plehwe, D., Slobodian, Q., & Mirowski, P. (Eds.). (2020). *Nine lives of neoliberalism.* Verso.

Poata-Smith, E. T. A. (2013). Inequality and Māori. In Rashbrooke, M. (Ed.), *Inequality: A New Zealand crisis*, pp. 148–58. Bridget Williams Books.

Poku, N. K., Renwick, N., & Glenn, J. (2000). Human security in a globalising world. In Graham, D., & Poku, N. (Eds.), *Migration, globalisation and human security*, pp. 9–22. Routledge.

Pool, I. (1991). *Te iwi Maori: A New Zealand population, past, present & projected.* Auckland University Press.

Pool, I. (2015). *Colonization and development in New Zealand between 1769 and 1900: The seeds of Rangiatea.* Springer.

Pool, I., & Jackson, N., (2018). Population change – Key population trends. *Te Ara – the Encyclopedia of New Zealand*, http://www.TeAra.govt.nz/en/graph/28720/new-zealand-population-by-ethnicity-1840-2013

Poot, J. (2010). Trans-Tasman migration, transnationalism and economic development in Australasia. *Asian and Pacific Migration Journal*, 19(3), 319–42.

Poot, J., & Sanderson, L. M. (2007). *Changes in social security eligibility and the international mobility of New Zealand citizens in Australia.* University of Waikato, Population Studies Centre.

Poot, J., Waldorf, B., & van Wissen, L. (Eds.). (2009). *Migration and human capital.* Edward Elgar.

Population Monitoring Group. (1991). *On the move: Migration and population – trends and policies.* New Zealand Planning Council.

Portice, J., & Reicher, S. (2018). Arguments for European disintegration: A mobilization analysis of anti-immigration speeches by UK political leaders. *Political Psychology*, 39(6), 1357–72.

Power, M. (1997). *The audit society: Rituals of verification.* Oxford University Press.

Prince, P. (2003). We are Australian – The constitution and deportation of Australian-born children. Research Paper, no. 3, 2003–04. Canberra, Parliamentary Library.

Prince, R. (2020). The geography of policy-making: Mobile policy, territory and state space. In Moisio, S., Koch, N., Jonas, A. E. G., Lizotte, C., & Luukkonen, J. (Eds.), *Handbook on the changing geographies of the state*, pp. 173–84. Edward Elgar.

Procházková, J. (2010). Bohemians in New Zealand – The history and present situation of the Puhoi village. *Český Lid*, 97(1), 19–34.

Pullman, M. (1996). Loyalty lies here: Peters. *New Zealand Herald*, 2 February, 9.

Radio New Zealand. (2013). McCully defends option to use detention centres. *Radio New Zealand*, 12 February, https://www.rnz.co.nz/news/political/127870/mccully-defends-option-to-use-detention-centres

Radio New Zealand. (2019). New Zealand's darkest day: A timeline of the Christchurch terror attacks. *Radio New Zealand*, https://shorthand.radionz.co.nz/NZ-DARKEST-DAY/index.html

Radio New Zealand. (2020a). How the Five Eyes countries share immigration data. *Radio New Zealand*, 30 December, https://www.rnz.co.nz/news/national/433786/how-the-five-eyes-countries-share-immigration-data

Radio New Zealand. (2020b). NZ to close its borders to anyone not a citizen or permanent resident, PM confirms. *Radio New Zealand*, 19 March, https://www.rnz.co.nz/news/national/412162/nz-to-close-its-borders-to-anyone-not-a-citizen-or-permanent-resident-pm-confirms

Radio New Zealand. (2022). RSE worker treatment like 'slavery', says Equal Employment Opportunities Commissioner. *Radio New Zealand*, 12 December, https://www.rnz.co.nz/news/national/480556/rse-worker-treatment-like-slavery-says-equal-employment-opportunities-commissioner

Ramasamy, S., Krishnan, V., Bedford, R., & Bedford. C. (2008). The Recognised Seasonal Employer policy: Seeking the elusive triple wins for development through international migration. *Pacific Economic Bulletin*, 23(3), 171–86.

Ran, G. J., & Liu, L. S. (2021). 'Forced' family separation and inter-generational dynamics: Multi-generational new Chinese immigrant families in New Zealand. *Kōtuitui: New Zealand Journal of Social Sciences Online*, 16(1), 148–67.

Rapson, V. (1998). New Zealand's migration policy: A revolving door? *People and Place*, 6(4), 52–62.

Rata, A. (2020). Dismantling Cook's legacy: Science, migration, and colonialism in Aotearoa. *New Zealand Science Review*, 76(1–2), 54–58.

Rata, A., & Al-Asaad, F. (2019). Whakawhanaungatanga as a Māori approach to indigenous–settler of colour relationship building. *New Zealand Population Review*, 45, 211–33.

Ratuva, S. (2022). The politics of imagery: Understanding the historical genesis of Sinophobia in Pacific geopolitics. *East Asia*, 39(1), 13–28.

Razzak, W. A. (2016). New Zealand labor market dynamics: Pre- and post-global financial crisis. *Journal of Business Cycle Research*, 12, 49–79.

Reed, I. A. (2020). *Power in modernity: Agency relations and the creative destruction of the king's two bodies*. University of Chicago Press.

Refugee Statistics. (2010). *New Zealand refugee statistics*. https://www.refugee.org.nz/Stats/stats.htm#%5B1%5D

Reinhoudt, J., & Audier, S. (2018). *The Walter Lippman Colloquium: The birth of neo-liberalism*. Palgrave Macmillan.

Reserve Bank of New Zealand. (1986). *Migration and the New Zealand labour market*. Vol. 49, 332–35. Reserve Bank of New Zealand.

Richmond, A. H. (1975). Canadian immigration: Recent developments and future prospects. *International Migration*, 13(4), 163–82.

Rizvi, F. (1997). Beyond the East/West divide: Education and the dynamics of Australia/Asia relations. *Australian Educational Researcher*, 24(1), 13–26.

Robertson, S. (2013). *Transnational student-migrants and the state: The education–migration nexus*. Palgrave.

Robertson, S. (2015). Contractualization, depoliticization and the limits of solidarity: Noncitizens in contemporary Australia. *Citizenship Studies*, 19(8), 936–50.

Rodger, S. (1988). Overstayers. *New Zealand Parliamentary Debates*, 490, 5723.

Rose, N., & Miller, P. (1992). Political power beyond the state: Problematics of government. *British Journal of Sociology*, 43(3), 173–205.

Ross, K., & Comrie, M. (2012). The rules of the (leadership) game: Gender, politics and news. *Journalism*, 13(8), 969–84.

Ross, R. (1972). Te Tiriti o Waitangi: Texts and translations. *New Zealand Journal of History*, 6, 129–57.

Royal Commission of Inquiry. (2019). *Ko tō tātou kāinga tēnei: Report: Royal Commission of Inquiry into the terrorist attack on Christchurch masjidain on 15 March 2019*. https://christchurchattack.royalcommission.nz/

Rudd, C. (2005). *Marketing the message or the messenger? The New Zealand Labour Party, 1990–2003*. Manchester University Press.

Ruddock, P. (2000). Refugee claims and Australian migration law: A ministerial perspective. *University of New South Wales Law Journal*, 23, 1.

Rudolph, C. (2003). Security and the political economy of international migration. *American Political Science Review*, 97(4), 603–20.

Sainsbury, D. (2012). *Welfare states and immigrant rights: The politics of inclusion and exclusion.* Oxford University Press.

Salesa, D. I. (2011). *Racial crossings: Race, intermarriage, and the Victorian British Empire.* Oxford University Press.

Salmond, A. (1997). *Between worlds: Early exchanges between Maori and Europeans, 1773-1815.* Penguin.

Salskov-Iversen, D., Hansen, H. K., & Bislev, S. (2000). Governmentality, globalization, and local practice: Transformations of a hegemonic discourse. *Alternatives, 25*(2), 183–222.

Scheel, S., & Ustek-Spilda, F. (2019). The politics of expertise and ignorance in the field of migration management. *Environment and Planning D: Society and Space, 37*(4), 663–81.

Schultz, T. W. (1972). *Economic research: Retrospect and prospect, Volume 6, Human resources,* pp. 1–84. NBER.

Scollay, R., Findlay, C., & Kaufmann, U. (2010). *Australia New Zealand Closer Economic Relations Trade Agreement (ANZCERTA) and regional integration.* ISEAS Publishing.

Scott, M. (2018). Assembling the Antipodes: Migration, finance and territoriality across Australia and New Zealand. *Territory, Politics, Governance, 6*(2), 240–58.

Shepherd, S. (2018). Managerialism: An ideal type. *Studies in Higher Education, 43*(9), 1668–78.

Siklodi, N., Ie, K. W., & Allen, N. (2023). From gender equity to gendered assignments? Women and cabinet committees in Canada and the United Kingdom. *Government and Opposition,* 1–24.

Simmons, L. (2007). Rogue Pakeha. *ARENA Journal, 28,* 45–64.

Simon-Kumar, R. (2015). Neoliberalism and the new race politics of migration policy: Changing profiles of the desirable migrant in New Zealand. *Journal of Ethnic and Migration Studies, 41*(7), 1172–91.

Simon-Kumar, R. (2020). Justifying inequalities: Multiculturalism and stratified migration in Aotearoa/New Zealand. In Simon-Kumar, R., Collins, F. L., & Friesen, W. (Eds.), *Intersections of inequality, migration and diversification: The politics of mobility in Aotearoa/ New Zealand,* pp. 43–64. Palgrave.

Simon-Kumar, R., Collins, F. L., & Friesen, W. (2020). *Intersections of inequality, migration and diversification: The politics of mobility in Aotearoa/New Zealand.* Palgrave.

Siu-lun, W. (1992). Emigration and stability in Hong Kong. *Asian Survey, 32*(10), 918–33.

Skeldon, R. (1990). Emigration and the future of Hong Kong. *Publica Affairs, 63*(4), 500–523.

Skeldon, R. (Ed.). (1994). *Reluctant exiles? Migration from Hong Kong and the new overseas Chinese*. M. E. Sharpe.

Skilling, P. (2010a). New Zealand's Fifth Labour Government (1999–2008): A new partnership with business and society? *Labour History*, 98, 39–53.

Skilling, P. (2010b). The construction and use of national identity in contemporary New Zealand political discourse. *Australian Journal of Political Science*, 45(2), 175–89.

Skilling, P. (2012). Immigration policy in New Zealand: Divergent narratives, shared assumptions and national identity. *Critical Policy Studies*, 6(4), 363–78.

Slobodian, Q. (2018). *Globalists: The end of empire and the birth of neoliberalism*. Harvard University Press.

Small, D. (2008). *Balancing national security and personal freedom in a low-risk society: The case of New Zealand*. Milan and Como, Italy: Research Committee on Sociology of Law Annual Conference: Law and Justice in the Risk Society, 9–12 July.

Smith, A. (1811). *An inquiry into the nature and causes of the wealth of nations*. United Kingdom: S. Doig and A. Stirling, Lackington, Allen and Company, Cradock and Joy, and T. Hamilton, London, and Wilson and Son, York.

Smith, K., & Haux, T. (2017). Evidence-based policy-making (EBPM). In Greve, B. (Ed.), *Handbook of social policy evaluation*, pp. 141–60. Edward Elgar Publishing.

Smith, P. V. (2021). The Dawn Raids. In Barber, S., and Davidson, M. (Eds.), *Through that which separates us*, pp. 29–40. Te Reo Kē/The Physics Room.

Spencer, S. (2011). *The migration debate*. Policy Press.

Spiro, P. J. (2008). *Beyond citizenship: American identity after globalization*. Oxford University Press.

Spivak, G. C. (1996 [1985]). Subaltern studies: Deconstructing historiography. In Landry, D., & MacLean, G. (Eds.), *The Spivak reader*, pp. 203–36. Routledge.

Spoonley, P. (2015a). A political economy of labour migration of New Zealand. *New Zealand Population Review*, 41, 169–90.

Spoonley, P. (2015b). New diversity, old anxieties in New Zealand: The complex identity politics and engagement of a settler society. *Ethnic and Racial Studies*, 38(4), 650–61.

Spoonley, P. (2020). *The new New Zealand: Facing demographic disruption*. Massey University Press.

Spoonley, P., & Bedford, R. (2012). *Welcome to our world? Immigration and the reshaping of New Zealand*. Dunmore.

Spoonley, P., Bedford, R., & Macpherson, C. (2003). Divided loyalties and fractured sovereignty: Transnationalism and the nation-state in Aotearoa/New Zealand. *Journal of Ethnic and Migration Studies*, 29(1), 27–46.

Spoonley, P., & Meares, C. L. (2011). Laissez-faire multiculturalism and relational embeddedness: Ethnic precincts in Auckland. *Cosmopolitan Civil Societies: An Interdisciplinary Journal*, 3(1), 42–64.

Spoonley, P., & Trlin, A. D. (2004). *Immigration, immigrants and the media: Making sense of multicultural New Zealand*. New Settlers Programme, Massey University.

Statistics New Zealand. (2022). *Net migration lowest in nine years*. https://www.stats.govt.nz/news/net-migration-lowest-in-nine-years

Statistics New Zealand. (2023). *International migration: October 2023*. https://www.stats.govt.nz/information-releases/international-migration-october-2023

Statistics New Zealand. (2024). *Permanent & long-term migration by country of residence, citizenship and birthplace (Annual-Jun)*. https://infoshare.stats.govt.nz/

Stedman Jones, D. (2012). *Masters of the universe: Hayek, Friedman, and the birth of neoliberal politics*. Harvard University Press.

Stevenson, T. (1992). *Exploratory report to the Waitangi Tribunal on a claim objecting to aspects of the Immigration Amendment Bill 1991*. Waitangi Tribunal.

Storey, K. (2016). *Settler anxiety at the outposts of empire: Colonial relations, humanitarian discourses, and the imperial press*. UBC Press.

Stringer, C. (2016). *Worker exploitation in New Zealand: A troubling landscape*. University of Auckland.

Stringer, C., & Michailova, S. (2019a). *Understanding the exploitation of temporary migrant workers: A comparison of Australia, Canada, New Zealand and the United Kingdom*. Ministry of Business, Innovation and Employment.

Stringer, C., & Michailova, S. (2019b). *Addressing the exploitation of temporary migrant workers: Developments in Australia, Canada, and the United Kingdom*. Ministry of Business, Innovation and Employment.

Swain, P. (2004). Questions for Oral Answer – Questions to Ministers. *New Zealand Parliamentary Debates*, 619, 14525.

Swain, P., & Hawkins, G. (2004). *Police and Immigration formalise practices*. New Zealand Government Press Release, 17 June, https://www.beehive.govt.nz/release/police-and-immigration-formalise-practices

Tagupa, W. (1994). Law, status and citizenship: Conflict and continuity in New Zealand and Western Samoa (1922–1982). *Journal of Pacific History*, 29(1), 19–35.

Tarling, N. (2004). *International students in New Zealand: The making of policy since 1950.* New Zealand Asia Institute, University of Auckland.

Tecun, A., Lopesi, L., & Shankar, A. (Eds.). (2022). *Towards a grammar of race in Aotearoa New Zealand.* Bridget Williams Books.

Templeton, H. (1995). *All honourable men: Inside the Muldoon Cabinet, 1975–1984.* Auckland University Press.

Templeton, H. (2000). Shand, Thomas Philip. *Dictionary of New Zealand Biography*, https://teara.govt.nz/en/biographies/5s12/shand-thomas-philip

Te Puni Kokiri (1998). *Economic gaps between Maori and non-Maori: A report to the Minister of Maori Affairs.* Te Puni Kokiri.

The Commonwealth. (2025). About us. Accessed 3 March. https://thecommonwealth.org/about-us

The Population Conference. (1997). People, communities, growth: Conference proceedings. Te Papa Tongarewa (Museum of New Zealand), Wellington, 12–14 November.

Thomsen, P. S., Lopesi, L., & Lee, K. L. (2022). Contemporary Moana mobilities: Settler-colonial citizenship, upward mobility, and transnational Pacific identities. *The Contemporary Pacific*, 34(2), 327–52.

Thorn, J. (1946). *Reports of the Dominion Population Committee.* New Zealand House of Representatives.

Tickell, A., & Peck, J. (2003). Making global rules: Globalisation or neoliberalisation. In Tickell, A., & Peck, J. (Eds.), *Remaking the global economy: Economic-geographical perspectives,* pp. 163–81. SAGE.

Tie, W. (2016). On the unbearable lightness of John Key. *Counterfutures*, 2, 143–70.

Tormey, A. (2007). 'Everyone with eyes can see the problem': Moral citizens and the space of Irish nationhood. *International Migration*, 45(3), 69–100.

Trevett, C. (2008). Troubled Pacific Immigration Division's third review. *New Zealand Herald*, 22 May, A06.

Trevett, C. (2020). Agent of chaos: Inside the story of the Labour NZ First coalition government. *The Spinoff*, 13 December, https://thespinoff.co.nz/politics/13-12-2020/agent-of-chaos-the-inside-story-of-the-labour-nz-first-coalition-government

Triandafyllidou, A. (Ed.). (2018). *Handbook of migration and globalisation.* Edward Elgar.

Trlin, A. D. (1997). For the promotion of economic growth and prosperity: New Zealand's immigration policy, 1991–1995. In Trlin, A. D., & Spoonley, P. (Eds.), *New Zealand and International Migration: A Digest and Bibliography*, (3), 1–27. Department of Sociology, Massey University, Palmerston North.

Trlin, A. D., & Kang, J. (1992). The business immigration policy and the characteristics of approved Hong Kong and Taiwanese applicants, 1986–1988. *New Zealand and International Migration: A Digest and Bibliography*, (2), 48–64.

Trlin, A. D., Spoonley, P., & Bedford, R. (1997). *New Zealand and international migration*. Palmerston North, Massey University Department of Sociology.

Tsai, M.-C. (2001). Dependency, the state and class in the neoliberal transition of Taiwan. *Third World Quarterly*, 22(3), 359–79.

Tsai, L. L., & Collins, F. L. (2017). Youth and mobility in working holidays: Imagined freedoms and lived constraints in lives of Taiwanese working holidaymakers in New Zealand. *New Zealand Geographer*, 73(2), 129–40.

Turia, T. (2007). *Maori concerns cannot be brushed aside*. The Māori Party press release. *Scoop*, https://www.scoop.co.nz/stories/PA0702/S00047.htm

Turia, T. (2008). *Maori values a foundation for all New Zealanders*. The Māori Party press release. *Scoop*, https://www.scoop.co.nz/stories/PA0806/S00480/maori-values-a-foundation-for-all-new-zealanders.htm?from-mobile=bottom-link-01

Vaggioli, Dom Felice (1896). *History of New Zealand and its inhabitants*. Translated into English by John Crockett in 2023. Otago University Press.

Vallelly, N. (2021). *Futilitarianism: Neoliberalism and the production of uselessness*. Goldsmiths Press.

Veracini, L. (2010). *Settler colonialism*. Palgrave Macmillan.

Vertovec, S. (2006). Is circular migration the way forward in global policy? *Around the Globe*, 3(2), 38–44.

Vosko, L. F. (2022). Temporary labour migration by any other name: Differential inclusion under Canada's 'new' international mobility regime. *Journal of Ethnic and Migration Studies*, 48(1), 129–52.

Vowles, J. (1997). Waiting for the realignment? The New Zealand party system, 1972–93. *Political Science*, 48(2), 184–209.

Vowles, J. (1998). *Voters' victory? New Zealand's first election under proportional representation*. Auckland University Press.

Vowles, J., & Aimer, P. (1993). *Voters' vengeance: The 1990 election in New Zealand and the fate of the Fourth Labour Government.* Auckland University Press.

Vowles, J., Coffé, H., & Curtin, J. (2017). *A bark but no bite: Inequality and the 2014 New Zealand general election.* ANU Press.

Vucetic, S. (2020). *The Anglosphere: A genealogy of a racialized identity in international relations.* Stanford University Press.

Waikato Times. (2004). Immigration fraud rising. *Waikato Times,* 12 April, 2.

Waitangi Tribunal. (2014). *He Whakaputanga me te Tiriti / The Declaration and the Treaty: The report on Stage 1 of the Te Paparahi o Te Raki Inquiry.* Legislation Direct.

Waitoki, W. (2019). 'This is not us': But actually, it is: Talking about when to raise the issue of colonisation. *New Zealand Journal of Psychology,* 48(1), 140–45.

Walia, H. (2021). *Border and rule: Global migration, capitalism, and the rise of racist nationalism.* Haymarket Books.

Walker, H. (2021). *Nau mai welcome home: Can Aotearoa New Zealand meet the needs of our diaspora, attract some of them home, and prepare for the trends of a post-pandemic future?* The Helen Clark Foundation.

Walker, R. (1984). The genesis of Maori activism. *Journal of the Polynesian Society,* 93(3), 267–81.

Walker, R. (1990). *Ka whawhai tonu matou: Struggle without end.* Penguin Books.

Walker, R. (1994). New Zealand immigration and the political economy. *The Social Contract,* 4(2), 86–97.

Walters, W. (2015). Reflections on migration and governmentality. *Movements: Journal for Critical Migration and Border Regime Studies,* 1(1).

Wang, B. (2018). *New Chinese migrants in New Zealand: Becoming cosmopolitan? Roots, emotions, and everyday diversity.* Routledge.

Wang, S. H. (2017). Fetal citizens? Birthright citizenship, reproductive futurism, and the 'panic' over Chinese birth tourism in southern California. *Environment and Planning D: Society and Space,* 35(2), 263–80.

Watts, A. (2021). *New Zealand's France: A different view of 1835–1935.* Aykay Publishing.

Weekes, J. (2016). Warning of 'education trafficking' scams hitting New Zealand. *Stuff,* 26 February, https://www.stuff.co.nz/dominion-post/76742569/warning-of-education-trafficking-scams-hitting-new-zealand

Wellwood, E. (2000). Aussies hint at changing free access. *The Dominion*, 21 September, Edition 2, 1.

Whāia Legal. (2021). *Legal advice on immigration policy and Te Tiriti o Waitangi*. New Zealand Productivity Commission Immigration Policy Inquiry, https://www.productivity.govt.nz/inquiries/immigration-settings/

Whyte, J. (2019). *The morals of the market: Human rights and the rise of neoliberalism*. Verso.

Wickramasekara, P. (2011). *Circular migration: A triple win or a dead end?* ILO, http://www.migration4development.org/sites/m4d.emakina-eu.net/files/no15-mar11-circular-migration-a-triple-win-or-a-dead-end.pdf

Williams, D. V. (1999). *'Te Kooti Tango Whenua': The Native Land Court 1864–1909*. Huia Publishers.

Williamson, M., & Guy, N. (2012). *Exercise barrier shows NZ's readiness for mass arrivals*. New Zealand Government Press Release, 20 June, https://www.beehive.govt.nz/release/exercise-barrier-shows-new-zealand%E2%80%99s-readiness-mass-arrivals

Winkelmann, R. (1999). *Immigration: The New Zealand experience*. Institute for Advanced Study of Labour (Bonn) Discussion Paper 61.

Wolfe, P. (1999). *Settler colonialism and the transformation of anthropology*. Bloomsbury Publishing.

Wolfe, R. (2005). *Battlers, bluffers and bully-boys: How New Zealand's Prime Ministers have shaped our nation*. Random House New Zealand.

Wonders, N. A. (2006). Global flows, semi-permeable borders and new channels of inequality. In Pickering, S., & Weber, L. (Eds.), *Borders, mobility and technologies of control*, pp. 63–86. Springer Netherlands.

Wong, L. T. (1984). Canada's guestworkers: Some comparisons of temporary workers in Europe and North America. *International Migration Review*, 18(1), 85–98.

Wood, A. (2011). 30,000 workers needed for Christchurch rebuild. *Stuff*, 2 August, http://www.stuff.co.nz/business/rebuilding-christchurch/5373259/30-000-workers-needed-for-Christchurch-rebuild

Woodhouse, M. (2016). *NZRP [New Zealand Residence Programme] changes to strike the right balance*. New Zealand Government Press Release, 12 October, https://beehive.govt.nz/release/nzrp-changes-strike-right-balance.

Woodhouse, M., & Finlayson, C. (2017). *Ministers attend Five Country Ministerial.* New Zealand Government Press Release, 29 June, https://www.beehive.govt.nz/release/ministers-attend-five-country-ministerial

Woods, R. J. H. (2015). From colonial animal to imperial edible: Building an empire of sheep in New Zealand, ca. 1880–1900. *Comparative Studies of South Asia, Africa, and the Middle East,* 35(1), 117–36.

Yanow, D. (1996). *How does a policy mean? Interpreting policy and organizational actions.* Georgetown University Press.

Yanow, D. (2007). Interpretation in policy analysis: On methods and practice. *Critical Policy Analysis,* 1(1), 110–22.

Yeoh, B. S. (2006). Bifurcated labour: The unequal incorporation of transmigrants in Singapore. *Tijdschrift voor Economische en Sociale Geografie,* 97(1), 26–37.

Young, A. (2008). Migration boss gave visa help to relatives. *New Zealand Herald,* 19 April, A04.

Young, A. (2008). Thompson's PhD claim raised by agency in 2004. *New Zealand Herald,* 19 May, A03

Yui, M., & Gregory, R. (2018). Quakes and aftershocks: Organisational restructuring in the New Zealand state sector, 1960–2017. *Policy Quarterly,* 14(3), 25–32.

Index

Entries in *italics* denote figures; entries in **bold** denote tables.

and immigrant settlement 152
Minister of Employment, as Minister of Immigration 94–95
Minister of Foreign Affairs 201, 229
Minister of Labour, as Minister of Immigration 46, 50, 63
Ministers of Immigration 1–3, 9–11, **39–41**; and the bureaucracy 105–7; changes in role of 175, 185, 199, 201, 203, 205, 251, 254; constituency pressures on 96–97; discretion of 60, 72; early 38, 44–47, 62; interviews with 18–20, 22–23, 66, 251; legal responsibilities of 10; political importance of 78; positionality of 96; women as 16
Ministry of Business, Innovation and Employment (MBIE) 10, 211–12, 233, 235, 239
Ministry of Foreign Affairs and Trade 10, 188, 197
Ministry of Social Development 10, 188
MMP (Mixed-Member Proportional) 135–36
Mont Pèlerin Society 13, 68
Moore, Mike 103
Muldoon, Robert 56, 60–61, 66, 69n7, 71–72, 86–87, 104, 253
multiculturalism 3, 9, 23, 60, 270; in Australia 108; and cosmopolitanism 125; laissez-faire 205; liberal 251–53, 256, 258; and Māori 91–92, 126–29; and migrant selection 83–84, 95–96, 118, 268; and neoliberalism 65, 67, 69, 71, 205, 253; and policy diffusion 265–67; use of term 12; see also economic multiculturalism
Mumbai 174, 197
Mutu, Margaret 208, 240

Nana, Ganesh 260
Nash, Walter 50, 52
National Government: 2023 coalition 259–60; coalition of 1996–1999 136–40, 142, 146; Fifth 193–94, 196, 202, 206, 211, 222, 230, 264; Third 66, 69; see also Fourth National Government
national identity 12, 24, 65, 67, 84, 150, 185
National Party 51; and asylum seekers 169; and citizenship 163–64; election campaign of 1975 60; formation of 49; and globalisation 141
Nauru 165
neoliberal governmentality 107
neoliberalism 2–3, 12–16, 63, 68, 173–74; and immigration policy 7, 9, 23, 73–74, 76–77, 79–83, 111–13, 251–53; race-free 82; and social liberalism 70–71; and the Third Way 151
neoliberal migration regime 11, 23, 71–75, 101, 105–10, 118
neoliberal orthodoxy 102, 110, 118, 129

neoliberal revolution 3, 65–66, 76, 79, 102–4
neoliberal triumphalism 193
Netherlands 53, 57
net migration in Aotearoa New Zealand 33; 1860-1901 36, 37–38; 1901–2023 44; 1982–1991 75–76, **76**, 80; in 1990s 115, **117**; in 2010s 206–8, 207, 215–16, 223–24, 238; with Australia 68, 73, 87, 263–64; and Covid-19 245; formula for calculating 215n23; losses 50, 56, 68, 73, 87; pledges to reduce 228, 231, 269; targets for 144, 264
New Growth Economics 155
NewLabour Party 102–3, 103n9
new public management approach 134
New South Wales 30, 34
New Zealand see also Aotearoa New Zealand
New Zealand and Australia Business Investment Forum 198
New Zealand Company 30, 32–34
New Zealanders, use of term 20, 49
New Zealand First 7–8, 104, 123–25, 129, 133; in 1996 coalition government 136–40, 145–46; in 1999 election 150; and 2005 Clark government 179, 181; in 2005 election 178; in 2008 election 191; in 2011 election 208; in 2014 election 212; and 2017 Ardern government 230–32, 236–37, 242; in 2017 election 228–29; in 2023 election 247–48; and asylum seekers 169; and citizenship 164; record in government 269
New Zealand Immigration Programme (NZIP) 152–53, 181
New Zealand models 267
New Zealand Nurses Organisation 229
New Zealand Planning Council 126
New Zealand Police 168, 176
New Zealand Productivity Commission 246, 260
New Zealand Qualifications Authority 220
New Zealand Residence Programme 181, 254, 266
New Zealand Settlements Act 1963 35
New Zealand Wars 6, 20, 34–35, 37
Ngata, Apirana 258
Ngā Tamatoa 70, 168
Niue 57, 60, 90
non-citizen arrivals 87, 216n25
nondecision-making 270, 272
non-discrimination 23, 78–79, 84, 90, 252, 268
non-Māori population 27, 42
non-White immigrants 7, 257
norms, informal 271
Northeast Asia 75–76, 116–17, 124
Northey, Richard 93
Nosworthy, William 48
Numerical Multifactor Assessment System 108
nurse aides 153

racial stereotypes 145

racism: anti-Asian 102, 136; and economic multiculturalism 102; in election campaigns 60; and immigration controls 42, 45, 67, 72, 237, 258; Labour Party and 93; as legacy of colonialism 5–6, 252; public expressions of 75; resurgent 2

rangatiratanga 30, 240

Rata, Arama 95, 238, 240

Rātana movement 50

Ray, Robert 87–88

Reagan, Ronald 151

Realm of New Zealand 60

recolonisation 48

Reeves, Paul 111

Refugee Convention 1951 52

Refugee Council 169

refugee policy 121, 165

refugee quota 75, 165, 225, 236

refugee resettlement 154, 210–11, 237, 239, 241

refugees: and demographic diversity 121; in Immigration Settlement Strategy 156; post-Cold War 174; racialised visions of 174; from Vietnam 59; from World War II 51

refugee status, applications for 60, 164–65, 168–69, 185

regulatory capture 271

Reid, Papaarangi 141

remittances 187, 189, 261

Residence Appeal Authority 113

residence applications 80, 105, 227

residence approvals: in 1980s 75–76, **76**, 80; in 1990s 116, **117**; in 2010s 216, 226, 238, 269; processing techniques 144; target for 153, 195, 231

residence pathways 162, 205, 217, 220–21, 223, 227, 233, 242

residence permits: fixed quota for 139; and Pacific countries 117–18, 162; staggered applications for 158

residency categories 113

responsibilisation 134, 211

Richardson, George 38

Richardson, Ruth 103–4

Robertson, Grant 246

Rodger, Stan 18–19, 66, 90n8; on diversity of electorate 96–97; and immigration bureaucracy 105, 107; on immigration review 78; on Māori and immigration policy 92, 128; on Pacific peoples 90, 160; and policy emulation 84–85, 266; and racism in immigration controls 258; on Roger Douglas 106; on trans-Tasman relations 87–88, 264

Rogernomics 103

Rolleston, William 38

Roosevelt, Franklin 50

Rowling, Bill 59–60

Royal Commission on Social Policy 126

RSE (Recognised Seasonal Employer) 186, 188–91, 268; cap on 231, 248, 261; and circular mobility 260–61; and Covid-19 247; international diffusion of 265; lobby groups 236; regulation of workers in 221; Woodhouse on 217–18, 227

Ruddock, Philip 159–60

Russell, George Warren 45

Ruthanasia 103–4, 129

same-sex couples 147

Samoa 55, 89–90, 162, 260; visa waivers 118

Samoan migrants 55, 61, 89, 117

Samoan Quota Scheme 55, 160, 162, 186, 225

Saudi Arabia 148

Savage, Michael Joseph 50

Saxenian, Anna 113

Schier, Gunter and Petra 149

Scottish settlers 27, 34

seasonal work 15, 55, 81, 175; see also RSE

Seasonal Work Permit 188

secondary sources 23

sectarianism 43

sector agreements 234

securitisation 3–4, 23–24, 167–68, 170, 175, 262; and family link policy 237; uneven 238; use of term 14

security discourses 173–74

security risks 166–69, 199, 268

Seddon, Richard 44–45

September 11, 2001 terrorist attacks 167, 174

settlement, uneven 133–34

settlement outcomes 152–53, 156, 175, 196

settler colonialism 8; confiscation of land for 35; consolidation of 42; and immigration policy 16, 39, 42, 84–85, 91, 95, 241; and state sovereignty 97; use of term 11–12; and White immigration 208

settler colonies 5; and Colombo Plan 53; migration between 259, 263; multi-culturalism in 12; policy diffusion between 8, 265–67; relationships between 62

Shand, Tom 54

Shanghai 148, 197

Sharples, Pita 192

Shaw, James 237

Shearer, David 192

Shipley, Jenny 104, 146, 149–50

short-term visas 16, 188

Shroff, Gordon 105

sibling category 209

silver fern visa 192, 196

Singapore 196n17, 227; visa waivers 82, 118

SIS (Security Intelligence Services) 167–68

skilled employment, offers of 117

Francis L. Collins is a professor of sociology at Waipapa Taumata Rau, the University of Auckland and has previously held positions in geography and population studies at the National University of Singapore and Te Whare Wānanga o Waikato, the University of Waikato. His research encompasses a focus on the regulation and experiences of temporary migration, racism and workplace exploitation; international student mobilities; and the relationship between migration and cities. Francis is the author of *Global Asian City: Migration, Desire and the Politics of Encounter in 21st Century Seoul* (Wiley, 2018). Co-edited volumes include *Intersections of Inequality, Migration and Diversification* (Palgrave, 2020), *Aspiration, Desire and the Drivers of Migration* (Routledge, 2020) and *Handbook on Transnationalism* (Edward Elgar, 2022).

Alan Gamlen is a social scientist specialising in migration, mobility and identity. He is a professor at The Australian National University, founding director of the ANU Migration Hub, and an ARC Future Fellow and College of Experts member. He has held appointments at Oxford, Stanford and the Max Planck Society, among others, and formerly served as founding editor-in-chief of the journal *Migration Studies* (Oxford University Press) and director of the Australian Population and Migration Research Centre. Gamlen is a member of the Tainui confederation of Māori tribes in Aotearoa New Zealand. His last book *Human Geopolitics: States, Emigrants, and the Rise of Diaspora Institutions* (Oxford University Press, 2019) won the ENMISA Distinguished Book Award.

Neil Vallelly is a lecturer in the sociology, gender studies and criminology programme at Ōtākou Whakaihu Waka, the University of Otago. He is the author of *Futilitarianism: Neoliberalism and the Production of Uselessness* (Goldsmiths Press, 2021), which has been translated into Italian, and his work has appeared in journals such as *Angelaki, Poetics Today, Critical Times, Journal of Gender Studies* and *Theory & Event*. Neil is the editor of the journal *Counterfutures: Left Thought & Practice Aotearoa*, a member of the executive committee for the Australasian Society for Continental Philosophy, and a recipient of a Rutherford Foundation Postdoctoral Fellowship (Royal Society Te Apārangi).